I SAW IT

*Ilya Selvinsky and the Legacy of
Bearing Witness to the Shoah*

WITH TRANSLATIONS OF MAJOR WORKS

Studies in Russian and Slavic Literatures, Cultures, and History

Series Editor – Lazar Fleishman (Stanford University)

I SAW IT

Ilya Selvinsky and the Legacy of Bearing Witness to the Shoah

WITH TRANSLATIONS OF MAJOR WORKS

MAXIM D. SHRAYER

Boston 2013

Library of Congress Cataloging-in-Publication Data:
A bibliographic record for this title is available from the Library of Congress.
ISBN 978-1-618111-69-2 (cloth)
ISBN 978-1-61811-191-3 (electronic)
ISBN 978-1-61811-307-8 (paper)
Book design by Adell Medovoy
Published by Academic Studies Press in 2013
28 Montfern Avenue
Brighton, MA 02135, USA
press@academicstudiespress.com
www.academicstudiespress.com

I Saw It: Ilya Selvinsky and the Legacy of Bearing Witness to the Shoah
By Maxim D. Shrayer

Copyright © 2013 by Maxim D. Shrayer. All rights reserved worldwide, including electronic. English translations copyright © 2010-2013 by Maxim D. Shrayer. All rights reserved worldwide, including electronic.

First Edition 2013

Works by Ilya Selvinsky are reprinted and translated by the permission of Tatiana Selvinskaya. Russian originals copyright © The Estate of Ilya Selvinsky.

Some of the illustrations used in this book come from sources in which the photographic materials or the names of the photographers were not identified. Every effort was made to seek appropriate permission to reproduce the illustrations used in this book.

Cover image: *The Bagerovo Anti-Tank Ditch*. Crimea, 14 December 2011
                 © by Maxim D. Shrayer.

IN MEMORIAM PYOTR (PEYSAKH) SHRAYER

CONTENTS

List of Illustrations ... ix

Introduction ... xv

CHAPTER ONE: *Selvinsky on the Shoah by Bullet* ... 1

   1. Selvinsky before the War: Poetics and Politics ... 1
   2. The Nazi Invasion and the Frontlines ... 15
   3. Jewish Poems in Praise of the Soviet Dictator? ... 24
   4. The Massacre at Kerch: History, Witnessing, Memory ... 30
   5. "I Saw It!" ... 82
   6. Revisi(ti)ng the Memories: "Kerch" and "The Trial in Krasnodar" ... 117

CHAPTER TWO: *The Price of Bearing Witness to the Shoah* ... 137

   1. Selvinsky's Troubles of 1943-1944 ... 137
   2. In the Moscow Exile ... 171
   3. (Re)reading Stalin ... 181

CHAPTER THREE: *The Victory and Beyond* ... 187

   1. Selvinsky and Jewish-Russian Shoah Poetry in 1944-1945 ... 187
   2. Kandava/Kandau ... 195
   3. Selvinsky during *zhdanovshchina* and the Anticosmopolitan Campaign ... 212
   4. The Ashes and Bones of Crimea ... 222

CHAPTER FOUR: *Selvinsky's Legacy and Soviet Shoah Poetry* ... 226

   1. The Anxiety of Noninfluence: Ozerov, Slutsky, Samoilov ... 226
   2. Selvinsky Agonistes ... 253

Appendix: *Two Shoah Poems by Ilya Selvinsky:*
　Russian originals and English translations 　263
　　1. "Я это видел!"—"I Saw It" 　263
　　2. "Керчь"— "Kerch" 　270

Works Cited 　278

Acknowledgments 　312

Index 　316

List of Illustrations

1. Ilya Selvinsky (center) with fellow members of the Literary Center of Constructivists. Moscow, 1925. From left to right: Vladimir Asmus, Aleksandr Kvyatkovsky, Eduard Bagritsky, Kornely Zelinsky, Nikolay Aduev, Ilya Selvinsky, Boris Agapov, Vladimir Lugovskoy, Grigory Gauzner (standing), Vera Inber, and Evgeny Gabrilovich. (Courtesy of Russian State Archive of Literature and the Arts, Moscow.)

2. Ilya Selvinsky (second from left) with fellow participants of the SS Chelyuskin expedition. Murmansk. Circa August 1933. (Courtesy of Tatyana Selvinskaya.)

3. Ilya Selvinsky with his family members. Moscow, April 1941. Left to right: Selvinsky, wife Berta, stepdaughter Tsetsiliya, mother-in-law Anna Moiseevna; facing away from camera, daughter Tatyana. (Courtesy of Tatyana Selvinskaya.)

4. Ilya Selvinsky. Identification as a special correspondent of *Krasnaia zvezda* (*Red Star*), issued on 22 October 1942. Signed "D. Vadimov," penname of Major General David Ortenberg, editor of *Red Star*. (Courtesy of Ilya Selvinsky Memorial Museum, Simferopol.)

5. Ilya Selvinsky. Army identification as a staff writer for *Syn otechestva* (*Son of Fatherland*), issued on 18 September 1941 by the 51 Separate Army. (Courtesy of Ilya Selvinsky Memorial Museum, Simferopol.)

6. Ilya Selvinsky (on the left) with Aleksandr Terlovsky, who headed the propaganda section at *Syn otechestva* (*Son of Fatherland*). Circa late 1941-early 1942. (Courtesy of Tatiana Selvinskaya.)

7. Ilya Selvinsky with colleagues at the office of *Boevoi natisk* (*Fighting Thrust*), newspaper of the Crimean Front. Circa early spring 1942. Left to right, bottom row: D. Berezin (editor), I. Selvinsky; top row: V. Machavariani, D. Dzhafarov, V. Losev. (Courtesy of Ilya Selvinsky Memorial Museum, Simferopol.)

8. Ilya Selvinsky (second from left). The Crimean Front. Circa late winter-early spring 1942. (Courtesy of Tatyana Selvinskaya.)

9. Ilya Selvinsky (fourth from right; annotated by Selvinsky) with the troops of Major General Vasily Kniga (first on right), commander of 72nd (Kuban Cossack) Cavalry Division. Crimea. Circa March 1942. (Collection of Maxim D. Shrayer.)

10. Crimea with principal urban centers. Contemporary map. (*The YIVO Encyclopedia of Jews in Eastern Europe*, vol. 1, New Haven, 2008, Courtesy of YIVO.)

11. Kerch and Environs, with reference to the Nazi occupation (1941-1944) and Ilya Selvinsky's experience as a military officer and witness to the Shoah on the Kerch peninsula. (Cartography based on www.ukrmap.com.ua, with annotations and legend by Maxim D. Shrayer.)

12. The first page of Ilya Selvinsky's wartime diary for 1942, with the poet's impressions of having seen the Bagerovo anti-tank ditch. (Courtesy of Ilya Selvinsky Memorial Museum, Simferopol.)

13. Sennaya (Haymarket) Square, Kerch. Plaque at 15 Proletarskaya Street, unveiled in 2002 to commemorate the murder of the Jews of Kerch in 1941. 14 December 2011. (Photo by Maxim D. Shrayer.)

14. The marker on the post-Soviet monument (2009) at the Bagerovo anti-tank ditch. 14 December 2011. (Photo by Maxim D. Shrayer.)

15. The marker on the Soviet-era monument (circa 1975-1976) at the Bagerovo anti-tank ditch. 14 December 2011. (Photo by Maxim D. Shrayer.)

16. The Bagerovo anti-tank ditch. The Soviet-era monument commemorating the murder of "over seven thousand peaceful Soviet citizens" (circa 1975-76) and the post-Soviet monument (2010) commemorating the murder of "thousands of Jews." 14 December 2011. (Photo by Maxim D. Shrayer.)

17. Sennaya (Haymarket) Square, Kerch, where the Jews of Kerch were ordered to appear on 29 November 1941 and from where they were marched to the city jail and subsequently trucked to the Bagerovo anti-tank ditch and murdered. 1947. (Courtesy of Vladimir Sanzharovets.)

18. View of Proletarskaya Street at Sennaya (Haymarket) Square. Kerch. 14 December 2011. (Photo by Maxim D. Shrayer.)

19. View of Kerch Embankment. Circa January 1942. (Courtesy of Vladimir Sanzhrovets.)

20. The Bagerovo anti-tank ditch, with mountains of the Katerlez Range in the background. From the January 1942 series of photos of the Bagerovo ditch. Photo by Evgeny Khaldey. (Konstantin Khodakovsky's album "Kerch during the Great Patriotic War," with notes by Vladimir Sanzharovets based on Khaldey's notebooks, http://fotki.yandex.ru/users/khodak.)

21. The Bagerovo anti-tank ditch, with mountains of the Katerlez Range in the background and Mt. Turkmenskaya on the far left. 14 December 2011. (Photo by Maxim D. Shrayer.)

22. Order No. 5 (early December 1941), signed "German security police" and posted around Kerch, ordering all the remaining Jews of Kerch to appear immediately at 2 Karl Liebknecht Street. (Courtesy of Boris Berlin.)

Illustrations

23. Grigory Berman over the bodies of his wife and children. From the January 1942 series of photos of the Bagerovo ditch. Photo by Evgeny Khaldey. (From Konstantin Khodakovsky's album "Kerch during the Great Patriotic War," with notes by Vladimir Sanzharovets based on Khaldey's notebooks, http://fotki.yandex.ru/users/khodak.)

24. Raisa Belotserkovskaya, one of the few Jewish survivors, standing over the Bagerovo anti-tank ditch in 1947. (Courtesy of Vladimir Sanzharovets.)

25. From the January 1942 series of photos of the Bagerovo ditch. Photo by Dmitri Baltermants. ("Dmitry Baltermants," http://club.foto.ru/classics/36.)

26. Kerch residents looking at the information window depicting the Nazi atrocities at Kerch. The window was coproduced by the Telegraph Agency of the USSR (TASS) and *Syn otechestva (Son of Fatherland)*, newspaper of the 51st Separate Army, where Selvinsky served until February 1942. January 1942. Photo by Evgeny Khaldey. (From Konstantin Khodakovsky's album "Kerch during the Great Patriotic War," with notes by Vladimir Sanzharovets based on Khaldey's notebooks, http://fotki.yandex.ru/users/khodak.)

27. German Atrocities in Kerch. A page spread printed in *Krasnyi Krym (Red Crimea)* on 24 January 1942. Photos and text by Mark Turovsky and Izrail Antselovich.

28. "We Shall Avenge!" A section of a page spread on Nazi atrocities with two uncredited photos (top by Evgeny Khaldey, bottom by either Mark Turovsky, Izrail Antselovich or Mark Redkin) depicting the aftermath of the Bagerovo mass execution. In the top photo Grigory Berman is identified by name. *Fotogazeta PURa (Photonewspaper of the Political Directorate of the Red Army)*. February 1942. (Courtesy of Vladimir Sanzharovets.)

29. Ilya Selvinsky. "I Saw It!" as published in *Krasnaia zvezda (Red Star)*, 27 February 1942.

30-31. Title page and table of contents of Selvinsky's *Ballads, Posters and Songs*. Krasnodar, 1942.

32-33. Cover and table of contents of Selvinsky's *Ballads and Songs*. Moscow, 1943.

34. Two pages from the collection *The Atrocities of German Fascists in Kerch* (Sukhumi, 1943) where Selvinsky's "I Saw It!" was reprinted. On the left side is a page of the poem, on the right, a photograph of a mother with her infant child murdered at the Bagerovo anti-tank ditch.

35-36. Ilya Selvinsky, "Once Again about Hitlerite Atrocities." *Boevoi natisk (Fighting Thrust)*, 24 February 1942. The image on the right shows a clipping with the closing section crossed out and a note in Selvinsky's hand: "the editor's insertion." In the inserted section the editor, Colonel Dmitri Berezin, placed a quote from Stalin. (Courtesy of Ilya Selvinsky Memorial Museum, Simferopol.)

37. Map of ancient Greek colonies in the Northern Black Sea, with the Crimean peninsula in the center. (Wikimedia).

38. View of Kerch Bay from Mount Mithridates. 14 December 2011. (Photo by Maxim D. Shrayer.)

39. View of modern Kerch from Mount Mithridates with the Great Mithridates Stairs. Photo by Sergey Sorokin. (Courtesy of Sergey Sorokin.)

40. View of the Panticapeum ruins in modern Kerch. 14 December 2011. (Photo by Maxim D. Shrayer.)

41. Aleksandr Romm. "Nadiusha." *Kerchenskii rabochii* (*Kerch Worker*), 15 January 1942.

42. Veniamin Goffershefer. "Bagerovo." *Syn otechestva* (*Son of Fatherland*), 29 January 1942.

43. Ilya Selvinsky. The North-Caucasus Front. Circa autumn 1942. (Courtesy of Tatyana Selvinskaya.)

44. Ilya Selvinsky (center) with poets Nikolay Aseev and Boris Pasternak, during Selvinsky's leave from the front. Chistopol, Tatarstan. Circa August 1942. (Courtesy of Tatyana Selvinskaya.)

45-46. Title page and first two pages of the table of contents of Ilya Selvinsky's *Crimea, Caucasus, Kuban*. Moscow, 1947.

47. Ilya Selvinsky's selected list of work and service experience, 1917-1945, with corrections and the three wartime entries written in by Selvinsky. There is a gap, from February 1944 to April 1945, in Selvinsky's military service. (Courtesy of Ilya Selvinsky Memorial Museum, Simferopol).

48-49. Pages 2-3 and 4-5 of Ilya Selvinsky's military registration card (*voennyi bilet*), issued on 15 November 1948. Pages 2-3 list Selvinsky's nationality as "Krymchak" and his native language as "Russian." Pages 4-5 refer to the period from February 1944 to April 1945 as being "a reservist." (Courtesy of the Ilya Selvinsky Memorial Museum, Simferopol.)

50. Ilya Selvinsky (first on left) with Yakov Khelemsky (center), their fellow officers and a driver. The 2nd Baltic Front, May 1945. (Courtesy of Tatyana Selvinskaya).

51. Page of Ilya Selvinsky's wartime diary entry for 12 May 1945, with a description and a drawing of the capitulation of a Nazi division at Kandava. (Courtesy of Ilya Selvinsky Memorial Museum, Simferopol.)

52. Ilya Selvinsky. 1940s. (Courtesy of Tatyana Selvinskaya.)

53. Ilya Selvinsky in his study, with a bust of Voltaire. Moscow, 1940s. (Courtesy of Tatyana Selvinskaya.)

54. Ilya Selvinsky with Tatyana Selvinskaya. 1949. (Courtesy of Tatyana Selvinskaya.)

55. Ilya Selvinsky. 1950s. (Courtesy of Tatyana Selvinskaya.)

56. Ilya Selvinsky. Portrait by Tatyana Selvinskaya. (Courtesy of Tatyana Selvinskaya.)

57. Ilya Selvinsky. Circa 1964. (Courtesy of Tatyana Selvinskaya.)

58. Lev Ozerov. Circa early 1960s. Lev Ozerov, *Lirika*, Moscow, 1964. Copy autographed to David Shrayer-Petrov. (Courtesy of D. Shrayer-Petrov.)

59. Boris Slutsky. Circa middle 1970s. (Boris Slutsky, *Neokonchennye spory*, Moscow, 1978.)

60. David Samoilov. *Pamiatnye zapiski*. Moscow, 1989

61. The anti-tank ditch at the 10th km. of the Simferopol-Feodosia Highway. 14 December 2011. Photo by Maxim D. Shrayer.

62. Front and back of the invitation to an evening commemorating the 70th anniversary of Ilya Selvinsky's birth at the Central House of Writers in Moscow. 24 October 1969. The participants include poets Semyon Kirsanov, Pavel Antokolsky, Lev Ozerov, and David Samoilov. (Collection of Maxim D. Shrayer.)

63. Ilya Selvinsky with grandson Kirill. July 1963. (Courtesy of Tatyana Selvinskaya.)

64. Ilya Selvinsky. A selection of poems published in *Ogonek* 60 (1960), with "Jewish Melody" in the central column.

Я очень бледно это описал
В стихотворении "Я ЭТО ВИДЕЛ!"
И больше не могу ни слова.
Керчь…

I have described this very hazily
In the poem "I SAW IT!"
And I cannot add even a single word.
Kerch…

                Ilya Selvinsky, "Kerch," 1942

Back at the headquarters of the front they told me that the family of [Colonel Abram] Khasin was murdered during the mass execution of the civilian population of the city of Kerch, carried out by the Hitlerites, and that by chance Khasin came upon a photograph of the dead lying in a ditch and recognized his wife and children. I was thinking: What must this person feel when he leads his tanks into battle.

                Vasily Grossman, *Years of War. Notebooks*, 1942

I walked on a stomped-out path … and 10,000 eyes that belonged to the vilest enemies of my people (both Russian and Jewish) stared at me from the formation.

                Ilya Selvinsky, *Wartime Diaries*, 1945

Introduction

OVER FIFTEEN YEARS AGO I wrote *Russian Poet/Soviet Jew: The Legacy of Eduard Bagritsky*. Published in 2000, it explored the political and cultural anxieties of a major Jewish-Russian poet living and working in the Soviet 1920s and early 1930s. Eduard Bagritsky and the protagonist of the present book, Ilya Selvinsky, were close in Moscow in the middle to late 1920s. Both were Jews originally from the coast of the Black Sea; both were members of the Literary Center of Constructivists, over which Selvinsky presided until its dismantlement in 1930; and both were talented poets famous on the early Soviet literary scene. It was Bagritsky who, in a poem of 1927, laid Selvinsky, along with Nikolai Tikhonov and Boris Pasternak, on the altar of the 1920s Soviet modernism: "To the alien West/ rushing over [fields of] harvested crops/ Tikhonov, Selvinsky, Pasternak...."

The career of Ilya Selvinsky (1899-1968) is emblematic of the experience of Jewish-Russian poets during World War II and the Shoah (Holocaust).[i] Selvinsky spent roughly the first two and a half years (summer 1941-autumn 1943) and the last month of the war (April-May 1945) at the frontlines. Serving as a staff writer and editor of army newspapers and also participating in combat, Selvinsky contributed only about twenty prose items during the wartime years. Poetry, not journalism or essayism, was Selvinsky's principal medium of writing and publishing about the events he witnessed and participated in. His poetic contributions to army newspapers ranged from lyrical, patriotic, or political poetry to rhymed captions to anti-Nazi cartoons.[ii] He composed longer and shorter poems with references to the Shoah, several of them explicit in their articulation of Jewish losses.[iii]

Selvinsky was able to steer his Shoah poems into print during and immediately after the Great Patriotic War (as the war against Nazi Germany and its allies became known in the Soviet Union), although he made compromises, some of them negotiating the official Soviet views of Jewish victimhood.[iv] During the war, he experienced political repression, paying a high price for his poems about the war and Shoah.

This book explores the dynamics of Selvinsky's wartime career by placing it first in the historical contexts of World War II and the Shoah, and subsequently in the cultural and ideological contexts of postwar Stalinism. The book's final section investigates Selvinsky's legacy as a poet-soldier and a witness to the Shoah in the occupied Soviet territories.

* * *

As I wrote and revised this book, and especially after I came upon tiers of new evidence during a research trip to Crimea, I had to remind myself that I was not writing a poet's biography. I wanted to tell the story of Soviet poetry of the Shoah through the prism of one poet's life and work. I did not set out to create a history of Shoah literature in the USSR, nor had I initially intended to write either a history of the Shoah in Selvinsky's native Crimea or a study of the cultural legacy of the Shoah in the Soviet Union. These topics, absorbing as they are and understudied as they still remain, left a lot still to be discovered and investigated. Such are, to a degree, the pains of interdisciplinary study, and these challenges are rendered more complex when the subject "Soviet Union" is coupled with the heading "Jews" and placed in the time frame of World War II and the Shoah.

* * *

Since my Moscow youth, both Eduard Bagritsky and Ilya Selvinsky have been among my favorite poets. My views of Bagritsky's poetry and Jewishness have evolved over the years, and I hope to revisit them before long. Having completed a book about Ilya Selvinsky as a principal Jewish-Russian poetic voice of the Soviet 1940s, I now realize that this volume is in a number of ways a sequel to my earlier book about Bagrtisky and

Jewish-Russian poetic identity. It is, perhaps, fitting that this book not only tells the story of Selvinsky as a witness to the Nazi atrocities but also includes English translations of Selvinsky's major Shoah poems.

M.D.S

December 2011; April 2012; January 2013
Brookline, Massachusetts

NOTES TO INTRODUCTION

i. Anglicized, reader-friendly spellings of Russian names are used in the main text; if a name has already gained a common spelling in English, this spelling is then used (e.g. Ehrenburg, not Erenburg; *Novy Mir*, not *Novyi mir*). In rendering the Russian-language bibliographical references, a slightly simplified version of the US Library of Congress transliteration system is used.

Unless indicated otherwise, all translations from the Russian are mine. As a general principle, literary translations of verse are printed as verse, whereas *literal* translations of verse are printed as prose with indications of the line boundaries. In some cases, preference is given to literary, not literal, English translations of poetic texts. Even though the literary translations I quote are metrically precise and relatively close to the Russian originals, one cannot rely on the English texts alone to draw accurate conclusions about the poem's structure, meaning, and significance.

Unless noted otherwise, I reference only the publications I have examined *de visu*, the latter circumstance being particularly significant in the case of original wartime publications in regional or army newspapers, some of which are extremely difficult to locate even in Russian and Ukrainian libraries or even in Crimean libraries and archives.

ii. As an example of Selvinsky's cartoon captions, see, for instance, "Fashisty—o blagodarnost' sud'be..." *Syn otechestva* 20 October 1941.

iii. I have previously discussed Selvinsky's experience as a Shoah poet; see Shrayer, "Jewish-Russian Holocaust Poetry in Official Soviet Venues: 1944-

1946 (Antokolsky, Ehrenburg, Ozerov)," paper delivered at the Annual Conference of the Association for Jewish Studies (AJS) (Washington, 21 December 2008); "Ilya Selvinsky," in *An Anthology of Jewish-Russian Literature: Two Centuries of Dual Identity in Prose and Poetry, 1801-2001*, 2 vols., ed. Maxim D. Shrayer, 1: 226-227 (Armonk, NY: M. E. Sharpe, 2007); Shrayer, "Selvinskii, Ilia Lvovich," in *The YIVO Encyclopedia of Jews in Eastern Europe*, 2 vols., ed. Gershon David Hundert, 2: 1684-1685 (New Haven: Yale University Press, 2008); Shrayer, "Bearing Witness: The War, the Shoah and the Legacy of Vasily Grossman," *The Jewish Quarterly* 217 (Spring 2011): 14-19; "Jewish-Russian Poets Bearing Witness to the Shoah, 1941-1946: Textual Evidence and Preliminary Conclusions," in *Papers from the VIII World Congress of the International Council for Central and East European Studies, Stockholm, July 2010*, ed. Stefano Garzonio, 59-11 (Bologna: Portal on Central European and Balkan Europe, 2011). http://www.iecob.net.

For a detailed, albeit not exhaustive, bibliography of works by and about Selvinsky, see "Sel'vinskii, Il'ia L'vovich," in *Russkie sovetskie pisateli. Poety (Sovetskii period). Bibliograficheskii ukazatel'*, vol. 23: 35-50 (St. Petersburg: Rossiiskaia natsional'naia biblioteka, 2000). The bibliography is missing some of the wartime publications. Selvinsky's wartime poems with explicit Shoah and Jewish references include: "Evreiskomu narodu" ("To the Jewish People," 1941); "Ia eto videl!" ("I Saw It!" 1942); "Kerch'" (1942; pub. 1945); "Otvet Gebbel'su" ("A Reply to Goebbels," 1942); "Sud v Krasnodare" ("A Trial in Krasnodar," 1943; pub. 1945); "Krym" ("Kak boi barabana, kak golos kartechi...," ["Like drumbeat, like the voice of canister shots..."] 1944, pub. 1945); "Krym" ("Byvaiut kraia, chto nedvizhny vekami...") ("Crimea" ["There are regions unchanged by centuries..."], 1945; pub. 1962); *Kandava* (1945); "Sevastopol'" (Sebastopol," 1944; pub. 1945).

iv. The primary published source of information about Selvinsky's war years is Vera Babenko, *Voina glazami poeta: Krymskie stranitsy iz dnevnikov i pisem I. L. Sel'vinskogo* (Simferopol': Krymskaia Akademiia gumanitarnykh nauk; Dom-muzei I. L. Sel'vinskogo, 1994). Babenko published—and commented on—extensive excerpts from Selvinsky's wartime diaries and letters. However, her valuable publication contains a number of errors, including those in the dating of diary excerpts. Babenko's book also includes Eduard Filat'ev's article "Taina podpolkovnika Sel'vinskogo," Babenko, 69-82. Filat'ev's article does not contain a scholarly apparatus or use footnotes, and the sources of his information stand in need of further verification.

See also Liudmila Daineko's investigation of Selvinsky's war experience in Kerch, 1941-1942: "Sel'vinskii i Kerch. Noiabr', 1941-mai, 1942," in *Vestnik Krymskikh Chtenii I. L. Sel'vinskogo*, vol. 1, 63-71 (Simferopol: Krymskii Arkhiv, 2002).

Parts of Selvinsky's wartime diaries and a few of his wartime letters to family members have previously appeared; the largest selection, which for the most part overlaps with the materials that Babenko quotes in *Voina glazama poeta*, appeared as Sel'vinskii, "*Ia eto videl*" (*Krymskie stranitsy voennykh dnevnikov*), ed. Ts. A. Voskresenskaia and R. M. Goriunova, *Krym-90. Al'manakh*, 76-85 (Simferopol': Tavriia, 1990); see Sel'vinskii, "Na voine. Iz dnevnikov i pisem rodnym," ed. Ts. Voskresenskaia, *Novy mir* 12 (1984): 163-175.

Maurice Friedberg might have been the first Western scholar to mention Selvinsky's World War II "moving poems dealing with the tragic fate of Russian Jewry"; see Friedberg, "Selvinskii, Ilya Lvovich," in *Encyclopedia Judaica*, 14: 1137 (Jerusalem: Keter Publishing House, 1972). Benjamin Pinkus included Selvinsky in a short list of Jewish-Russian poets who wrote about the Shoah; see Pinkus, *The Soviet Government and the Jews 1948-1967: A Documentary Study*, 389 (Cambridge: Cambridge University Press, 1984). Some of Selvinsky's poems about the Shoah have been identified in an entry in the Russian-language Jewish encyclopedia published in Israel; see "Sel'vinskii, Il'ia L'vovich," in *Kratkaia evreiskaia entsiklopediia*, vol. 7: 742-743 (Jerusalem: Obshchestvo po issledovaniiu evreiskikh obshchin; Evreiskii universitet v Ierusalime, 1994) [unsigned; entry by Mark Kipnis] and also in an entry in the recent Russian encyclopedia of the Shoah, M[aria] M. Al'tman, "Poeziia," in *Kholokost na territorii SSSR. Entsiklopediia*, 2nd ed., ed. I. A. Al'tman, 789 (Moscow: Rosspen, 2011). Ada Kolganova included "I Saw It!" in her anthology; see Sel'vinskii, "Ia eto videl!" in *Menora. Evreiskie motivy v russkoi poezii*, ed. Ada Kolganova, 130-134 (Moscow-Jerusalem: Evreiskii universitet v Moskve, 1993). Feliks Kandel' touches on Selvinsky's "I Saw It!" in the opening of his overview of the Soviet cultural response to the Shoah; see Kandel', "Ocherk shest'desiat chetvertyi. 'Chernaia kniga'. Deiateli kul'tury i Katastrofa," in *Kniga vremen i sobytii. Vol. 5. Istoriia evreev Sovetskogo Soiuza, 1939-1945*, http://felixkandel.org/index.php/books/295.html, last accessed 28 January 2012. In his recent book, *"I am to be read not from left to right but in Jewish: from right to left": The Poetics of Boris Slutsky* (Boston: Academic Studies Press, 2011), Marat Grinberg comments on Selvinsky's experience as a Shoah poet. I read Harriet Murav's book, *Music from a Speeding Train: Jewish Literature in Post-Revolutionary Russia* (Stanford: Stanford University Press, 2011), in November 2011 as I revised this manuscript for publication. I noted Murav's readings of three of Selvinsky's Shoah poems, "I Saw It!," "Tribunal in Krasnodar," and *Kandava* (Murav, 134; 154-165). I further noted the absence of references to "Kerch," Selvinsky's second principal poem about the Bagerovo anti-tank ditch massacre. Finally, I noted that Murav does not discuss Selvinsky's wartime troubles and punitive dismissal from the army.

For additional sources of information on Selvinsky's wartime years and Crimean connections, see M. F. Arkharova, "Vmeste s nami shli v nastuplenie stikhi Sel'vinskogo," in *O Sel'vinskom: vospominaniia*, ed. Ts. A. Voskresenskaia and I. P. Sirotinskaia, 106-112 (Moscow: Sovetskii pisatel', 1982); "Avtory 'Boevoi Krymskoi," *Literaturnaia gazeta*, 6 May 1970: 5 [selection of interviews]; Vera Babenko and Vladislav Gavriliuk, "'Net, ia ne legkoi zhizn'iu zhil...,'" *Krymskie penaty* 2 (1996): 88-107; D. Berezin, "Oruzhiem stikha," in *O Sel'vinskom*, ed. Ts. A. Voskresenskaia and I. P. Sirotinskaia, 101-105; I. A. Dobrovol'skaia, *"Eshche moi brig ne trogalsia s prichala...": O iunosti poeta Il'ii Sel'vinskogo* (Simferopol': Krymskaia akademiia gumanitarnykh nauk, 1999); Vera Katina, "'Kazhdyi chelovek imeet pravo na tumannyi ugolok dushi' (evreiskaia tema v zhizni i tvorchestve Il'i Sel'vinskogo)," in *Dolia evreis'kykh gromad tsentral'noi ta skhidnoi Evropy v pershii polovyne XX stolittia. Materialy konferentsii 6-28 serpnia 2003 r., Kyiv*, http://www.judaica.kiev.ua/Conference/Conf2003/46.htm, last accessed 26 February 2011; Iakov Khelemskii, "Kurliandskaia vesna," in Voskresenskaia and Sirotinskaia, eds., *O Sel'vinskom*, 125-175; E. A. Nekrasova, "Voennaia zhurnalistika Il'I Sel'vinskogo," in *Vestnik Krymskikh chtenii I. L. Sel'vinskogo*, vol. 2: 76-84 (Simferopol: Krymskii arkhiv, 2003); M. A. Novikova, "Zagadki biografii Il'i Sel'vinskogo (nekotorye novye metody eksursionnoi raboty)," in *Vestnik Krymskikh chtenii I. L. Sel'vinskogo*, vol. 2: 95-101 (Simferopol: Krymskii arkhiv, 2003); Evdokiia Ol'shanskaia, "Mne zhizn' podarila vstrechi s poetom," *Zerkalo nedeli* (1998), http://www.litera.ru/stixiya/articles/397.html, last accessed 7 April 2010; Lev Ozerov, "Stakan okeana," in *O Sel'vinskom*, ed. Ts. A. Voskresenskaia and I. P. Sirotinskaia, 366-396; Lev Ozerov, "Il'ia Sel'vinskii, ego trudy i dni," in *Il'ia Sel'vinskii, Izbrannye proizvedeniia v dvukh tomakh*, ed. Ts. Voskresenskaia and I. Mikhailov, 2 vols., 1: 5-20 (Moscow: Khudozhestvennaia literatura, 1989); Osip Reznik, *Zhizn' v poezii: Tvorchestvo I. Sel'vinskogo* (Moscow: Sovetskii pisatel', 1981); L. A. Rustemova, "Krymskii 'kontekst' I. Sel'vinskogo," in *I. L. Sel'vinskii i literaturnyi protsess XX veka. V mezhdunarodnaia nauchnaia konferentsiia, posviashchennaia 100-letiiu I. L. Sel'vinskogo. Materialy* 73-80 (Simferopol': Krymskii arkhiv, 2000); Margarita Shitova, "Neiasnaia bol' nadezhdy," *Krymskie izvestiia*, 4 November 2006, http://www-ki.rada.crimea.ua/nomera/2006/205/bol.html, last accessed 7 April 2010; Mikhail Solomatin, "My eto videli," *Zhurnal Mikhaila Solomatina*, 21 October 2009, http://mike67.livejournal.com/261554.html, last accessed 29 June 2010; David Shraer-Petrov, "Karaimskie pirozhki. Il'ia Sel'vinskii," in David Shraer-Petrov, *Vodka s pirozhnymi: roman s pisateliami*, 272-282 (St. Petersburg: Akademicheskii proekt, 2007); P. P. Sviridenko, "Stroka poeta v boevom stroiu (Iz frontovykh vospominanii)," in O Sel'vinskom, ed. Ts. A. Voskresenskaia. and I. P. Sirotinskaia, 115-121. See also Evgenii Evtushenko, "Nesostoiavshiisia velikii. Il'ia Sel'vinskii," *Novye izvestiia* 24 March 2006, http://www.newizv.ru/culture/2006-03-24/43038-nesostojavshijsja-velikij.html, last accessed 10 April 2011. For a useful overview of Selvinsky's political troubles and censorial difficulties in 1943-1946, see P. S. Reifman, "Glava piataia: Vtoraia mirovaia. Chast' vtoraia," in P. S. Reifman, *Iz istorii russkoi, sovetskoi i postsovetskoi tsenzury*. http://www.gumer.info/bibliotek_Buks/History/reifm/16.php, last accessed 6 April 2010. To the best of my knowledge, Herman Ermolaev was the first Western scholar to discuss Selvinsky's wartime troubles in the context of Soviet censorship. See Ermolaev, *Censorship in Soviet Literature, 1917-1991*, 73-74 (Lanham, MD: Rowman & Littlefield, 1997).

CHAPTER ONE

SELVINSKY ON THE SHOAH BY BULLET

1. Selvinsky before the War: Poetics and Politics

Before turning our attention to the Nazi invasion of the Soviet Union, let us briefly consider aspects of Selvinsky's prewar career while taking stock of the treatment of Jewish and Judaic questions, of Selvinsky's place on the prewar Soviet literary pantheon, and of official repressions against the poet. A poetic virtuoso and an innovator of Russian versification, Selvinsky was born in 1899 in Crimean capital Simferopol, the grandson of a Krymchak. (Krymchaks are Crimea's indigenous, rabbinate non-Ashkenazi Jews, who speak a Turkic language.) Selvinsky grew up in Simferopol and in Evpatoria in the family of an entrepreneurial tailor who later became a furrier. As an adult, Selvinsky indicated that Russian was his native language, remembered some Hebrew, and retained some knowledge of spoken Yiddish (and also the Krymchak language).[1] Whenever possible, Selvinsky listed "Krymchak" as his nationality in his Soviet documents. At the same time, Selvinsky clearly regarded the Krymchaks as a subgroup of the broader category of the Jewish people, and spoke of both the Jewish and the Russian people as "my own." As a young boy, Selvinsky was given instruction in the Torah and into his early teen years attended services with his father at both Ashkenazi and Krymchak prayer homes and synagogues.[2] In 1905, in response to the wave of pogroms then sweeping over parts of the Russian Empire, Selvinsky's father sent him, his mother, and his younger sister

---

1 On Selvinsky's command of Yiddish, Tatyana Selvinskaya, Personal Interview, Simferopol, 15 December 2011.
2 Vera Katina and Marina Novikova recently investigated Jewish aspects of Selvinsky's childhood and early youth. See Katina, "Kazhdyi chelovek imeet pravo...."; Novikova, "Zagadki biografii Il'ia Sel'vinskogo."

to Constantinople, Turkey, where Selvinsky briefly attended school at the French Catholic mission. As a young man Selvinsky had his share of adventures, ranging from wrestling in the circus and working as a sailor, a longshoreman, and an itinerant actor to participating in the Civil War (first, briefly, in an anarchist troop, later in the the Red Army). He published his first poem in 1915, and in the 1920s experimented with the use of Yiddishisms and thieves' lingo in Russian verse.[3] In 1923, Selvinsky graduated in law from Moscow University.

Selvinsky was the leader of the Literary Center of Constructivists (LTsK), an early Soviet modernist group, from 1924 until its derailment in 1930, and edited landmark anthologies by constructivist authors.

1. Ilya Selvinsky (center) with fellow members of the Literary Center of Constructivists. Moscow, 1925. From left to right: Vladimir Asmus, Aleksandr Kvyatkovsky, Eduard Bagritsky, Kornely Zelinsky, Nikolay Aduev, Ilya Selvinsky, Boris Agapov, Vladimir Lugovskoy, Grigory Gauzner (standing), Vera Inber, and Evgeny Gabrilovich. (Courtesy of Russian State Archive of Literature and the Arts, Moscow.)

In the mid- to late 1920s, with the publication of the collection *Records* (1926), the epic poem *The Lay of Ulyalaev* (1924, pub. 1927), the narrative poem *Notes of a Poet* (1927), and the novel-in-verse *Fur Trade* (1928;

---

3 Yuri Tynianov first spoke about Selvinsky's "new intonation" in the article "Interval" (1924). See Iu. N. Tynianov, "Promezhutok," in *Poetika, Istoriia literatury. Kino*, ed. V. A. Kaverin, A. S. Miasnikov, 7 (Moscow: Nauka, 1977).

pub. 1929), he achieved national Soviet fame. The poet Aleksandr Revich recently suggested that "*The Lay of Ulyalaev*, alongside *And Quiet Flows the Don* [by Mikhail Sholokhov], is probably the best literary work about the Civil War, having most shockingly portrayed its horror."[4] *The Lay of Ulyalaev* and especially *Fur Trade* remain unsurpassed masterpieces of Russian epic and narrative poetry. Soviet leaders who took a keen interest in the new letters, among them Lev Trotsky and Nikolai Bukharin, expressed admiration for Selvinsky's poetry. Lazar Fleishman, in whose study of Boris Pasternak in the 1930s Selvinsky makes numerous appearances, highlights a characteristic episode. At an event hosted by Lev Trotsky in 1926, which brought together editors of leading Moscow "thick" journals Aleksandr Voronsky (*Krasnaia nov'* [*Red Virgin Soil*]) and Vyacheslav Polonsky (*Novy Mir* [*New World*]) and the poets Boris Pasternak, Semyon Kirsanov, and Ilya Selvinsky, Trotsky singled out Selvinsky and asked him to recite a section of *The Lay of Ulyalaev* for the second time.[5] Vyacheslav Polonsky (1886-1932), one of the dominant literary critics of the 1920s, lauded Selvinsky's contribution:

> *The Lay of Ulyalaev*, long poems and a whole range of shorter works speak of Selvinsky as a rising star of Russian poetry. [...] At that Selvinsky is from head to toe a creation of our epoch. He grew up in the Revolution. Revolutionary is not only the material he uses; revolutionary is his very approach to literary mastery. The least traditional of the contemporary poets, one who disregards all of the existing or past canons, [a poet] heavyish and difficult, in the development of Russian poetry Selvinsky represents a step forward from the marvelous intimate art of Pasternak and from Mayakovsky's achievements. [...] Selvinsky is one of the poets who not only has a past, but also has a future.[6]

---

4   Aleksandr Revich, "Sedoe s detstva pokoleni'e," in Il'ia Sel'vinskii. *Iz pepla, iz poem, iz snovidenii*, ed. A. M. Revich, 15 (Moscow: Vremia, 2004).
5   Lazar' Fleishman, *Boris Pasternak v tridtsatye gody*, 12-14 (Jerusalem: Magnes Press/Hebrew University, 1984). Fleishman quotes from the memoirs of Mariia Ioffe.
6   Viasheslav Polonskii, *Ocherki literaturnogo dvizheniia revoliutsionnoi epokhi*, 2nd ed., 46 (Moscow: Gosudarstvennoe izdatel'stvo, 1929).

Selvinsky's polemic and rivalry with Vladimir Mayakovsky was one of the highlights of the Soviet literary scene in the late 1920s, while his grudging recantation of the Constructivist program in 1930-1931 did not earn him much trust from the regime.

The wreath of sonnets *Bar Kokhba* (1920, pub. 1924) occupies a special place among Selvinsky's works. While perhaps influenced by both the Yiddish drama *Bar Kokhba* (1887) by Abraham Goldfaden and by Vladimir (Ze'ev) Jabotinsky's Russian-language poem "In Memory of Herzl" (1904), Selvinsky's *Bar Kokhba* has no equivalents in early Soviet writing. Against the backdrop of a growing campaign against traditional Jewish life and Judaism in the Soviet Union, the work became a powerful monument to Jewish—and Judaic—survival. Selvinsky's other major Jewish works of the pre-World War II years included "Mot'ka Malkhamoves" ("Motke the Angel of Death," 1926; from the Hebrew and Yiddish "Malech-hamovess"), "Anecdotes about the Karaite Philosopher Babakai-Sudduk" (1931), *The Lay of Ulyalaev*, and *Fur Trade*. Selvinsky's poem "Portrait of My Mother" (1933) contained a bitter comment about Jewish assimilation in the USSR: "Henceforth her son's face will remain defiled/Like the Judaic Jerusalem,/Having suddenly become a Christian holy site." In 1930, trying to redeem himself after the onslaught against the independent literary groups of the 1920s, Selvinsky composed the opportunistic poem "From Palestine to Birobidzhan"(1930, pub. 1933).

In 1939 Selvinsky created the play *The Tushino Camp*, known in manuscript as *A Version of False Dmitri II* and set in the 1600s, during Russia's "Time of Troubles." In the introduction, Selvinsky turned to Shakespeare in order to explain his motivation in giving literary credence to theories of the Jewish origin of the impostor-tsar False Dmitri II (who came to be known as *tushinskii vor*—the Tushino thief). "Shylock is an entirely different matter," Selvinsky argued. "The depth of this image is not only in his being a father fighting to avenge his daughter's seduction, but also in his being a Jew, avenging his national oppression. Here one could not change any significant shadings. Othello's national particularity is a color; Shylock's national particularity is an idea."[7] Not surprisingly, *The Tushino Thief* was officially dismissed as lacking "un-

---

7   Il'ia Sel'vinskii, *Tushinskii lager'*, *Zerkalo* 15-16 (2000), http://magazines.russ.ru/zerkalo/2000/15/14selv.html, last accessed 20 February 2012.

derstanding of history,"[8] and remained unpublished until 2000, when Selvinsky's daughter, the visual artist and poet Tatyana Selvinskaya, unearthed it from the archive and offered it to a Russian-Israeli journal for publication. One of the play's principal subtexts is S. An-sky's *The Dibbuk* (1911-1919), which in and of itself is a remarkable fact for a Soviet play written in 1930 for the stage. In a short appreciation of Selvinsky that appeared as a preface to *The Tushino Camp*, the Russian-Israeli critic Aleksandr Goldshtein noted:

> [... A]bove all, let us stress that obvious eye-catching [feature]: the high class of the writing. Classics write this way (and those avant-gardists who have become classics). And one more, equally important point: if Ilya Lvovich's attempts to perceive the epochal tempo-rhythm tended, as a rule, to be successful, he only succeeded every other time to embrace the ideological tenets mandatory for all. An enthusiastic appeal to rebellious values and a Jewish-Messianic substratum of a foreigners' invasion was in 1939, at the time of the forming of a new, post-revolutionary, national-state mythology, absolutely out of place.[9]

Throughout his literary career, Selvinsky had his share of official chastisement and ostracism, denunciations and near-misses.[10] In the words of Arlen Blium, starting with the mid-1920s, "Selvinsky constantly remained on the radar screen of the organs of censorship."[11] On 20 May 1945, as Selvinsky looked back at his rollercoaster prewar literary career

---

8   See Selvinsky, Wartime Diaries, 27 April 1942; cf. Babenko, *Voina*, 42. Selvinsky recalled in his diary that Aleksandr Shcherbakov scolded him and thrust a middle school textbook of history "under [his] nose." Wartime Diaries, Authorized corrected photocopy at the Selvinsky Memorial Museum, Simferopol (hereafter Selvinsky, Wartime Diaries). Throughout this book, whenever possible, I will cross-reference Selvinsky's published diaries and letters with their manuscripts. In many cases, diaries and letters have been published with errors, omissions, lacunae, and editorial/censorial intrusions, most of which can only be clarified by going directly to archival sources.

9   Aleksandr Gol'dshtein, "O Sel'vinskom," *Zerkalo* 15-16 (2000), http://magazines.russ.ru/zerkalo/2000/15/14selv.html, last accessed 20 February 2012.

10 For a useful overview of Selvinsky's troubles with Stalin's regime, see Babenko and Gavriliuk, 91-107.

11 Arlen Blium, "Index librorum prohibitorum russkikh pisatelei," Part 4, *NLO* 62 (2003), http://magazines.russ.ru/nlo/2003/62/blum.html, last accessed 19 September 2011.

while already anticipating the postwar ambush of creative artists by the Stalinist regime, he reminisced in his diary:

> When in 1928 my *Fur Trade* came out, Kerzhentsev raised a scream in the newspapers [Platon Kerzhentev was at the time Deputy Chief of the Directorate of Propaganda and Agitation of the Central Committee of the Communist Party], that it was supposedly the intelligentsia's claim to power. All newspapers picked up this scream and turned it into a call for action. Then I wrote a letter to *Komsomolskaya Pravda* [*Komsomol'skaia Pravda*]—"A Reply to Comrade Kerzhentsev"—in which I strenuously objected to his thesis. [...] Naturally *Komsomolskaya Pravda* did not print the letter but forwarded it to Kerzhentsev."[12]

What followed, according to Selvinsky's diary, was an invitation to become Chairman of the Union of Writers. After Selvinsky repeatedly turned down Kerzhentsev's invitation, this exchange took place:

> —Why are you refusing? [Kerzhentsev asked]—Odd question. You have just done everything to undermine my reputation as a writer in the eyes of the society, and now this "thrashed" wise man is to become Chairman of the Union!—We shall restore your reputation, Kerzhentsev said, unperturbed.—And *Fur Trade*?—We shall find a formula for it, too.
> I did not expect such cynicism and was literally stunned. I said many insolent things to K. and then left.[13]

In his public conduct and in his writings, Selvinsky remained a proud poet—and a proud Jew—despite rounds of direct official ostracism. Due to his personal bravery, chutzpah, and competitive nature, and also his hubristic ambition to be a tribune and voice of the people, Selvinsky periodically attempted to articulate in poetry what he thought might

---

12 Selvinsky, Wartime Diaries, 20 May 1945.
13 Selvinsky, Wartime Diaries, 20 May 1945.

influence or at least inform official Soviet rhetoric. Selvinsky's ideological bets with history, some of which in retrospect appear both naïve and miscalculated, did not serve him well with Stalin and his henchmen.

Throughout the 1930s, Selvinsky's official status proved to be precarious while he continued to enjoy great literary acclaim. The (founding) First Congress of the Union of Soviet Writers, which convened in August-September 1934 in Moscow, offers ample evidence of Selvinsky's position. In the proceedings of the congress, Selvinsky's name was the fourth-most-frequently evoked of all the living Soviet poets, trailing Boris Pasternak's and Nikolai Tikhonov's, and closely competing with Nikolay Aseev's. At the congress Nikolai Bukharin, one of the leading Bolsheviks and editor-in-chief of the daily *Izvestia*, delivered a long speech about poetry. At the time Bukharin, whose career had entered a downward spiral in 1928-1929 and would eventually end with his purging in 1938, still wielded much influence, not least in the realm of literary politics. To "Tikhonov, Selvinsky, Pasternak," the three poets fatefully conjoined in a poetic line by Eduard Bagritsky, Bukharin added Nikolay Aseev, labeling Pasternak, Selvinsky, Tikhonov, and Aseev as the four living Soviet poets of "the very highest caliber" who influenced the poetic scene in "the most decisive fashion." Bukharin praised Pasternak's originality and mastery most highly, yet favored Selvinsky's longer and shorter poetry with an almost equal enthusiasm: "I. Selvinsky is to a certain measure B. Pasternak's antipode. He is a poet with a big poetic voice, seeking to burst out to the expanses of wide roads, mass scenes, where one hears screaming, where horses stomp their hooves, where a dashing song is pouring out, where enemies fight, where a living life is boiling and where history kneads its tough dough." Bukharin also chided Selvinsky, if gently, for sometimes "failing his own directive" and substituting "rhymed factory wall newspaper" for "attempts [...] at vast canvasses." Bukharin closed the Selvinsky section of his speech by calling him "an undoubtedly revolutionary, very big, real—and at that cultured—master of verse."[14]

A number of Soviet poets, most memorably Selvinsky's coeval Aleksey Surkov, took umbrage at Bukharin's position and at his being partial to Pasternak and Selvinsky and short-shrifting (rightfully, one might add)

---

14 See Bukharin's speech in I. K. Luppol et al., eds., *Pervyi vsesoiuznyi s"ezd sovetskikh pisatelei. 1934. Stenograficheskii otchet*, 479-503 (Moscow: Gosudarstvennoe izdatel'stvo "Khudozhestvennaia literatura", 1934; Rpt. Moscow: Sovetskii pisatel', 1990).

some of the ideologically more orthodox and formally inferior poets.[15] The response to Bukharin's poetry speech in fact adumbrated a turn in Stalinist cultural policy after the First Congress; as Fleishman notes, "from the autumn of 1934 Bukharin's speech was being referenced in a markedly negative fashion."[16] Selvinsky's unapologetic remarks at the First Congress sum up his stance: "I consider the main challenge of working in poetry [the fact] that the wide reading public absorbs the new verse with difficulty. Take any thought, express it in normal human speech, and everybody understands. Yet the poet speaks in an abnormal, rhythmical language. [...] But the trouble is that the critics do not promote our wealth among the masses [Selvinsky uses this expression to refer to the achievements of Soviet poetry]."[17]

From the late 1920s and throughout the rest of his life, its middle part intersecting with the years of Stalin's rule, Selvinsky advanced an artistic platform that could be described by three ideological-aesthetic principles. He argued, through thick and thin, that artistic form must be experimental, and that Soviet art must possess a complex structure and texture. He emphasized that the *narodnost'* (here understood as an artistic sense of nationhood or peoplehood) of Soviet literature cannot be restricted to the interests and aspirations of workers and peasants and must give voice and form to the intelligentsia. Finally Selvinsky warned, sometimes through his criticism of other authors, that Russian cultural chauvinism threatens not only the ideology of Soviet national unity but also the development of Soviet art.[18]

As a young poet Selvinsky was so impressed with *Das Kapital* that he added the name Karl to his first name and for a long period of time signed his works "Eli-Karl Selvinsky," a form binding together his wor-

---

15 See Surkov's speech in Luppol et al., *Pervyi vsesoiuznyi s"ezd sovetskikh pisatelei. 1934*, 512-514; see also Aleksandr Eshanov, "V preddverii zamysla," *Alef* 991 (2009), http://www.alefmagazine.com/pub1917.html, last accessed 29 January 2012; Valentin Domil', "Zvezdy i ternii Il'i Sel'vinskogo. Evreiskii vopros 'korolia poetov'," *Sekretnyi portal. Zhurnal Vladimira Pletinskogo* 16 April 2010, http://velelens.livejournal.com/45472.html, accessed 29 January 2012.
16 Fleishman, *Boris Pasternak*, 219.
17 See Selvinsky's speech in Luppol et al., *Pervyi vsesoiuznyi s"ezd sovetskikh pisatelei. 1934*, 554-557.
18 Selvinsky's position comes across very clearly in his letter to Ilya Ehrenburg of 25 November 1956, expounding upon and explaining his own polemical article "Sense of Nationhood and Poetry" (1956), which in turn had been occasioned by Ehrenburg's article "On the Poems of Boris Slutsky" (1956); both articles had appeared in *Literary Gazette*. See Selvinsky, Letter to Ehrenburg, 25 November 1956 in B. Ia. Frezinskii, ed., *Pochta Il'i Erenburga. Ia slyshu vse...1916-1967*, 331-334 (Moscow: Agraf, 2006); Il'a Erenburg, "O stikhakh Borisa Slutskogo," *Literaturnaia gazeta* 8 July 1956; Sel'vinskii, "Narodnost'" i poeziia," *Literaturnaia gazeta* 18 October 1956.

ship of Marx with the traditional style of Jewish double or hyphenated first names.¹⁹ (In Isaac Babel's story of 1931, a Jewish boy is given the name "Karl-Yankel"—after Karl Marx and Jacob the Patriarch—and is secretly circumcised by his grandmother). As late as in his 1940s identification papers, Selvinsky's full name still appears as "Ilya-Karl Lvovich Selvinsky." A blazing modernist and a classicist, an intellectual and an artist, a Marxist by heart's conviction, a Jew, a Russian, and a Soviet, like an icebreaker Selvinsky pressed for a navigational path of his own. He tried to take cues from the regime, yet insisted on his inalienable right to an aesthetic of his own, and also on featuring members of the intelligentsia, and not workers and peasants, as his chosen heroes.

Characteristic is the story of the creation of Selvinsky's epic work based on his participation, as a special correspondent for *Pravda*, in the SS *Chelyuskin* Arctic expedition of 1933-1934.

2. Ilya Selvinsky (second from left) with fellow participants of the SS Chelyuskin expedition. Murmansk. Circa August 1933. (Courtesy of Tatyana Selvinskaya.)

---

19 About Selvinsky's hyphenated first name see, for instance, Tsetsiliia Voskresenkaia, "Oproverzhenie," *Canadian Slavonic Papers* 27.1-2 (1995): 281-282. In the poem "Youth" ("Iunost'," 1920) and elsewhere in poetry Selvinsky wrote of studying Karl Marx in his youth.

———————————— CHAPTER ONE ————————————

Selvinsky began work on the epic poem *Chelyuskiniana* in 1934, soon after his return from the expedition, which ended with the sinking of the ship and the survival of its crew. Selvinsky and a small group of comrades had left the expedition earlier upon the order of the leader, the Polar explorer Otto Shmidt. Shmidt later came to Selvinsky's defense when unfounded public charges and rumors of cowardice were leveled against the poet.[20] Still, Selvinsky's aborted participation in the expedition became something of a pretext for an orchestrated critical campaign against him and his writings. This campaign reached a peak at the February 1937 Pushkin Plenary Meeting of the Governing Body of the Union of Soviet Writers. The Pushkin Plenary Meeting, as Fleishman has shown, became the forum for the dismantling of what one might call the Bukharin line in Soviet literature, and Pasternak and Selvinsky were the principal targets.[21] In his response, quoted in the Soviet press as an example of his allegedly disingeneous attempts to portray himself as a "victim" of ostracism (which he was), Selvinsky said: "It is bitter for me to realize that I, a thirty-seven-year-old adult, a healthy, physically strong, absolutely Soviet man, have no creative perspectives whatsoever. I know in advance that whatever I would write, there would always be people who would pull four lines from me and cover with spit whatever I do."[22]

In fact, Selvinsky had been having a hard time publishing his Arctic epic. In 1936 he placed short excerpts in newspapers, and part one appeared in the January 1937 issue of *Novy Mir*. Then the publication was stalled for a year. There were several factors behind Selvinsky's difficulties. It did not go unnoticed that Selvinsky's epic refused to concoct a proletarian or peasant hero. As Susanne Frank recently argued, "Selvinsky's long poem turns Otto Iulievich Shmidt into a prototype of a Soviet hero, Stalin's envoy, juxtaposed to the Norwegian conqueror of the South and North poles Amundsen. [...] The epic's other heroic figure is the radio operator [Ernst] Krenkel [...]."[23] Neither Shmidt nor Krenkel is an ethnic Russian, and both have foreign, Germanic names. However, it appears that the main reason for the publishing difficulties stemmed

---

20 O[tto] Iu. Shmidt, "Pisateli na 'Cheliuskine'," *Literaturnaia gazeta* 28 June 1934.
21 See Fleishman, *Boris Pasternak*, 196-199.
22 "Na pushkinskom plenume pravleniia Soiuza sovetskikh pisatelei," *Izvestiia* 27 February 1937, quoted in Fleishman, *Boris Pasternak*, 399.
23 Siuzanna Frank [Susanne Frank], "Teplaia Arktika: k istorii odnogo starogo literaturnogo motiva," tr. Tatiana Lastovka, *NLO* 108 (2011), http://magazines.russ.ru/nlo/2011/108/fr7.html, last accessed 29 January 2012.

from the sections of the epic devoted to Stalin, and to Selvinsky's approach to praising the Soviet leader. Although different in verse texture and voice, this approach may be likened to the one Boris Pasternak attempted in his four-part cycle "The Artist" published in *Izvestia* on 1 January 1936. There Stalin, although unnamed, appeared as an "artist" of history. The quality of Pasternak's and Selvinsky's verse, the loftiness of Pasternak's allegory in the Stalin cycle, and the might of Selvinsky's epic voice in the Stalin pages of *Chelyuskiniana* had the potential to lend more aesthetic validity to the tyrant than hundreds of cultist hymns, and yet neither work had struck its goal.[24]

This brings us to the 28 December 1937 report on Selvinsky's *Chelyuskiniana* sent to three Soviet leaders by Lev Mekhlis,[25] then a member of Stalin's inner circle. The note was addressed to the Soviet Premier and Politburo member Vyasheslav Molotov, to Lazar Kaganovich, Politburo member and one of Stalin's closest party generals, and to Andrei Zhdanov, Secretary of the Central Committee and Leningrad party boss after the murder of Sergey Kirov in 1934. Selvinsky had complained to Molotov about the difficulties he experienced with his epic work, and Mekhlis was responding to Molotov's consequent inquiry. In 1930-1937 Mekhlis had been editor of *Pravda*, and was afterward appointed Deputy People's Commissar of Defense and Chief of the Army's Political Directorate (PUR). Mekhlis's note is a fascinating document which shows the extent to which Selvinsky was known and knowable to the top echelon of the Stalinist leadership:[26]

> In connection with the note by the poet Selvinsky addressed to comrade Molotov, I have the following to

---

24 Neither Pasternak's nor Selvinsky's 1930s poetry about Stalin was selected for the 1936 anthology *Poems and Songs about Stalin*, which featured sycophantic texts by such talented Russian-language poets as Nikolay Zabolotsky and Aleksandr Prokofiev and poetry translated from a number of languages of the USSR, including many from Georgian and two from Yiddish. See Efim Zozulia and Aleksandr Chachikov, eds., *Stikhi i pesni o Staline* (Moscow: Zhurnal'nogazetnoe ob"edinenie, 1937); see also Fleishman, *Boris Pasternak*, 284-285.

25 In his recent book about Mekhlis, engaging albeit tainted by an anti-Jewish prejudice, Iurii Rubtsov makes no mention of Mekhlis's 1937 note on Selvinsky or of Mekhlis's subsequent encounters with Selvinsky, including those at the Crimean war theater in 1942; see Iu. V. Rubtsov, *Mekhlis. Ten' vozhdia* (Moscow: Veche, 2011).

26 Evgeny Dobrenko, in his study of the "forging of the Soviet writer," touches on Selvinsky's engagement with the regime and on the attention paid to Selvinsky by the apparatus of Soviet censorship. See Evgenii Dobrenko, *Formovka sovetskogo pisatelia: Sotsial'nye i esteticheskie istoki sovetskoi literaturnoi kul'tury* (St. Petersburg: Akademicheskii proekt, 1999), 450, 476, and passim.

report. [...] A chapter in the long poem *Chelyuskiniana* is devoted to a literary portrait of comrade Stalin. Previously Selvinsky negotiated [the publication of this long poem]. At the time *Pravda* did not agree to print the [submitted] version of the long poem. That which Selvinsky is now passing for a long poem about comrade Stalin differs radically from the original text. The author has either deleted or modified the most atrocious, illiterate places. [...] It would be difficult for me to quote in a letter everything that Selvinsky has corrected, as this would take up a huge amount of space. I shall quote only the most characteristic [excerpts]. [...] The part, concerning a description of how comrade Stalin walked through a [military] formation, has been radically redone by the author. I would not say that it is entirely satisfactory. [...] Selvinsky is a formalist [a very negative Soviet term referring to active formal quest in literature and the arts—MDS], he writes in a language completely unintelligible to the masses. [...] Even in the latest version of the long poem about Stalin, substantially corrected, he all the time dubs Stalin "Soso" [Georgian diminutive of Stalin's first name—MDS]. [...] Of Stalin's appearance at the first congress of collective farms [First All-Union Congress of Collective Farm Shock Brigadiers, 1933] he writes this way: "There sits a man with the face of a portrait." Thereafter he continues: "Touched with drumbeat, a rough-hewn face." [...] There are good instances in the long poem, but on the whole it is written in such a language that it is difficult to read it. The mass reading public will not understand many places; some are marked by ambiguity. I suppose that Selvinsky needs to work on the long poem some more, mainly in the direction of turning it into a work accessible to the mass reading public."[27]

---

[27] L[ev] Mekhlis, "[Zapiska] Molotovu, Kaganovichu, Zhdanovu o poeme Sel'vinskogo 'Cheliuskiniana.' 28 December 1937," Fond Aleksandra N. Iakovleva, http://www.alexanderyakovlev.org/fond/issues-doc/1015940, accessed 29 January 2012.

Did Mekhlis recognize a connection between Selvinsky's refusal to portray Stalin in a simplistically cultist fashion and the centrality of verbal technique in Selvinsky's poetry? Several days later Molotov wrote a short (and slightly ungrammatical) resolution on Mekhlis's report: "To comrades Kaganovich and Zhdanov: In the least this much needs to be done without allowing into print the 'long poem' and without a new scrutiny of it."[28] Excerpts from part two and part three of *Chelyskiniana* appeared in the leading monthlies *Novy Mir* and *October (Oktiabr')* in 1938, but Selvinsky was unable to publish a complete text of the revised and re-revised text of his "epic poem about Stalin."[29] In 1957 a further reworked version, titled *Arctic: A Novel*, was published in Thaw-era Moscow, stripped of its Stalinist sections. The revisions of *Arctic* were part of Selvinsky's larger postwar project of revamping his epic poems, whereby a lot of the intricacy, poignancy, and originality was purged from his texts.[30]

In the 1930s Selvinsky was twice targeted by separate party resolutions. On 21 April 1937, the Politburo issued the resolution "Concerning Selvinsky's play *Umka the Polar Bear*." Stick and carrot, carrot and stick were applied to some of the leading Soviet writers in the 1930s, and Selvinsky was among them. In 1938 he was decorated with the Order of the Red Banner of Labor. On 4 August 1939, on the eve of World War II, Selvinsky was chastised in the resolution of the Orgburo of the Central Committee titled "On the Magazine *October* and Poems by I. L. Selvinsky," and his poems were deemed "anti-artistic and harmful."[31]

Despite the official denunciations, in 1938-41 Selvinsky was professor at the Literary Institute in Moscow and poetry editor at *October*, and a principal mentor to the younger generation of Soviet poets, the

---

28 Mekhlis, "[Zapiska] Molotovu, Kaganovichu, Zhdanovu o poeme Sel'vinskogo 'Cheliuskiniana.'" 28 December 1937."
29 See *"Selvinskii, Il'ia L'vovich,"* in *Bibliograficheskii ukazatel'*, 39; Frank.
30 Selvinskii, *Arktika. Roman* (Moscow: Sovetskii pisatel', 1957).
31 See Andrei Artizov, Oleg Naumov, eds., *Vlast' i khudozhestvennaia intelligentsia: dokumety TsK RKP(b)-VKP(b), VChK-OGPU-NKVD o kul'turnoi politike, 1917-1953 gg.*, 359; 430; 433 (Moscow: Mezhdunarodnyi fond "Demokratiia", 1999); D. L. Babichenko, *"Literaturnyi front". Istoriia politicheskoi tsenzury 1932-1946 gg. Sbornik dokumentov*, 22; 40 (Moscow: Entsiklopediia rossiiskikh dereven', 1994); see also Babenko and Gavriliuk. See a discussion of Selvinsky's position in the late 1930s by the poet Vladimir Kornilov. Kornilov brings to light a critique of Selvinsky by the then-young and relatively unknown Konstantin Simonov, published in *Literary gazette* on 15 January 1938. Simonov argued that Selvinsky needs to "seek a path to the heart of the mass reader." See Kornilov, "Dvoe. Kniazhii vnuk i vnuchka prachki," http://www.chukfamily.ru/Lidia/Biblio/kornilov_dvoe.htm, last accessed 29 January 2012.

generation of Lev Ozerov (1914-1996), David Samoilov (1920-1990), and Boris Slutsky (1919-1986). In 1939-40 when, following the outbreak of World War II and then during the Soviet-Finnish War, Soviet writers were given military ranks, Selvinsky was made *intendant* second class (an administrative non-combat rank corresponding to major or battalion commissar).[32]

3. Ilya Selvinsky with his family members. Moscow. April 1941 Left to right: Selvinsky, wife Berta, stepdaughter Tsetsiliya, mother-in-law Anna Moiseevna; with the back to the camera: daughter Tatyana. (Courtesy of Tatyana Selvinskaya.)

At the time of the Nazi invasion Selvinsky may have remained, as Tatyana Selvinskaya reminisced, an "ardent admirer of Stalin."[33] Selvinsky's diaries and private letters bear out the notion of Selvinsky's faith in the Soviet system much more than they simply expose his ardent Stalinism. Selvinsky kept going back and forth in his assessment of

---

32 See Filat'ev, 70.
33 Tatyana Selvinskaya, Personal Interview, Simferopol, 15 December 2011.

Stalin and of how to write and not to write about Stalin. The war and the Shoah put to the final test Selvinsky's vision of Stalin, of Soviet history, and of his own triple identity.

2. The Nazi Invasion and the Frontlines

In the 1930s, the reaction of Jewish-Russian poets to Nazism was muted at best and virtually absent at worst. In the USSR, poets were not having an easy time confronting the growing misfortunes of European Jewry or placing antifascist verses with specific Jewish references in Soviet publications. In 1936 Ilya Selvinsky traveled to Berlin and composed—perhaps concocted says it better—poems of political protest, including two short satires of Nazi Germany's anti-Jewish climate: "Antisemites" and "The Jewish Question." In "The Jewish Question," a brown-clad doorman first proclaims that no songs by "the Jew Heine" would be performed in a Berlin café, then mutters a song with Heine's lyrics—as though unaware of the irony of his performance. Selvinsky's poems based on his impressions from this visit to Berlin would remain unpublished until 1956.[34]

The outbreak of World War II and the Soviet annexation of Eastern Poland, North Bukovina, and the Baltic areas with their still-unSovietized Jewish populations did not elicit a response from Selvinsky. Had he and the vast majority of the Jewish-Russian poets in the USSR—Ilya Ehrenburg and the young Boris Slutsky excepting—not been aching to write about the looming tragedy west of the Soviet borders? This question is not easy to answer without a degree of speculation. We can definitely observe that in the atmosphere of the first weeks and months of the Nazi invasion of the Soviet Union, which were quite disastrous for

---

34   See Il'ia Sel'vinskii, "Antisemity"; "Evreiskii vopros," in *Izbrannye proizvedeniia*, 2 vols., 1: 155; 156 (Moscow: Goslitidat, 1956); cf. Il'ia Sel'vinskii, *O vremeni, o sud'bakh, o liubvi*, 69-70 (Moscow: Sovetskii pisatel', 1962). In a letter dated 9 June 1936 and sent from Paris to Nikolai Bukharin in Moscow, Ehrenburg reacted to the official displeasure with Selvinsky's work: "Why would one first send Selvinsky abroad, and then print in the newspaper that this is 'gallimaufry'? The fascists quote our papers and ask the leftist intelligentsia: 'Is this what you applauded a month ago' and so forth"; see I. G. Erenburg, *Pis'ma*, ed. B. Ia. Frezinskii, 2: 222 (Moscow: Agraf, 2004). The political context surrounding the composition of Selvinsky's "The Jewish Question" is very briefly discussed in Rainer Grübel, "Genij-Geije. Zur Struktur und zur Strukturbildenen Funktion eines Reims in dem Gedicht 'Evreiskij vopros' von Il'ja Sel'vinskij." *Die Welt der Slaven* 18 (1973): 183-184.

the Red Army, Selvinsky and many other Jewish-Russian authors were overcome with a new spiritual and cultural fervor. On 9 December 1942 Selvinsky spoke of this wartime upsurge of triple self-awareness in a letter he sent from Crimea to his wife Berta Selvinskaya:

> On 27, 28, and 29 September very heavy fighting took place, in which I had the happiness to participate. I underscore, happiness! These three days have enriched my soul. That I have survived and even remained unscathed is almost a miracle. [...] I, for instance, simply cannot imagine not being at the front! This is not the Finnish Campaign, but a war, striking all of our motherland, a war on the outcome of which depends the whole future of our people and its cultutre. In such a war being at the front is not only a fulfillment of one's duty but also an achievement of personal happiness. It is all about how one understands this very happiness.[35]

It was a military country at war, and many poets became soldiers. Some of them volunteered, others were drafted; others yet, including some of the leading authors of the older generation who did not volunteer, were evacuated to the hinterlands. Many Jewish-Russian authors served as military journalists during the war, becoming voices of the Soviet people fighting at both the war front and the home front. They viewed the war and their calling not only in Russian and Soviet terms, but also in Jewish ones. This new sense of mission (and commission) was liberating, yet it expressed itself in different ways, not all of them literary and some of them directly or indirectly propagandistic. As Mordechai Altshuler observes, "Upon the Nazi invasion of the USSR, the Soviet propaganda system stepped up its activity. Quite a few Jews enlisted very willingly in this system, sensing now, perhaps more than ever, that their sentiments and their country's policies were fully aligned."[36]

Soon after the Nazi invasion, Selvinsky volunteered for the war front.

---

35   Sel'vinskii, "Na voine. Iz dnevnikov i pisem rodnym," 166-167; cf. excerpts in Babenko, *Voina*, 11-12.
36   Altshuler, "The Shoah in the Soviet Mass Media during the War and in the First Postwar Years Reexamined," *Yad Vashem Studies* 39.2 (2011): 125.

Tatyana Selvinskaya reminisced that her father inspired the members of his poetry seminar at the Literary Institute to volunteer immediately—and many in fact did so.[37] Initially Selvinsky was not sought after as a staff writer or correspondent either by *Krasnaia Zvezda* (*Red Star*), the army's main newspaper, or by the national civilian newspapers. In fact, though Selvinsky arrived at the front in August 1941, he did not become a special correspondent for *Red Star* until October 1942, when he had already been serving as a rank-and-file writer for an army newspaper.

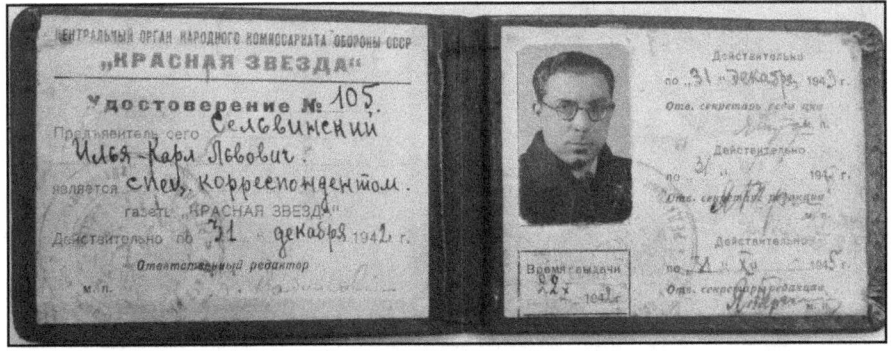

4. Ilya Selvinsky. Identification as a special correspondent of *Krasnaia zvezda* (*Red Star*), issued on 22 October 1942. Signed on the bottom left side "D. Vadimov," penname of Major General David Ortenberg, editor of *Red Star*. (Courtesy of Ilya Selvinsky Memorial Museum, Simferopol.)

Vying for greater fame and military glory, Selvinsky saw action in battle—not just the newsroom behind the frontlines—in Crimea, at North Caucasus, and in Russia's Kuban region. (Previously part of the Russian Federation, in 1954 the Crimean peninsula was transferred to what was then the Ukrainian SSR, and it is presently an autonomous republic within the independent Ukraine). Selvinsky was initially assigned as a staff writer to *Syn otechestva* (*Son of Fatherland*), the newspaper of the 51st Separate Army.[38] He had apparently asked to be assigned to the Black Sea navy, but the then-powerful Mekhlis had a hand at placing

---

37 Tatyana Selvinskaya, Personal Interview, 15 December 2011.
38 See Selvinsky, Wartime Diaries, 23 September 1941 and 7 November 1941; cf. Babenko, *Voina*, 16; 22.

him at *Son of Fatherland*, which was certainly not a particularly visible assignment for a famous Soviet poet.[39]

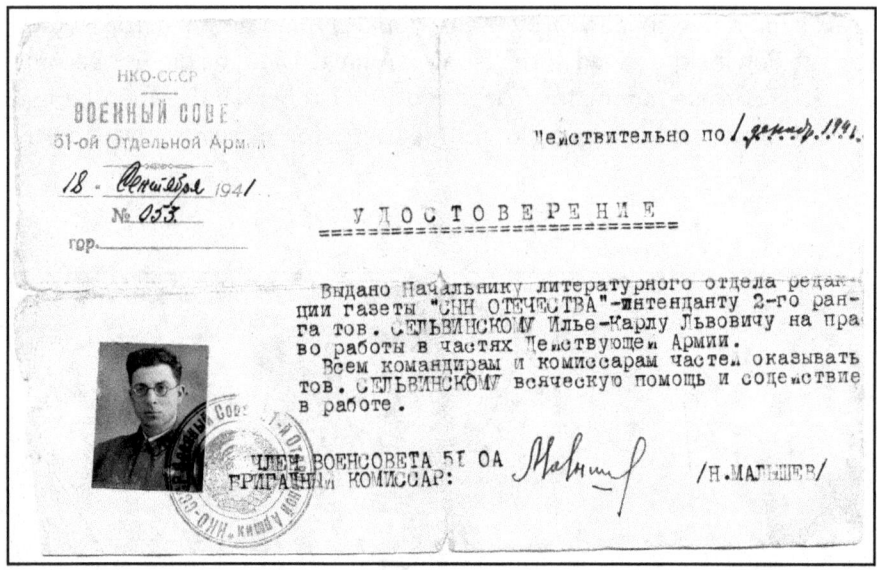

5. Ilya Selvinsky. Army identification as a staff writer for *Syn otechestva* (*Son of Fatherland*), issued on 18 September 1941 by the 51 Separate Army. (Courtesy of Ilya Selvinsky Memorial Museum, Simferopol.)

Surviving wartime diaries offer examples of Selvinsky's assessment of his literary affairs. Soon after arriving in Crimea, Selvinsky recorded this in a notebook titled "Diary. 1941. Soviet-Fascist War": "[...T]here was also something promising in my life before the war. But, like a stone on my heart, lay three tragedies that could not even be printed, never mind staged. [...] What can one do to forget one's sad musings? How

---

39 At the outbreak of the war with Nazi Germany the Soviet press and propaganda apparatus found itself not very well staffed to cover the frontlines, and hence there was a certain initial chanciness in the assignment of correspondents. See, for instance, Irina Shirokorad's comments in her dissertation prospectus, "Tsentral'naia periodicheskaia pechat' SSSR v gody Velikoi Otechestvennoi voiny, 1941-1945 gg." Avtoreferat (Moscow, 2002), http://www.dissercat.com/content/tsentralnaya-periodicheskaya-pechat-sssr-v-gody-velikoi-otechestvennoi-voiny-1941-1945-gg., last accessed 27 October 2011.

memory sometimes gets in the way [...]."[40] Selvinsky's diary entries for August-September 1941 reflect the poet's displeasure with both his rank and his placement:

> So I am in Crimea again. Just like back in 1918, it is once again my destiny to defend the same Turkish Rampart from the Germans. I was appointed, as is stated in PUR's order No. 00738 [PUR is the acronym for the Chief Political Directorate of the Red Army], "to the position of staff writer [pisatel']" for the editorial office of the army newspaper." My rank is *intendant* second class. Oh, well… Considering that Pushkin's rank was *Kammerjunker* [a court rank appropriate for a younger aristocrat, not a great poet], and Lermontov's was simply *junker* [Lermontov's rank during his years of study in junior officer's school], I cannot fret too much. Second class, so be it.[41]

Selvinsky probably could not imagine that his native Crimea was to fall within months and that Sebastopol, the principal base of the Soviet Black Sea navy, would be besieged and eventually lost in July 1942. He speculated that some of his peers working at military newspapers might spend the war without ever tasting gunpowder. "I'm writing [this] in Sebastopol (I was given the assignment to prepare a page spread about the navy for the paper)," the poet noted on 23 October 1941. "I'm staying in the palace where [Admiral] Kolchak once stayed, and where the culture department of the front's headquarters is presently housed. Writers are staying here [...]. I saw Fedka [Fyodor] Reshetnikov, the cartoonist with whom I sailed on the *SS Chelyuskin*. The boys are living in comfort. They do not visit the frontlines. Evidently, they would live through the war in contentment."[42]

---

40 Selvinsky, Wartime Diaries, August 1941.
41 Babenko, *Voina*, 6.
42 Selvinsky, Wartime Diaries; cf. Babenko, *Voina*, 16; cf. Sel'vinskii, "Ia eto videl (Krymskie stranitsy voennykh dnevnikov)," 78.

6. Ilya Selvinsky (on the left) with Aleksandr Terlovsky, who headed the propaganda section at *Syn otechestva* (*Son of Fatherland*). Circa late 1941-early 1942. (Courtesy of Tatiana Selvinskaya).

Selvinsky regretted not having been allowed to stay in Sebastopol and defend the city-port. The trajectory of the Soviet retreat brought him to the eastern part of the Crimean peninsula, where the Kerch peninsula forms a eastward-pointing protrusion. During the retreat of Soviet troops from the Kerch peninsula in November 1941, Selvinsky crossed the Strait of Taman with forces of the 51st Separate Army and arrived on the Taman peninsula.[43] Less than two months later, during the Kerch-Feodosia Landing Operation, he returned to Kerch, the site of his most traumatic wartime experiences (see Ill. 11).

Selvinsky's path crossed with that of Mekhlis in February 1942, when Mekhlis, then head of PUR and Deputy People's Commissar of Defense, was sent to the Crimean Front as Stalin's representative. In his diary on 3 February 1942 Selvinsky noted a conversation with Mekhlis: "He spoke with me politely, but a bit on the dry side. Said that it was a crime on my part not to contribute to *Red Star*. Offered to transfer me from *Son of Fatherland* to *Fighting Thrust* (trading army for front) and stated that [with the transfer] he would change my status from that

---

43 See Babenko, *Voina*, 21-23.

of an *intendant* to that of a political officer."⁴⁴ In early February 1942 Selvinsky was in fact transferred to *Boevoi natisk* (*Fighting Thrust*), organ of the recently formed Crimean Front.

7. Ilya Selvinsky with colleagues at the office of *Boevoi natisk* (*Fighting Thrust*), newspaper of the Crimean Front. Circa early spring 1942. Left to right, bottom row: D. Berezin (editor), I. Selvinsky; top row: V. Machavariani, D. Dzhafarov, V. Losev. (Courtesy of Ilya Selvinsky Memorial Museum, Simferopol.)

The Kerch peninsula, owing to its strategic position and access to the Black Sea coast of Russia and to North Caucasus, was a site of exceptionally tenacious fighting, with parts of its territory changing hands four times during the war.⁴⁵ It was Selvinsky's destiny to be on the Kerch peninsula in November 1941, January-May 1942, and then again in November 1943.

---

44 Selvinsky, Wartime Diaries, 3 February 1942; cf. Babenko, *Voina*, 33-34.
45 For details, see Vsevolod Abramov, *Kerchenskaia katastrofa 1942* (Moscow: Iauza; Eksmo, 2006), http://militera.lib.ru/h/abramov_vv/index.html, last accessed 9 June 2010. Abramov references Selvinsky's wartime diaries. I was unable to substantiate some of Abramov's claims, especially those he makes in footnote 153 about Selvinsky's troubles.

8. Ilya Selvinsky (second from left). The Crimean Front. Circa late winter-early spring 1942. (Courtesy of Tatyana Selvinskaya).

Selvinsky was profoundly affected by both the Nazi atrocities he witnessed in and around Kerch in January 1942, when the area was temporarily liberated, and the subsequent collapse of the Crimean Front and the Soviet military catastrophe at Kerch. Brooding over the disaster, which resulted in colossal human and material losses on the Soviet side, Selvinsky noted on 12 May 1942, having just arrived in Krasnodar from the falling Kerch, "Thus, the second stage of the struggle for Crimea will end as unfortunately as the first did. In both cases our talentless and poorly educated generals are to blame, who fear Stalin more than they do the enemy. [...] Who will now answer for all of this? Well, let us suppose that Mekhlis and Kozlov [Lieutenant General Dmitri Kozlov, commander of the Crimean Front] will be shot, but does it really matter?"[46] On 16 May 1942 Selvinsky wrote down this

---

46 Selvinsky, Wartime Diaries, 12 May 1942; cf. Babenko, *Voina*, 46.

verse-like comment: "Kerch has fallen. Crimea has, once again, become foreign. Everything starts all over again. The blood of the landing has not resulted in anything."[47] Kozlov was demoted and transferred to a different army, and Mekhlis was severely demoted, removed from his high posts, and also transferred. After the Soviet troops left the Kerch peninsula for the second time in May 1942, Selvinsky found himself fighting on and reporting from the coast of the Black Sea and the Kuban region. He subsequently served, in 1942-1943, on the staff of *Vpered k pobede!* (*Forward to Victory!*), the newspaper of the political department of the North-Caucasus Front, into which the troops of the former Crimean Front were coopted, and then on the staff of its successor, the newspaper *Vpered za rodinu!* (*Forward for the Motherland!*).[48]

9. Ilya Selvinsky (fourth from right; annotated by Selvinsky) with the troops of Major General Vasily Kniga (first on right), commander of 72nd (Kuban Cossack) Cavalry Division. Crimea. Circa March 1942. (Collection of Maxim D. Shrayer.)

---

47 Selvinsky, Wartime Diaries, 16 May 1942; cf. Babenko, *Voina*, 47. Selvinsky refers to Crimea having, once again, become "foreign [zarubezhnym]" in the poem "To the Fighters of the Crimean Front"; see "K boitsam Krymskogo fronta," in Sel'vinskii, *Krym Kavkaz Kuban'*, 57.

48 In November 1943 the North-Caucasus Front was reconfigured as the Separate Maritime Army. See also Selvinsky's own recollections of his work at the newspapers in 1942-1943, Sel'vinskii, "Na chetyrekh iazykakh. O gazete Severo-Kavkazskogo fronta 'Vpered k pobede'," in *Literaturnoe nasledstvo. Sovetskie pisateli na frontakh Velikoi Otechestvennoi voiny*, vol. 1: 520-523 (Moscow: Nauka, 1966); see also Nekrasova.

Selvinsky participated with paratroopers and with troops of Major General Vasily Kniga's 72nd (Kuban Cossack) Cavalry Division[49] in frontal attacks of Nazi positions, in particular during the Soviet landing operations and counter-offensives in the Kerch area in February-March 1942. In March 1942, after Selvinsky volunteered for and showed personal bravery in a mounted charge against the enemy, he was promoted, and his rank was officially changed from *intendant* (as was common for military journalists) to that of a combat political officer, *senior battalion commissar* (lieutenant colonel).[50] During his service in the Black Sea region he was twice wounded and decorated for valor, with the Order of the Red Star and the Order of the Great Patriotic War (First Degree).

3. Jewish Poems in Praise of the Soviet Dictator?

Did Selvinsky know and understand, during his first months at the front in August-October 1941, that the Nazis were annihilating the Jewish populations of the occupied Soviet territories?[51] Could he fathom that once Crimea had been occupied, its Jews would be murdered? It is difficult to answer this question. A diary entry from 1 September 1941 describes a visit to the Jewish collective farm Fraybelen in the Dzhankoy district of Crimea (after the liberation of Crimea in 1944, when former Jewish rural communities were being given Russian names, Frayleben was renamed Volnoe):

> The peasants, by the way, are the same all over Russia. These ones are Jews. But agricultural labor has left a

---

[49] See Selvinsky, Wartime Diaries, 22 February, 2-16 March 1942; cf. Babenko, *Voina*, 37-38. Also see Sel'vinskii, "Na chetyrekh iazykak"; Boris Serman, "Adzhimushkai," in *O Sel'vinskom: vospominaniia*, ed. Ts. A. Voskresenskaia and I. P. Sirotinskaia, 113; "Kniga, Vasilii Ivanovich," http://ru.wikipedia.org/wiki/Книга,_Василий_Иванович, last accessed 24 January 2012. Selvinsky wrote "The Song of the 72 Kuban Cossack Division," in which he mythologized the division's commander, Vasily Kniga; see "Pesn'a 72-i Kubanskoi Kazachei Divizii," in *Krym Kavkaz Kuban'*, 100-101.

[50] See Selvinsky, Letter to Berta Selvinskaya, 28 March 1942, Ilya Selvinsky Memorial Museum. See also Babenko, *Voina*, 37-38. See Selvinsky's farewell letter to his wife, dated 1 March 1942 and written on the eve of an attack in which he though he would be killed. The attack was delayed; Babenko, *Voina*, 37-38.

[51] For a very useful overview of the onset of the Shoah in the occupied Ukraine in the summer and autumn of 1941, see Wendy Lower, *Nazi Empire-Building and the Holocaust in Ukraine*, 69-96 (Chapel Hill: The University of North Caroline Press, 2007).

deposit of something ancient and overgrown on them. These horses, cows, sheep, pigs, this smell of manure, this endless procession of minute, but undelayable things to do—all of this introduces you into the daily living that had been typical of Jewry perhaps only in the biblical times. Yet how quickly the Jews have changed! Initially, by their curls and noses you still recognize the Jews in them. But already half an hour later you feel something new, more significant: that their entire psychology had adjusted to the new conditions of labor. As far as the children are concerned, even their noses have become shorter.[52]

The Nazis would occupy the area of Dzhankoy by the beginning of November 1941 and shortly proceed to eradicate its Jewish population. On the eve of the Shoah, Selvinsky spoke in concert with Soviet rhetoric on the Jewish question and did not display, at least in his diaries and letters, anxiety over the fate of the Crimean Jews. The events of the late autumn of 1941 would forever change his world.

In September 1941 Selvinsky wrote and published, originally in the army newspaper *Son of Fatherland* on 22 September 1941, the poem "K evreiskomu narodu" ("To the Jewish Nation"). Not a great poem by any stretch of imagination, its intonation and its blank trochaic tetrameter almost parodically recalling Maxim Gorky's "Song about a Falcon" of Soviet middle school fame, it deserves attention most of all for the sheer fact of its publication and reprinting in two of Selvinsky's three wartime collections. In Selvinsky's poem one hears echoes of Ehrenburg's milestone speech "To the Jews" originally read at a rally in Moscow and printed in *Izvestia* on 26 August 1941. (Selvinsky had already left for the front and was not at the rally. Pasternak had been also invited to speak, but declined to attend, apparently explaining his refusal as unwillingness to limit his antifascist feelings to the Jewish question.[53]) "My mother tongue is Russian," Ehrenburg said at the rally. "I am a Russian writer. Like all Russians, I am now defending my homeland. But the Hitlerites

---

52 Selvinsky, Wartime Diaries, 1 September 1941.
53 See Leonid Katsis, "'Doktor Zhivago' B. Pasternaka: ot M. Gershenzona do Ben-Guriona," *Evreiskii knigonosha* 8 (2005), http://echo.oranim.ac.il/main.php?p=news&id_news=47&id_personal=9, last accessed 24 February 2011.

have reminded me of something else: my mother's name was Hannah. I am a Jew. I say this with pride. Hitler hates us more than anything. And this adorns us."⁵⁴ In a diary entry dated October 1941, Selvinsky acknowledged taking inspiration from Ehrenburg's essays and journalism during the early months of the Nazi invasion: "Every day newspapers arrive with Ehrenburg's articles. What a fighting temperament, what an inexhaustible wealth of associations. What brilliance of style! This is a genius writer of essays [...] Here's someone to be envied. He alone does more for victory than all of us writers, taken together."⁵⁵ In January 1961, Selvinsky would echo his wartime response to Ehrenburg's essays and journalism in a tribute to the Ukrainian poet Pavlo Tychyna (1891-1967): "But for a Communist there is no greater pride than the hatred of the enemies of the revolution. At war I passionately envied Ilya Ehrenburg, whom fascists so hated. Every day he appeared in the big newspapers, and his every article struck the target with the might of a tank division. I dreamed about achieving the same as a poet, but I did not succeed."⁵⁶ Selvinsky was never an admirer of Ehrenburg's poetry, yet his poem's title recalled—and Selvinsky may not have intended this—the title of Ehrenburg's poetic entreaty "Evreiskomu narodu" ("To the Jewish Nation," 1911), written at a very different time and voicing a call for Jews to gather strength, rise, and "return to Jerusalem, your native land."⁵⁷ In Selvinsky's poem, which also has some of its sources in Soviet poetry about the Civil War (e.g., the work of Boris Kornilov), the rhetoric is not only one of a wartime reawakening of Jewish self-consciousness during the Soviet war against Nazism, but also one of Jewish militancy and extreme bravery on the battlefields of the war:

---

54 Ehrenburg, "To the Jews," tr. Joshua Rubenstein, in Shrayer, *An Anthology*, 1: 532; cf. Erenburg, "Evreiam," *Izvestiia* 26 August 1941; Erenburg, *Staryi skorniak i drugie proizvedeniia*, ed. M. Vainshtein, 2 vols., 2: 251-252 (Jerusalem: n.p., 1983). This motif, and the specific mention of the name of the poet's mother, Hannah, is also found in Ehrenburg's poem "Brodiat Rakhili, Khaimy, Lii..." ("Rachels, Hayims, and Leahs wander..."), an earlier version of which appeared in Ehrenburg's 1941 collection *Vernost' (Loyalty)*; see Erenburg, *Vernost' (Ispaniia. Parizh). Stikhi*, 52 (Moscow: OGIZ, 1941).
55 Selvinsky, Wartime Diaries, October 1941; cf. Sel'vinskii, "Ia eto videl (Krymskie stranitsy voennykh dnevnikov)," 78. In the poem "Ballad of KV Tank" (1942) Selvinsky wrote of "Ehrenburg's quill pen/And news broadcasts [svodki] of the Sovimformburo" reaching the heroic crew of a Soviet tank; Sel'vinskii, "Ballada o tanke 'KV'," in *Krym Kavkaz Kuban'*, 55.
56 Sel'vinskii, "Sila poeta," *Literaturnaia gazeta* 28 January 1961.
57 Erenburg, "Evreiskomu narodu," in Erenburg, *Ia zhivu* (St. Petersburg: n.p., 1911), 51-52.

Там несется крик фашистов,
Дикий, шалый, оголтелый:
"Коммунистам и евреям
    Смерть!"
[…]
И когда, рыча проклятья,
Людоеды ставят рядом
Имя целого народа —
Как, евреи, не гордиться
Этим вражеским признаньем?
Сочетание такое —
    Честь!
[…]
Так вперед, на батареи!
Будьте там, где в дыме галок
Смерть со свастикой на шлеме
Жаждет выбить все живое;
Будьте там, где коммунисты,
Точно статую из стали,
Льют победу. Ваше место —
    Здесь! [58]

(There the screaming of fascists is heard,/ A wild, frenzied, frantic [call]:/ "To Communists and Jews/ Death!"/ […] And when, roaring their damnations,/ Cannibals put forth/ The name of an entire people [nation]—/ How, Jews, can one not be proud/ Of the enemy's acknowledgment?/ Such a pairing —/ Is an honor! […] So forward, to battlefields!/ Be there where amid smoke of the bombs/ Death with a swastika on its helmet/ Is desperate to destroy everything living;/ Be there where the Communists,/ Cast the victory,/ Like a statue of steel. Your place is—/Here!)

---

58   Selvinskii, "Evreiskomu narodu," in *Ballady, plakaty i pesni*, 21-23 (Krasnodar: Kraevoe izdatel'stvo, 1942); "Evreiskomu narodu," in *Voennaia lirika*, 41-43 (Tashkent: Gosudarstvennoe izdatel'stvo UzSSR, 1943).

It should not escape one's attention that in addressing the Jews collectively, Selvinsky writes *vashe mesto* ("your place"), not *nashe mesto* ("our place"), in contrast to Ehrenburg's "I am a Jew. I say this with pride. Hitler hates us more than anything. And this adorns us [Eto nas ukrashaet]."

To dismiss Selvinsky's "To the Jewish People" as merely opportunistic would be an oversimplification, especially because keeping silent about Jewish questions would have been simpler and safer for a Soviet Jew, poet, and military officer. A propensity to link the wartime destiny of Jews—perhaps even Jewish survival—with Stalin's role in history is already emergent in this poem and must therefore be noted. Selvinsky's poetic address to the Jews signals the authorial intention to praise the leader. The antepenultimate and penultimate lines, "Tochno statuiu iz stali, /L'iut pobedu..." ("Cast the victory,/ Like a statue of steel..."), evoke Stalin's name through the implied rhyming of *stali* (genitive of *stal'*) with "Stalin" (the leader's adopted last name, derived from the Russian noun *stal'* = steel). During the war years, Selvinsky recycled the "Stalin-steel" rhyme and the allusion in at least two other dithyrambic poems. In the poem "Stalin u mikrofona" ("Stalin at the Microphone," 1941), apparently composed in Moscow prior to Selvinsky's departure for the front but not published in book form until the second half of 1942, the name "Stalin" is not implied but rather rhymed directly with *stali* (of steel).[59] In "Za rodinu, za Stalina" ("For Motherland, for Stalin," 1941), a touch more interesting for its versification and constructivist echoes, yet more boiler-plate in its cultism, we find this stanza:

> За родину, за Сталина,
> Пошла она [авиация] в полет!
> Нацеливает сталь она,
> Стальную лаву льет.[60]

(For motherland, for Stalin,/ It [the air force] went on missions!/ It aims its steel,/ It pours its steel lava.)

---

59 Sel'vinskii, "Stalin u mikrofona," in Il'ia Selvinskii, *Ballady, plakaty i pesni*, 6-7 (Krasnodar: Kraevoe izdatel'stvo, 1942); *Oktiabr'* 12 (1942): 3; *Ballady i pesni*, 3 (Moscow: Goslitizdat, 1943); *Voennaia lirika*, 4-5 (Tashkent: Gosudarstvennoe izdatel'stvo UzSSR, 1943). The Stalin-steel rhyme would also appear in the closing stanza of Selvinsky's translation of the long poem *Voice of Motherland* by the Armenian poet Nairi Zarian; see *Krym Kavkaz Kuban'*, 79.
60 Sel'vinskii, "Za rodinu, za Stalina," in *Ballady, plakaty i pesni*, 8-9 (Krasnodar: Kraevoe izdatel'stvo, 1942).

Selvinsky must have hesitated or procrastinated with the publication of these embarrassing poems, and apparently "For Motherland, for Stalin" never appeared in a periodical and was printed only once, in the collection *Ballads, Posters, and Songs* (1942). But he did not hesitate to join the chorus of other Soviet authors in voicing loyalty to Stalin not through poetry but through formulaic prose. Selvinsky's short essay "Golos Stalina" ("The Voice of Stalin") ran in Moscow's *Literaturnaia gazeta* (*Literary Gazette*) on 6 July 1941 under an epigraph from his own poem "Stalin at the Microphone." Selvinsky ended the piece this way: "One felt like saying to him right there, near the loudspeaker: 'Our dear one, our very own, our Stalin! Lead us! We trust your every word, we shall face victory or death at your every call! For your voice is the voice of each of us! For the people and Stalin are inseparable and indivisible.'"[61]

In his personal letters and diaries Selvinsky kept going back to a phrase Stalin had allegedly dropped about him in a conversation with the writer Fyodor Panfyorov: "Selvinsky is talented. Almost a genius. But he goes past the soul of the people.'" Selvinsky's diary for the autumn of 1941 reflects his ruminations about both the eternal problem of poet versus ruler (he mentions Pushkin and Nicholas I). Selvinsky also polemicizes—with himself and with Stalin—about Stalin's view of his writings. In his wartime diaries Selvinsky elaborated at length on what Stalin had said about him:

> But as far as going "past the soul of the people"... no! With this I will never agree. Stalin's mistake in my case is very understandable. Lenin said: "Politics is there where the millions are! Not tens or even hundreds of thousands, but precisely millions." But millions mean workers and peasants. Therefore for a politician the people are necessarily the masses. Thus a people's [narodnyi] poet is one for the masses. A proletarian or a peasant poet. [...] Neither Shakespeare, nor Goethe, nor Pushkin, nor a single great poet was an agitator [ne byl agitatorom]. In particular, neither Shakespeare, nor Goethe, nor Pushkin described the life of the whole people as peas-

---

61 Sel'vinskii, "Golos Stalina," *Literaturnaia gazeta* 6 July 1941.

CHAPTER ONE

ants, soldiers or artisans [...] But can comrade Stalin really say about them that they went past the soul of the people? [...]

And if we can now turn to my works, then of course, it would be easy to notice that the problem of the intelligentsia, its destiny in the revolution, is central for me. But first of all, central does not mean all-encompassing. Does *Umka the Polar Bear* only portray members of the intelligentsia? Gorky once said to me: "I read your *Umka*. A major work." [...] And *The Lay of Ulyalaev*? Is it only about the intelligentsia?

During the autumn of 1941 the question of how to write Stalin into war lyrics preoccupied Selvinsky, and it continued to be on his mind throughout 1941-1945. While praising Stalin may have amounted to taking out an insurance policy, no paeans to the leader guaranteed artistic freedom or protected Selvinsky against repressions.

4. The Massacre at Kerch: History, Witnessing, Memory

The first poet to publish extensively about the Shoah in the occupied Soviet territories,[62] in 1942-1943 Selvinsky bore witness to the Nazi atrocities on the Crimean peninsula and the south of Russia. His poems were published and republished in newspapers, magazines, anthologies, and the poet's own collections. They were read in radio broadcasts and disseminated among the Soviet troops. Most significant for the experience of bearing witness to the Shoah are the poems "Ia eto videl!" ("I Saw It!" 1942) and "Kerch" (1942), in both of which Selvinsky depicted the aftermath of the execution of thousands of Jews who had remained in the occupied Kerch and its environs after the first retreat of Soviet troops in November 1941.[63]

---

62 On the Shoah by bullet, see, for instance, the recent book by Father Patrick Desbois, *The Holocaust by Bullets: A Priest's Journey to Uncover the Truth Behind the Murder of 1.5 Million Jews* (New York: Palgrave Macmillan, 2009). It is noteworthy that, with the exception of a brief interview with a woman from Feodosia and a vignette about a Krymchak girl murdered outside Simferopol, the book offers very little investigative information on the Shoah in Crimea, and none on Kerch.

63 The Russian originals of "I Saw It!" and "Kerch" and the poems' English translations are found in the Appendix following the main text. The Crimean scholar Liudmila Daineko has investigated the

10. Crimea with principal urban centers. Contemporary map. (*The YIVO Encyclopedia of Jews in Eastern Europe, vol. 1*, New Haven, 2008, Courtesy of YIVO.)

To reconstruct the historical context of the war and Shoah in Crimea, suffice it to say that by November 1941 the Axis forces had occupied all of Crimea except Sebastopol. At the end of December 1941 the Soviet troops mounted an ambitious if only partially successful landing operation in the areas of Kerch and Feodosia. By 1 January 1942 Kerch was liberated. It remained under Soviet control until the middle of May 1942, when the Nazi forces retook it. A section of the northeastern part of the Kerch peninsula was re-conquered in November 1943 over the course of the Kerch-Eltigen Landing Operation, whereas the city of Kerch, like much of Crimea, would remain Nazi-occupied until the spring of 1944.[64]

---

military context of Selvinsky's service on the Kerch peninsula in 1941-1942. See L. I. Daineko, "Sel'vinskii i Kerch. Noiabr', 1941-mai, 1942," in *Vestnik Krymskikh Chtenii I. L. Sel'vinskogo*, vol. 1: 63-71 (Simferopol: Krymskii Arkhiv, 2002).

64 See, for instance, a concise and very useful summary of the history and documentation of World War II in Crimea by S. A. Androsov, "Arkhivy Kryma v gody Velikoi Otechestvennoi voiny (1941-1945)," in *Istoricheskoe nasledie Kryma. Zhurnal* 8 (2004), http://old.commonuments.crimea-portal.gov.ua/rus/index.php?v=1&tek=87&art=324, last accessed 12 January 2012.

11. Kerch and Environs (see the Legend on p. 33).

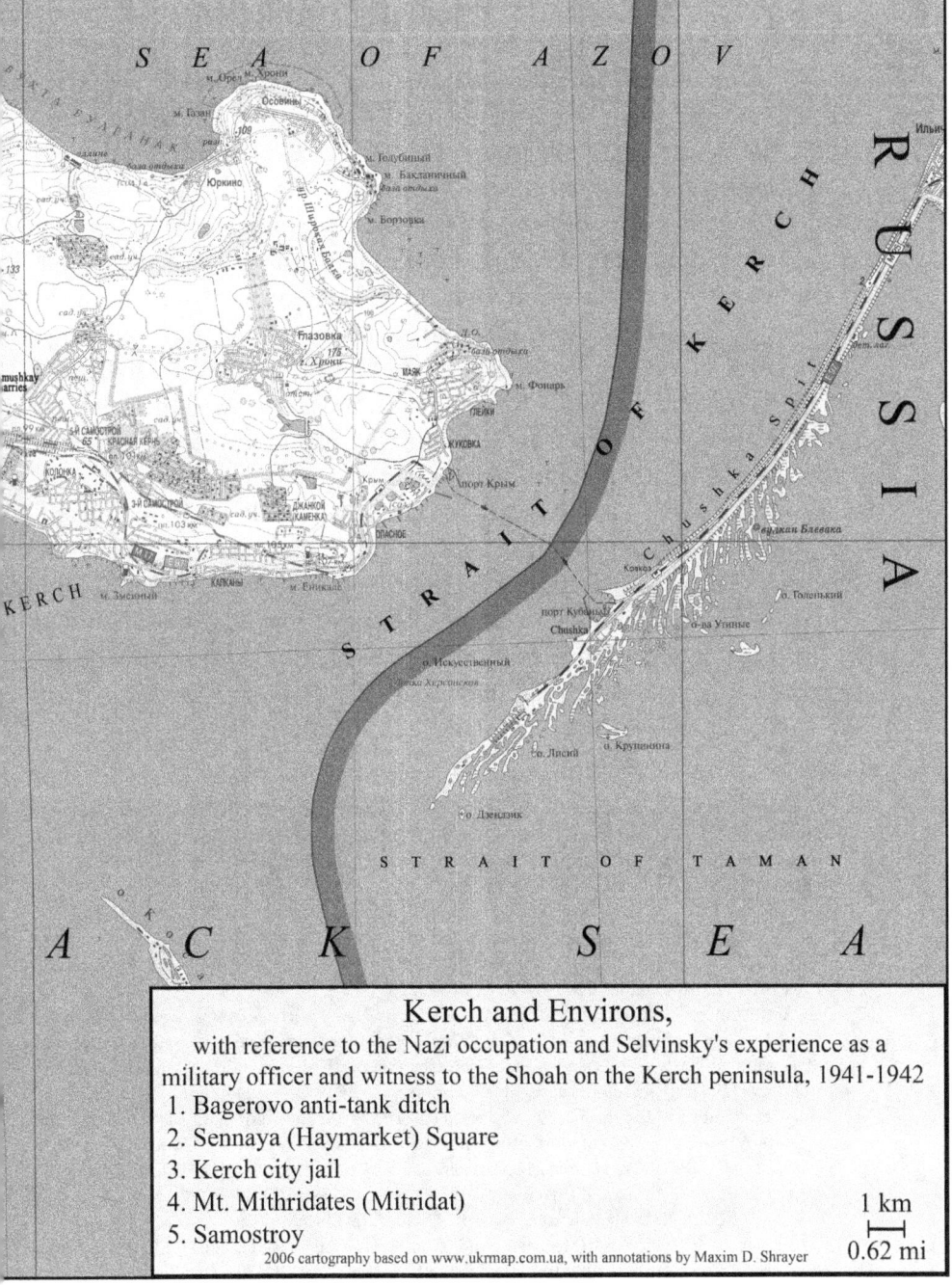

Kerch and Environs,
with reference to the Nazi occupation and Selvinsky's experience as a military officer and witness to the Shoah on the Kerch peninsula, 1941-1942
1. Bagerovo anti-tank ditch
2. Sennaya (Haymarket) Square
3. Kerch city jail
4. Mt. Mithridates (Mitridat)
5. Samostroy

2006 cartography based on www.ukrmap.com.ua, with annotations by Maxim D. Shrayer

According to the Soviet census of 1939, 65,452 Jews resided in Crimea (making up 5.8 percent of its total population). With its two Jewish autonomous districts and 86 Jewish agricultural colonies, Crimea was then the pride of the Soviet campaign for Jews on land. Unlike the Birobidzhan project, largely a failure, Crimea had true Jewish-Soviet successes to show to the world. Following the June 1941 invasion and the swift advances of the Axis troops in the summer and early autumn, only some of Crimea's Jews managed to be evacuated and escape to safety. The task of Einsatzgruppe D,[65] which carried out most of the genocide with the assistance and support of regular German army units and local collaborators, was to make Crimea *Judenrein* ("Jew-free") by the early spring of 1942. Murdered with the local Jewish population were also Jewish refugees from Ukraine who had found temporary refuge in parts of Crimea before its occupation, as well as Jewish-Polish refugees.[66] Living in Crimea alongside the larger Ashkenazi community were the Krymchaks, whom the Nazis regarded as Jews and who were likewise subjected to extermination. Altogether, between 30,000 and 40,000 Jews were murdered in Crimea; of the estimated prewar population of 6,500 Krymchaks, 5,500 or more were exterminated. The largest action, killing between 12,000 and 14,000 Jews, was carried out in Crimea's capital city of Simferopol in December 1941.[67]

---

[65] For a detailed study of the activities of Einsatzgruppe D, see Andrej Angrick, *Besatzungspolitik und Massenmord. Die Einsatzgruppe D in der südlichen Sowjetunion 1941-1943* (Hamburg: Hamburger Edition, 2003); as an example of post-Soviet scholarship on Crimea during the occupation, see O. V. Roman'ko, *Krym pod piatoi Gitlera. Nemetskaia okkupatsionnaia politika v Krymu, 1941-1944 gg.*, 81-83 (Moscow: Veche, 2011).

[66] See, for instance, the testimony of M. Kotel' about a Jewish family from Warsaw murdered in Kerch: "Gorod mertvykh," in *Zverstva nemetskikh fashistov v Kerchi. Sbornik rasskazov postradavshikh i ochevidtsev*, 75-79 (Sukhumi: Krasnyi Krym, 1943).

[67] See, for instance, Jonathan Dekel-Chen, "Crimea," 1: 363-364; Michael Zand, "Krymchaks," in 1: 948-951; Gitel' Gubenko, *Kniga pechali* (Simferopol: Redotdel Krymskogo upravleniia po pechati, 1991); Mikhail Tiaglyi, *Mesta massovogo unichtozheniia evreev Kryma v period natsistskoi okkupatsii poluostrova (1941-1944). Spravochnik*, 11-12 (Simferopol': BETs "Khesed Shimon", 2005); Joshua Rubenstein and Ilya Altman, eds., *The Unknown Black Book: The Holocaust in the German-Occupied Soviet Territories*, 337-338 (Bloomington: Indiana University Press, 2008); Yitzhak Arad, *The Holocaust in the Soviet Union*, 202-211 (Lincoln: University of Nebraska Press; Jerusalem: Yad Vashem, 2009); Il'ia Al'tman, *Zhertvy nenavisti: Kholokost v SSSR. 1941-1945*, 287 (Moscow: Fond "Kovcheg", 2002); "Istreblenie evreev Rossii i Kryma," in *Kholokost i evreiskoe soprotivlenie na okkupirovannoi territorii SSSR* (Moscow: Fond "Kholokost"; Kaleidoskop, 2002), http://jhistory.nfurman.com/shoa/hfond_100.htm, last accessed 15 July 2010. The Karaites, with whom the Krymchaks are sometimes confused, were not regarded as Jews by the Nazis and were by and large spared the fate of both the Ashkenazi Jews and the Krymchaks during the occupation. For a recent assessment of the survival of the Karaites during the Shoah, see Kiril Feferman, "Nazi

The murder of the Jews of Kerch and its environs was carried out as part of a series of mass executions of Jews outside Crimean cities, among them Simferopol, Feodosia, Evpatoria, and Yalta, and in rural areas and Jewish agricultural districts, in November-December of 1941.[68] Yet only on the Kerch peninsula, after its temporary liberation, were the Soviets able to come upon and document overwhelming evidence of the recent Nazi atrocities within days after these atrocities had been carried out. Bloodcurdling descriptions and very graphic visual images of the Bagerovo anti-tank ditch filled with corpses verbally and iconically represented all the other ditches, ravines, and wells across Crimea into which the victims fell after they were murdered.

The critic Veniamin Goffenshefer, who like Selvinsky served on the staff of *Son of Fatherland* and witnessed the immediate aftermath of the Nazi atrocities in Kerch, stated as early as January 1942 that "[...] the Soviet people who liberated the Kerch peninsula saw for the first time the horrifying aftermath left by the bloody fascist beast [krovavogo fashistskogo zveria]."[69] Almost seventy years later, Goffenshefer's point was echoed in the words of the American historian David Shneer: "On December 31 [1941], [Kerch] was one of the first areas with a significant prewar Jewish population to be liberated from Nazi occupation, which meant that it was one of the first places in which Soviet soldiers, journalists, and photographers saw with their own eyes the effects of Nazi occupation and the war against European Jewry."[70] Given the number of victims killed at the Bagerovo anti-tank ditch (hereafter referred to as the Bagerovo ditch), and also given the ample documentation of the massacre undertaken in early January-February 1942, it is puzzling that the massacre has received little attention from Shoah historians. In reversing this trend, Shneer recently reassessed the place of the massacre in the Soviet wartime

---

Germany and the Karaites in 1938-1944: Between Racial Theory and *Realpolitik*," *Nationalities Papers* 39.2 (March 2011): 277-294. For an overview of the history of Karaites in Russian lands, see Golda Aikhiezer, "Karaites," in *The YIVO Encyclopedia of Jews in Eastern Europe*, ed. Gershon David Hundert, 2 vols, 1: 860-862 (New Haven: Yale University Press, 2008).

68   On the Shoah in the rural and agricultural areas of Crimea, see Mikhail Tiaglyi, "Kholokost evreiskikh obshchin Kryma v dokumentakh GAARK," Part 2, http://www.holocaust.kiev.ua/bulletin/vip2/vip2_2.htm, last accessed 7 April 2010.
69   V[eniamin] Goffenshefer, "Bagerovo," *Syn otechestva* 29 January 1942.
70   David Shneer, *Through Soviet Jewish Eyes: Photography, War, and the Holocaust*, 100-101 (New Brunswick: Rutgers University Press, 2010).

perception of the Shoah. "[I]mmediately after its liberation," Shneer argues, "Kerch became the symbolic reference point for Nazi atrocities, the place at which Soviet witnesses saw with their own eyes and their own cameras that the rumors, innuendo, and even the published trophy photographs were true. [...] These images, poems, and articles figured Kerch as the symbolic site of Nazi atrocities until 1943, when Babi Yar [...] would come to overshadow what had been discovered before."[71]

In the first week of January 1942 Selvinsky arrived in the Kerch area.[72] During the second or third week of January Selvinsky made the first entry in his diary for 1942:

> About myself and how I've been doing, what I've seen—later. The important part is the excruciating impact [potriasaiushchee vpechatlenie] of the sight of Kerch after the Germans. I got to Kerch with the landing troops of the second echelon. The city is half-destroyed. That's that—we shall restore it. But near the village of Bagerovo in an anti-tank ditch—7000 executed women, children, old men, and others. *And I have seen them*. Now I do not have the strength to write about it in prose. Nerves can no longer react. What I could—I have expressed in verse (see 'I Saw It!')."[73]

Both in the diary and in the poem to which he refers in the diary, Selvinsky writes of the aftermath of both the large-scale massacre which took place outside Kerch in the beginning of December 1941 and the smaller-scale massacres which continued there through the end of the first occupation. Evidence collected in 1942-1944 and subsequently revisited by historians adds up to what is still an incomplete account of how in November-December 1941 the Nazis and their accomplices murdered predominantly members of the Ashkenazi Jewish

---

[71] Shneer, *Through Soviet Jewish Eyes*, 107-108. Shneer discussed the Kerch photography in more detail in "Picturing Grief: Soviet Holocaust Photography at the Intersection of History and Memory," *The American Historical Review* 115.1 (February 2010): 28-52.

[72] Selvinsky, Wartime Diaries, January 1942; Daineko, 65-66; Babenko, 25; Sel'vinskii, "'Ia eto videl' (Krymskie stranitsy voennykh dnevnikov)," 81.

[73] Selvinsky, Wartime Diaries, January 1942; the first dated entry for 1942, following the undated entry about having seen the Bagerovo ditch, is for 16 January 1942; cf. Babenko, 25.

community of Kerch. (The majority of the area's Krymchaks were murdered in the summer of 1942, during the second occupation of the Kerch peninsula, at the Adzhimushkay anti-tank ditch northeast of Kerch.[74]) To this day historians, especially local Crimean historians, some of them propelled by a mixture of the residual Soviet rhetoric of not dividing the dead, revisionism, and unease with the possibility of a Jewish- and Shoah-centered narrative of wartime Crimean history, continue to debate the massacre at the Bagerovo anti-tank ditch. Local Jewish historians and activists also participate in an ongoing reevaluation of the history of the Shoah in Crimea. Journalists and bloggers share horrific photographs and documents and variously interpret the known data.[75]

The number 7000 was apparently first cited in the news dispatches of TASS, the Telegraph Agency of the Soviet Union, on 5 January 1942.[76] On 5 January 1942 an unsigned report, "Bloody Atrocities of Germans in Kerch," appeared in *Pravda*, stating: "According to preliminary data, altogether in Kerch the fascist scumbags killed up to 7000 people. Many children were poisoned by German brutes."[77] In fact, the *Pravda* report appeared one day before the issuing, and two days before the publication, of a note by Vyacheslav Molotov, then People's Commissar (Minister) of Foreign Affairs. Distributed worldwide, Molotov's note of 6 January 1942 cited the number of Kerch victims as 7000, and this

---

74 See Arad, *The Holocaust in the Soviet Union*, 207; Tiaglyi, *Mesta massovogo unichtozheniia evreev Kryma*, 43-45; Tiaglyi, "Kerch," in *Kholokost na territorii SSSR. Entsiklopediia*, 2nd ed., ed. I. A. Al'tman, 402-403 (Moscow: Rosspen, 2011).

75 To this end, of interest are discussions on the online genealogical forum "Evreiskie korni": "Bagerovskii rov g. Kerch," http://forum.j-roots.info/viewtopic.php?f=26&t=144, last accessed 7 April 2010; see also "Kerchenskie evrei otmetili godovshchinu Kholokosta," http://www.kerch.com.ua/articleview.aspx?id=10066, last accessed 7 April 2010; "Kerch v gody Velikoi otechestvennoi voiny," in Forum vypusknikov Bagerovskoi srednei shkoly, http://bagerovo-school.ru/phpBB3/viewtopic.php?f=27&t=1371, last accessed 20 October 2011. See also Izia Katsap, "Ia eto videl svoimi glazami. Ia eto sam perezhil," *Forum: Evreiskaia gazeta na russkom iazyke dlia semeinogo chteniia* 22-28 April 2010, 15. A somewhat tendentious memoir by Petr Kotel'nikov, who as a teenager lived through the occupation of the Kerch peninsula, offers recollections of the murder of the Jews of Kerch; see *Kerch 1935-1945 (Vospominaniia ochevidtsa)* (Simferopol: n.p., 2007), especially pp. 23-26.

76 "London, January 5. The Germans massacred nearly 7000 Russians during the occupation of Kerch, says the TASS news agency," reads the opening of a short and vague report in *The Evening Post* (Wellington, New Zealand); see "Massacre by Germans in Kerch," *The Evening Post* [Wellington, New Zealand], 6 January 1942: 6; article image at http://paperspast.natlib.govt.nz, last accessed 20 February 1942.

77 "Krovavye zverstva nemtsev v Kerchi," *Pravda* 5 January 1942, 3.

number was subsequently repeated in numerous publications. Compiled in August 1944 and based in part on the materials documented in early 1942, the Act of the Extraordinary State Commission concerning Kerch also referred to 7000 people who were gathered at Kerch's Sennaya (Haymarket) Square on 29 November 1941, and the deputy chief Soviet prosecutor Lev Smirnov drew on the conclusions of the Commission and quoted them at the Nuremberg Military Tribunal in February 1946.[78] A number of authors, including Yitzhak Arad and Ilya Altman, historians of the Shoah in the Soviet Union, and the memory-keeper Gitel Gubenko, cite 7000 as either the number of victims of the November-December massacres outside Kerch or the number of Jews gathered up at Haymarket Square on 29 November 1941 following a Nazi order.[79] The inscription on the memorial plaque put up in 2002 by the local Jewish community opts out of putting an exact number on the victims in favor of a totalizing language of memory: "On 29 November 1941 the German-Fascist invaders gathered in this square and executed in the Bagerovo ditch all the Jews of Kerch."

---

78 See *Niurnbergskii protsess. Prestupleniia protiv chelovechestva*, vol. 5, ed. N. S. Lebedeva et al. (Moscow: Iuridicheskaia literatura, 1991), http://lib.ru/MEMUARY/1939-1945/NURNBERG/np5.txt, last accessed 5 October 2011. In an official list of the sites of mass executions prepared on 11 September 1946 by the then-director of the Crimean Regional State Archive A. D. Belikova, the number of people murdered at the Bagerovo ditch was cited as 7000. See "Spravka o mestakh massovykh ubiistv sovetskikh grazhdan nemetsko-fashistskimi okkupantami na territorii Kryma za 1941-1944 gody," in *Gor'kaia pamiat' voiny. Krym v Velikoi otechestvennoi*, ed. V. K. Garagulia et al., 83-89 (Simferopol: Krymskaia akademiia gumanitarnykh nauk, 1995).

79 See Arad, *The Holocaust in the Soviet Union*, 206-207; and Al'tman, *Zhertvy nenavisti*, 287. The Shoah in Crimea has been the subject of archival research and memorialization by the US-based émigré Gitel Gubenko, whose parents and other family members perished at the Bagerovo ditch; see Gitel' Gubenko, *Kniga pechali* (Simferopol: Redotdel Krymskogo upravleniia po pechati, 1991), where an account of the Bagerovo ditch massacres is found on pp. 21-31. Drawing on the materials of the State Archive of the Crimean Autonomous Republic (GAARK), Gubenko published partial lists of Jewish civilians, victims of the executions in various parts of Crimea, including Kerch (82-88). Bentsion M. Vol'fson, in his article of 1942, was the first to make a distinction between the total number of victims murdered in the Bagerovo ditch (about 7000), and the number of people who were gathered in Haymarket Square on 29 November 1941 and then sent to the Kerch city jail (about 5000); see B. M. Vol'fson, "Krovavye prestupleniia nemtsev v Kerchi," *Istoricheskii vestnik* 8 (1942): 33-34.

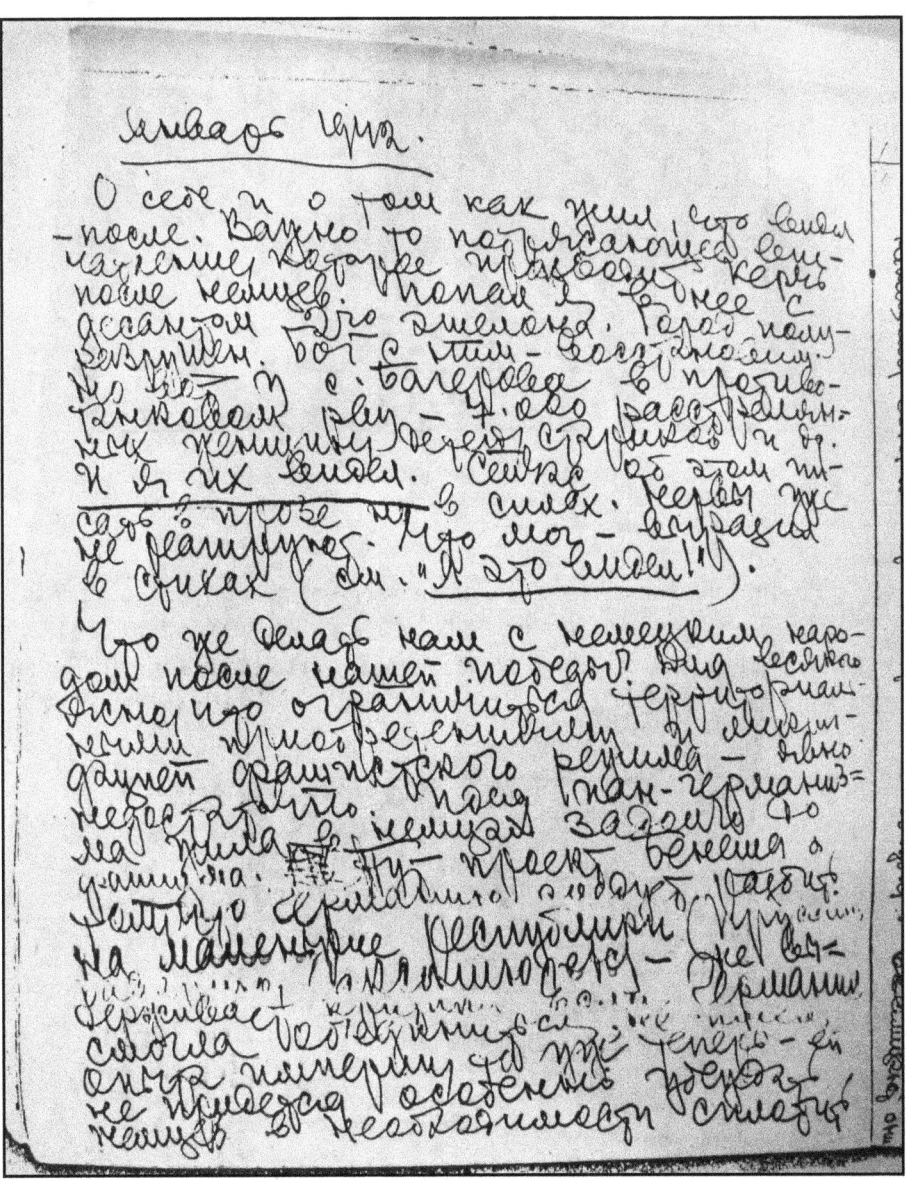

12. The first page of Ilya Selvinsky's wartime diary for 1942 with the poet's impressions of having seen the Bagerovo anti-tank ditch. (Courtesy of Ilya Selvinsky Memorial Museum, Simferopol.)

13. Sennaya (Haymarket) Square, Kerch. Plaque at 15 Proletarskaya Street, unveiled in 2002 to commemorate the murder of the Jews of Kerch in 1941. 14 December 2011. Photo by Maxim D. Shrayer.

First publicized in early January 1942, the signifying number, 7000, has been severed from its signified, the Jews killed at Kerch in 1941, and imprinted on the collective Soviet memory. It appeared on the Soviet-era marker placed at the Bagerovo anti-tank ditch in the middle 1970s:

14. The marker on the post-Soviet monument (2011) at the Bagerovo anti-tank ditch. 14 December 2011. Photo by Maxim D. Shrayer.

"Here in the Bagerovo anti-tank ditch, in November-December 1941, the fascist barbarians executed over 7000 peaceful Soviet citizens: women, old people, children. Memory eternal to the victims of fascism." The marker is placed at the foundation of a white stella monument with a red five-point star.

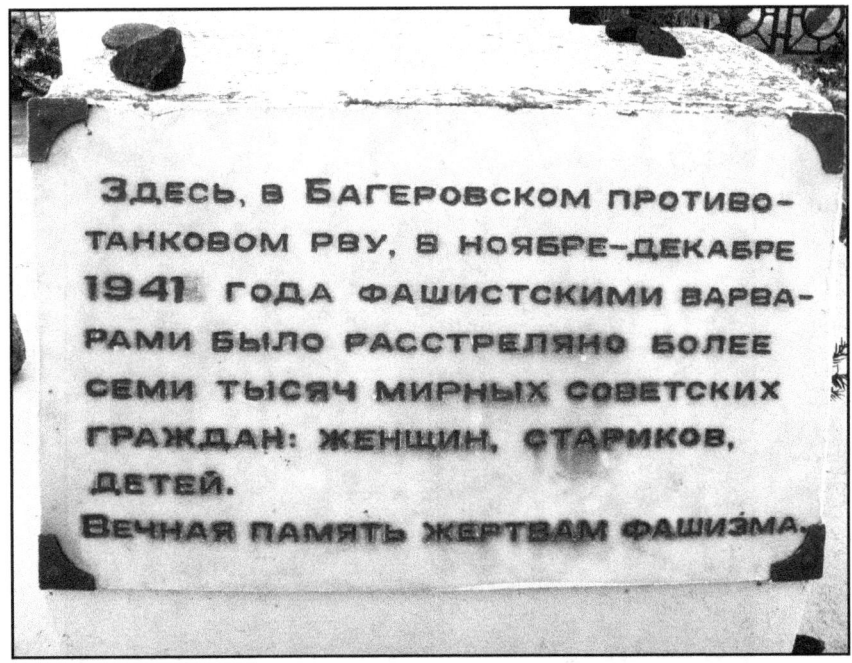

15. The marker on the Soviet-era monument (circa 1975-1976) at the Bagerovo anti-tank ditch. 14 December 2011. Photo by Maxim D. Shrayer.

In 2010 a second monument, adorned with the Star of David, was added. Carved on this marker are the words, "Here at this spot in December 1941, in the Bagerovo anti-tank ditch, were murdered with horrible cruelty, by the hands of German executioners and their assistants, murderers from the other nations, thousands of Jews: men and women, girls and boys, young men and women, old people and infants, who resided in the city of Kerch and its environs. They were annihilated so as to root out the Jewish people, wipe of the memory of Jewry and

---- CHAPTER ONE ----

end the life of every one who bears the name of Israel. So may their memory be for a blessing and may in their lot they remain until the end of the days."

16. The Bagerovo anti-tank ditch. The Soviet-era monument commemorating the murder of "over seven thousand peaceful Soviet citizens" (circa 1975-76) and the post-Soviet monument (2010) commemorating the murder of "thousands of Jews." 14 December 2011. Photo by Maxim D. Shrayer.

The two inscriptions, their language and the information they communicate, capture some of the dynamics of the memory of the Shoah in the Soviet Union and, specifically, in Crimea.[80]

In 2003, in a study of the activities of Einsatzgruppe D in the south of the Soviet Union, the German historian Andrej Angrick cited three different sets of numbers as based on German military archives and testimonies of former members of Sonderkommando 10B of Einsatzgruppe D. Angrick's narrative of the atrocities carried out in and around Kerch took very little notice of wartime Soviet evidence and survivors' and witnesses's testimonies. According to Angrick, following the first occupation of Kerch the German Ortskommandatur (military commandant's office) estimated there to be 10,000-12,000 Jews in the city.[81] Angrick then cites a 27 December 1941 report of the Ortskommandatur which assumed that of the city's 50,000 people, 15% were Jews, and that it would "soon have 7500 less people to feed."[82] Finally, Angrick refers to a 7 December 1941 Nazi report of "2500 Jews" of Kerch having undergone "resettlement" in the early days of December ("resettlement" [Umsiedlung] being a coded term for murder), and also to a German soldier's subsequent testimony citing the execution of "2000 Jews." In recent years, lower estimates of the number of Jews murdered in Kerch in November-December 1941, around 2500, have been arrived at, in part via questionable math, by historians based in Crimea.[83] Mikhail Tiaglyi, who has written extensively on the Shoah in Crimea and specifically in Kerch, now believes that the number 7000, used in the Kerch

---

80 For a local report on the commemorations of the 70th anniversary of the massacre at the Bagerovo ditch, see "Bagerovskii rov," http://sarafanews.ru/Bagerovskij-rov.html, last accessed 27 January 2012; "Bagerovskii rov," *Murzik Media*, 29 November 2011, http://murzikmedia.blogspot.com/2011/11/blog-post.html, last accessed 27 January 2012.

81 Angrick, *Besatzungspolitik und Massenmord*, 357; Arad also cited this report in his work, see *The Holocaust in the Soviet Union*, 206 and 575, n. 31.

82 Angrick, 356.

83 V. N. Gurkovich, "Istoricheskii kommentarii k stikhotvereniiu I. L. Sel'vinskogo 'Ia eto videl!'" in *Vestnik Krymskikh chtenii I. L. Sel'vinskogo*, vol. 2, 89-95 (Simferopol: Krymskii arkhiv, 2003); "K voprosu o rasstrelakh mirnogo naseleniia v Bagerovskom rvu v 1941 godu," in *Kerch voennaia. Sbornik statei. 60-letiiu osvobozhdeniia goroda posviashchaetsia*, 27-31 (Kerch: Kerchenskii gosudarstvennyi istoriko-kul'turnyi zapovednik, 2004); G. V. Korotkova, "Okkupatsionnyi rezhim v Kerchi v period Velikoi Otechestvennoi voiny i ego posledstviia," in *Kerch voennaia. Sbornik statei. 60-letiiu osvobozhdeniia goroda posviashchaetsia*, 304-339 (Kerch: Kerchenskii gosudarstvennyi istoriko-kul'turnyi zapovednik, 2004); "K voprosu o rabote chrezvychainykh komissii v Kerchi (1944 g.)," in *Na kerchenskom platsdarme. K 60-letiiu osvobozhdeniia Kerchi. Sbornik nauchnykh statei*, 166-183 (Kerch: Kerchenski gosudarstvennyi istoriko-kul'turnyi zapovednik, 2004).

report of the Central Executive Commission, is "probably [...] significantly inflated."[84] Reports of a number of victims far in excess of 7000 in fact were already circulating at the time of the first liberation of Kerch. Fyodor Reshetnikov, a rising star of Soviet academy painting, who as a staff artist of the navy newspaper *Red Black Sea Navyman (Krasnyi chernomorets)* was sent to Kerch in early January, remembered: "I got to see the aftermath of [the Nazis'] terrible crimes [...]. Near the small town of Bagerovo 14,000 residents of [Kerch] were executed and dumped into an anti-tank ditch [...]."[85] The highest number of victims was given by Vasily Shevchuk, subsequently Lieutenant General of the Soviet air force, who reminisced about the devastating sight of the Bagerovo ditch in a memoir published in 1980:

> What life was like in the occupied territories we already knew. Not everything, for sure. Later my heart would shudder from the pain of Khatyn and Babi Yar, Mauthausen and Buchenwald. Then we did not know everything. [...] In early [1942] our regiment was stationed at the Bagerovo airport outside Kerch, right after our troops had liberated the city. On one of the non-flying days our regimental commissar Vasily [...] Merkushev gathered the pilots and, without explaining anything, suggested that we get into the back of a battered 1.5-ton truck. [...] That which we saw cannot be described. It was a wide ditch filled with corpses. Dead people, among whom, under a thin layer of sand and the snow [...] one could make out children, women, old people. [...] How did the nerves bear it?! [...] I wanted to close my eyes and

---

84 Tiaglyi, "Kerch," in *Kholokost na territorii SSSR. Entsiklopediia*; see also Tiaglyi, "Mesta massovogo unichtozheniia...," 42; "Kholokost evreiskikh obshchin Kryma v dokumentakh GAARK," Part 1, http://www.holocaust.kiev.ua/bulletin/vip1/vip1_2.htm, last accessed 7 April 2010. At least one Crimean historian with archival expertise, Boris Berlin, makes a distinction between the number of Jews gathered at Haymarket Square on 29 November 1941, around 5000, and the total number of Jews murdered at the Bagerovo ditch, which he believes to be significantly higher than 7000, in part because of the Jewish refugees. See Boris Berlin, "Kholokost v Krymu," Paper delivered at 17 Krymskie mezhdunarodnye nauchnye chteniia I. L. Sel'vinskogo "Tragicheskii opyt Velikoi otechestvennoi voiny v istoriko-literaturnom osmyslenii," Simferopol, 16 December 2011; Boris Berlin, Personal Interview, 15-17 December 2011, Simferopol. Berlin follows the distinction between 5000 and 7000 initially made by Bentsion M. Vol'fson in 1942.
85 *Fedor Reshetnikov*, ed. B. V. Vishniakov (Moscow: Izobrazitel'noe iskusstvo, 1982), note to ill. 90-91.

thrust myself far away from there, as far as possible.... But an unknown force powerfully stopped me: "Stand, Shevchuk. Stand and watch. Watch and remember. This is what the beasts are doing with your people." No, no one fainted. No one ran away. We stood there, teeth and fists clenched. Each of us thought: "These could have been your parents, your wife, your children...." The Bagerovo ditch.... In less than three months the invaders shot and buried alive 25,000 peaceful civilians on the Kerch soil.[86]

While some data supports the presence of over 10,000 Jews in Kerch at the time of the first occupation, it is difficult to speak conclusively about accurate numbers and especially about the methods by which these numbers have been subsequently revised. Some of the data available in Crimean archives, including surviving lists of Jews compiled by the Nazi administration, has not been analyzed. Furthermore, some of the victims, especially Jewish-Polish refugees who ended up getting stuck in the bottleneck of the Kerch peninsula in the autumn of 1941, will probably never be accounted for. Nor will we know whether the number 7000 is inclusive just of the Jews murdered at the Bagerovo ditch during the 29 November 1941 action or encompasses those killed throughout the first occupation of the Kerch peninsula up until 30 December 1941.

My purpose in this book is to reconstruct what Selvinsky and other witnesses to the immediate aftermath of the massacre knew and understood, what they saw in and around Kerch, and what they heard from survivors and eyewitnesses—all in early 1942. This much I have been able to reconstruct from various sources, interviews, and on-site research.

In many ways the murder of the Jews of Kerch followed the scheme the Nazis used in other Crimean cities and towns in the late fall of 1941. To reiterate, the principal difference lies in the fact that Kerch was temporarily liberated and the atrocities documented in their immediate

---

86 V[asilii] M. Shevchuk, *Komandir atakuet pervym* (Moscow: Voenizdat, 1980), http://militera.lib.ru/memo/russian/shevchuk_vm/01.html, last accessed 22 February 2012. See also the discussion of the number of victims in the wartime diary of I. A. Kozlov, one of the leaders of the Soviet underground in occupied Kerch; G. V. Korotkova, ed., "Dnevnik I. A. Kozlova iz fondov Kerchenskogo zapovednika," in *Nauchnyi sbornik Kerchenskogo zapovednika*, 2: 502-503 (Kerch: Kerchenskii istoriko-kul'turnyk zapovednik, 2008).

aftermath. On 25 November 1941 all the Jews of Kerch were ordered to register within three days and to wear six-pointed stars. On 28 November 1941, Order No. 4, signed "nemetskaia politsiia bezopasnosti" (German security police) and posted around town, ordered "all Jews (regardless of age) with children to appear on Saturday 29 November from 8 AM to 12 PM at Haymarket Square (marketplace) with a 3-day supply of food. Note: persons in mixed marriages [v smeshannom brake] are not subject to reporting requirements. Those not carrying out the present order will be publically executed." Rumors circulated that the Jews would be resettled or sent to work at the Mariental collective farm.

17. Sennaya (Haymarket) Square, Kerch, where the Jews of Kerch were ordered to appear on 29 November 1941 and from where they were marched to the city jail and subsequently trucked to the Bagerovo anti-tank ditch and murdered. 1947. (Courtesy of Vladimir Sanzharovets.)

Thousands of Jews, mostly women, children, and the elderly, were gathered at Haymarket Square; thence the victims were marched down Proletarskaya Street to Kirova Street and then along the embankment to the city jail.

18. View of Proletarskaya Street at Sennaya (Haymarket) Square. Kerch. 14 December 2011. Photo by Maxim D. Shrayer.

19. View of Kerch Embankment. Circa January 1942. (Courtesy of Vladimir Sanzhrovets.)

There some women and teenage girls were raped and tortured. From the city jail trucks took groups of victims to the anti-tank ditch located west of the city of Kerch, where they were murdered during the first days of December.[87] Members of Sonderkommando 10B were aided by auxiliaries from the local population, who clubbed the victims, pushing them toward the anti-tank ditch, and also apparently by Wehrmacht riflemen of the 46 Infantry Division.[88]

Very soon the Kerchians, including those Jews still remaining in hiding, heard about the executions. "On the next day," as Z. Gold, who lost 16 family members at the Bagerovo ditch, recounted the events, "rumors reached us from eyewitnesses of the beastly execution. They said that the Germans had cordoned off the road to Bagerovo and did not allow the population to walk or drive by the anti-tank ditch. Collective farmers residing close to Bagerovo heard the machine gun shots, screams of women, children, and groans of the wounded."[89] Consider the detailed testimony of Sofya Lifshits (Livshits):

> On the morning of 1 December [1941] the commandant of the jail called me, the children and my husband out to the corridor. There he took away our things, apartment keys, wrote down our address and placed us in a truck. When 20 people had gathered in the truck, the Germans drove us to the Bagerovo ditch. As soon as the truck arrived there, the police [it is possible that Lifshits refers to the Russian-speaking *Hiwis*, drawn from the ranks of the local collaborators—MDS] started to pull us from the truck, some by the hands, others by the legs. The

---

87 See Tiaglyi, *Mesta massovogo unichtozheniia*... 41-46, notes on 91-92; "Kerch," in *Kholokost na territorii SSSR. Entsiklopediia*; "Kholokost evreiskikh obshchin Kryma," Part 1, http://www.holocaust.kiev.ua/bulletin/vip1/vip1_2.htm, last accessed 7 April 2010; Arad, *The Holocaust in the Soviet Union*, 206-207; Gubenko, 21-23; Vol'fson; *Zverstva nemetskikh fashistov v Kerchi. Sbornik rasskazov postradavshikh i ochevidtsev*, esp. pp. 8, 12-20; 45-50; 55-56; 61-62; 65-68; 75-78; 93-102; V[asilii] Iakovlev, *Prestupleniia. Bor'ba. Vozmezdie*. (Simferopol: Krymizdat, 1961); 25-38, 233-234; Al'tman, "Istreblenie evreev Rossii i Kryma." On 14 December 2011 the Simferopol-based historian Vladimir Gurkovich, the Kerch-based historian Vladimir Sanzharovets, and the Simferopol-based activist of the Krymchak community Arkady Achkinazi accompanied me on a tour of Kerch's Shoah sites. I have subsequently benefited from a series of email conversations with V. Sanzharovets. In a 21 January 2012 electronic communication, Sanzharovets clarified some of the details of the route from Sennaya Square to the Kerch city jail.
88 Angrick, 356-357.
89 Z. Gol'd, "Palachi," in *Zverstva nemetskikh fashistov v Krymu*, 99.

fascists also pulled me down from the truck. I fell onto the ground and with tears started to beg the policeman to release my children. But he chased me after the crowd toward the ditch. Then a second policeman ran up to me and stared to pull off my overcoat. I tell him: "Why are you taking my coat off? What do you need it for? You won't live for a thousand years." In response to these words the policeman hit me hard on the head with a rubber stick. My eyes grew dark, and I tumbled into the ditch, passing out. The children, who had been beside me, holding my skirt, tumbled into the ditch with me. When the Germans started to undress my husband, he started to yell "Help!" and fight them off. He managed to wrest himself from the hands of the bandits and run up to me and the children. [...] He was all covered in blood. Standing beside me he yelled: "My babies, where are you going? Where are they taking you? There's the road for you, run and save yourselves!..." Then I passed out for the second time. Later I came to and started to gnash on the snow. I lay there for a long time. The whole time I heard the screaming of women who were being executed, the crying of children. [...] After the execution of each group the Germans came up to the ditch and finished off the small children who were still alive. [...] I was wounded by shots in both calves. [...] When it grew dark I felt that I was being covered with soil. I started to suffocate and then carefully, quietly freed my head. I saw that it was night already and the moon was shining. [...] I crawled up to the children. My Abrasha lay there with his eyes open. I thought he was alive and started to whisper his name, calling him: "Abrasha, Abrasha!" but he didn't answer. Abrasha and Marik were dead. The fascists shot my little kids through the head. To warm myself up I pulled the overcoat from Abrasha, put it on myself, kissed the kids and walked, not knowing where to go."[90]

---

90   Originally published in Vol'fson, 35-36; cf. S. Livshits, "Ubiitsy zhenshchin i detei," *Zverstva*

Five anti-tank ditches, intended to deter German tanks but failing to do so, had been dug on the Kerch peninsula prior to the Nazi advance, and four of those five became execution sites and mass graves.[91] The so-called Bagerovo anti-tank ditch received its name from the small town of Bagerovo (known in the postwar Soviet years for its classified military airfield) because in 1941, when the ditch was dug, Bagerovo was the town nearest to it west of Kerch, even though the village of Skasiev-Fontan (presently the district of Michurino within Kerch) was only about 2 km east of the ditch. The name is therefore a bit misleading. The ditch, 4 meters wide and 2 meters deep, extended for 1.5 kilometers from south to north, perpendicular to the tracks of the Dzhankoy-Kerch Railroad and the Vokzalnoe Highway (which runs from Kerch to Bagerovo and Chistopolie). At the present time, the ditch is located about 1 km west of the city boundary of Kerch, and about 6 km east of the town of Bagerovo. Only the section of the ditch north of both the highway and the railroad tracks remains; the village of Oktyabrskoe presently abuts the highway on the south side, with houses built directly across what remains of the ditch. Oktyabrskoe and the "87 km" bus stop and railroad junction are presently the landmarks closest to the site of massacre at the Bagerovo anti-tank ditch. The section of the ditch where the murders took place extends for about 1 km in the direction of the Katerlez Mountain Range.[92]

---

nemetskikh fasistov v Krymu, 65-67; cf. Iakovlev, 30-32.
91 Vladimir Sanzharovets, e-mail communication, 21 January 2012.
92 This description of the area and the map with my annotations and added landmarks are based on my field research during a visit to Kerch and the Bagerovo anti-tank ditch on 14 December 2011, and also on a subsequent comparison of a number of prewar, wartime, and postwar maps, contemporary atlases, and satellite maps. Vladimir Sanzharovets has furnished me with valuable information on the history of the area and with rare maps. Sanzharovets has written extensively about the history of the name "Bagerovskii rov" (Bagerovo ditch). See Sanzharovets, V. F. "Antropotoponimy kerchenskogo poluostrova: proiskhozhdenie nekotorykh istoricheskikh i sovremennykh oikonimov (opyt istoriko-toponimicheskogo issledovaniia)," *Nauchnyi sbornik kerchenskogo zapovednika* 3 (2011): 389-411.

20. The Bagerovo anti-tank ditch, with mountains of the Katerlez Range in the background. From the January 1942 series of photos of the Bagerovo ditch. Photo by Evgeny Khaldey. (Konstantin Khodakovsky's album "Kerch during the Great Patriotic War," with notes by Vladimir Sanzharovets based on Khaldey's notebooks, http://fotki.yandex.ru/users/khodak.)

21. The Bagerovo anti-tank ditch, with mountains of the Katerlez Range in the background and Mt. Turkmenskaya on the far left. 14 December 2011. Photo by Maxim D. Shrayer.

CHAPTER ONE

In December 1941, following the mass round-up of the Jews of Kerch on 29 November 1941, Order No. 5 was issued and posted, requiring that "all Jews still residing in the city of Kerch and near environs appear immediately at Karl Liebknecht Street, 2"—the former offices of the city's Party committee.

> **ПРИКАЗ № 5**
>
> 1. Все евреи, проживающие еще в городе Керчи и в ближайших местностях, должны немедленно явиться по адресу: ул. Карла Либкнехта, № 2.
>
> 2. Все население города, знающее место нахождения евреев, должно заявить в Немецкую полицию безопасности.
>
> 3. За невыполнение настоящего приказа РАССТРЕЛ.
>
> *Немецкая полиция безопасности*

22. Order No. 5 (early December 1941), signed "German security police" and posted around Kerch, ordering all the remaining Jews of Kerch to appear immediately at 2 Karl Liebknecht Street. (Courtesy of Boris Berlin.)

Residents who had knowledge of the Jews' whereabouts were ordered to report them or likewise face execution, and some apparently did. Even today in Crimea one hears of non-Jewish relatives having surrendered children of mixed marriages to the Nazi authorities. Some evidence suggests that following the murder of the Jews of Kerch, Soviet prisoners of war and members of the local Roma community may also have been executed at the Bagerovo anti-tank ditch. Evidence also suggests that at the very end of December, with the Kerch-Feodosia Landing Operation already on the way, the Nazis rounded several hundred male residents of the workers' settlement of Samostroy near the town of Kamysh-Burun, and subsequently executed them at the Bagerovo ditch.[93] As late as 29 December 1941, the Jews rounded up after the mass action of 29 November were still being taken from the city jail to the ditch and killed, and most of the survivors came from among the Jews who were being sent to their death on 29 December 1941.[94]

The Soviet sailors and soldiers of the first echelon of the Kerch landing came upon the Bagerovo ditch on 30 December 1941.[95] The first investigators arrived at the scene in the earliest days of January. Some of them, like the photographers Evgeny Khaldey and Dmitri Baltermants, both dispatched to photograph the liberation of Kerch, apparently chanced upon the anti-tank ditch and decided to document what they initially could not fully comprehend. Lev Borodulin, a colleague of Dmitri Baltermants, recalled that Baltermants "photographed [the aftermath of the massacre at the Bagerovo ditch] mechanically ["snimal mashinal'no"; can also denote doing something "in a trance"], but vague premonitions did not leave him."[96] Khaldey, who had arrived from the northern port of Murmask, spoke with some of the survivors and eyewitnesses he photographed, recording their names and information in a

---

93 Samostroy, literally "self-built," was a common prewar Soviet name for a workers' settlement, and there were several such neighborhoods in Kerch proper, which resulted in confusion with the reporting of the atrocities committed against residents during both the first and the second occupations. It is therefore not easy to sort out which Samostroy is being mentioned in the accounts and historical and popular literature. In a recent article, Oksana Sheremet clearly links the "Samostroy" mentioned in Selvinsky's "I Saw It!" with the Samostroy settlement in Kamysh-Burun, "Za den' do svobody," *Bospor* 1 December 2011, http://www.bospor.com.ua/articles/4300.shtml, accessed 27 January 2011. On the murder of the residents of the Kamysh-Burun Samostroy, see also varying data and accounts in Lev Ish, "Krovavye zverstva fashistov v Kerchi," *Krasnyi Krym* 29 January 1942, 2; Veniamin Goffenshefer, "Bagerovo," *Syn otechestva* 29 January 1942; Vl[adimir] Mitrofanov, "Krym pered ob"ektivom," *Literatura i iskusstvo* 21 March 1942, 3; *Zverstva nemetskikh fashistov v Kerchi*, 17-18; 51-54; 57-58; 69-70; 79-80; 85; "Spravka o mestakh massovykh ubiistv…"; Vol'fson, 34; Iakovlev, 36; Korotkova, "Okkupatsionnyi rezhim v Kerchi." 311.

94 Finally, some evidence indicates that as the Nazi forces retreated, they stopped a truck carrying local collaborators from Kerch, executed them, and dumped their bodies into a "ravine" (balka), which may or may not have been the Bagerovo ditch; see Vol'fson, 36, n. 1; Iakovlev, 38.

95 Vol'fson, 33; also see Mosia Gol'dshtein's testimony in *Zverstva nemetskikh fashistov v Kerchi*, 44. For a recent account of the landing, see Anatolii Kuptsov, Liubov' Semenova, "O morskoi baze, desante, pervom osvobozhdenii goroda," *Kerchenskii rabochii* 14 January 2012, http://www.krab.crimea.ua/?p=3687, last accessed 12 February 2012.

96 Lev Borodulin, "O Dmitrii Bal'termantse," http://www.sem40.ru/famous2/m736.shtml, last accessed 27 January 2012.

notebook.[97] He was taken with the story of Grigory Berman, director of the Larindorf junior high school (before the war, Larindorf, which was renamed Krestyanovka in 1944, was the center of the Larindorf Jewish National District).

23. Grigory Berman over the bodies of his wife and children. From the January 1942 series of photos of the Bagerovo ditch. Photo by Evgeny Khaldey. (Konstantin Khodakovsky's album "Kerch during the Great Patriotic War," with notes by Vladimir Sanzharovets based on Khaldey's notebooks, http://fotki.yandex.ru/users/khodak.)

---

97 See Shneer, *Through Soviet Jewish Eyes*, 102; Vladimir Sanzharovets, Personal Interview, Kerch, 14 December 2011, and electronic communication, 28 December 2011.

Berman, whom Khaldey photographed over the bodies of his wife Khana Shmukler and their children, was having trouble finding transportation to move his family's bodies to bury them.[98] He kept returning to the ditch and grieving, which attracted the eye of Khaldey's camera—and also that of the documentary filmmaker Mikhail Oshurkov, who in January 1945 would film the liberation of Auschwitz.[99] The documentary film director Vladimir Mitrofanov headed a film crew at the Crimean Front and was subsequently killed during the retreat of Soviet troops from Kerch in May 1942.[100] Mitrofanov and his colleagues Leon Arzumanov and Vladimir Oshurkov filmed the Bagerovo ditch in the early days of January. In an article published in *Literature and Art* (*Literatura i iskusstvo*), as *Literary Gazette* was called in 1942-1944, Mitrofanov described the aftermath of the massacre and a conversation with Raisa (Raya) Belotserkovskaya, wife of a Red Army

---

98   Vladimir Sanzharovets based this information on conversations with Khaldey, who was consulting notes in his journal.
99   Footage of G. Berman grieving over the bodies of his wife and children was included in the Soviet documentary film, "Film Documents about the Atrocities of the German-Fascist Invaders," submitted and shown as part of the evidence at the Nuremberg Military Tribunal. Ilya Gutman's 1986 documentary *Nuremberg: 40 Years Later* featured footage from the Soviet documentary shown at the Nuremberg Military Tribunal, including several shots of the Bagerovo ditch. The first documentary included the image of a written testimony by 16 Soviet documentary cameramen from the Central Studio of Documentary Films, dated 21 December 1945 and signed by all of them, including the well-known Soviet documentary filmmaker Roman Karmen. This signed testimony does not include the names of Mikhail Oshurkov or Leon Arzumanov, both of whom filmed the aftermath of the Bagerovo ditch massacre for the Central Studio of Documentary Films. Mikhail Oshurkov and Vladimir Mishchenko are listed as cameramen in the credits of a January-February newsreel filmed in Kerch in early 1942 and containing footage of the Bagerovo ditch. See "Kinosiuzhet. Ianvar'-fevral' 1942 g., 2 ch.," in *Ukraina i Druga Svitova viina. Kinolitopys. Anotovanyi katalog kinozhurnaliv, dokumenalnykh fil'miv, kinosiuzhetiv, spetsvypuskiv (1939-1945)*, ed. Tetiana Emel'ianova, 56 (Kyiv: Derzhavnyi komitet arkhiviv Ukrainy; Tsentral'nyi derzhavnyi kinofotofonoarkhiv Ukrainy imeni G. S. Pshenichnogo, 2005). Leon Arzumanov and Aleksandr Adzhibegishvili are listed as cameramen in the credits of another newsreel filmed in Kerch in early 1942 also containing footage of the Bagerovo ditch; see "Kinosiuzhet. Ianvar'-fevral' 1942 g., 2 ch.," in Emel'ianova, 55. Jeremy Hicks examines the Soviet documentary footage from the liberation of Majdanek and presents his research in "From Atrocity to Action: How Soviet Cinema Initiated the Holocaust Film: Imagining the Unimaginable in the Soviet Context," in *Justice, Politics and Memory in Europe after the Second World War. Landscape after Battle*, volume 2, ed. Suzanne Bardgett, David Cesarini, et al., 249-266 (London: Vallentine Mitchell, 2011). I look forward to reading his forthcoming book on the Shoah and Soviet documentary cinema.
100 See Aleksandr Grishin, "...Etot fil'm o voine tak i ne byl sniat," *Krymskie izvestiia* 19 February 2011, http://www-ki-old.rada.crimea.ua/nomera/2011/031/this.html, last accessed 22 February 2012. Some evidence indicates that the footage filmed by Mitrofanov and his crew was buried in the Adzhimushkay Quarries and never saw the light of day.

soldier, who lost her children and crawled out of the ditch, wounded but alive:

> Before us is a young woman. [...] Grief and an injury have prematurely bent her back. What a pity that we do not have a sound recording device with us. Her terrifying account calls for revenge, arousing an insatiable desire to pay the fascist executioners back in plenty for everything they did. One wants millions of people to hear this account with their own ears.
>
> Raya Belotserkovskaya is one of seven thousand Soviet civilians whom the Germans executed in Kerch. She literally rose from the coffin. [...] "On the morning of 29 December," Raya recalls, "we were put in a vehicle and driven to the execution. The bandits usually took off one's left shoe—this was a sign of a condemned person. On the way I threw my brother Izya [Gofman] out of the vehicle [...] The executioners put us with our backs to them, beside the ditch. A burst of submachine-gun shots. A bullet burned my neck. I fell on top of my already dead children....
>
> "This spot right here. Film it," Raya points. She is standing next to her brother beside a long anti-tank ditch filled to the top with corpses. [...] Raya slowly walks with Izya along a continuing row of bodies. Then she kneeled, peering at the corpses of the people she knew.[101]

In his research on Jewish Soviet photographers, David Shneer noted a mixture of confusion, disbelief, —and what comes across as self-correction— in the recollections of Baltermants and Khaldey, who both participated in taking photographs of the Bagerovo ditch.[102]

---

101 Vl[adimir] Mitrofanov, "Krym pered ob"ektivom," *Literatura i iskusstvo* 21 March 1942, 3.
102 See Shneer, *Through Soviet Jewish Eyes*, 100-108; "Picturing Grief," 34-37.

24. Raisa Belotserkovskaya, one of the few Jewish survivors, standing over the Bagerovo anti-tank ditch. 1947. (Courtesy of Vladimir Sanzharovets.)

25. From the January 1942 series of photos of the Bagerovo ditch. Photo by Dmitri Baltermants. ("Dmitry Baltermants," http://club.foto.ru/classics/36.)

Shneer has investigated some of the photographs that Khaldey, Baltermants, Mark Redkin, Izrail Antselovich, and Izrail Ozersky—all of them Jews and Soviet photojournalists—took at the site of the Bagerovo ditch in the early days of January 1942.

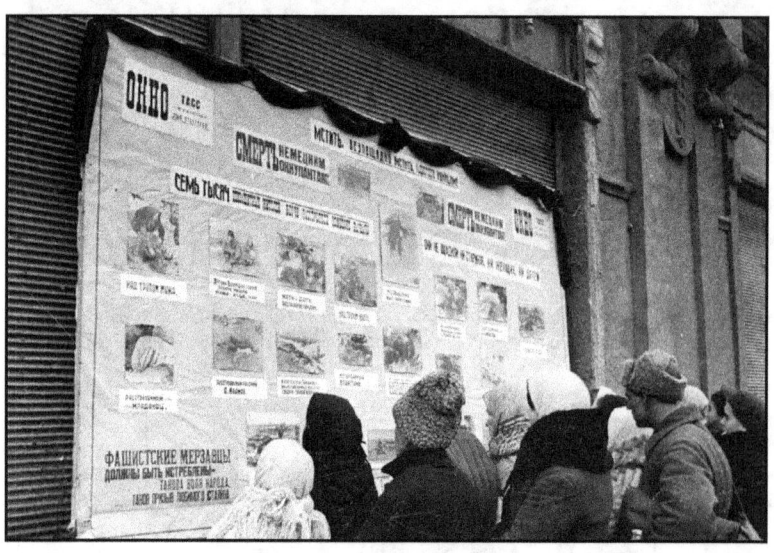

26. Kerch residents looking at the information window depicting the Nazi atrocities at Kerch. The window was coproduced by the Telegraph Agency of the USSR (TASS) and *Syn otechestva* (*Son of Fatherland*, newspaper of the 51st Separate Army, where Selvinsky served until February 1942. January 1942. Photo by Evgeny Khaldey. (Konstantin Khodakovsky's album "Kerch during the Great Patriotic War," with notes by Vladimir Sanzharovets based on Khaldey's notebooks, "http://fotki.yandex.ru/users/khodak" http://fotki.yandex.ru/users/khodak.)

Shneer's research invited questions about the attention given to Kerch by the Soviet media and also about the paucity and inadequacy of the coverage of the Bagerovo ditch massacre. Indeed, in January 1942 TASS dispatched to Kerch additional correspondents and photographers attached to the Southern Front; at its peak TASS would have as many as six people covering the Crimean Front. Some of the reporters, including Mark Redkin and Izrail Ozersky, only took photographs, whereas others, including Izrail Antselovich and Mark Turovsky, took photographs and wrote articles.[103] The national civilian newspapers like *Pravda*, *Izvestia*

---

103 See list of correspondents in Shirokorad. Note that overall Shirokorad takes a starkly Russocentric

and *Komsomolskaya Pravda*, the popular weekly magazine *Ogonek* (*Little Flame*), and the main army newspaper *Red Star* had correspondents in the area or dispatched them to Kerch immediately at the start of the Kerch-Feodosia Landing Operation; these publications and others reported on the liberation of Kerch in January 1942 and would have been in the position to shed light on the Bagerovo anti-tank massacre. *Izvestia*, for instance, had special correspondents filing reports from Kerch as early as 31 December 1941, but it was not until 7 January 1942 that two sentences about "unheard-of atrocities committed by the Nazis in Feodosia and Kerch" appeared in an unsigned report "In Crimea."[104] *Komsomolskaya Pravda*, the central organ of the Young Communist League (Komsomol), had two reporters covering the area, and published its first report on the storming of Kerch and Feodosia on 3 January 1942. On 6 January 1942 its Crimea-based reporters Anatoly Kalinin and Boris Vakulin wrote that "[a]ccording to incomplete data, during their brief time in Kerch the Germans hanged, executed, massacred 7000 Soviet civilians. Small children were poisoned."[105] Some correspondents of the national publications, such as the *Red Star* reporter Lev Ish (who would be killed at Sebastopol later in 1942) or the TASS correspondents Mark Turovsky and Izrail Antselovich, managed to publish much more revealing articles in the local Kerch and Crimean press in January 1942.[106]

Consider, as one characteristic example, the coverage of the Kerch atrocities in the newspaper *Krasnyi Krym* (*Red Crimea*).

---

view of the war and the Soviet wartime press, and apologetically treats Stalin's wartime grand-Russian chauvinism.

104 Stepanov, A., Galyshev, S[ergei]. "Operatsii Krasnoi Armii i Flota v Krymu," *Izvestiia* 1 January 1942, 2; "V Krymu." *Izvestiia* 7 January 1942, 3. On 9 January 1942 *Izvestia* reported separately on the Nazi atrocities in Feodosia, described the murder of civilians at an anti-tank ditch, and avoided specific mention of the word "Jew" and its cognates. It mentioned one name which hints at the victim's Jewish (Krymchak) origins. Two days later the same paper specified atrocities against Jews in Kharkov; see K[onstantin] Taradankin, "Chto proiskhodit v Khar'kove," *Izvestiia* 11 January 1942, 2.

105 A[natolii] Kalinin, B[oris] Vakulin, "Kak byli vziaty Kerch' i Feodosia," *Komsomol'skaia pravda* 3 January 1942, 2; "Boi v Krymu," *Komsomol'skaia pravda* 6 January 1942, 2. See also the collective letter of five Kerch physicians, all of them with Jewish-sounding names, found in O. I. Gol'dina et al., "Chudovishchnye zverstva fashistov v Kerchi (pis'mo vrachei goroda Kerchi)," *Komsomol'skaia pravda* 8 January 1942, 1.

106 See Ish, "Krovavye zverstva fashistov v Kerchi"; Turovskii and Antselovich [text and photos], "Zverstva nemtsev v Kerchi," *Krasnyi Krym* 24 January 1942, 3.

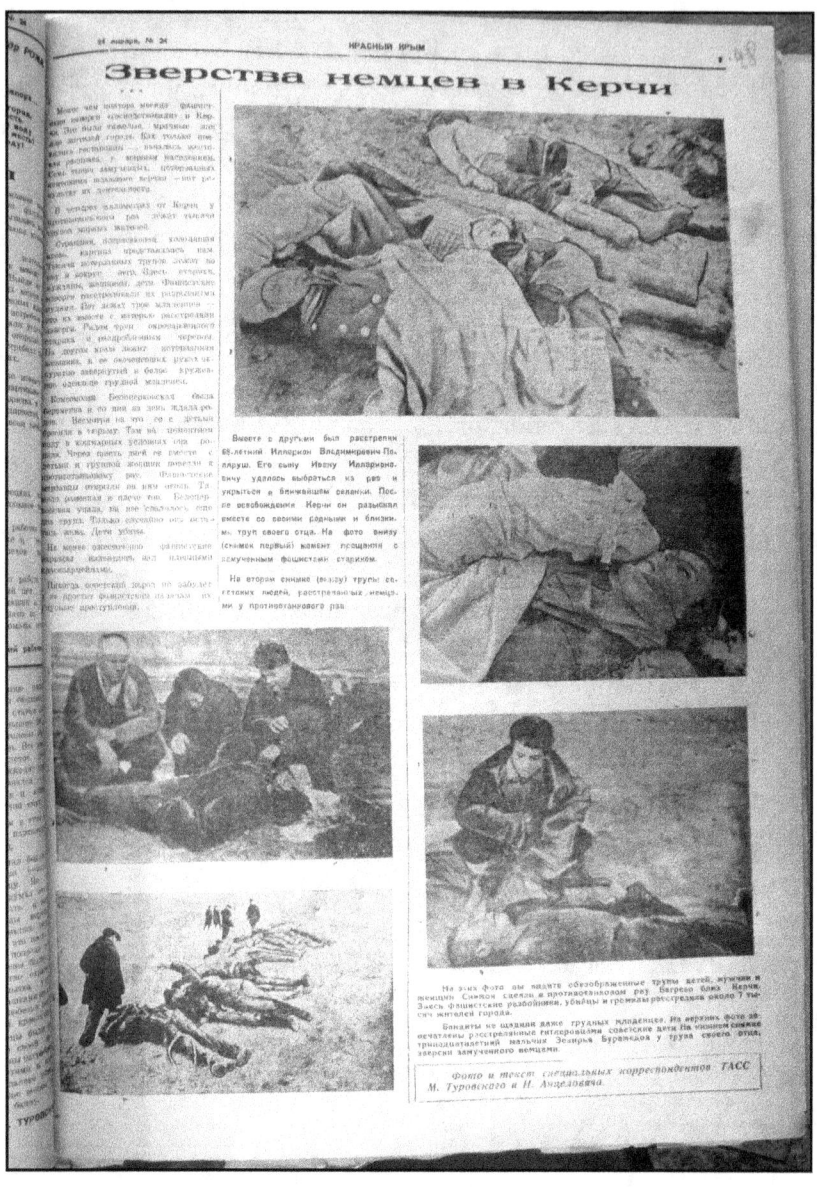

27. German Atrocities in Kerch. A page spread printed in *Krasnyi Krym* (*Red Crimea*) on 24 January 1942. Photos and text by Mark Turovsky and Izrail Antselovich.

On 24 January 1942 *Red Crimea* ran a page of materials, by Turovsky and Antselovich, on the Bagerovo anti-tank ditch. Featured were five photographs, including two very graphic shots of murdered children and a mother murdered with an infant: "A terrifying, striking, blood-chilling scene revealed itself to us. Thousands of mauled corpses are lying in the ditch and around it. There are old people, men, women, children. The fascist brutes executed them with exploding bullets. [...] On the other edge there lies a mauled woman, and in her frozen arms—an infant neatly wrapped in a white lacy blanket."[107] Nowhere in the article or the captions is the word "Jew" or its cognates used, whereas Russian and Tatar names populate the captions. The materials repeatedly cited 7000 as the number of victims. On 29 January 1942, *Red Crimea* published Lev Ish's article "Blood Atrocities of Fascists in Kerch." Ish's article showed a different level of detail and a fairly explicit articulation of Jewish losses. Ish explained that on 28 November 1941 the Nazis "ordered the Jewish population of the city" to gather on Haymarket Square on the following day, and drew on the 30 December 1941 testimony of the Kerch doctors to evoke a picture of the executions at the Bagerovo ditch. He spoke of a "wild pogrom" in the streets of the city. Only then did Ish introduce an equalizing rhetorical gesture, "[t]he rabid Hitlerite scum spared no one: neither Jews, not Russians, nor Ukrainians, nor Tatars." Ish ended his article in the vein of Ehrenburg's writings in *Red Star*: "Let us annihilate all Germans who crept onto our land as occupiers! Death to fascists!" *Red Star* did not carry Ish's reports of the massacre at the Bagerovo ditch.

In his chronicle *The Year 1942*, David Ortenberg (penname D. Vadimov, 1904-1998), who was the editor of *Red Star* from June 1941 to July 1943, indirectly acknowledged that *Red Star* correspondents did not cover the aftermath of Nazi atrocities against the Jews in the temporarily liberated parts of Crimea. A perusal of all the issues of *Red Star* for January and February 1942 attests to the fact that no specific coverage of the mass murder at Kerch was printed in the paper, even though the *Red Star* special correspondent Pavel Slesarev reported on the liberation of Kerch on 3 January 1942.[108] When on 11 January

---

107 Turovskii and Antselovich. "Zverstva nemtsev v Kerchi."
108 See P.[avel] Slesarev, "Bor'ba za Kerch'," *Krasnaia zvezda* 3 January 1942. In his article "When the Wolf Starts Bleeting...," published in *Red Star*, Ehrenburg mentioned Kerch in connection with the recent advanced of Red Army; see Erenburg, "Kogda volk nachinaet bleiat'...." *Krasnaia zvezda* 6 January 1942.

1942 the paper ran Slesarev's report "The Funeral of the Victims of the German Occupation of Kerch," it made no mention of the systematic murder of the Jews of Kerch even while citing a local party official's speech in which the execution of "seven thousand men, women, children, and elderly" was decried.[109]

Konstantin Simonov (1915-1979), the poet, playwright, and novelist who became one of the most famous literary voices of the fighting country and as such one of Stalin's favorites, was a staff writer for *Red Star*. After Ortenberg dispatched Simonov to cover the Kerch-Feodosia Landing Operation, Simonov was unable to reach Kerch and did not see the Bagerovo ditch in January 1942.[110] Simonov ended up reporting from Feodosia, where he wrote and filed by telegraph a two-part "Letter from Crimea."[111] He reported that "in an anti-tank ditch behind the [former] Bedrizov lime works [...] there lay 917 corpses of Russians, Tatars, and Jews ages 12 to 80, executed there by machine guns back on 8 December [1941]. On a different outskirt of the city, this time not in a ditch but simply on the ground, not far from a cemetery, there lay 230 corpses of Krymchaks. They were executed separately, 8 days later."[112] In Feodosia Simonov interviewed the arrested collaborator Vasily Gruzinov and also queried an NKVD officer about the murder of the Jews of Feodosia. Chapter 1 of Simonov's diary for 1942 captured many vivid details and data related to the murders of the Ashkenazi Jews and Krymchaks of Feodosia, but this material did not make it to print during the war. In February 1942 Simonov was sent to Kerch again, and this time he visited the Bagerovo ditch, as his plane landed at the military airport in the vicinity of the site. "I spent several days in Kerch," Simonov wrote in his diary for 1942. "During those days I visited with the commander of the air force of the Crimean Front [...], talked to pilots, walked above the Kerch ditch [sic]. It had already been

---

109 See P. Slesarev," "Pokhorony zhertv nemetskoi okkupatsii v Kerchi," *Krasnaia zvezda* 11 January 1942, 3; see also a photograph of the funeral in *Zverstva nemetskikh fashistov v Kerchi*, 101.
110 See Konstantion Simonov, *Raznye dni voiny. Dnevnik pisatelia*, 2 vols. (Moscow: Khudozhestvennaia literatura, 1982), http://militera.lib.ru/db/simonov_km/index.html, last accessed 22 February 2012. Simonov describes his January 1942 visit to Crimea in chapter 1 of his diary for 1942, http://militera.lib.ru/db/simonov_km/2_01.html.
111 Konstantin Simonov, "Pis'mo iz Kryma. Posledniaia noch'," *Krasnaia zvezda* 9 January 1942, 3; "Pis'mo iz Kryma. Predatel'," *Krasnaia zvezda* 10 January 1942, 3.
112 Simonov, "Pis'mo iz Kryma. Posledniaia noch'," *Krasnaia zvezda* 9 January 1942, 3. On the murder of the Jews of Feodosia, see Tiaglyi, *Mesta massovogo rasstrela...*, 72-78.

covered but still looked terrifying—jutting from under the soil was now a leg, now a frayed piece of clothing."[113] Simonov did not write about the Bagerovo ditch in his *Red Star* reportages from Kerch.[114] Ironically, if such maudlin irony can capture the refusal of the army's main paper to publicize the truth, *Red Star* came the closest to acknowledging that specified atrocities had been committed against the Jewish population of Kerch when it printed Molotov's note of 6 January and discussed it in a special editorial.

Selvinsky arrived in the Kerch area from the Taman peninsula with troops of the second echelon, landing at Cape Kamysh-Burun.[115] By the time Selvinsky saw the Bagerovo anti-tank ditch—and the poet may have visited it more than once in the second and third week of January—he would have had at least some access to coverage of the massacre in the press. He was unlikely to have seen central civilian newspapers like *Pravda* or *Izvestia*, but he was very likely to have read *Red Star*. There can be little doubt that Selvinsky had already been familiar with the Molotov note, and was going to the scene of the massacre cognizant of the number of victims, 7000, cited in the note. Furthermore, Selvinsky also sensed the outer limits of what the central Soviet media considered printable. Let us pause and reflect on the impact of the Molotov note on a 42-year-old educated Jewish military officer who has just arrived in the (temporarily) liberated Kerch.

As I have already mentioned, on 6 January 1942 Molotov issued a note on German atrocities. The note was printed or excerpted in central, regional, and army Soviet newspapers on 7-9 January 1941 and

---

113 Simonov, *Raznye dni voiny*, http://militera.lib.ru/db/simonov_km/2_03.html, last accessed 22 February 2012.
114 In 1976 the Soviet filmmaker Aleksey German made the film *Twenty Days without War*, based on the screenplay by Konstatin Simonov, which, in turn was based on Simonov's short novel of the same title. The novel's protagonist Lopatin, a writer and frontline journalist, is commonly believed to have been based on Simonov himself. Yet a number of parallels, including Lopatin's past experiences in Crimea during the Kerch-Feodosia Landing Operation, also point to Ilya Selvinsky. The screenplay and especially German's film, where Yuri Nikulin, who played Lopatin, bore an uncanny resemblance to Selvinsky's photographs of 1941-1942, fleshed out the Selvinsky connection in a way that Simonov's short novel had not.
115 Selvinsky, Wartime Diaries, 22 January 1942. For details of the Kerch landing operation, see Leonid Melkov, *Kerch'. Povest'-khronika v dokumentakh, vospominaniakh i pis'makh uchastnikov geroicheskoi zashchity i osvobozhdeniia goroda v 1941-1944 godakh*, 57-70 (Moscow: Izdatel'stvo politicheskoi literatury, 1981). In the recollections, Selvinsky's colleagues on the staff of *Son of Fatherland* differ as to whether he arrived in the area of Kerch right before or immediately after 1 January 1942; see Arkharova 107-108; Sviridenko 119-121.

covered in worldwide media.¹¹⁶ This was the only Soviet official note to speak to the world of specified Nazi atrocities against the Jews, to cite preliminary numbers of Jewish victims in the context of Nazi atrocities, and to refer to such atrocities as having been committed not just against unspecified "Soviet citizens" or "Soviet civilians," but specifically against the Jews in the occupied territories:

> Many mass murders were committed by the German occupants in other Ukrainian cities. These bloody executions were especially directed against unarmed and defenseless Jewish working people. According to incomplete figures, no less than 6000 persons were shot in Lvov, over 8000 in Odessa, over 8500 killed or hanged in Kamenets-Podolsk, over 10,500 persons shot down with machine guns in Dnepropetrovsk, and over 3000 local residents shot in Mariupol, including many old men, women and children, all of whom were robbed and stripped naked before execution. According to preliminary figures, about 7000 persons were killed by the German fascist bandits in Kerch."¹¹⁷

Molotov's note pointed to the murder of the Jews outside Kerch. On the day after its publication an editorial in *Red Star*, "Pack of Murderers and Pillagers," cited "preliminary data" of 7000 people "murdered by German-Fascist robbers" at Kerch. What is more significant, however, is

---

116 See "Nota narodnogo komissara inostrannykh del tov. V. M. Molotova o povsemestnykh grabezhakh, razorenii naseleniia i chudovishchnykh zverstvakh germanskikh vlastei na zakhvachennykh imi sovetskikh territoriiakh," *Pravda*, 7 January 1942, 1-2; *Krasnaia zvezda* 7 January 1942, 1-2; *Izvestiia* 7 Janury 1942, 1-2; *Komsomol'skaia pravda* 7 January 1942; cf. text of the note in *Dokumenty obviniaiut*, 1: 33-45. For an example of a summary of the note printed in a local or regional newspaper, see "Peredaem soderzhanie noty Narodnogo komissara inostrannykh del tov. V. N. Molotova," *Kerchenskii rabochii* 8 January 1942, 1. The Western press reported on the note; see, for instance, "Molotoff [sic] Accused Nazi of Atrocities—Note Detailing 'Crimes' Handed to All Foreign Diplomats," *The New York Times* 7 January 1942, 8; "More Nazi Crimes Listed by Soviet; Molotoff Note to All Friendly Countries Charges Germany Orders Terrorism—Vast Looting Is Alleged Attacks on Women and Girls Said to Be Part of Program—Mass Murders Described," *The New York Times* 8 January 1942, 7. The first of the *New York Times* reports was filed from London and cites "several thousand" [murdered] in Kerch." The second, filed from Moscow and much more detailed, refers to 7000 vicims in Kerch.
117 I quote from this English translation: "Note on German Atrocities in Occupied Soviet Territory," http://www.ibiblio.org/pha/policy/1942/420106b.html, last accessed 7 April 2010.

the likening, in the editorial, of the mass murders committed in towns and cities of Ukraine and Crimea to "St. Bartholomew's night, when in nighttime Paris about 10,000 Huguenots were murdered."[118] Without spelling out the parallel between Jews and Huguenots, the editorial implicitly suggested that the victims of the Nazi genocide belonged to a singled-out identity group.

But perhaps more importantly to this reconstruction, by the time Selvinsky saw the Bagerovo ditch, he had already heard accounts from the survivors and local residents and from the members of the Soviet underground in the Kerch area, and read first testimonies and descriptions of the massacre that were detailed in the pages of the local press. A separate look is therefore in order on the coverage of the atrocities in the Kerch press in January 1942, when Selvinsky was based there.

The Kerch newspaper *Kerchenskii rabochii* (*Kerch Worker*) was quickly re-launched on 3 January 1942.[119] On 7 January it ran a statement by a group of the city's Jewish doctors, who had survived "from among the 7000 brutally executed people" because their services were needed and the Gestapo had temporarily released them. Dated 30 December 1941 and signed with seven names, the "Act on Fascist Atrocities" is the first known official document providing details on the murders of Jews in Kerch. The act clearly stated that "all Jews, regardless of age, were ordered to appear at Haymarket Square" and that "starting with 1 December groups were being driven to be executed [...,] at first women with infants, then teenagers separately, then only women, and finally, men alone."[120] On 8 January 1942, in the same issue of *Kerch Worker* in which the contents of Molotov's note were summarized, the funeral commission of the city Party committee and city council ran a brief announcement that "on 9 January 1942 at 11 a.m. at the Club of Industrial Cooperation" a memorial service for the victims of

---

118 "Svora ubiits i grabitelei," *Krasnaia zvezda* 8 January 1942, 1.
119 See Melkov, 74; N. A. Sirota, "Kogda front priblizilsia vplotnuiu....," in *Kerch' geroicheskaia. Vospominaniia. Ocherki. Dokument, 31* (Simferopol': Tavriia, 1974).
120 Mukhat, M. et al. "Akt o fashistskikh zverstvakh. 30/XII-41 g." *Kerchenskii rabochii* 7 January 1942: 1. A different letter from five "doctors of the city of Kerch," dated 8 January 1942, was sent to *Komsomolskaya Pravda*; O. I. Gol'dina et al, "Chudovishchnye zverstva fashistov v Kerchi (pis'mo vrachei goroda Kerchi)," *Komsomol'skaia Pravda* 8 January 1942: 1; cf. "Iz pis'ma vrachei goroda Kerchi v redaktsiiu gazety 'Komsomol'skaia pravda' ot 8/1/1942," *Dokumenty obviniaiut. Sbornik dokumentov o chudovishchnykh zlodeistvakh germanskikh vlastei na vremmenno zakhvachennykh imi sovetskikh territoriikh*, 1: 190-192 (Moscow: Gosudarstvennoe izdatel'stvo politicheskoi literatury, 1943).

fascist terror will take place. Bodies will be carried out at 3 p.m."[121] On the following day *Kerch Worker* ran an editorial, "Wrath of the People," focusing on the funerals of "eight out of thousands of the tortured, brutally rent [zverski rasterzannykh] victims."[122] The word Jew figures nowhere in the editorial, and yet there is a coded message in its language.[123] On 12 January the front page of *Kerch Worker* carried the article "Fascist Murderers" by Izrail Antselovich, which anticipates Antselovich's subsequent report, "Vile Murderers," to be published in *Little Flame* on 8 March 1942. Both the earlier article in the local paper and the subsequent piece in the national illustrated weekly suffer from the same tendency to obfuscate Jewish losses or present them in a multiethnic Soviet context. "You want to know how they ran things here," says "the old railroad worker Ivan Alekseevich Tkachenko" to a group of journalists whom Antselovich refers to as "we": "Go over there, toward Bagerovo. There those beasts executed several thousand people." Antselovich describes approaching the site: "We walk along the highway. Walking together with us are hundreds of residents of Kerch and Kamysh-Burun. Walking there are Russians, Ukrainians, Jews, Tatars, Greeks, Armenians. There, at the anti-tank ditch, fascist officers and soldiers—those human lowlifes—were executing their relatives and loved ones."[124] Antselovich cited several testimonies of survivors and eyewitnesses. One of them was Kaplunovsky, "an elderly doctor," whose name suggested his Jewish identity while the identity itself was not revealed. Finally, on 14 January 1942, just a few days after Selvinsky's documented visit to the Bagerovo anti-tank ditch, *The Kerch Worker* published a photograph by Leonid Yablonsky; it depicted two corpses with the following caption: "During the month and a half of controlling Kerch the German barbarians tortured thousands of peaceful citizens to death, among them children, women, and old people. In

---

121 See announcement by "Komissia po pokhoronam" in *Kerchenskii rabochii* 8 January 1942.
122 See a photograph of the funeral in *Zverstva nemetskikh fashistov v Kerchi*, 101.
123 "Gnev naroda," *Kerchesnkii rabochii* 10 January 1942.
124 I[zrail'] Antselovich, "Fashistskie ubiitsy," *Kerchenskii rabochii* 12 January 1942, 1; cf. Antselovich, "Gnusnye ubiitsy," *Ogonek* 8 March 1942, 7.

the photo: corpses of citizens brutally murdered by fascists in one of the cells of the Kerch jail."¹²⁵

During a visit to Kerch in December 2011, exactly seventy years after the massacres, I sought to reconstruct Selvinsky's path to the Bagerovo anti-tank ditch. Selvinsky and his fellow military journalists walked from the editorial office of *Son of Fatherland*, at first probably down the Mithridates (Mitridat) Stairs and along the embankment and eventually along the railroad tracks, to come upon a sight of utter horror and confusion. The winter of 1941-42 was unusually cold and snowy for Crimea, and specifically for the Kerch region.¹²⁶ Selvinsky and his colleagues saw an anti-tank ditch partially covered with snow, and partially dug out, with bodies lying beside the ditch and visible under the removed snow. In the words of Veniamin Goffenshefer, "We only saw the corpses of those whom the fascists killed during the final days before their retreat. Thousands of corpses still lie under the snow. Over there, a hole has been dug out in the snow, and from its walls hands, feet, and heads of the murdered ones jut out."¹²⁷ They may have also seen freshly dug-out mass graves into which some unidentified bodies were deposited. It was early in the morning, and Selvinsky and those with him were not likely to see many people near the ditch. But if they did see any people, these people would have included relatives of the victims, seeking to identify and claim the bodies of their loved ones, locals digging and moving the corpses, and perhaps some investigators in uniform or plain clothes. "Solitary grieving women who had remained alive walked like shadows along the endless ditch, hoping to identify their family members and loved ones amid the undressed frozen bodies piled one on top of the other," recalled Fyodor Reshetnikov, who was there within days before or after Selvinsky's visit.¹²⁸

Even the best informed witnesses among the Soviet writers, photographers, cinematographers, and visual artists who visited the Bagerovo anti-tank ditch in early January 1942 had trouble understanding why there were hardly any Jewish mourners, and also why some of the bodies lying on top of and beside the ditch were those of ethnic Russians,

---

125 L[eonid] Iablonskii, ["Photo of Nazi atrocities"], *Kerchenskii rabochii* 14 January 1942.
126 See, for instance, a memoir by Vladimir Samarinov, which contains interesting details: *Prervannoe detstvo*, http://www.proza.ru/2011/03/27/1786, last accessed 28 December 2011.
127 Goffenshefer, "Bagerovo."
128 *Fedor Reshetnikov*, ed. Vishniakov, note to ill. 90-91.

Ukrainian, and Tatars—whose mourning relatives were present. There were indeed so few known Jewish survivors and eyewitnesses that each one figures prominently in most accounts of the massacre.[129]

The Jewish survivor who became best known was Raisa Belotserkovskaya; her letter, published in *Red Star* on 17 January 1942, was apparently the first personal account of the massacre printed in the national Soviet press."[130] Belotserkovskaya's letter, which would subsequently be reprinted in wartime volumes documenting Nazi atrocities in the occupied territories, ended this way: "I am not even thirty yet now, after the horrors of the German occupation, I look like an old woman. The Germans murdered my three children; a German bullet left a trace in my body. Where is one to find the words that would subject to damnation this gang of killers, these cannibals drinking the blood of women and children! [...]"[131] In the early days of January, Reshetnikov met Belotserkovskaya near the Bagerovo ditch and did a pencil drawing of her in his sketchpad, noting her first name incorrectly. He titled the sketch "The Terrifying Memories of A. Belotserkovskaya. 1942" and wrote beneath the sketch, "Along with her three children the Hitlerites executed this woman and threw her in the anti-tank ditch filled with 14,000 women, old people and children—residents of Kerch. After regaining consciousness she, having lost a lot of blood, found the strength to crawl out from under the corpses and inch her way to the nearest village, where she was given shelter until our troops liberated the city."[132]

The Jewish survivors and eyewitnesses also included: Grigory Berman; Iosif Vaingardten (Vaingartner); Vaingardten's niece Z. Gold; Sofya Lifshits (Livshits); R. Goldshtein; Izya Gofman (Raisa Belotserkovskaya's brother); and Mosia Goldshtein, these last two teenagers. Apparently only those bodies that could be identified were buried in individual graves, and that was a very small fraction of all the Jews killed at the Bagerovo ditch. To quote the testimony of Z. Gold,

---

129 Vol'fson (35) writes that "of the mass of 7000 executed people several dozen survived by chance [sluchaino utselelo neskol'ko detiatkov chelovek]."
130 Ortenberg, *God 1942*, 96-97 (Moscow: Izdatel'stvo politicheskoi literatury, 1988).
131 R. Belotserkovskaia, "Budem mstit' fashistam. Pis'mo zheny krasnoarmeitsa R. Belotserkovskoi," *Krasnaia zvezda* 17 January 1942; cf. R. Belotserkovskaia, "Istrebliaite fashistov," in *Zverstva nemetskikh fashistov v Kerchi*, 55-56; "Pis'mo zheny krasnoarmeitsa R. Belotserkovskoi," in *Dokumenty obviniaiut* 1: 190-194; cf. Ortenberg, *God 1942*, 97.
132 Reshetnikov, ed. Vishniakov, note to ill 90-91.

> [A]fter the arrival of the Red Army I went to the Bagerovo ditch to the site of the execution of the victims of fascism. With great difficulty I was able to find from all of my relatives only Mosia Rokhlin. By all signs he had been executed on the eve of the fascists' flight, i.e. 28 December. [...] The fascists had subjected Mosia to torture. We buried him in a mass grave with seven partisans who had been tortured to death. After that I kept going back to Bagerovo, in order to find mama and my other relatives, but it was impossible to find them.[133]

We know little about the public funerals reported as early as 8 January 1942, and Selvinsky left no information about them in his diary or letters. The ditch was covered and left as a huge mass grave, and even today we do not know what lies beneath the thin layer of soil and steppe grass lining the ditch.

Several photojournalists were at the scene with Selvinsky or at other times during those first two weeks of January, and Selvinsky deliberately described a Soviet photographer in one of his two poems about the Bagerovo ditch massacre. A separate note about the photographic coverage of the massacre is therefore in order. The first explicit photojournalistic coverage of the Nazi atrocities committed in and around Kerch appeared in the central Soviet press on 20 January 1942, when *Komsomolskaya Pravda* published three photographs of the Bagerovo ditch with a brief editorial introduction and captions. The publication bore the title "The Fascists will Pay for This with Their Heads!" The editorial introduction stated that "[d]ocumentary evidence has shown that in Kerch alone the vile fascist executioners killed 7000 women, children, and old people."[134] Neither the editorial introduction nor the captions said anything about the victims' ethnic identity. On 4 February 1942 *Little Flame* ran a page with two photographs by Mark Redkin, both of them reprinted from the *Komsomolskaya Pravda* publication of 20 January 1942.[135] "The caption writers," Shneer explains, "obscured

---
133 Gold, 100.
134 Mark Redkin, phot., "Fashisty poplatiatsia za eto golovami! Otomstim za krov' bezvinnykh zhertv. Fotodokumenty o zverstvakh nemtsev v Kerchi," *Komsomol'skaia pravda* 20 January 1942.
135 Mark Redkin, phot., "Strashnye prestupleniia gitlerovskikh palachei," *Ogonek* 4 February 1942, 4.

the perpetrators of the crimes. [...] And no mention is made of the fact that most of the dead women and children [...] were Jewish."¹³⁶

On 8 March 1942, celebrated in the Soviet Union as International Women's Day, *Little Flame* carried a more extensive layout on Bagerovo, entitled "Evildoings of Hitlerites in Kerch." The targeted anti-Jewish nature of the Nazi atrocities was obfuscated again. The publication carried eight photographs, by Izrail Antselovich, Izrail Ozersky, and Dmitri Baltermants, and an article by Antselovich.¹³⁷ "They were killed in cold blood in a premeditated fashion," read the article. "They were killed indiscriminately—Russians and Tatars, Ukrainians and Jews. The Hitlerites have indiscriminately murdered the Soviet population in many cities, villages, and the countryside."¹³⁸ The caption under one of the photographs on the first page of the two-page spread identified the victim as the "67-year-old I. Kh. Kogan." To some extent, as Shneer has argued, "[i]n the newspapers published during the war, writers, photographers, and editors suggested that this was a massacre of Jews in other ways."¹³⁹ But such gestures and suggestions, sometimes emanating from a subtle interplay between the images, captions, and other materials published on neighboring pages, were limited and became even more constricted as the war went on.¹⁴⁰ When two photos, one by Dmitri Baltermants and one by Izrail Antselovich, from the 8 March 1942 *Little Flame* spread were reprinted in the British *Picture Post* on 20 June 1942 in an article on "What the Advancing Russians Found," the photographers' names were missing, the captions were utterly misleading, and the names were Russian and Tatar: "The Germans came to the village, they looted it, and took some of the men away. [...] Now the village women came out in search for husband and son. One of them, S. Afanasyeva, cries for a youth who was only eighteen years old [...]"; "He was called Rakhman [...] Then the Germans said he had a pair of

---

136 Shneer, *Through Soviet Jewish Eyes*, 103.
137 I[zrail'] Antselovich, I[zrail'] Ozerskii, and D[mitrii] Bal'termants, phot., "Zlodeiianiia gitlerovtsev v Kerchi," *Ogonek* 8 March 1942, 6-7; Antselovich, I[zrail'], "Gnusnye ubiitsy," *Ogonek* 8 March 1942, 7.
138 Tr. David Shneer; quoted in Shneer, *Through Soviet Jewish Eyes*, 104.
139 Shneer, *Through Soviet Jewish Eyes*, 105.
140 As Shneer notes, "[O]n December 27, 1942, for the one-year anniversary of the [temporary] liberation of Kerch, *Unity* [*Eynikayt*, the Yiddish-language newspaper of the Jewish Antifascist Committee] republished Redkin's photograph of the dead women and children. Although the caption spoke about the victims in a universal sense, the well-known Soviet Yiddish writer Itsik Fefer's poem 'I Am a Jew' was published on the preceding page. Associating the photograph with Fefer's poem rendered the scene Jewish." See Shneer, "Picturing Grief," 40.

felt boots and was keeping them for himself."[141]

Some of the early witnesses who came upon the aftermath of the massacre at the Bagerovo ditch were equipped with more knowledge and understanding; some were more confused and dumbfounded than others. The level of both detail and comprehension tended to decrease as one moved from the coverage in the local Crimean press to the national press—and, also as a tendency, the obfuscation of the Jewish losses increased proportionally. Consider the second paragraph of a distorted report from Kerch by a *Pravda* special correspondent: "Every day outside the city, residents of Kerch have been extracting from the anti-tank ditch corpses of their relatives executed by the fascists. Mass graves have been erected [*vozdvignuty*, an odd verb choice—MDS], and the wreaths which the city laid on them are still showing green."[142] There were, to be sure, inconsistencies in the national coverage of the atrocities, and in some cases the victims' and mourners' explicitly Jewish names were not edited out.[143] Such was the case, for instance, with two photographs printed in February 1942 in *Photonewspaper of the Political Directorate of the Red Army*.

But as a strong tendency, by the time one got to the coverage in central newspapers—*Pravda* hinted at the murder of Jews at Kerch on January 5 and 20 January, *Izvestia* described it in starkly nonspecific terms on 7 January and 31 January, *Komsomolskaya Pravda* printed three photographs on 20 January, *Little Flame* ran a page on 4 February and a two-page spread on 8 March—an uninformed reader would have a difficult time understanding that what had taken place in Kerch and was carried out at the Bagerovo anti-tank ditch was genocide of the Jews.[144]

---

141 "What the Advancing Russians Found," *Picture Post* 15:12 (20 June 1942): 7-9.
142 "V osvobozhdennoi Kerchi," *Pravda* 20 January 1942, 3; signed "spetsial'nyi korrespondent" (special correspondent).
143 See "Otomstim!" *Fotogazeta Glavnogo politicheskogo upravleniia armii* 19 (February 1942): 1. Here the caption under the top photograph explicitly states the name and prewar residency of the "teacher of the Larindorf incomplete middle school comrade Berman [pictured] over the bodies of his wife and children executed by the Germans."
144 Also as a tendency, Jewish readers and some readers with background knowledge of Jewish civilization would have been able to decode the Jewish writers' signals. For instance, in an essay linking Nazi atrocities with the decline of German civilization and morality under Nazism, Vladimir Lidin spoke of the anti-tank ditches outside Kerch and Feodosia, referring to the latter as having become "the wailing wall" ("stenoi placha stal etot protivotankovyi rov"); see Vl[adimir] Lidin, "Plevely," *Izvestiia* 31 January 1942, 2.

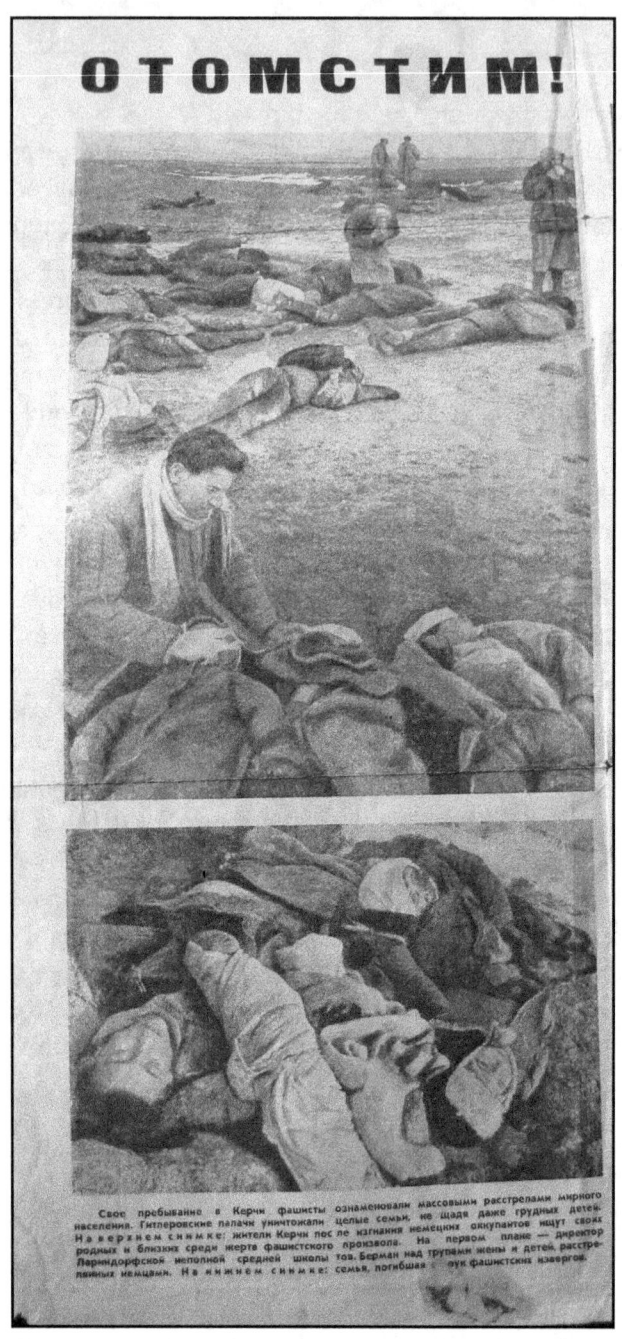

28. "We Shall Avenge!" A section of a page spread on Nazi atrocities with two uncredited photos (top by Evgeny Khaldey, bottom by either Mark Turovsky, Izrail Antselovich or Mark Redkin) depicting the aftermath of the Bagerovo mass execution. In the top photo Grigory Berman is identified by name. *Fotogazeta PURa (Photonewspaper of the Political Directorate of the Red Army)*. February 1942. (Courtesy of Vladimir Sanzharovets.)

As early as January 1942, as evidenced by Molotov's note of 6 January 1942 and by the coverage in national civilian and military publications, the Soviet leadership, in presenting the mass murder of the Jewish population in the occupied territories, was already engaged in obfuscating the genocidal and exclusive nature of the Nazi atrocities against all Jews. Even Ehrenburg, the principal Soviet anti-Nazi propagandist and voice of the people's resistance, could not speak unequivocally of the massacre at the Bagerovo ditch in the pages of the Soviet press. On 4 March 1942, in a dispatch submitted for publication not in the Soviet but the Western press, Ehrenburg finally wrote this: "In a ditch outside Kerch 7004 corpses of the city residents were found—Russian, Tatar, Jews, old men, women, infants. At Feodosia the Germans killed all the Jews, from infirm old women to newborns, all 704. Then they queried Berlin: Should the Krymchaks be considered Jews? Berlin replied: Yes, to be considered. 242 Krymchaks were killed."[145]

Scholars of the Shoah have suggested that even though the Soviet leadership was well aware of the ongoing annihilation of the Jewish population in the occupied Soviet territories by the end of the summer of 1941, it "softpedaled the Jewish aspect" (Altshuler's expression).[146] The extent to which the official presentation of Nazi crimes and atrocities would change over the course of 1942 can be gleaned from Molotov's note of 27 April 1942, "On Horrendous Evil Crimes, Atrocities and Violence Committed by the German Fascist Occupants in the Occupies Soviet Regions, and on the Responsibility of the German Government and Command for These Crimes." In the latter note, the emerging if unwritten policy of being silent about Jewish losses already finds ample expression: no atrocities against Jews are specified, *none at all*. Arad has argued that "it can be assumed that in the period between January 1942, when the [6 January 1942 Molotov] note was published, and April 1942, when the [27 April 1942] note was published, a decision had been made to conceal even further the fact that Germany policy against the Jews differed from that toward other nations in the occupied territories."[147]

---

145 Erenburg, *Letopis' muzhestva. Publitsisticheskie stat'i voennykh let*, 2nd ed., ed. L. Lazarev, 83-84 (Moscow: Sovetskii pisatel', 1983).
146 Altshuler, "The Holocaust in the Soviet Mass Media," 123; see Karel C. Berkhoff's discussion of the reports of the annihilation of the Jews in the occupied territories, reaching Stalin in July 1941 and subsequently Berkhoff, "'Total Annihilation of the Jewish Population': The Holocaust in the Soviet Media, 1941-45," *Kritika: Explorations in Russian and Eurasian History* 10:1 (Winter 2009): 66-67.
147 Arad, *The Holocaust in the Soviet Union*, 537-538.

If we can speak of an unwritten Soviet policy on (not) discussing both the specific Jewish losses and Jewish military valor, such a policy was already emergent in the spring of 1942. Nazi plans were being presented as aimed at "the extermination of the Soviet population, prisoners of war and partisans through bloody violence, torture, executions and mass murders of Soviet citizens, regardless of their nationality, social status, gender, or age."[148] In a separate, lengthy section of the 27 April 1942 note, titled "Beastly Crimes and Violence against the Local Population in the Occupied Soviet Areas," Jewish victims were not identified as Jews or were subsumed into the overall numbers of Soviet civilian losses in the occupied territories. When mentioned, Jews never topped the list of Nazi victims—contrary to the historical facts: "According to incomplete data, in three Belarusian cities alone, German occupants executed over 28,000 civilians: in Vitebsk, 6000 in Pinsk, 10,000, in Minsk over 12,000. Hundreds of Ukrainians, Russians, Jews, Moldovans and civilian citizens of other nationalities perished by the hand of Hitlerite executioners in the cities of Ukraine. In Kharkov alone the Hitlerites executed 14,000 people just in the early days of the occupation."[149] The same note twice mentioned the details of the massacre outside Kerch, calling it "one of the bloodiest crimes of the German army on the Soviet land." The note referred to "documents and photographs in possession of the Soviet Government," and spoke, predictably, of the execution of "over 7000 local citizens."[150]

When we think of Selvinsky as a principal literary witness to the Shoah in Crimea, we should also keep in mind that the Nazi atrocities in the Kerch peninsula, including the Bagerovo ditch massacre, were being officially investigated and documented during Selvinsky's stay in the area of Kerch, in January-February 1942. On 25 February 1942 the People's Commissar of Internal Affairs Lavrenty Beria approved the instruction "Concerning the Manner of Collecting, Assessing and Storing of the Documentary Materials about the Atrocities, Destruction, Pillaging and Violence by German Authorities in Soviet Districts Occupied by Them."

---

[148] "Nota narodnogo komissara inostrannykh del tov. V. M. Molotova o chudovishchnykh zlodeianiiakh, zverstvakh i nasiliiakh, 27 aprelia 1942 g.," in *Dokumenty obviniaiut*, vol.1, 9-32. 9-10.

[149] "Nota narodnogo komissara inostrannykh del tov. V. M. Molotova o chudovishchnykh zlodeianiiakh, zverstvakh i nasiliiakh, 27 aprelia 1942 g.," 26.

[150] "Nota narodnogo komissara inostrannykh del tov. V. M. Molotova o chudovishchnykh zlodeianiiakh, zverstvakh i nasiliiakh, 27 aprelia 1942 g.," 26; 28

This gave the investigators and archivists on site a broad mandate to collect any relevant documents and materials related to the Nazi occupation and committed atrocities. As the Crimean archivist Sergey Androsov recently demonstrated, on 27 February 1942 Dmitry Belugin, who had been chief of the Crimea's archives prior to the peninsula's occupation and who returned to Kerch from Krasnodar in early 1942, was already reporting to the NKVD's Directorate of State Archives: "At the moment I am in the city of Kerch [...] and am engaged in collecting materials relevant to the Great Patriotic War."[151] The materials Belugin collected apparently included copies of the orders issued by the Nazi authorities during the first occupation of Kerch, photographs of the aftermath of the massacre at the Bagerovo ditch, and survivors' testimonies. According to Androsov, on the basis of the collected materials the Kerch city Party committee intended to publish the volume *Atrocities of the German Fascists in Kerch* in 1942, but the collapse of the Crimean Front in May 1942 resulted in the evacuation of the materials to Krasnodar and a year-long delay in publication.[152]

The first professional historian to describe the Nazi atrocities in Kerch and to cite the number of victims was Bentsion M. Volfson, who in 1942 contributed an article to *Istoricheskii zhurnal* (*Historical Journal*).[153] Originally from Bobruisk, Belarus, Volfson had graduated from Moscow University. A party member since 1932, before the war he had served in the party apparatus in Crimea while also teaching, working in Crimean State Archive, and actively publishing on Crimean history. Having collected documentary evidence and testimonies on

---

151 See S[ergei] A. Androsov, "Arkhivy Kryma v gody Velikoi Otechestvennoi voiny (1941-1945)," *Istoricheskoe nasledie Kryma. Zhurnal* 8 (2004), http://old.commonuments.crimea-portal.gov.ua/rus/index.php?v=1&tek=87&art=324, last accessed 12 January 2012. On the 25 February 1942 instruction, see Marina Sorokina, "People and Procedures: Toward a History of the Investigation of Nazi Crimes in the USSR," *Kritika: Explorations in Russian and Eurasian History* 6.4 (Fall 2005): 813.
152 See also Melkov, 75.
153 See B[entsion] Volfson, "Krovavye prestupleniia nemtsev v Kerchi," *Istoricheskii zhurnal* 8 (1942): 33-36. About Volfson, see A. A. Nepomniashchii, "Istoriia nauki v Krymu. Nerealizovanye krymovedcheskie proekty 1930-kh godov: deistvuiushchie litsa," *Istoricheskoe nasledie Kryma. Zhurnal* 20 (2007), http://old.commonuments.crimea-portal.gov.ua/rus/index.php?v=1&tek=105&par=74&l=&art=613, last accessed 7 January 2012; Androsov, "Arkhivy Kryma"; Az Nevtelen, "Dnevniki imperatritsy. Romanovy v Krymu v opisanii Vol'fsona," http://ru-history.livejournal.com/3272322.html, accessed 7 January 2012. In his passing comments on the coverage of Kerch, Altshuler ("The Holocaust in the Soviet Mass Media," 136) refers to Volfson, a professional historian, as a "reporter."

Kerch in early 1942 and personally interviewed some of the survivors, Volfson summarized his findings in a concise article which should have made the facts of the Nazi atrocities available to the larger academic community by the end of 1942. Volfson's article, "Bloody Crimes of the Germans in Kerch," is highly valuable as an early published account by a trained historian and archivist, a Jew proficient in Yiddish, and something of a party functionary. "The fascists exterminated everyone: Russians, Jews, Ukrainians, Tatars, Karaites, Krymchaks, and Greeks," wrote Volfson. "Jews were being exterminated with particular malice and subjected to especially humiliating and beastly torments prior to the execution."[154] Volfson's article betrayed the author's great effort, through both argument and statement of fact, to indicate that Jews were being annihilated. At the very same time, Volfson conformed to the emerging official rhetoric of not dividing the dead and thus obfuscating the overwhelming Jewish losses.

Some of the Kerch-based original findings, including survivors' testimonies, eyewitness accounts, and photographic materials (with captions but without credits), originally slated for publication in 1942, were eventually published only in the second half of 1943.[155] The volume was released by the Crimean regional publishing house Red Crimea and appeared in Sukhumi, Abkhazia under the auspices of the Crimean Regional Committee of the Communist Party, which had been evacuated from Krasnodar further down the coast of the Black Sea after Krasnodar's occupation in August 1942. Published under the title *Atrocities of the German Fascists in Kerch: A Collection of Accounts by Victims and Eyewitnesses*, the volume had a print run of only 1600 copies and enjoyed a limited circulation. A brief foreword, "From the Crimean Regional Committee of the Communist Party," spoke of "the most nightmarish evildoings of the fascists on our soil—the execution by them of 7000 peaceful residents of the city of Kerch." The foreword introduced the authors of the volume as "the city's modest [skromnye] workers who had faced execution in the terrible Bagerovo ditch and only by accident having remained alive."[156] The volume's unsigned introduction was in fact a version of Volfson'a article "Bloody Crimes of Germans

---

154 Vol'fson, 35.
155 See *Zverstva nemetskikh fashistov v Kerchi. Sbornik rasskazov postradavshikh i ochevidtsev* (Sukhumi: Krasnyi Krym, 1943).
156 *Zverstva nemetskikh fashistov v Kerchi*, 5.

in Kerch," and there is reason to believe that Volfson played a prominent role in the gathering and preparation of the volume's testimonies. Naum Sirota, secretary of the Kerch Party committee and himself a Jew, contributed a propagandistic essay in which not a word was said about Jewish victimhood in Kerch.[157] Twenty-three photographs were printed in the volume. The photographers' names were missing, even though some of the images had appeared previously and were recognizable as the works of Baltermants, Khaldey, Turovsky, Yablonsky and other photographers. Jewish names of victims or mourners were also missing in the captions, and only Russian/Ukrainian and Tatar names were printed. Among the contributors of testimonies, three (Iosif Vaingardten [Vaingartner], Raisa Belotserkovskaya, and Sofya Lifshits [Livshits]) were Jews who had personally survived the massacre and lost their families at the Bagerovo ditch. The contributors also included four Jews who had survived by not following the Nazi orders and apparently remaining in hiding and three Jewish doctors who had also survived. Of special interest was the testimony of R. Goldshtein, which focused on the role of collaborators in identifying Jews to the Nazi authorities. Testimonies by six Russian, Ukrainian, and Tatar witnesses focused on the murder of civilians from the area of Kamysh-Burun. Given the fact that the vast majority of the victims were Jews, the high proportion of non-Jewish voices gave an uninformed reader a skewed idea of the Nazi atrocities. At the same time, a close analysis of Volfson's introduction and the testimonies would have given a Soviet reader sufficient information to understand that the Nazis were exterminating *all* the Jews in the occupied territories while also committing atrocities against the local residents and Red Army POWs. In addition to documentary materials and testimonies, the volume featured the text of Selvinsky's "I Saw It!" (which was the volume's third entry, following the articles by Volfson and Sirota) and a short poem by Boris Serman, another Jewish-Russian poet with Crimean roots. To this day, *Atrocities of the German Fascists in Kerch* has not been reprinted. It remains the most extensive published compendium of testimonies by survivors and eyewitnesses

---

157 N[aum] A. Sirota, "Otomstim za krovavye zlodeianiia," in *Zverstva nemetskikh fashistov v Kerchi. Sbornik rasskazov postradavshikh i ochevidtsev*, 23-31. In his subsequent memoirs, Sirota continued to circumnavigate the anti-Jewish nature of the massacres; see "Kogda front priblizilsia vplotnuiu...." in *Kerch' geroicheskaia. Vospominaniia. Ocherki. Dokumenty*, 14-36 (Simferopol': Tavriia, 1974).

of the massacres committed during Kerch's first occupation.

In 1943 one testimony from this volume, four photographs, and a separate letter from a group of Kerch physicians were included in the first book of a voluminous collection of materials, *Documents Accuse*, published in Moscow by the State Publishing House of Political Literature.[158] Also noteworthy is a special propaganda booklet devoted to the atrocities in Kerch, one in a series of such booklets released in Moscow in 1942 following the liberation of some of the occupied Soviet territories. Titled *We Shall Not Forget, We Shall Not Forgive!: Fascist Atrocities in Kerch*, the propaganda booklet had a print run of 45,000 copies. The booklet unfolded into a poster and featured materials on the Bagerovo ditch massacre: 22 photographs, Antselovich's article "Fascist Atrocities in Kerch," and a slightly abridged version of Selvinsky's "I Saw It!"[159] Finally, there is reason to believe that materials about the Bagerovo ditch had originally been slated for the second wartime collection devoted to the Nazi occupation of Crimea, *German Barbarians in Crimea*, published in 1944 in Simferopol following Crimea's liberation.[160] In fact, in April 1944 Selvinsky's old army newspaper, *Son of Fatherland*, featured, under the rubric "We Saw It" (echoing Selvinsky's poem), a preview of materials about the Bagerovo ditch massacre from what was then described as a "book about the German atrocities in Crimea."[161] In the newspaper the volume was said to have already appeared, while the reprinted excerpts actually came from three items published in 1943 in *Atrocities of the German Fascists in Kerch*. In the 1944 Crimean collection, no separate materials on the Bagerovo ditch massacre were included (the Bagerovo anti-tank ditch was only mentioned once, in Mark Turovsky's article about the Adzhimushkay Quarries); the Nazi atrocities in Kerch were not covered, and only sections of three testimonies depicted the

---

158 See "Iz pis'ma vrachei goroda Kerchi v redaktsiiu gazety 'Komsomol'skaia pravda' ot 8/1/1942" and "Pis'mo zheny krasnoarmeitssa R. Belotserkovskoi," in *Dokumenty obviniaiut. Sbornik dokumentov o chudovishchnykh zlodeistvakh germanskikh vlastei na vremmenno zakhvachennykh imi sovetskikh territoriakh*, 1: 190-194 (Moscow: Gosudarstvennoe izdatel'stvo politicheskoi literatury, 1943).
159 Sel'vinskii, "Ia eto videl"; Antselovich, "Zverstva fashistov v Kerchi," both in *Ne zabudem, ne prostim* [*Zverstva fashistov v Kerchi*] (Moscow: Goskinoizdat, 1942 [booklet-poster]). This poster-booklet is rare, and I am most grateful to Vladimir Sanzharovets for providing a copy; Sanzharovets estimates the publication date to be between February and May 1942. Only one caption ("the old tailor Nokhum Rappoport") explicitly suggests the victim's Jewishness.
160 *Nemetskie varvary v Krymu*, 7; 14-15; 89-91.
161 See "My eto videli. Rasskazy ochevidtsev o zverstvakh nemtsev v Krymu," *Syn otechestva* 7 April 1944.

extermination of the Jews of Simferopol.[162] One can speculatively link the disappearance of materials on the Bagerovo ditch with a broad shift in Soviet coverage of the Shoah in the occupied Soviet territories, a shift we shall examine below in greater detail.[163]

After the Soviet troops had permanently liberated all of Crimea in the spring of 1944, the reports on Nazi atrocities at Kerch were collected and parsed by the Extraordinary State Commission. In 1946 portions of these reports were submitted as part of the Soviet evidence presented at the Nuremberg Military Tribunal. The conclusions of the investigation by the Kerch commission were apparently compiled in August 1944, following the liberation of Crimea, based in part on the materials documented and photographed in early 1942.[164] Jumping ahead of this book's chronology of events, let us turn for a moment to "Crimes against the Civilian Population," the speech by the deputy chief Soviet prosecutor Lev Smirnov at the Nuremberg Military Tribunal. In the section "Establishing the Regime of German-Fascist Terror," delivered on 15 February 1946, Smirnov drew on and quoted parts of document "USSR-63," the Act of the Extraordinary State Commission concerning Kerch, devoted to the first occupation of Kerch in November-December 1941. The Kerch section of the Soviet accusatory speech is remarkable in its total omission of any facts or telltale signs indicating that the Nazi

---

162 See *Nemetskie varvary v Krymu*, 98.
163 Finally, in *The Black Book*, Ehrenburg and Grossman included a testimony by a Kerch fisherman, Iosif Vaingardten (Vaingertner), a survivor of the Bagerovo massacre. See "The Story of Iosif Vaingertner, a Fisherman from Kerch," in *The Complete Black Book of Russian Jewry*, ed. Ilya Ehrenburg and Vassily Grossman, tr. and ed. David Patterson, 223-226 (New Brunswick, NJ: Transaction Publishers, 2002). A different version of Vaingardten's testimony had previously appeared in *Atrocities of the German Fascists in Kerch*. See I. Vaingardten, "Nikogda ne zabudu," in *Zverstva nemetskikh fashistov v Kerchi*, 45-50.
164 The Extraordinary State Commission (Chrezvychainaia gosudarstvennaia komissiia) for the investigation of the crimes of the Nazis and their accomplices in the occupied territories was founded by the ukase of the Presidium of the Supreme Soviet of 2 November 1942. For a comprehensive overview of the history, see Sorokina. Drawing in part on the research of Niels Bo Poulsen, Karel C. Berkhoff notes that the "[...] publication of its findings (as booklets and press articles) began only in April 1943"; Berkhoff also notes that "fully half of its reports—including those on Crimea, Moldavia, western Ukraine, and Leningrad—never appeared at all"; see Berkhoff, 84-85. In a recent overview of the Shoah-related holdings of the State Archive of the Autonomous Republic of Crimea (GAARK), Tiaglyi reports that the Crimean Republic Extraordinary Commission was founded in accordance with the 2 November 1942 ukase and was active from June 1944 to May 1945. Under its auspices, 25 city and district commissions were operational, including a separate Kerch investigative commission. Tiaglyi also indicates that testimonies gathered from eyewitnesses and survivors were commonly doctored, and references to the murdered Jews replaced with references to unspecified Soviet civilians. See also Gubenko, 21.

occupying forces were conducting genocide of the Jewish population. The word "Jew" and its cognates were all absent from the act and from Smirnov's presentation, and the Nazi genocidal actions were portrayed as being directed against the entire Soviet civilian population:

> On the night of 28 November 1941 a Gestapo order was posted around town. According to it, the residents, who had previously been registered with the Gestapo, were ordered to appear at Sennaya [Haymarket] Square from 8 to 12 a.m. with a 3-day supply of provisions. All males and females, regardless of age and health conditions, were ordered to appear. [...] Those who came to the square on 29 November were sure that they were summoned to be sent to work. By 12 noon over 7000 people had gathered in the square. There were young men and women, children of all ages, very old men and pregnant women. [...]
>
> Upon the entrance of the Red Army to Kerch, in January 1942, at the examination of the Bagerovo [antitank] ditch, it was discovered that for the length of one kilometer this ditch, 4 meters wide and 2 meters deep, was filled up with corpses of women, children, elderly, and teenagers. Near the ditch were pools of frozen blood. Scattered nearby were children's hats, toys, ribbons, ripped-off buttons, gloves, bottles with nipples, little children's boots, galoshes and chopped-off feet, hands, and other body parts. All of this was spattered with blood and brains.
>
> Fascist scoundrels executed the defenseless population with exploding bullets [...]."[165]

---

165 *Niurnbergskii protsess. Prestupleniia protiv chelovechestva*, vol. 5, ed. N. S. Lebedeva et al. (Moscow: Iuridicheskaia literature, 1991), http://lib.ru/MEMUARY/1939-1945/NURNBERG/np5.txt, last accessed 5 October 2011; cf. "Nuremberg Trial Proceedings. Vol. 7. Sixtieth Day. Friday, 15 February 1946" [The Avalon Project], http://avalon.law.yale.edu/imt/02-15-46.asp, last accessed 20 February 2012. Following the main part of Smirnov's presentation, a Soviet documentary film about Nazi atrocities, *Film Documents about the Atrocities of the German-Fascist Invaders*, was shown as part of the submitted evidence and included footage of the aftermath of the massacre at the Bagerovo ditch. Roman Karmen described the Soviet documentary in an article published in the central Soviet press, "Mertvye obviniaiut," *Izvestiia* 20 February 1946; Karmen's article

In the postwar Soviet years, when the Shoah on the Kerch peninsula was discussed in popular and historical books and in memoirs by former military officers, guerilla fighters, and members of the Soviet underground who remained in Kerch during the occupation, accounts similar in their obfuscation of the truth were recycled. Testimonies by a very limited number of witnesses and survivors were presented in a decontextualized fashion.[166] Selvinsky's poem "I Saw It!" was referenced or cited in postwar Soviet literature about the war in Crimea and in Kerch, although it, too, was almost invariably divorced from its historical context. The most detailed—and the most odious—example of this concealment of the Nazis' agenda is a chapter on the occupation of Kerch in Vladimir Yakovlev's *Crimes. Struggle. Retribution*, published in Crimea in 1961. The chapter takes its title, "Sorrow—without end," from a line of Selvinsky's "I Saw It!" Yakovlev, who was familiar with the history of the occupation of Crimea and with the Kerch sources, makes no mention of the Jewishness of the victims, except by identifying some of the survivors and eyewitnesses by their Jewish names. In referring to Order No. 4 of 28 November 1941, Yakovlev (and his editors and censors) came up with the following equivocation: "The order demanded, that all the residents [and not all Jews, as was stated in the order—MDS], previously registered with the Gestapo, appear on 29 November from 8 AM to 12 PM at Haymarket Square [...]."[167] Needless to say, as late as the 1980s an unfamiliar Soviet reader would have had a difficult time understanding that the vast majority of the victims murdered at the Bagerovo anti-tank ditch were Jews. This brings us back to the moral, intellectual, and artistic challenges Selvinsky faced

---

devoted a paragraph to the aftermath of the Bagerovo ditch massacre, cited 7000 as the number of victims, yet failed to identify them as Jews; see also an informative memoir by Iosif Gofman, former bodyguard of the chief Soviet prosecutor Roman Rudenko, *Niurnberg predosteregaet. Vospominaniia telokhranitelia glavnogo obvinitelia ot SSSR R. A. Rudenko o Niurnbergskom sudebnom protsesse*, 2nd ed. (Poltava: n.p., 2007); see "Nuremberg Trial Proceedings, vol. 7. Sixty-Second Day. Tuesday, 19 February 1946" [The Avalon Project], http://avalon.law.yale.edu/imt/02-19-46.asp, last accessed 20 February 2012. Sections of the Soviet documentary, including images of the Bagerovo ditch, were subsequently incorporated into Ilya Gutman's 1986 documentary film *Nuremberg: 40 Years Later*"; see Il'ia Gutman [dir.], Niurnberg: 40 let spustia (Moscow, 1986); http://films.academic.ru/film.nsf/9268/Нюрнберг%3A+40+лет+спустя, last accessed 20 February 2012.

166 Very typical of this trend is Leonid Melkov's 1981 narrative of Kerch in 1941-1944, where in a two-page summary of the rounding up and murder of the Jews of Kerch, the author managed to say nothing at all about the victims' Jewish identity; see Melkov, 49-50.

167 Iakovlev, 29.

as a witness in January 1942 and continued to face during the postwar decades until his death in 1968.

The dearth of postwar Soviet information and testimony about the atrocities in Crimea further complicated the status of Selvinsky's eyewitness poems about the Nazi atrocities on the Kerch peninsula as sources of public knowledge and awareness of the Shoah. Therefore visual evidence and verbal accounts and testimonies gathered in Kerch and published in early 1942 are crucial for our understanding of both the immediate context and the legacy of Selvinsky's Shoah poems. Some of the most valuable published evidence comes from local Kerch and Crimean newspapers and army and navy newspapers based in Crimea or nearby. This evidence is not easy to obtain and has never been examined systematically. As I have sought to show, by and large the published journalistic reportages and photographs obfuscated or suppressed explicit indications that the Nazis were eradicating the entire Jewish population in the occupied Soviet territories. The situation was more complex with literary texts, especially poetic accounts of the massacres, where an editor or a censor could not merely change a line of verse or a quatrain the way they could delete or rewrite a sentence, change a caption, or even disallow a photograph to be printed. As I will argue below, Selvinsky's achievement as an early poetic witness to the Shoah consisted in speaking of the murder of Jews in the occupied Soviet territories with an openness that was unrivaled in the Soviet journalism of 1941-42, some of Ehrenburg's essays excepted.

5. "I Saw It"

Ilya Selvinsky, Vasily Grossman, Ilya Ehrenburg and other Jewish-Russian writers wishing to write about the Shoah in the occupied Soviet territories faced hard choices: palliative truth versus partial silence; the rhetoric of a united Soviet people versus a Jewish perspective; not dividing the dead versus giving the victims a Jewish burial in language and memory.

In a letter to his wife Berta, dated 12 January 1942, Selvinsky wrote: "Yesterday I saw the ditch outside Kerch, where lie 7000 [people] executed by the Germans. An excruciating impact. All day I've been ill from the sight."[168] One notes immediately that Selvinsky's wartime diary and letters, which elsewhere contain very revealing and politically dangerous statements, some of them critical of the Soviet military command and even of Stalin, make no mention of the identity of the murdered people lying in the Bagerovo anti-tank ditch. Moreover, Selvinsky never discussed the murder of Jews in his wartime journalism, although on several occasions he did write of the Nazi atrocities against both civilians and Soviet military personnel.[169] Was poetry the only medium though which Selvinsky could communicate some of the truth about the Shoah?

According to those who were with him on that morning, Selvinsky began to take notes for or to compose the poem "Ia eto videl!" ("I Saw It!") while standing over the ditch filled with executed victims.[170] In 1944 Goffenshefer, whom Selvinsky called by the familiar nickname "Gof,"[171] reminisced about Selvinsky as he revisited the memories of January 1942: "Standing next to me is the poet Ilya Selvinsky. A strongly built man who had seen much, who had sailed on the *SS Chelyuskin*, he stares at the terror of Bagerovo. Wrath is in his eyes, red from cold wind and hot tears. His lips whisper soundlessly. Perhaps one of his most powerful poems, 'I Saw It!' is being born."[172] Maria Arkharova, who was Selvinsky's colleague on the staff of the army newspaper *Son of Fatherland*, recalled:

> Yet what we saw in the cursed ditch.... "About this one cannot—with words" [from Selvinsky's poem]. I felt that this could only have been a terrible nightmare; that I was about to wake up. There was only one thought: it cannot be that this is reality! I remember how Ilya Lvovich [Selvinsky] froze over the ditch, and I will never forget

---

168 Quoted in Daineko, 66; cf. commentary in Sel'vinskii, *Sobranie sochinenii v shesti tomakh*, 1: 677-678; cf. Osip Reznik, *Zhizn' v poezii: Tvorchestvo I. Sel'vinskogo*, 228 (Moscow: Sovetskii pisatel', 1981). I am grateful to Ludmila Daineko for checking the quotation against the original postcard at the Central Museum of Taurida, Simferopol' (Fondy Krymskogo respublikanskogo uchrezhdeniia "Tsentral'nyi muzei Tavridy").
169 See, for instance, Sel'vinskii, "Shest' dokumentov," *Boevoi natisk* 22 February 1942, 2; "Eshche raz o zverstvakh gitlerovtsev," *Boevoi natisk*, 24 February 1942, 2.
170 See Arkharova, 107-108. See also Berezin; Shitova; Gubenko, 29-30; Ozerov, *Biografiia stikhotvoreniia*, 48 (Moscow: Znanie, 1981).
171 Selvinsky mentioned Goffenshefer in his report to the Military Commission of the Union of Soviet Writers on 13 July 1942; see V. Korshunova and M. Sitkovetskaia, pub. "O voine, o literature, o sebe....Vystupleniia A. Tvardovskogo, I. Sel'vinskogo, I. Erenburga," *Voprosy literatury* 5 (1975): 232.
172 V[eniamin] Goffenshefer, "Ne gasi ego, pamiat'!" *Syn otechestva* 16 March 1944.

his eyes filled with suffering. We were all so shocked by what we had seen that we walked back in burdensome silence. I had no words, nor tears [...]. The same night Ilya Lvovich brought his poem "I Saw It!" to our portable printing office.[173]

V. Machavariani, who as a military journalist and editor worked closely with Selvinsky on the tetralingual edition of the front's newspaper, later reminisced about visiting the Bagerovo ditch:

I happened to be in that area soon after the landing. The victims of the barbarian execution had been thrown into a ditch that remained open—the fascists, fleeing in panic, did have time to cover the ditch. With me was Ilya Selvinsky, at the time a mighty, burly fellow. At the sight of the thousands of murdered people he was so shocked that he fainted. And on the following day the pages of our newspaper were already carrying across the entire front the red-hot lines of the poem, burning with desire for revenge.[174]

Machavariani might have used poetic license to recollect these events and might have also compressed the time line, but the spirit of his account confirms Selvinsky's own diary notes and the accounts of

---

173 Arkharova, 108. Another wartime colleague, P. P. Sviridenko, wrote in 1979 that "'I Saw It!' could be placed as an epigraph to the majority of Selvinsky's works created at the war front;" Sviridenko, "Stroka poeta v boevom stroiu (iz frontovykh vospominanii)," 121.

174 V. Machavariani, [interview] in "Avtory 'Boevoi Krymskoi," *Literaturnaia gazeta*, 6 May 1970, 5; see also V. Machavariani "Stikhi o liubvi k Rodine i nenavisti k vragam" [Rev. of *Ballady, plakaty i pesni* by Il'ia Sel'vinskii], *Vpered k pobede!* 15 July 1942. Not surprisingly, in the pages of his extensive book about Selvinsky, which went through three editions between 1967 and 1981, Osip Reznik did not discuss Selvinsky's experience as a witness to the Shoah, and only quoted Machavariani's comments (Reznik, 231). Reznik touched on the subject of the Shoah only in connection with Selvinsky's postwar tragedy *Reading Faust* (*Chitaia Fausta*, 1947), which focused on the moral choices of nuclear physicists in Nazi Germany and engaged the subject of the Nazi concentration camps. I quote Reznik's comments below as illustrative of both his rhetoric and the limits of what Selvinsky's Soviet biographer could say in print: "The losses were so immense, and the evildoings of the fascists so horrific, that when the tragedy of Majdanek, Auschwitz, Buchenwald and countless death camps was completely revealed, the people at the forefront of humankind could not but ponder the question of what had birthed and forged the beastly face of fascism, which overshadowed the barbarism of the Middle Ages. Selvinsky was one of those Soviet artists who were among the first in the world to venture answering this question through artistic means" (Reznik, 411).

others who were present at the scene. In his recollection Machavariani, a Georgian, went further than most of his Soviet contemporaries, including Selvinsky's authorized biographer Osip Reznik, a Jew, in drawing attention to the poet's discussion of specified Jewish losses: "In 1941, literally a day or two before the December landing operation of our troops in Kerch, the SS men and local *Polizei*-traitors committed one of their numerous beastly crimes. The herded to a place not far from Kerch 7500 old men, women, children, predominantly of Jewish origin ... [and murdered them]."[175] The accounts and reminiscences by Selvinsky's wartime colleagues vary not only in certain factual details, which in some of the accounts appear to have been reconstructed in part on the basis of Selvinsky's own poems, but also in the degree of their authors' reticence or silence about the poem's subject and about the Shoah in general. For instance, Dmitri Berezin, Selvinsky's editor at *Fighting Thrust* and its successor editions, with whom Selvinsky, during his tenure there, clashed over matters of censorship and discipline, remembered this in 1968:

> There is [Selvinsky], standing before the Kerch ditch [sic], and his gaze takes in thousands of corpses of infants, mothers, old people—victims of the Hitlerites' atrocities. No, their heads were not sheared, their clothes had not been removed. At the time the fascist barbarians had not yet expanded their infernal industry, had not started to make from human skin purses and gloves for their fair-haired wenches ["dlia svoikh belokurykh sterv"]. The horrid beastliness shocked the poet. And several hours later his accusatory judgment in verse was ready, the judgment which astounded not only the soldiers at the front, but the whole world.[176]

Furthermore, other poets and prose writers, both Jews and non-Jews, stood over the Bagerovo ditch in January and February 1942, and silence was the dominant response to the sight of the massacre. Vasily Shevchuk, an ace air force pilot, recalled a wartime conversation with Konstanin Simonov:

---

175 V. Machavariani, [interview] in "Avtory 'Boevoi Krymskoi'."
176 Berezin, 101-102.

It turned out that we had both been [in Kerch] at the same time and we recalled the Bagerovo ditch—a place of sad memories. Simonov talked about arriving there right when they were removing the corpses. "No means of expressing human feelings—neither music, nor painting, nor literature—are capable, in my opinion, of conveying to the people that which you have personally seen there [chto ty videl sam—cf. the title of Selvinsky's poem "I Saw It!"—MDS]. [...] No matter what we write about fascism, about its atrocities, it will all be too little and actually not the way it was.... But write about it we must and write about it we shall. Human memory is short. [...] It remembers the good for a long time but tries to forget the vile, mean, beastly. And not to speak of fascism, to subject it to forgetting—it means to give other degenerate monsters a chance to repeat it in a new, even more inhuman version...."[177]

Simonov's silence and Selvinsky's poetry of bearing witness are a double case in point.

"I Saw It!" may have been the first published Russian-language poetic account of a massacre of Jews in the occupied Soviet territories. And one can speak with greater certainty that Selvinsky's poem about the Bagerovo ditch was the first published literary text about the Shoah in Crimea. The poem was first printed in *Bolshevik*, the newspaper of the Krasnodar Regional Party Committee, on 23 January 1942.[178] In February 1942 Selvinsky opened an evening of writer-soldiers in Kerch with a reading of "I Saw It!" In the program, the poem appeared under the title "Bagerovskii rov" ("The Bagerovo Ditch").[179] "I Saw It!" was reprinted in *Red Star* on 27 February 1942.

---

177 Shevchuk, *Komandir atakuet pervym*, http://militera.lib.ru/memo/russian/shevchuk_vm/08.html, last accessed 22 February 2012.

178 See "Sel'vinskii, Il'ia L'vovich," in *Russkie sovetskie pisateli. Poety (Sovetskii period). Bibliograficheskii ukazatel'*, vol. 23: 40 (St. Petersburg: Rossiiskaia natsional'naia biblioteka, 2000). D. Berezin recalled that "two days after [Selvinsky's visit to the Bagerovo ditch] [...] 'I Saw It!' was published in the newspaper *Fighting Thrust*"; see Berezin, 102. I was unable to verify this information, and the bibliographical guide to Selvinsky does not list it.

179 "Vecher pisatelei-frontovikov," 20 February 1942, Poster, exhibited at the Selvinsky Memorial Museum, Simferopol, 2012.

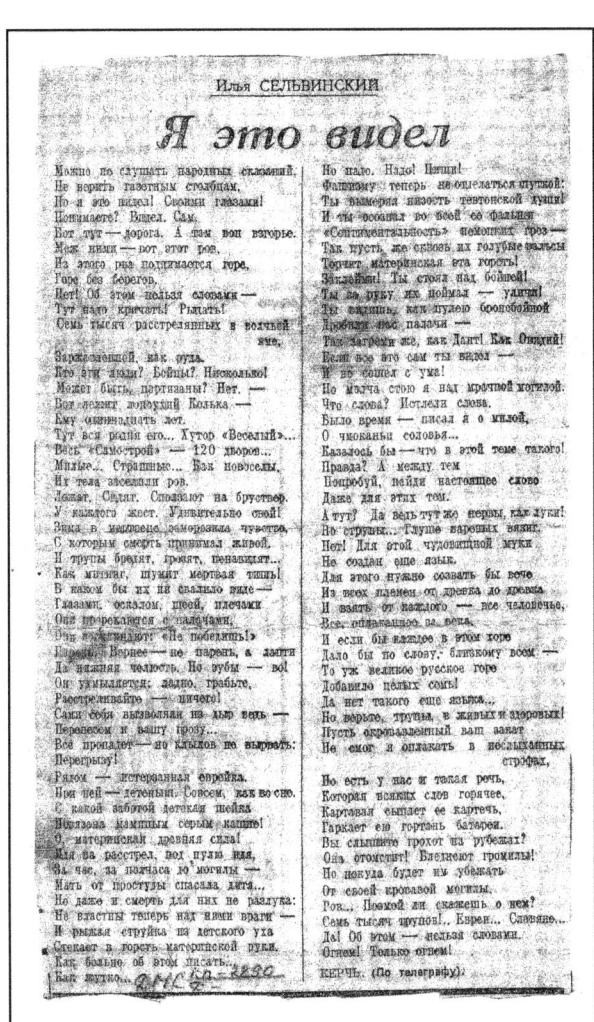

29. Ilya Selvinsky. "I Saw It!" as published in *Krasnaia zvezda* (*Red Star*), 27 February 1942.

Just two weeks before that, Selvinsky had debuted in *Red Star* with the poem "Ballad about Leninism," written after "I Saw It!" and also incorporating Selvinsky's experiences during and after the landing at Kerch.[180] Ortenberg noted receiving Selvinsky's poem: "Ilya Selvinsky sent us the poem 'I Saw It!' whose tragedian might struck all of us deeply.

---

180   Selvinskii, "Ballada o leninizme," *Bolshevik* [Krasnodar] 27 January 1942, 2; cf. *Krasnaia zvezda*, 13 February 1942, 3.

It was printed in today's issue."[181] Although *Red Star* had not reported on the atrocities at the Bagerovo anti-tank ditch, the massacre had been on Ortenberg's radar screen by the time Selvinsky's poem had reached the editor's desk. "'Where is one to find the words?'" Ortenberg asked in his chronicle of 1942, echoing the testimony of Raisa Belotserkovskaya. "Ilya Selvinsky found them," the former *Red Star* editor concluded.[182]

In early 1942, "I Saw It!" was also reprinted in the year's first (double) issue of *October*. With its publication in *October*, one of Moscow's (and the country's) three leading "thick journals," "I Saw It!" had become not only an event of the Soviet military media and mass media, but also a literary event. In some of the original publications, including the *October* version, on which I will base my analysis, "I Saw It!" carried an epigraph from Heine's "The Silesian Weavers" ("Die schlesischen Weber," 1844): "Deutschland, wir weben dein Leichentuch, / Wir weben hinein den dreifachen Fluch" ("Germany, we [now] weave you a shroud, / And into it we weave a threefold curse").[183] One can imagine the poignancy of Heine's spirit of Judaic unrest and social militancy hovering over writings by a Jewish poet publishing in the Soviet Union during the war with Nazi Germany. The Heine epigraph did not appear in the *Red Star* publication and a number of other reprintings of the poem.

After *October*, "I Saw It!" was reprinted several more times throughout 1942-1943, both in Selvinsky's own collections, starting with *Ballads, Posters, and Songs* (1942), and in edited volumes.[184]

---

181 Ortenberg, *God 1942*.
182 Ortenberg, *God 1942*, 97.
183 The epigraph comes from the opening stanza of Heine's poem, in which Silesian weavers sing a song-curse to Germany as they work at the loom and grind their teeth. Selvinsky quotes the poem in a free Russian rendition by Petr Lavrov (1823-1900), a sociologist and essayist, and a key leader of Russian revolutionary populism (*narodnichestvo*). Known in Russian as "Tkachi" ("Weavers"), Lavrov's rendition was a very popular Russian revolutionary song throughout the late nineteenth and early twentieth centuries.
184 See Sel'vinskii, "Ia eto videl!" in Works Cited. The *October* version was missing eight lines that Selvinsky included in both the previous and some of the subsequent publications of the poem. They follow immediately after the description of a Jewish mother murdered with her child: "How painful [it is] to write of this…How terrifying…./ But you must. Must! Write!/ Fascism will now not get away with a joke:/ You have measured the baseness of the Teutonic soul back and forth!/ And you realized in all its falseness/ The 'sentimentality' of German [in some editions, of Prussian] daydreams —/ So let it jut out of their blue waltzes,/ This mother's cupped hand"; see, for instance, *Krasnaia zvezda* 27 February 1942; *Ballady, plakaty pesni*, 90. Despite the powerful message, the diction of these lines betrays an odd departure from what is otherwise an unmistakably Selvinskian poetic language. I would situate the sources of these lines in Ehrenburg's wartime propagandistic essays.

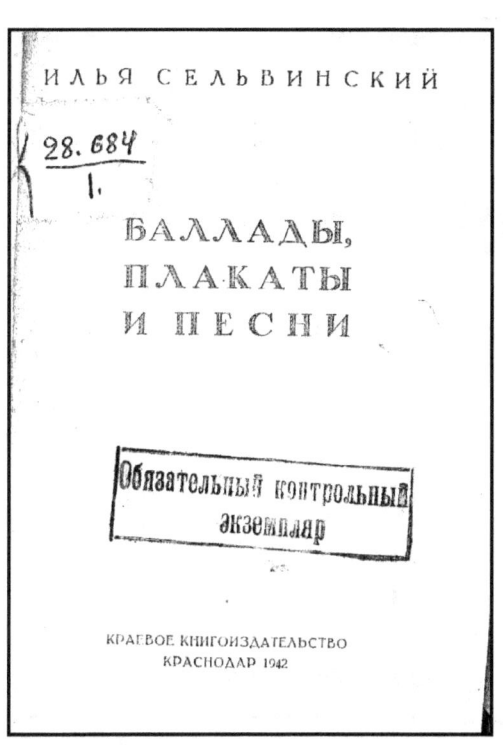

30-31. Title page and table of contents of Selvinsky's *Ballads, Posters and Songs*. Krasnodar, 1942.

32-33. Cover and table of contents of Selvinsky's *Ballads and Songs*. Moscow, 1943.

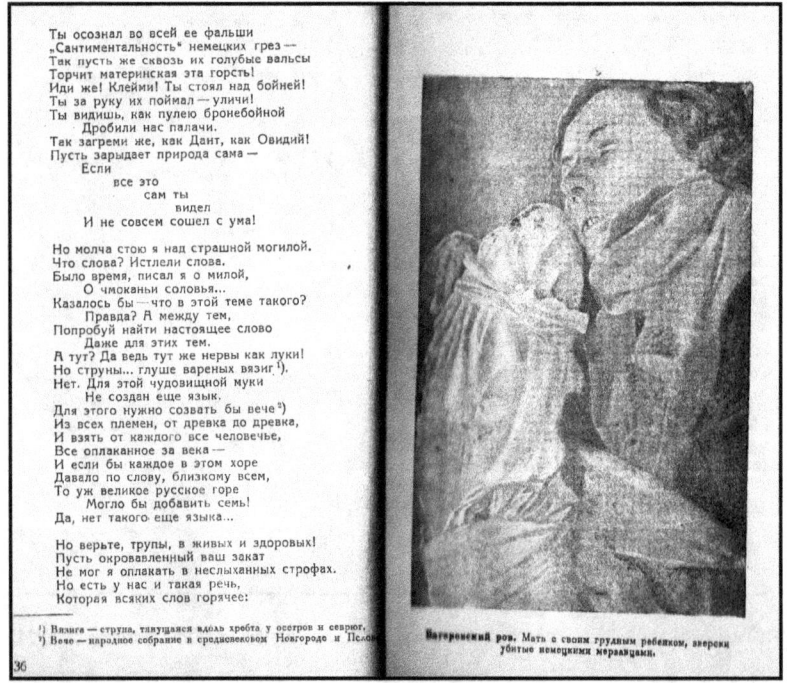

34. Two pages from the collection *The Atrocities of German Fascists in Kerch* (Sukhumi, 1943) where Selvinsky's "I Saw It!" was reprinted. On the left side is a page of the poem, on the right, a photograph of a mother with her infant child murdered at the Bagerovo anti-tank ditch.

The legendary actor Vasily Kachalov (1875-1948) read Selvinsky's poems over the radio.[185] The poet and critic Lev Ozerov praised Selvinsky's wartime poetry in two articles published in 1942 in Moscow. In an extensive article printed in *Literature and Art*, Ozerov argued that Selvinsky's wartime poems "reveal a new Selvinsky for us." A section of Ozerov's article analyzed "I Saw It!": "A native of Crimea, the poet found himself there during the hard days of the Crimean epic campaign of 1941-1942," Ozerov wrote. "He saw with his own eyes, he was a witness to and a participant in great events. [...] And Selvinsky made sure that his poetic word would be absolutely truthful, direct, convincing. ... [In "I Saw It"...] the poet conveys the 'naked sense' of what he saw, speaking of all the fascist evildoings with passion, immediacy and the documentary [precision] of an eyewitness."[186] The Russian language tries to make a distinction between an immediate eyewitness (*ochevidets*, derived from *oko* [eye] and *videt'* [to see], and another type of witness (*svidetel'*, also derived from *videt'* [to see] and often used in the legal context). Ozerov called Selvinsky both an *ochevidets* and a *svidetel'* of the Bagerovo ditch massacre, and he could not have been more precise in using both terms. In *Literature and Art* Ozerov could not mention anything specific about the murder of Jews by the Nazis. Five months later Ozerov returned to Selvinsky's poetry in an article published in the newspaper of the Moscow city party committee, *Moskovskii Bol'shevik (Moscow Bolshevik)*. This second article incorporated some points and even phrases from the first one, yet in the second article Ozerov might have been the first to identify Selvinsky's mission as both a poet-soldier and a witness to the murder of Jews in the occupied territories:

> Having grown up in Crimea, the poet found himself there during the Crimean heroic campaign of 1941-1942. He was a witness to and a participant in great events. "I Saw It Myself," was the title the poet gave to one of his poems [Ozerov slightly misquotes the title of 'I Saw It!'] In this poem he succeeded in making the word direct, convincing, and simple—as a blood-stirring eyewitness testimony about the fascist atrocities should be. [...]

---

185 See Ozerov, "Sila slova," *Moskovskii bol'shevik*, 11 December 1942, 3.
186 Ozerov, "Voennaia lirika Il'ia Sel'vinskogo," *Literatura i iskusstvo* 25 July 1942, 3.

> What did the poet see? The Crimean land. A ditch filled with Soviet civilians. That's the general background. And the details of this picture. A corpse of a Jewish woman [evreiki], who, not long before death, tied with a warm scarf the neck of her son who lay next to her.[187]

That "I Saw It!" enjoyed national fame may be gleaned not only from its reprintings or its critical reception in Moscow, but also from the reactions of Selvinsky's colleagues in the army press. Consider a review of Selvinsky's collection *Ballads, Posters and Songs* (1942) by V. Machavariani, who referred to "I Saw It!" as a *poema*, a long (epic) poem: "The striking verses of the long poem resound with wrath, denunciation and passion, like large epic canvasses."[188] Consider also the comments by Petr Pavlenko (1899-1951), a Soviet writer and a prominent cultural functionary of the Stalin era who was a high-ranking special correspondent for *Pravda* and *Red Star*. Pavlenko stated this about Selvinsky's wartime poems: "… and if he had only written 'Ballad about Leninism' and 'I Saw It!' one would have to say that undying poems had been born, which history would immortalize in marble or bronze monuments devoted to the Great Patriotic War."[189]

In the *Red Star* publication, "I Saw It!" shared the page with Ehrenburg's essay "Signs of Distinction," which ended with the hopeful words "The Red Army is moving westward."[190] Selvinsky reached a mass military and civilian audience. He subsequently heard that Goebbels, the Reich Minister of Propaganda, targeted him in a radio address, dismissing Selvinsky's account of Nazi atrocities and promising "the so-called Soviet writers […] a noose."[191] Selvinsky responded with the poem

---

187 Ozerov, "Sila slova," *Moskovskii bol'shevik*, 11 December 1942, 3. *Moskovskii bol'shevik* was subsequently renamed *Moskovskaia pravda*.
188 V. Machavariani, "Stikhi o liubvi k Rodine i nenavisti k vragam" [Rev. of *Ballady, plakaty i pesni* by Il'ia Sel'vinskii], *Vpered k pobede!* 15 July 1942.
189 Quoted in Ozerov, *Biografiia stikhotvoreniia*, 48. According to Ozerov, Pavlenko's review was published in *Forward to Victory!*
190 Il'ia Erenburg, "Znaki otlichiia," *Krasnaia zvezda* 27 February 1942, 3.
191 In his Wartime Diary for 1943, Selvinsky mentions hearing about this on the way back from Tbilisi to the North-Caucasus Front; see also Babenko, *Voina*, 30. At the same time, Berezin later recalled that Selvinsky was there when the operator, "while turning the radio receiver […] caught a Berlin station" (Berezin, 102). Selvinsky and others subsequently revisited the episode. See, for instance, Sel'vinskii, "Sila poeta." Goebbels' radio address targeting Selvinsky has become something of a commonplace of Soviet criticism. I have not been able to locate the original source.

"Otvet Gebbel'su" ("A Reply to Goebbels,"), which was first published in *Forward to Victory!* alongside "I Saw It!"[192] In it he wrote of Goebbels: "The terrifying Bagerovo ditch/ Is too big for the dwarf's imagination."[193]

In the opening quatrain of "I Saw It!" (the complete Russian and English texts are found in the Appendix), Selvinsky introduces himself as an eyewitness while questioning both the widely known popular versions of historical events and the newspaper coverage. He fashions himself as both a poet and a reporter who arrived on the scene in the immediate aftermath of the massacre so as to see the murdered people and to record the atrocities:

> Можно не слушать народных сказаний,
>   Не верить газетным столбцам.
> Но я это видел! Своими глазами!
>   Понимаете? Видел! Сам!
> Вот тут дорога. А там вон — взгорье.
>   Меж нами вот этак — ров.
> Из этого рва подымается горе.
>   Горе — без берегов.[194]

> One may choose to dismiss people's tales
>   Or disbelieve printed columns of news.
> But I saw it! With my own eyes.
>   Do you understand? I saw it. Myself.
> Here—the road. Over there—a higher plain.
>   Between them, just so—a ditch.
> From the ditch rises boundless pain
>   And sorrow—without end.
>   *(here and hereafter tr. Maxim D. Shrayer).*[195]

---

192 Sel'vinskii, "Otvet Gebbel'su" *Vpered k pobede!* 31 December 1942; *Bolshevik* 1 January 1943.
193 Sel'vinskii, "Otvet Gebbel'su," In *Krym Kavkaz Kuban'*, 13-17(Moscow: Sovetskii pisatel', 1947).
194 Here and hereafter I quote the text of "Ia eto videl!" from its publication in *Oktiabr'* 1-2 (1942): 65-66; I have added the exclamation sign in the title, which did not appear in the *Oktiabr'* or *Krasnaia zvezda* publications, but has appeared in most of the poem's publications. See also the principal wartime publications of the poem: in *Krasnaia zvezda* 27 February 1942, 3; in Il'ia Sel'vinskii, *Ballady, plakaty i pesni* (Krasnodar: Kraevoe izdatel'stvo, 1942), 87-92; in *Zverstva nemetskikh fashistov v Kerchi*, 33-38; in *Ballady i pesni*, 42-45 (Moscow: Goslitizdat, 1943); and in *Voennaia lirika* (Tashkent: Gosudarstvennoe izdatel'stvo UzSSR, 1943), 18-22.
195 For a previously published English translation of "I Saw It!" see Ilya Selvinsky, "I Saw It!" tr. Denis Johnson & IWP, in *Twentieth-Century Russian Poetry*, ed. John Glad and Daniel Weissbort, 178-

Right away Selvinsky strikes a chord that both he and other writers bearing poetic witness to the Nazi atrocities would strike, time and again, in their wartime journalism and diaries and in their poetry. Words do not and cannot capture the sight of the catastrophe:

> Нет! Об этом нельзя словами...
>   Тут надо рычать! Рыдать!
> Семь тысяч расстрелянных в волчьей яме,
>   Заржавленной, как руда.

> No! About this one cannot—with words....
>   One must sob. Roar.
> 7000 murdered ones—in a wolf's hollow,
>   A hollow rusty like ore....

In bearing both poetic and documentary witness to the atrocities against the Jews in the occupied Soviet territories, Selvinsky made smaller compromises and bigger concessions. Some of these concessions must have been made under censorial pressure. A military journalist and political officer, Selvinsky reported to his newspaper editors and superiors. To imagine what Selvinsky was up against—editorial interference and censorship in the army newspapers—consider Selvinsky's article "Once again on the Hitlerite Atrocities," which ran on 24 February 1942 in *Fighting Thrust*.[196]

A clipping of the article has survived among Selvinsky's wartime papers. In it the final passage is crossed out by Selvinsky's own hand, and a note is appended: "inserted by the editor." The inserted passage contained a quotation from a speech by Stalin. Poetry certainly fared better in the conditions of wartime military censorship than prose, and one would be repeating a useful truism by suggesting that as a medium poetry is more resistant to censorial interference than nonfiction or fiction.

---

182 (Iowa City: University of Iowa Press, 1992).
196 Selvinskii, "Eshche raz o zverstvakh gitlerovtsev," *Boevoi natisk*, 24 February 1942, 2. Cf. a later short article in the same newspaper, accompanying and commenting on an eyewitness account of Nazi atrocities against Soviet soldiers. Sel'vinskii, "Ubiitsy rasplatiatsia svoei chernoi krov'iu. Novyi dokument of chudovishchnykh zverstvakh gitlerovskikh palachei," *Boevoi natiski* 30 March 1942, 2.

35-36. Ilya Selvinsky, "Once Again about Hitlerite Atrocities." *Boevoi natisk* (*Fighting Thrust*), 24 February 1942. The image on the right shows a clipping with the closing section crossed out and a note in Selvinsky's hand: "the editor's insertion." In the inserted section the editor, Colonel Dmitri Berezin, placed a quote from Stalin. (Courtesy of Ilya Selvinsky Memorial Museum, Simferopol.)

Following its original publication, Selvinsky kept changing and revising the poem; revising and re-revising was a strong tendency of his career, not only a consequence of his survivalism. A comparison of the published versions tells a compelling story of Selvinsky's negotiations among historical facts, among the Jewish-, Russian-, and Soviet-centric points of view, and changing censorship conditions and ideological expectations.

In January 1942, in the immediate aftermath of the massacre at the Bagerovo ditch, Selvinsky faced daunting, multiple tasks as a poetic witness. Jewish poets rarely coin official rhetoric in a non-Jewish state, but they sometimes couch emergent tendencies or policies in a rhetoric that sears the popular imagination. This is one of the bigger challenges of studying Soviet Shoah poetry, especially today, when the poets are gone and much of the immediate historical and cultural context has been lost or obscured. As one seeks to reconstruct Selvinsky's artistic laboratory in 1942, one should not only weigh the documented evidence of the Shoah in Crimea and specifically on the Kerch peninsula, but also take into account what we know of the official Soviet investigation of the Nazi atrocities and presentation of facts to the Soviet public.

In giving the victims lying in the ditch imaginary or composite identities, Selvinsky fashioned some as Slavs and others as Jews. Here one must unavoidably resort to the craft of conjecture. In fashioning examples of Nazi atrocities, Selvinsky's poem "I Saw It!" conjured up four principal individuals. First came the image of a "kurnosyi" ("pug-nosed") eleven-year-old boy by the name of "Kolka" (diminutive of Nikolay), and this image suggested that the murdered boy was not a Jew but a Slav. (In other versions, published both earlier and later, the sobriquet "lop-eared" ["lopoukhii"] appeared instead of "pug-nosed.") Kolka was murdered with his entire extended family:

> His kin is all here, Merriment Homestead,
> All the Samostroy houses—120 of them.

The translation "Merriment Homestead" renders, albeit imperfectly, the Russian "Хутор Веселый," which is a very common name and may or may not refer to a specific location. At the same time, Samostroy (Самострой; literally "self-built") most likely points to the Kamysh-Burun neighborhood of Samostroy and possibly to several neighborhoods of the same name within the prewar boundaries of the city of Kerch. In revisions of the poem, Selvinsky replaced the lines "So dear … so scary…. Like new residents,/ Their bodies have moved into the ditch" with "Nearby stations, nearby villages—/All of them like hostages have been thrown into the ditch," while not capitalizing the name Samostroy and keeping the quotation marks ("самострой"), as though underscoring that it is not a specific but a generic term referring to a workers' town or neighborhood.[197]

---

197 See Sel'vinskii, "Ia eto videl!" *Sobranie sochinenii v shesti tomakh*, 1: 352.

After the Slavic boy slain with his whole kin, Selvinsky describes a murdered handicapped man who is ethnically unmarked, and then introduces a massacred old woman who is marked as an Orthodox Christian (and Selvinsky intensified this charactarization in the subsequent versions). Later in the poem Selvinsky openly describes a "massacred [or mauled] Jewish woman" ("isterzannaia evreika") lying in the ditch with her small child:

> Рядом истерзанная еврейка.
> Тут же — детеныш. Совсем как во сне:
> С какой заботой детская шейка
> Повязана маминым серым кашне.

> Nearby, a mauled Jewish woman,
> And a small child with her. Is he awake?
> The mother's grey shawl is wrapped with such care
> Around the babe's neck.

The description is particularly heart-rending because Selvinsky mentions how the small child's neck is carefully wrapped with a gray scarf: "Half an hour before the grave/ The mother was protecting her child from catching a cold." In the 1943 volume *Atrocities of the German Fascists in Kerch*, a photo depicting murdered children and a photo of a young woman killed with her baby illustrated Selvinsky's poem (see Ill. 34).[198]

It is illuminating to compare Selvinsky's "I Saw It!" with the journalistic coverage of the Nazi atrocities in Kerch which appeared in army publications and the local Kerchian, Crimean, and national press in January-March 1942. Consider, for instance, Izrail Antselovich's article which ran in *Little Flame* on 8 March 1942, on the same page as four photographs of the corpses of murdered victims and their relatives looking for or mourning their loved ones. In Antselovich's account:

> For a month and a half the Germans were in Kerch. [...]

---

198 See Sel'vinsklii, "Ia eto videl!" in *Zverstva nemetsikh fashistov v Krymu*, 33-38; "Bagerovskii rov. Deti, rasterzannye nemetskimi banditami," ibid., 35; "Bagerovskii rov. Mat' so svoim grudnym rebenkom, zverski ubityе nemetskimi merzavtsami," ibid., 37.

> As per instructions from Berlin the Gestapo chief in Kerch [...] devised an exact schedule of the annihilation of the residents of Kerch. According to this schedule, first the Soviet citizens of one nationality were supposed to be executed, then another one, then the third one. And in all the cases they executed entire families. Then the murderers got tired of investigating who is Russian, Ukrainian, Armenian, Jew, Greek, or Tatar. Entire streets were led to the execution [...]."[199]

In rendering nonspecific the truth about the Nazi murder of the Jews of Kerch, Antselovich, a Jew, described women murdered with their children in a language reminiscent of Selvinsky's poem, which by 8 March 1942 had already appeared in the national Soviet press. Consider this passage, which was meant to serve as a commentary to one of the photographs published in the *Little Flame* spread: "Here a mauled body of a woman ["isterzannoi zhenshchiny"; cf. Selvinsky's "isterzannaia evreika" "mauled Jewish woman"] lies on the edge of the ditch. In her frozen hands [she clutches] an infant neatly swaddled in a white blanket spattered with blood. He, too, was murdered by the Germans. Next lie a defaced girl of eight and a boy of about five. With great care his mother wrapped him in a warm scarf [on zabotlivo ukutan mater'iu v teplyi sharfik"; cf. Selvinsky's "S kakoi zabotoi detskaia sheika/ Poviazana maminym serym kashne"]. Next is a corpse of another woman [...]." In Selvinsky's poem the victims, whom Antselovich described as two mothers massacred with their children without identifying their Jewishness, appeared as a single image of a "Jewish woman" ("evreika") murdered with her young child. A portrait of a murdered young woman lying next to her murdered children would subsequently appear in the Kerch report of the Extraordinary State Commission and in other reports on and accounts of the massacre, wherein all Jewish markers of the victims' identities were deliberately removed: "A massacred young woman [isterzannaia molodaia zhenshchina] lay on the edge [of the ditch]. In her arms there was an infant neatly swaddled in a white lacy blanket. Next to the woman there lay an eight-year-old girl and a boy of about five, both pierced with exploding bullets. Their little hands clutched

---

199 I[zrail'] Antselovich, "Gnusnye ubiitsy," *Ogonek* 8 March 1942, 7.

their mother's dress."[200] Only Selvinsky's poem identifies the murdered mother and child as Jews.

In the remaining sections of "I Saw It!" Selvinsky brings the volume several notches up, once again stressing the poet-soldier's imperative:

> Иди же! Клейми! Ты стоял перед бойней!
> Ты за руку их поймал — уличил!
> Ты видишь, как пулею бронебойной
>   Дробили нас палачи.
> Так загреми же, как Дант, как Овидий!
> Пусть зарыдает природа сама,
> Если
>   все это
>   сам ты
>   видел,
> И не сошел с ума!

> Go now. Brand them! You have seen the blood bath.
> You have caught them red-handed—an eyewitness.
> You see how with armor-piercing bullets
> The executioners decimate us.
> So thunder now, like Dante, like Ovid,
> Let nature itself weep and moan,
> If
>   you
>   saw
>   all of this,
> And have not gone mad.

In these imperative, commanding phrases addressed by the eyewitnessing poet to himself or to fellow-witnesses, the reader of Russian poetry will hear notes of Isaiah 6 as mediated by Pushkin's "Prophet" (1825):

---

200 Quoted in *Niurnbergskii protsess. Prestupleniia protiv chelovechestva*, Vol. 5, http://lib.ru/MEMUARY/1939-1945/NURNBERG/np5.txt, last accessed 5 October 2011.

> Восстань, пророк, и виждь, и внемли,
> Исполнись волею моей,
> И, обходя моря и земли,
> Глаголом жги сердца людей

(Arise, Prophet, see and hearken,/ Be filled with my will,/ And going around seas and lands,/ Sear people's hearts with the Word.)

In fact, in some of the versions of the poem the weapons are said to thunder like the "word of the prophets" ("glagolom prorokov gremiat batarei"), as though Selvinsky deliberately extracts his diction from Pushkin's Isaianic poem.[201] One is reminded not only of the poem's literary pedigree but also of the poet's own ostentatiously stated ambition to be—or to become—a voice of the people. Selvinsky wrote to his wife in a letter of 6 April 1942: "For the first time in my life I have begun to feel in me the features of a people's tribune."[202]

Moreover, and this is particularly important for the continuity of Jewish poetry from biblical times across the many languages and cultures of the diaspora, in Selvinsky's "I Saw It!" one hears powerful echoes of *Skazanie o pogrome*, Jabotinsky's translation of Hayim Nahman Bialik's long poem *Tale of a Pogrom* (Hebrew original title *Be Ir HaHarigah* [*In the City of Slaughter*], 1904). Between 1911 and 1922, Jabotinsky's classic translation was reprinted five times and was certainly better known to the young Selvinsky than was Bialik's Hebrew original. The opening lines of Bialik's long poem (rendered through rhyming lines of iambic pentameter in Jabotinsky's creative translation) pulse through the texture of Selvinsky's verse. I am deliberately offering a literal translation of Jabotinsky's Russian version, which has been ensconced in the Russian literary canon:

---

201 See, for instance, these versions of "Ia eto videl!" in Sel'vinskii, *Izbrannye proizvedeniia* 1: 165; *Lirika*, 253; *Sobranie sochinenii v shesti tomakh*, 1: 355; *Izbrannye proizvedeniia*, 1971: 209; *Stikhotvoreiia. Tsarevna-lebed'. Tragediia*, 114; *Ia eto videl!* 100; *Izbrannye proizvedeniia v dvukh tomakh* 1: 179; in *Antologiia russkoi sovetskoi poezii*, 2 vols., ed. L. O. Belov et al., 1: 451 (Moscow: Gosudarstvennoe izdatel'stvo khudozhestvennoi literatury, 1957).

202 Selvinsky, Letter to Berta Selvinskaya, 6 April 1942, Ilya Selvinsky Memorial Museum; cf. Sel'vinskii, "Na voine. Iz dnevnikov i pisem rodnym," 171.

...Встань, и пройди по городу резни,
И тронь своей рукой, и закрепи во взорах
Присохший на стволах и камнях и заборах
Остылый мозг и кровь комками; то — они.[203]

(Arise and go to the city of slaughter,/ And touch with your hand, and fasten on your eyes,/ Dried to the tree trunks, stones, and fences/ Cold spattered brains and clumps of clotted blood; that's—them [i.e. the dead victims].)[204]

Selvinsky's intonation of uncomprehending despair in "I Saw It!" also rings close to Jabotinsky's rendering of Bialik's closing lines, with their call on the poet to run to the steppe (desert) and rip himself open with mournful sobs:

Что в них тебе? Оставь их, человече,
Встань и беги в степную ширь, далече:
Там, наконец, рыданьям путь открой,
И бейся там о камни головой,
И рви себя, горя бессильным гневом,
За волосы, и плачь, и зверем вой —
И вьюга скроет вопль безумный твой
Своим насмешливым напевом...[205]

---

[203] Bialik, Kh. N. *Skazanie o pogrome*, in Bialik, *Pesni i poemy*, tr. Vl. Zhabotinskii, 3rd ed., 167 (St. Petersburg: S. D. Zaltsman, 1914).

[204] The complete Hebrew text of Bialik's poem may be found at http://benyehuda.org/bialik/beir.html, courtesy of Project Ben-Yehudah. See the same lines in Atar Hadari's literary English translation: "Rise and go to the town of the killings and you'll come to the yards/ and with your eyes and your own hand feel the fence/ and on the tree and on the stones and plaster of the walls/ the congealed blood and hardened brains of the dead (Hayim Nahman Bialik, *Songs from Bialik*, ed. and tr. Atar Hadari, 1 (Syracuse: Syracuse University Press, 2000).

[205] Bialik, tr. Zhabotinskii [Jabotinsky], 177. A detailed investigation of the trace of Bialik—specifically *In the City of Slaughter*, both the original Hebrew and Jabotinsky's Russian translation—in Selvinsky's Shoah poetry goes beyond the scope of this study and awaits its investigator. In addition to the observations made here, one should take stock of at least three other points. First, it would be fruitful to examine Selvinsky's dialogue with Bialik about being unable to find "words" to describe the "nightmare." Second, in "I Saw It!" Selvinsky follows Bialik's diegetic strategy of describing the impressions of the poet as he bears witness to the aftermath of the mass violence and renders individual portraits of massacred Jews; specifically, Bialik describes a murdered mother and with her an infant with his lips pressed to her breast. Third, like Bialik in *In the City of Slaughter*, Selvinsky in "I Saw It!" takes stock of the biblical motif of man as grass, and also of dead/murdered men likened to lifeless/plucked grass. In an article about Jabotinsky's literary legacy,

(What business are they of yours? Leave them, o son of man,/ Arise and run to the steppe expanses, far:/ There, finally, release your sobbing,/ And beat your head against the rocks,/ And tear out your hair, burning with powerless wrath,/ And weep, and howl like a beast—/ And the blowing storm will muffle your mad wails,/ With its mocking melody.)[206]

The epic volume of the poet's witnessing voice (note the evocation of both Dante and Ovid in the same line) has been turned up, yet Selvinsky, much like the Bialik of *In the City of Slaughter*, cannot find words to render the sight of the massacre:

> Но молча стою я над страшной могилой.
> Что слова? Истлели слова.

> But silent I stand over the [terrifying] burial pit.
> What words? The words have turned to rot [or: to ashes].

Selvinsky the Jewish-Russian poet, military officer, and eyewitness to the Shoah concludes that "…для этой чудовищной муки/ Не создан еще язык" ("… no, for this unbearable torment/ No language has been devised"). Perhaps inadvertently, Selvinsky already in 1942 identifies not only a numbing intersection of poetics and politics, but also a vexing problem lying at the crossroads of poetics and trauma theory. In the years immediately following the Shoah and World War II, and subsequently in the 1980s and 1990s, first survivors and witnesses and then students of their testimonies stressed the extent to which human language, be it poetic or ordinary, is incommensurate with the task of

---

Mikhail Vaiskopf rather carelessly called Selvinsky one of "Jabotinsky's late epigones," mentioning Selvinsky's poem "Vor" ("Thief") and his verse epic *The Lay of Ulyalaev*, but not the wartime poetry; in the latter category Vaiskopf also included Eduard Bagritsky, citing *Duma pro Opanasa* (*The Lay of Opanas*); see Vaiskopf, "Liubov' k dal'nemu: literaturnoe tvorchestvo Vladimira Zhabotinskogo," *Vestnik evreiskogo universiteta* 29 [11] (2006), http://gazeta.rjews.net/Lib/Jab/vaisk.shtml, last accessed 22 June 2010.

206 Cf. Adari's literary English translation: "And now what have you left here, son of man, rise and flee to the desert/ and take with you the cup of sorrows, and tear your soul in ten pieces/ your heart give for food to a helpless fury/ and your great tear spill there on the heads of the boulders/ and your great bitter scream send forth—to the lost in the storm" (Bialik, *Songs from Bialik*, 9).

bearing witness. In *Remnants of Auschwitz: The Witness and the Archive* (1998) Giorgio Agamben argues that

> [...] testimony is the disjunction between two impossibilities of bearing witness; it means that language, in order to bear witness, must give way to non-language in order to show the impossibility of bearing witness. The language of testimony is a language that no longer signifies and that, in not signifying, advances into what is without language, to the point of taking on a different insignificance—that of the complete witness, that of he who by definition cannot bear witness.[207]

In 2006, in the Preface to the new translation of *Night*, originally written in the 1950s, Elie Wiesel discusses his trials of writing about and bearing witness to the Shoah:

> Convinced that this period in history would be judged one day, I knew that I must bear witness. I also knew that, while I had many things to say, I did not have the words to say them. Painfully aware of my limitations, I watched helplessly as language became an obstacle. It became clear that it would be necessary to invent a new language.[208]

Wiesel's description of the tangle of existential and artistic challenges that he faced as a writer-witness, and especially his emphasis on "inventing a new language," rings close to Selvinsky's own admission of the poet's dead-end of bearing witness.

Let us return to the text of Selvinsky's "I Saw It." In order to create a language that in bearing witness would adequately respond to such a catastrophe and such unimaginable victimhood, Selvinsky proposes to summon a gathering of all "tribes" ("plemen"). He uses the old Russian term *veche*, originally referring to a popular assembly in medieval

---

207 Giorgio Agamben, *Remnants of Auschwitz: The Witness and the Archive*, tr. Daniel Heller-Roazen, 39. (New York: Zone Books, 1999).
208 Elie Wiesel, "Preface to the New Translation." In *Night*, vii-ix (New York: Hill and Wang, 2006).

Slavdom, notably in the Republic of Novgorod. As he thinks out loud about such an assembly of all tribes, he projects that if each segment of humankind brought "one word," to this "chorus," then "the great Russian sorrow/ To each word would add seven." It is here that one becomes especially aware that in this poem about a Nazi massacre, in which the vast majority of the targeted victims were Jews, Selvinsky implements a rhetoric stitched through with Russocentric sentiments.

It is possible, of course, to argue that the expression "the great Russian sorrow" merely refers to the great sorrow of Russia the land and the country, and is not meant specifically to augment a sense of ethnic Russianness. But I do not think that Selvinsky's use of this expression was either nonspecific or gratuitous. Such a rhetoric, where the words expressing the "great Russian sorrow [or: woe]" ("velikoe russkoe gore") subsume the implied yet unidentified voices of the Jewish sorrow, was part of the price Selvinsky paid for bearing poetic witness to the Shoah. As Selvinsky revised (or restored?) the poem in the post-Stalinist years, the lines about the "great Russian sorrow" gave way to a distinctly universal "dialect of bottomless suffering" ("narech'e muki bezdonnoi").[209] Not surprisingly, in many of the reprintings that followed Stalin's death and appeared during the Thaw and subsequently, Selvinsky cleansed the poem of the Russocentric rhetoric of suffering. In place of the lines about the great Russian sorrow contributing seven words for each word offered by the other "tribes," Selvinsky now placed lines proposing universal sources for a composite language of suffering: "Wails, wheezes, sighs and moans,/ Repercussion of invasions, echoes of bloodbaths...."[210] And as a further indication that the poet kept searching for a way to continue referencing Jewish history and Jewish suffering in a stream of universal echoes, one finds in place of the line "Repercussion of invasions, echoes of bloodbaths" ("Otgul nashestvii, echo rezni") a direct reference to a pogrom: "Echo of invasions, pogroms, bloodbaths" ("Ekho nashestvii, pogromov, rezni").[211]

In the 1942 *October* version of "I Saw It!" here under scrutiny, Selvinsky concludes that "no such language"— a universalizing language oddly spiked with a sevenfold dose of Russian—"has been devised" ("da net

---

209 See Sel'vinskii, *Izbrannye proizvedeniia*, 1972, 209.
210 See, for instance, Sel'vinskii, *Izbrannye proizvedeniia* 1956, 1: 165; Sel'vinskii, *Izbrannye proizvedeniia* 1972, 209, and others.
211 See Sel'vinskii, "Ia eto videl!" in *Antologiia russkoi sovetskoi poezii* 1: 451.

takogo eshche iazyka…"). Hence the poet's inability to mourn in verses:

> Пусть окровавленный ваш закат
> Не мог я оплакать в неслыханных строфах…

> Even if in unheard-of stanzas
> I have failed to mourn your blood-soaked sunset.

In place of the unavailable poetic language Selvinsky nominates the language of Soviet military fire aimed at the Nazis:

> Но есть у нас и такая речь,
> Которая всяких слов горячее:
> Картавя, сыплет ее картечь!
> Гаркают ею гортань батареи!

> We do have just the kind of speech,
> More scorching than any verbal artistry:
> Canister shots, *r*'s misrolled, keep
> Rattling the larynx of the battery.

Note the ambiguous interplay between the forms of the collective pronoun *vy*=you plural and *my*=we. Does the pronoun *vash*=yours in *okrovavlennyi vash zakat* ("your blood-soaked sunset") refer collectively to the Bagerovo victims? And if so, why does Selvinsky not choose to call it *nash* "krovavyi zakat" (*our* "blood-soaked sunset"), which would have pointed to a sunset over Russian/Soviet land—in this case, over Crimea? When Selvinsky writes, "[w]e do have just the kind of speech," is he making a distinction between two collective entities, the thousands of victims lying in the ditch, and the Red Army, in which he is a poet-soldier while his weapons are both words and ammunition? Selvinsky's use of the verb *kartavit'* (to misroll one's *r*'s) manifests that voices of the massacred Jews linguistically and metaphorically join the Red Army's avenging artillery fire.[212] In the popular imagination, a

---

212 Echoes of Selvinsky's "I Saw It!" can be heard in the powerful poem "Di blayene platn fun Roms drukeray" ("The Lead Plates of the Rom Printers," 1943) by Abraham (Avrom) Sutzkever (1913-2010), written in the Vilna Ghetto. The Yiddish poet calls on the Jewish fighters to melt, literally and figuratively, the lead plates from which the famous Rom publishing house and printing press

particular misrolling of the Russian *r*'s is commonly associated with a "Jewish accent": some native speakers of Yiddish or their children display a characteristically misrolled, uvular (grunted) *r* instead of the lingual (tongue-trilled) Russian consonant. This would make them targets for taunting, and "anecdotes" about identifying a Jew by his misrolled *r*'s belong to the common repertoire of anti-Jewish jokes.[213] Hardly unintentionally or gratuitously, Selvinsky marks the sound of canister shots as Jewishly-accented, thus further complicating what might have already seemed like a slippery distinction between the collectivized, "Jewish and Slavic" identity of the victims, and the collective, implicitly internationalist Soviet identity of the Red Army. Furthermore, the misrolled *r*'s of the Soviet artillery have pushed to the sidelines if not ousted what had previously seemed like a dominant Russian rhetoric of sorrow and loss in place of a specific language of Jewish mourning. (In a number of the subsequent reprintings of the poem, Selvinsky altered the image of the shots of artillery batteries sounding like misrolled r's.)

As Selvinsky nears the poem's finale, the poet-witness speaks directly to the victims of the massacre:

> Вы слышите грохот на рубежах?
> Она отомстит! Бледнеют громилы!
> Но некуда будет им убежать
> От вашей кровавой могилы.
> Ослабьте же мышцы. Прикройте веки.
> Травою взойдите у этих высот.
> Кто вас увидел — отныне навеки
> Все ваши раны в душе унесет.

> Can you hear this blast at the boundary?
> The avenging fire.... Murderers grow pale!
> But they will have nowhere to flee
> From your blood-soaked burial.

---

used to print the Babylonian Talmud, and to use both the molten lead and the molten Jewish voices as bullets. See A. Sutzkever, "The Lead Plates of the Rom Printers," in *Selected Poetry and Prose*, tr. and ed. Barbara and Benjamin Harshav, 168-170 (Berkeley: University of California Press, 1991).

213 In Soviet poetry, something of a locus classicus for the treatment of the Jewishly-misrolled *r* is Semyon Kirsanov's poem "R" (1929).

> Now relax your muscles. Lower your eyelids,
> Rise like grass over these heights.
> He who saw you, henceforth forever
> Shall carry your wounds in his heart.[214]

In the publication in *Red Star*, which occurred within the same two months as the *October* publication, the quatrain starting with the words "Now relax [or: loosen] your muscles" was missing, but it reappeared in other reprintings, including Selvinsky's summarial collection *Crimea, Caucasus, Kuban* (1947). One can assume that in the context of the poem's publication in the main army newspaper rather than in a literary journal, the mournful pathos of the victims' loosening muscles and lowering eyelids would have clashed with the bombastic tone and journalistic grandiloquence of the avenging "speech" in the preceding lines. At the same time, unlike the *October* version, the *Red Star* as well as some of the subsequent wartime and postwar publications of the poem carried the line "But [do] believe, corpses, in those alive and healthy!" ("No ver'te, trupy, v zhivykh i zdorovykh!") immediately after the quatrain about "the great Russian sorrow." Selvinsky must have thought that some reaffirmation of the power of the living avengers and rememberers was rhetorically necessary so as to balance the emphasis on the metaphysical survival of the victims. Yet the tone of this line disagreed with the mournful pathos of the poem, and Selvinsky wavered about its inclusion in the poem.

Beneath the surface of a Soviet rhetoric of remembering Nazi crimes with powerful words (poetry) and of avenging the victims with artillery fire, there lie traces of biblical poetry. For centuries these sources—their traces—had been nurturing both the Russian and the Jewish cultural imagination, and they continued to do so during the Soviet decades. In the line calling on the victims to "rise like grass" ("travoi vzoidite") over the terrain of their death, one hears echoes of several passages in the Tanakh (Hebrew Bible).[215] In particular, one might consider passages

---

214 In the *October* publications, this line read as "Все наши раны в душе унесет" ("Shall carry our wounds in his heart [literally: soul]"). In subsequent editions "наши" ("our"), which would have referred to the "we" in "Но есть у нас и такая речь" ("We do have just the kind of speech"), was changed or corrected to "ваши" ("yours") as referring to the Bagerovo victims. In quoting the *October* version of the poem, I have corrected what seems like a typo.

215 I am deliberately limiting my analysis to the texts of the Hebrew Bible shared by both Jews and Christians. Here I am not looking at subtexts from the New Testament.

in the Book of Isaiah and the Book of Psalms, in which human physical life/death is likened to the life/death of grass, and contrasted with the undying spirit, word, and love of God. A likely biblical source comes from chapter 40 in the Book of Isaiah:

> [...] A voice rings out: "Proclaim!"
> Another asks, "What shall I proclaim?"
> All flesh is grass,
> All its goodness like flowers of the field:
> Grass withers, flowers fade
> When the breath of the Lord blows on them.
> Instead, man is but grass:
> Grass withers, flowers fade—
> But the word of our God is always fulfilled!" [...] (Is. 40:6-8).[216]

Another antecedent may be found in Psalm 103:

> [...] Man, his days are like those of grass;
> he blooms like a flower of the field;
> a wind passes by and it is no more,
> its own place no longer knows it.
> But the Lord's steadfast love is for all eternity
> Toward those who fear Him [...]. (Ps. 103:15).[217]

Unlike the biblical prophet or the ancient psalmist, Selvinsky's eyewitnessing poet, a Soviet Jew writing in Russian and leaning upon a suppressed memory of Judaism, cannot and may not put faith in God's benevolence and omnipotence.

Previously in the poem, in the lines immediately preceding the description of a murdered Jewish woman lying in the ditch with her murdered small child, Selvinsky also sketched a portrait of a massacred old woman, whom he identified as a Christian. In the revisions of this section of the poem, Selvinsky kept changing the description of the woman's clothes and appearance or deleting the section altogether. In

---

[216] *Tanakh: A New Translation of the Holy Scriptures According to the Traditional Hebrew Text*, 698-699 (Philadelphia: The Jewish Publication Society, 1985).
[217] *Tanakh*, 1229.

the version printed in *October*, the massacred old woman is dressed in "ragged nun's garb," and this is supposed to suggest either that she is dressed in all black or that she is a pious person—or both. Selvinsky needs the characterization of the old woman as religiously observant so as to place in her mind a dismissal of divinity which occurred as she met her death in the Bagerovo ditch. In the *October* version, the near-death clarity of the old woman's consciousness is described as "through this ancient, mossy, overgrown/ Black-crow mysticism—light has burst," whereas in alternative versions the stamp of death on the face of the murdered old woman is called "a reproach to the purest maiden [i.e. Madonna],/ a destruction of the faith of the ancient years."[218] In all versions where the section appeared, Selvinsky stuck these words in the gullet of the murdered old woman:

"Коли на свете живут фашисты —
    Стало быть, бога нет!... "

"If fascists live in this world,
    Then there is no god...."

The poem's rejection of organized religion is not only an obvious and expected consequence of the prescribed Soviet atheism but at least to some extent a consequence of the aftermath of the catastrophe itself— and of the poet's experience of standing over a ditch filled with corpses of executed Jews. Selvinsky's poet may not be assured, and in turn may not assure the victims, of either God's supreme powers or God's ability to effect punishment on the Nazi murderers. In the quatrain deleted in the *Red Star* publication, Selvinsky's poet-witness seems confident of only one thing: that the memory of having eyewitnessed the aftermath of the massacre would live eternally, "henceforth forever" ("otnyne naveki") stored in a spiritual realm he conventionally labels "soul" ("dusha"). Imagine Selvinsky's military editors and censors stumbling upon and poring over these lines: "Now relax your muscles. Lower your eyelids,/ Rise like grass over these heights./ He who saw you, henceforth forever/ Shall carry your wounds in his heart." Selvinsky's mournful voice conflates a somewhat tired image of physical death and

---

218 See Sel'vinskii, 1972, 207.

unremembrance (grass growing over a field of death) with a symbol layered with religious meaning and cultural significance. To elucidate some of the biblical roots of the quatrain in question, and of Selvinsky's poem as a whole, one would benefit from turning to the opening of Psalm 102, subtitled "A prayer of the lowly man when he is faint and pours forth his plea before the Lord"):

> O Lord, hear my prayer;
> let my cry come before You.
> Do not hide Your face from me
> in my time of trouble;
> turn Your ear to me;
> when I cry, answer me speedily.
> For my days have vanished like smoke
> and my bones are charred like a hearth.
> My body is stricken and withered like grass;
> too wasted to eat my food;
> on account of my vehement groaning
> my bones show through my skin.
> I am like a great owl in the wilderness,
> an owl among the ruins.
> I like awake; I am like
> a lone bird upon a roof.
> All day long my enemies revile me;
> my deriders use my name to curse.
> For I have eaten ashes like bread
> and mixed my drink with tears,
> because of Your wrath and Your fury;
> for You have cast me far away.
> My days are like a lengthening shadow;
> I wither like grass.
> But you, O Lord, are enthroned forever;
> Your fame endures throughout the ages.
> You will surely arise and take pity on Zion,
> for it is time to be gracious to her;
> the appointed time has come (Ps. 102:1-14).[219]

---

[219] *Tanakh*, 1227. Consider also this section from Psalm 90: 5-6: "O Lord, You have been our refuge

In the poetry of the ancient psalmist, the Jewish-Russian poet would have gleaned signs and symbols of an ancient catastrophe,[220] and those signs and symbols would have fed the Soviet witness's diction and imagery as he wrote the poem in January 1942.[221]

It is a small miracle that Selvinsky managed to rescue from editors and censors the quatrain about "rising like grass over these heights" in most of the published versions of "I Saw It!" In terms of the political gestures expected of Soviet poets, pointing to Stalin as the embodiment of both absolute strength and total goodness would have been prescriptively appropriate. Yet Selvinsky, who did not shun Stalinist panegyrics in his writings, avoided speaking of Stalin or other Soviet leaders in his Shoah poems. Did he find the act of mourning the Jewish victims to be morally and aesthetically incompatible with singing Stalinist dithyrambs?

Perhaps more so than Selvinsky's immediate Soviet readers during World War II, today's readers of "I Saw It!" recognize how especially challenging it must have been to bear witness and yet to remain compliant to the ideological and censorial expectations of the Stalinist state—especially with the emerging taboo on discussing Jewish losses apart from Soviet (Russian) losses. How excruciatingly difficult it must have been to witness truthfully while satisfying the demands of wartime censorship and the pragmatics of one's own internal censor:

Ров... Поэмой ли скажешь о нем?
7000 трупов... Евреи... Славяне...

---

in every generation./ Before the mountains came into being,/ Before You brought forth the earth and the world,/ from eternity to eternity You are God./ You return man to dust;/ You decreed, 'Return you mortals!'/ For in Your sight a thousand years/ are like yesterday that has past,/ like a watch of the night./ You engulf men in sleep;/ at daybreak they are like grass that renews itself;/ at daybreak it flourishes anew;/ By dusk it withers and dries up [...]" (*Tanakh*, 1217).

220 For a classic study of the Jewish response, see David G. Roskies, *Against the Apocalypse: Responses to Catastrophe in Modern Jewish Culture* (Cambridge, MA: Harvard University Press, 1984).

221 Another question awaiting further investigation is the prophesy of "dry bones" in Ezekiel 37 as a subtext for the ending of Selvinsky's "I Saw It!": "And He said to me, 'O mortal, these bones are the whole House of Israel. They say, 'Our bones are dried up, our hope is gone; we are doomed.' Prophesy, therefore, and say to them: Thus said the Lord GOD: I am going to open your graves and lift you out of the graves, O My people, and bring you to the land of Israel. You shall know, O My people, that I am the LORD, when I have opened your graves and lifted you out of your graves. I will put My breath into you and you shall live again, and I will set you upon your soil. Then you shall know that I the LORD have spoken and have acted'—declared the LORD" (Ezekiel 37: 11-14), *Tanakh*, 957-958.

> Да! Об этом нельзя словами:
> Огнем! Только огнем!

> The ditch.... Tell about it in meter [literally: "long poem"]?
> 7000 corpses ... Jews ... Slavs ...
> No! About this one cannot—with words:
> Fire! Only with fire.

Here the Jewish poet's agony of witnessing as captured in Bialik's *In The City of Slaughter* springs to mind again in Selvinsky's concluding quatrain, where the word Jew is repeated after the description of the murdered Jewish mother with her child. Selvinsky states more explicitly, loudly, and clearly than almost any Soviet source published in 1941-1942 that Jews topped the list of Nazi victims. Having placed "Slavs" (slaviane), and not Jews (evrei) first in the line would not have disrupted the prosody, yet it would have underemphasized Jewish losses. Selvinsky deliberately placed "Jews" first, before "Slavs" and in direct violation of the official perspective on the Nazi atrocities. Furthermore, Selvinsky did not list any other nationalities, even though the official reports and news coverage of the Nazi atrocities in Crimea and specifically at the Bagerovo ditch spoke of the Nazis' murdering Soviet people of many nationalities, including Tatar names beside Russian, Ukrainian, and Jewish names. Do the words "disbelieve printed columns of news" in the second line of "I Saw It!" daringly point to official coverage in the Soviet press and to the 6 January 1942 Molotov note? While in citing the number of victims, 7000, Selvinsky probably could not have deviated from the number released in the Molotov note and other official documents. Yet he did his best to shed more historical light on the systematic murder of Jews by the Nazis and their accomplices.[222]

I have examined *de visu* 23 separate publications of "I Saw It!" Among them, three were printed in wartime periodicals (*Red Star, October,* and *Forward to Victory!*), two in wartime collections (*Atrocities of the German Fascists in Kerch; A Volume of Poems*[223]), one in a pro-

---

222   I discussed this with Vladimir Sanzharovets on 14 December 2011, and he also felt that a different number could not have appeared *in light* of the 6 January 1942 Molotov note.
223   In the extensive 1943 anthology of poetry titled *Sbornik stikhov* (*A Volume of Poems*), two of Selvinsky's prewar poems were featured, along with "Ballad about Leninism" and "I Saw It!" (both

paganda booklet-poster, thirteen in books by Selvinsky published between 1942 and 2004, two in anthologies of Soviet poetry from the 1950s and 1960s, one in a Soviet-era critical study, and one in a post-Soviet anthology of Jewish motifs in Russian poetry. There were other publications both during and after the war. Since its inclusion in Selvinsky's *Ballads, Posters, and Songs* (1942), "I Saw It!" has appeared in 18 out of 26 collections, volumes, and selected and collected editions of Selvinsky's poetry, and in all six of his poetry books published during the Great Patriotic War and the postwar 1940s.[224] Around 1953, the year of Stalin's death, and during the Thaw, Selvinsky is believed to have introduced (or restored) substantial changes in the text of the poem. "Jews" became "Semites" in the line "7000 trupov ... Evrei ... Slaviane ...," and it became "7000 trupov ... Semity ... Slaviane ...." The change did not alter the line metrically, but it did change the meaning significantly, both by placing the historical legacy of antisemitism behind the massacre and by sidestepping the Soviet construction of Jewish identity.[225]

On its surface, the change from Jews to Semites could be interpreted as a restoration of congruence or balance: Slavs as a larger group including not only Russians but Ukrainians, Belorussians, and others would be matched by Semites as a larger category than Jews. It is further conceivable that the change from Jews to Semites would offer Selvinsky a way to subsume the Crimea's native Jews, the Krymchaks, into the collective group of victims alongside the Ashkenazi Jews, thereby not limiting the Shoah to the latter. At the same time, the choice of "semity" ("Semites") over "evrei" ("Jews"), especially if it had been made in the wartime publications, would have highlighted the Nazi racial ideology and genocidal nature of the atrocities against the Jews. As compared to "Semites," the use of "Jews" was a less resounding choice.

---

of 1942). Some of the lines in the version of "I Saw It!" used in this anthology do not seem to have appeared elsewhere. See Sel'vinskii, "Ia eto videl!" in *Sbornik stikhov*, 373-375, ed. V[asilii] Kazin and V[iktor] Pertsov (Moscow: Gosudarstvennoe izdatel'stvo khudozhestvennoi literatury, 1943).

224 Excluded from these calculations are the 1957 edition of Selvinsky's novel in verse *Arktika* (*Arctic*), the thematic collection *Kazakhstan* (1958), and the volume for children *Chto pravil'no?* (*What's Right?*).

225 I am grateful to Kirill Ospovat for pointing out, during my lecture at Institut für Slawistik Humboldt-Universität zu Berlin on 17 April 2012, that in making the change to "7000 trupov... Semity... Slaviane" Selvinsky was also enchancing the line's alliterative power.

Selvinsky's poems about the aftermath of the Nazi atrocities in Crimea further reveal that despite the pressure, he managed to say much more in them than in his occasional pieces of journalism or essays printed in the army newspapers. In the aforementioned article "Once Again on the Hitlerite Atrocities," Selvinsky cited the execution of 50,000 people in Kiev and other massacres, yet stuck to the most general (or, perhaps, ambiguous) of terms in speaking of the Nazi genocide: "our people" ("nash narod").[226] We also know of Selvinsky's stated dissatisfaction with what he was able to say in his poems about the victims killed at the Bagerovo ditch—and with how he said it.

Sources dating to the wartime years testify to the impact of "I Saw It!" Soon after its publication in the central press it entered the repertoire of wartime lyrics heard on the radio and in public performances by actors.[227] The poem was studied in schools and universities. On 28 March 1942 Selvinsky wrote to his wife that "in Krasnodar in schools they are reading 'I Saw It!' It appears that it has deeply touched the *soul of the people*. I underscore this in connection with the second part of the formula 'almost a genius.'"[228] Earlier in the same letter Selvinsky mentions that Stalin has personally overruled the decision of the censors from Glavlit (The Main Directorate for Literary and Publishing Affairs) and instructed *Red Star* to publish his poem "Ballad about Leninism."[229] Thus, to a person familiar with Selvinsky's literary affairs, the reference to "almost a genius" contextually (and polemically) points to Stalin's reported view of Selvinsky's poetry. The poet was still hoping that Stalin would not only read his wartime poems such as "I Saw It!" but recognize their national value.

On 6 April 1942, Selvinsky wrote to his wife:

> About the poem "I Saw It!" Your impressions of how the writers have reacted to it coincide with the general attitude to the poem. When [Pyotr] Pavlenko came to

---

226 Selvinskii, "Eshche raz o zverstvakh gitlerovtsev," *Boevoi natisk* 24 February 1942, 2.
227 See, for instance, a memoir by Selvinsky's stepdaughter Tsetsiliia Voskresenskaia, *Moi vospominania. Dokumental'nyi roman*, 198-199 (Moscow: Vremia, 2006); see also Boris Militsyn, "Tatarstanskie stranichki iz zhizni sem'i Il'i Sel'vinskogo," *Kazanskie istorii* 5 February 2011, http://history-kazan.ru/2011/02/татарстанские-странички-из-жизни-сем/, last accessed on 3 October 2011.
228 Selvinsky, Letter to Berta Selvinskya, 28 March 1942, Ilya Selvinsky Memorial Museum.
229 Sel'vinskii, "Ballada o leninizme," *Krasnaia zvezda* 13 February 1942.

Krasnodar and visited the editorial office of *Bolshevik*, they proudly showed him my poem, which had been published there, and started reading it to him out loud. Then Pavlenko hushed them: 'You cannot read! This is a true hymn of hatred [gimn nenavisti]! Let me read it!' [...] In Krasnodar they recorded me with a shorinophone, reciting the poem. At 4 o'clock in the afternoon I stood in the crowd in the street near a radio loudspeaker and listened to my voice, as usual not recognizing it. But that's not the point. Cars rushed by, streetcars were clanking, but the people stood like during prayer, listened and cried. Hundreds of letters from Red Army soldiers say the same. It seems that I had touched something very deep. But I myself cannot hear this poem. I see through it only those who I saw in the ditch, and I know that I have not expressed even one hundredth of what I should have expressed."[230]

In the same letter, Selvinsky also wrote that he had been "thinking of a poet's destiny and of the people [*o narode*; this collective form in the Russian can also mean "nation"] to whom [he] had grown so close during the war." Even if what Selvinsky writes is meant not only for his wife but also for those unwanted yet expected readers perlustrating his correspondence, his comments gain a particular resonance when steeped simultaneously in the context of his aspirations as a national poet and the context of Jewish death and Jewish survival in the Soviet Union: "No matter how horrific, how monstrous is what the war has brought, it has nevertheless done one great thing: the people have understood all the happiness which Soviet power, Lenin, Stalin, the Bolshevik party have brought."[231]

Selvinsky's younger contemporary, the poet Aleksandr Yashin (1913-1968), said this at a writers' meeting in 1943: "I heard the sailors of the Red Navy select the best among the poems by our Soviet poets and recite them on the radio. I heard a sailor recite Selvinsky's poem 'I

---

230 Selvinsky, Letter to Berta Selvinskaya, 6 April 1942, Ilya Selvinsky Memorial Museum; cf. incomplete version in Selvinskii, "Na voine. Iz dnevnikov i pisem rodnym," 171. See also Ozerov, *Biografiia stikhotvoreniia*, 45-48; Sel'vinskii, "Na chetyrekh iazykakh," 520.
231 Selvinsky, Letter to Berta Selvinskaya, 6 April 1942, Ilya Selvinsky Memorial Museum.

Saw It!'—the most wrathful of Selvinsky's poems."²³² In 1998 the poet Evdokia Olshanskaya (1929-2003) reminisced about the influence of Selvinsky's "I Saw It!":

> I first heard the name of Ilya Selvinsky during the war, in the early spring of 1945. We were living in Shatura, outside Moscow, I was in seventh grade. [...] My sister, who was five years older and stimulated my interest in poetry, had already returned to Kiev from evacuation and entered the university. She sent me poems she liked [...]. One time she sent me a poem by Ilya Selvinsky. It was called 'I Saw It!' [...] It told about the execution of Jews in Crimea. But Kievans received it as a description of the tragedy of Babi Yar (poems had already been written about it by Olga Anstey and Lyudmila Titova, young Russian women who remained in occupied Kiev who also saw it with their "own eyes," but it would be years before their poems would reach the reader). Therefore in Kiev the poem "I Saw It!' was passed from hand to hand, people copied it, memorized it, which is how it had reached me.²³³

In a short memoir of Selvinsky penned in 1969, Pavel Antokolsky (1896-1978), another principal Jewish-Russian Shoah poet who chose his words more and more carefully as he grew old, called "I Saw It!" a "sobbing requiem in memory of women, old men, and children, executed by the Nazis in a ditch at Kerch."²³⁴ In retrospect one can see clearly that with "I Saw It!" Selvinsky introduced the topic of the Shoah into Soviet poetry by blending the documentary and the lyrical in a first-person witnessing perspective.

6. *Revisi(ti)ng the Memories: "Kerch" and "The Trial in Krasnodar"*

---

232 Quoted in Sel'vinskii, "Na voine. Iz dnevnikov i pisem rodnym," 163. Yashin apparently said this during an official discussion of Selvinsky's work at the Military Commission of the Union of Soviet Writers on 7 June 1943, following Selvinsky's own presentation.
233 Evdokiia Ol'shanskaia, "Mne zhizn' podarila vstrechi s poetom." *Zerkalo nedeli* (1998). http://www.litera.ru/stixiya/articles/397.html. Last accessed 7 April 2010.
234 Antokol'skii, "Il'ia Sel'vinskii," 11.

Later in 1942, Selvinsky revisited the subject of the Shoah in Crimea, and specifically the Bagerovo ditch massacre, in the poem "Kerch." "Kerch" is both more descriptive and more meditative than "I Saw It," altogether a superior literary text if such comparisons are worth anything, given the gravity of the subject matter. According to one source, "Kerch" first appeared in December 1943 in *Forward for the Motherland!*, the newspaper of the Separate Maritime Army and a successor to *Forward to Victory!* The poem reached a wide Soviet audience only in February 1945, when it was published in the prominent Moscow monthly *Znamia (Banner)*.[235] Despite the poem's centrality in the corpus of Selvinsky's wartime poems, "Kerch" was not reprinted until 1984. In the 1972 posthumous, academic edition of Selvinsky's poetry, a section of "Kerch" was quoted in the commentary to "I Saw It!": "In the poem 'Kerch' [...], not included in the present edition, I. Selvinsky describes how he became a witness to fascist crimes at the village of Bagerovo."[236] Unlike "I Saw It!," to which Selvinsky specifically directs the reader in the text of "Kerch," the latter remained largely unknown to postwar Soviet readers.[237]

In contrast to "I Saw It!" "Kerch" does not specify the identity (identities) of the victims. When speaking of concrete Nazi victims, Selvinsky renders the victims' individuality in palpably human, yet ethnically and religiously non-specific terms. In two places in the poem Selvinsky's authorial voice bestows upon the thousands of victims of the Bagerovo ditch massacre the collective, non-specific identity of

---

235 See [Commentary by I. L. Mikhailov in] Sel'vinskii, *Izbrannye proizvedeniia v dvukh tomakh*, 1: 585 (Moscow: Khudozhestvennaia literatura, 1989); see also [Commentary by I. L. Mikhailov and N. G. Zakharenko] in Il'ia Sel'vinskii, *Izbrannye proizvedeniia*, ed. I. L. Mikhailov, 900-901 (Leningrad: Sovetskii pisatel', 1972); Selvinskii, "Kerch'," *Znamia* 2 (1945): 78-79; *Stikhotvoreniia. Tsarevna-lebed': tragediia*, ed. Ts. Voskresenskaia, 108-111 (Moscow: Khudozhestvennaia literatura, 1984), in *Izbrannye proizvedeniia v dvukh tomakh*, 2 vols., ed. Ts. Voskresenskaia, 1: 193-196 (Moscow: Khudozhestvennaia literatura, 1989); in Sel'vinskii, *Iz pepla, iz poem, iz snovidenii*, ed. A. M. Revich, 150-154 (Moscow: Vremia, 2004). To the best of my knowledge, Yakov Khelemsky was the first to offer an extensive analysis of "Kerch" in his memoir of Selvinsky. See Iakov Khelemskii, "Kurliandskaia vesna," in *O Sel'vinskom: vospominaniia*, ed. Ts. A. Voskresenskaia and I. P. Sirotinskaia, 125-175. Knowing that Selvinsky had contemplated an epic work about the war, Khelemsky proposed that a number of Selvinsky's wartime poems, including "I Saw It!" and "Kerch," formed a cycle of epic proportions (170).
236 [Commentary by Mikhailov and Zakharenko] in Sel'vinskii, *Izbrannye proizvedeniia*, 1972, 900-901. There is a mistake in the commentary: the crimes were committed not at the town of Bagerovo but at the so-called Bagerovo anti-tank ditch.
237 Critics and commentators, Ozerov and Khelemsky excepting, also avoided "Kerch." See Ozerov, *Biografiia stikhotvoreniia*, 47; Khelemskii, "Kurliandskaia vesna," 170-172.

the dead ("mertvetsy"). In a central episode of the poem, Selvinsky inserts, in quotation marks, a direct account by a survivor describing the death of his mother, wife, and two daughters; the survivor's Jewish identity may only be surmised through context and conjecture and also, perhaps, through his speech. At the same time, and especially when illuminated by the history of the massacre, the notable absence of official Soviet rhetoric on the Shoah makes "Kerch" a more powerful act of bearing witness despite the vigilance of its diction. That Selvinsky was content with the results may also be inferred from the fact that he made no substantive changes in the text of the poem.[238] The latter circumstance seems especially significant when we think of Selvinsky's jittery revisions in the text of "I Saw It!" The publication history of "Kerch" illustrates both Selvinsky's awareness of the poem's vulnerability and his esteem for the poem's integrity.

Without knowing the historical context, one can fail to read "Kerch" as a poem about the Shoah. Without knowing the history of the place—and of the massacre to which Selvinsky refers in the poem—one would be inclined to read "Kerch" not as a poem about the Shoah but as a meditation, both nostalgic and scornful, on the relationship between culture and catastrophe, civilization and cruelty, poetry and history.

The poem opens with a reminiscence of Selvinsky's Crimean youth:

> У нас в гимназии делили Крым
> На эллинский и дикий. Все приморье
> От Евпатории и до Керчи
> Звалось Элладой. Если же случалось,
> Перевалив за горную преграду,
> Спуститься в степь, то называлось это —
> "Поехать в Скифию."

> In high school we divided the Crimea
> Into Hellenic and Wild. The coast
> From Eupatoria down and all the way to Kerch
> Was called Hellas. And then, if one should happen

---

[238] Cf. Sel'vinskii, "Kerch'," *Znamia* 2 (1945): 78-79; Sel'vinskii, *Stikhotvoreniia. Tsarevna-lebed': tragediia*, ed. Ts. Voskresenskaia, 108-111 (Moscow: Khudozhestvennaia literatura, 1984); Sel'vinskii, *Iz pepla, iz poem, iz snovidenii*, ed. A. M. Revich, 150-154 (Moscow: Vremia, 2004).

To steal across the mountains and descend
Onto the steppe, we used to call this:
"Going to Scythia"

(*here and hereafter tr. Maxim D. Shrayer*).

The Crimean coast evokes Graeco-Roman civilization; the wild expanses of the Scythian steppe stand for lack of culture and refinement.

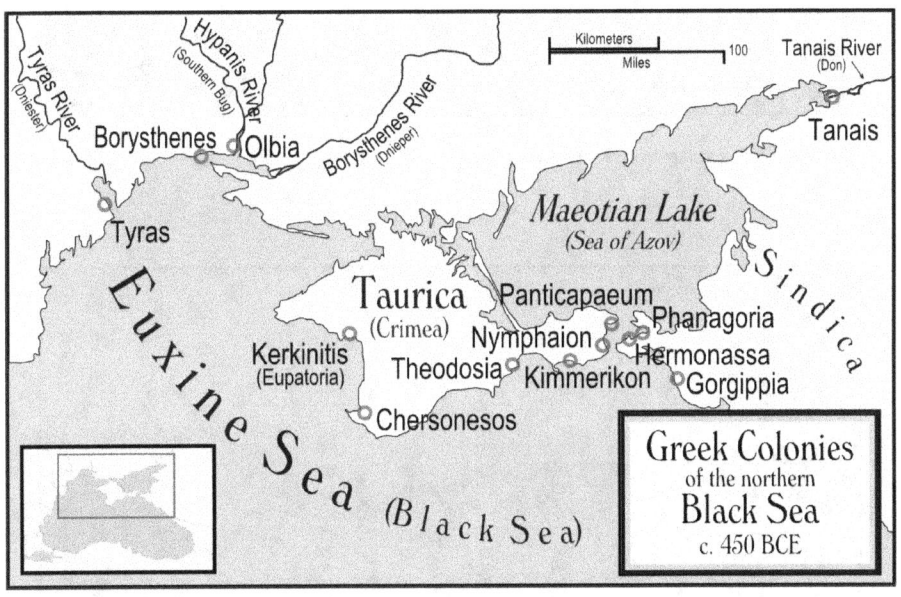

37. Map of ancient Greek colonies in the Northern Black Sea, with the Crimea peninsula in the center. (Wikimedia).

Following his arrival from Taman in early January 1942, Selvinsky was reminded of this dichotomy when the Soviet forces landed near Kerch.

38. View of Kerch Bay from Mount Mithridates. 14 December 2011. Photo by Maxim D. Shrayer.

39. View of modern Kerch from Mount Mithridates with the Great Mithridates Stairs. Photo by Sergey Sorokin. (Courtesy of Sergey Sorokin.)

As the poet looks at the liberated Kerch (liberated only temporarily, but he does not know that) from the top of Mount Mithridates (Midridat), where he had previously stood in early November 1941, he recalls the ciy's ancient Greek name:

> ...Хотя и в шутку,
> Мы называли наши города
> По-гречески, как это было древле.
> Об этом я давно уж позабыл.
> И вдруг, когда десантные войска,
> Форсировав пролив, обосновались
> На Крымском берегу, и я увидел
> Невдалеке перед собою Керчь, —
> Мой голос прошептал: "Пантикапея..."

> ... although in jest
> We called our towns and cities
> By their Greek names, as in days of yore.
> I had long forgotten all about this.
> But suddenly when our landing forces
> Traversed the strait and took their position
> On the Crimean shore, when I saw
> Not far ahead of me the city of Kerch,
> My voice whispered "Panticapaeum."

Then follows a particularly gorgeous description of the view from the ancient Mount Mithridates, and of life in the ancient Greek city as Selvinsky envisioned it, a description which superimposes the heritage of Tauric Chersonese onto the wartime reality of a (temporarily) liberated Soviet Kerch.

> В лиловом и оранжевом тумане
> Над морем воспарил амфитеатр
> Пленительного города. Гора
> С каким-то белым и высоким храмом
> Курилась облаками. Дальний мыс
> Чернел над хризолитовым заливом.
> А очертанья зданий на заре

Подсказывали портики, колонны
И статуи на форуме. Эллада
Дышала сном. Один туман, как грезы,
Описывал громады парусов,
Орду козлов или толпу сатиров, —
И я был старше на пять тысяч лет.

In lilac and orange fog, above the sea
An amphitheater of a resplendent city
Soared, while some white and lofty temple
Rose from a mountain into the sky
Amid smoking clouds. A distant cape
Shone black over the bay of chrysolite.
And silhouettes of buildings at daybreak
Suggested porticoes and columns
And statues in the forum, while Hellas
Breathed in her deep slumber. Only the fog,

40. View of the Panticapeum ruins in modern Kerch. 14 December 2011. (Maxim D. Shrayer.)

Like reveries, encircled colossal sails,
A horde of billy goats or a crowd of satyrs,
And I was older by five thousand years.

Ludmila Rustemova argues that Selvinsky "inscribed" into the centuries-old context of Crimean history, "where peoples and nations ousted one another in ways far from peaceful," "the tragic events of World War II, the shock and horror he experienced at Bagerovo, not far from Kerch, the ancient Panticapeum."[239] One of the tensions in the poem's opening, that between civilization and absence of civilization, manifests itself in the juxtaposition of the cultured, Hellenic Crimea and the wild, Scythian Crimea. It would be tempting to suggest that Selvinsky implicitly equates the devastation of Bosporus by Goths and Huns, whom representatives of the Graeco-Roman civilization regarded as hordes of barbarians, with the destruction brought upon modern Crimea by the Nazis, whom the Soviet press commonly labeled barbarians, ruffians, or bandits. However, I suspect that Selvinsky has something else in mind as he reconstructs Crimea's Graeco-Roman past. Selvinsky's point is *not* to equate Nazis and the peoples and tribes whom the Greeks viewed as uncivilized, but rather to establish, in the context of the Shoah, that Nazism had developed in culturally refined Germany and Austria, in the lap of Western civilization, which was the heir apparent to the Graeco-Roman civilization. Selvinsky's point, as I see it, is to suggest preemptively, before he describes the site of the massacre, that the legacy of culture and beauty has not prevented the Nazis from committing genocide. What does Selvinsky signal to the reader when he calls the Graeco-Roman past "grub[aia] epokh[a]" ("ruffian days") and "uzhasnyi vek!" ("a terrible age!")? A reader of Selvinsky recognizes that Graeco-Roman motifs go back not only to his childhood and youth on the coast of Crimea but also to his early literary works, notably his *Bar-Kokhba*, one of whose central motifs is the confrontation of the Graeco-Roman and Judaic civilizations, in which Rome seeks to root out Judeans. The poem also contains subtle references to Selvinsky's novel in verse *Fur Trade*, where recollections of the poet's Crimean youth fig-

---

239 L.A. Rustemova, "Krymskii 'kontekst' I. Sel'vinskogo," in *I. L. Sel'vinskii i literaturnyi protsess XX veka. V mezhdunarodnaia nauchnaia konferentsiia, posviashchennaia 100-letiiu I. L. Sel'vinskogo. Materialy*, 77 (Simferopol': Krymskii arkhiv, 2000). Again, there is a mistake: not at Bagerovo but at the Bagerovo anti-tank ditch.

ure very prominently, and where Selvinsky reflected on the interplay of the Scythian, Hellenic, and Judaic civilizations in the making of his Crimean identity.

Having brought the reader back to the poem's present—the Soviet takeover of Kerch in late December 1941—Selvinsky approaches the heart of this poem.

> […] И когда из дыма
> Опять он появился над заливом
> И танки с красным флагом потянулись
> По набережной, а увидя ров,
> Ушли сквозь стену банка в переулок, —
> У берега уже лежала Керчь.
> Так за один лишь день я увидал
> Два лика города. Но мне война
> Готовила еще и третий.

> […] And when out of the smoke
> The city once again appeared over the bay,
> And tanks with red flags rolled in, one after another
> Along the embankment, then encountered a ditch
> And drove through a bank's façade into a side street—
> By now Kerch was lying there by the shore.
> Thus, in one day I got to see two faces
> Of the same city. But the war
> Held a third one in store for me.

Selvinsky has actually shown us three, not two, disparate faces of Kerch: an ancient Greek city, a city of Selvinsky's youth in the last years of the Russian Empire, and a Soviet city prior to the first Nazi occupation. The fourth face of Kerch is that of the war and Shoah:

> […] Ночью,
> В армейскую газету, очень тихо
> И как-то лунатически, как будто
> Одно и то же неотступно видя
> И об одном задумавшись навеки,
> Вошел не бледный, нет, а просто белый,

Невероятный чем-то человек.
Далеким голосом (таким далеким,
Что нам казалось, будто бы не он,
А кто-то за него) — он нам поведал
Пещерным слогом каменного века,
Рубя на точках:
"В десяти верстах
Тут Багерово есть. Одно село.
Не доходя, направо будет ров.
Противотанковый. Они туда
Семь тысяч граждан".

[...] That night
To the office of the army newspaper, very quietly—
Like a somnambulist, as though before him
The same vision stood incessantly, forever
Stuck on the same unceasing thought—
Came someone not pale, but simply white,
A man who was in some ways unimaginable.
In a faraway voice (so faraway
That we felt it wasn't he who spoke,
But someone else spoke for him)—he told us
In a caveman's speech of Stone Age intonations,
Incising the full stops:
"Six miles from here.
There's Bagerovo. A small town.
Before you get there, to the right there's a ditch.
Anti-tank. They took over there
Seven thousand folks."

Here the poet's guide is not Virgil, as one might have expected from Selvinsky's epic ambitions and the infernal tour of the ditch filled with corpses (recall the invocation of Dante and Ovid in "I Saw It!"). Rather, the guide is a Jewish man who has lost his family and speaks in a voice starkly devoid of artistry or style. (In 1944, in "The Hell of Treblinka," Vasily Grossman would also emphasize that in spite of the deliberately Dantesque parallels, not Ovid but only the voices of the dead Jews and the survivors and eyewitnesses of the horror could serve as his guides through the death camp.²⁴⁰) The survivor points Selvinsky and his colleagues to the site of the massacre, and they walk there, following his directions. (Selvinsky gets the directions and topography right, except that he misjudges the distance from the ditch to the town of Bagerovo, probably having assumed that the adjacent village of Oktyabrskoe was a section of Bagerovo). At this point in Selvinsky's account, the poet's individual I/eye, both the voice of identity and the ocular point of view, morphs into the collective "we" of a group of witnesses: "Мы тут же и пошли. Писатель Ромм,/ Фотограф, я и критик Гоффеншефер" ("We set out right away. The writer Romm. / The photographer, myself, and the critic Goffenshefer"). Romm is identified as the "writer," which here refers less to a distinction between poetry and prose than to his position as a staff "writer" ("pisatel'," as the position was called in the nomenclature of military newspapers). Goffenshefer is clearly "the critic." And Selvinsky did not explicitly state his own craft or literary medium, in part because his rank had by that point changed to political officer and in part because calling himself a "poet" would have been ostentatious. All three literary practitioners in the poem (Ilya Selvinsky, Aleksandr Romm, and Veniamin Goffenshefer) were Jews. Aleksandr Romm (1898-1943), poet, literary scholar, literary translator, and brother of the film director Mikhail Romm, served in the Black Sea navy in 1941-1943. Veniamin Goffenshefer (1905-1966), well known as a critic in the 1930s-60s, was the author of the study *Mikhail Sholokhov* (1940) and other works. Selvinsky's close colleague, Goffenshefer was a staff writer at *Son of Fatherland* throughout the war. Romm, a writer for the *Red Black Sea Navyman* (*Krasnyi chernomorets*), was in Kerch on an assignment to cover the landing operation and the liberation of the Kerch peninsula. Romm's writings about the Bagerovo ditch massacre, if there were any, have not been found.²⁴¹

---

240 See Shrayer, "Bearing Witness: The War, the Shoah and the Legacy of Vasily Grossman."
241 Romm died by suicide in October 1943; see http://ru.wikipedia.org/wiki/Ромм,_Александр_Ильич, last accessed 8 April 2010; M. Gasparov, "Aleksandr Romm. Stikhi 1927-28 gg.," *Toronto Slavic Quarterly* 2 (Fall 2002), http://www.utoronto.ca/tsq/02/romm.shtml, last accessed 8 April 2010. About Romm's experiences as a military reporter in Crimea and in Kerch, see V. F., "Pisateli-chernomortsy," *Literatura i iskusstvo* 13 June 1942; Aleksandr Romm, "Pisatel'-voin," *Literatura i iskusstvo* 4 July 1942, 3. During his stay in Kerch in early January 1942, Romm contributed poetry to the local press. See A. Romm, "Nadiusha," *Kerchenskii rabochii* 15 January 1942.

> **Александр РОММ**
>
> # НАДЮША
>
> Девушка простилась с мамой, с братом,
> Застегнула жесткую шинель
> И пошла — под пули и гранаты,
> В зной, под ветер, на мороз, в метель.
>
> Девушка была на смерть готова,
> Научилась раненых носить,
> Легкою рукой, приветным словом,
> Взглядом и улыбкою лечить.
>
> ...Бой гремел у сопки, над проселком,
> Помогала девушка бойцам.
> Там ее поранило осколком,
> И попалась бедная врагам.
>
> Раненую немцы истязали,
> Долго издевались, как могли,
> Смелую — бесстыдно унижали,
> Ласковую — мучили и жгли,
>
> А потом на немцев налетела
> Сотня моряков — и, кончив бой,
> Брошенное маленькое тело
> Мы нашли в канаве, под горой.
>
> Каждой ранкой к мести призывая,
> Грязною рукой обнажена,
> Девушка лежала неживая:
> Немцами замучена она.
>
> Бей врага! Пускай бежит, как заяц, —
> Загораживай ему пути!
> Бей его, чтоб ни один мерзавец.
>
> Не успел укрыться и уйти!
>
> Бей их так, чтоб в них дрожали души!
> Не уйти врагам от наших рук!
> Отомстим за девушку Надюшу,
> Отомстим за всех ее подруг!

41. Aleksandr Romm. "Nadiusha." *Kerchenskii rabochii* (*Kerch Worker*), 15 January 1942.

Goffenshefer contributed the essay "Bagerovo" to the army paper on 29 January 1942; his essay did not mention the word "Jew."[1]

---

1   Goffenshefer, "Bagerovo." In 1944 Goffenshefer revisited the Bagerovo ditch massacre in another article: "Ne gasi ego, pamiat'!" *Syn otechestva* 16 March 1944.

42. Veniamin Goffenshefer. "Bagerovo." *Syn otechestva* (*Son of Fatherland*), 29 January 1942.

The photographer Selvinsky refers to without naming him was also a Jew, most likely Leonid Yablonsky or Mark Turovsky. After the Nazi invasion Turovsky, who had been based in Crimea and knew the area well, was assigned to cover Crimea for TASS. Yablonsky was a staff photographer of *Son of Fatherland*, where Selvinsky headed the literary section at the time described in the poem "Kerch".[1] In fact, the "window" of TASS depicting the Nazi atrocities at Kerch, which was displayed in

---

1 "Turovskii Mark Il'ich," in "Крымовед: Personalia." http://www.krimoved-library.ru/books/evrei-kryma14.html, last accessed 27 January 2012; "Iablonskii Leonid Isaakovich," in "Крымовед: Personalia," http://www.krimoved-library.ru/books/evrei-kryma14.html, last accessed 27 January 2012.

that city in January 1942, was a coproduction of the Crimean office of TASS and Selvinsky's paper *Son of Fatherland*—information which may be gleaned from a close examination of a well-known photograph by Evgeny Khaldey (see Ill. 26). In addition to the journalists, writers, photographers, and documentary filmmakers, visual artists were sent to the scene of the massacre to bear witness. One of them was Fyodor Reshetnikov, whom Selvinsky had known since the *SS Chelyuskin* expedition of 1933-1934. Reshetnikov did sketches of the ditch and the survivors, and he devoted at least one large oil painting to the massacre. Titled "Germans in Kerch (Bagerovo)", it was exhibited at the Tretyakov Gallery in Moscow in 1943. More importantly for the purpose of this investigation, Reshetnikov's study for the painting, "Bagerovo. Fascists in Kerch" (1942), was published in *Forward to Victory!* on the same page as Selvinsky's poems "I Saw It!" and "A Reply to Goebbels." In Reshetnikov's study, the phenotypical features of some of the victims are blurred, while others look distinctly like Russian peasants. In the editor's unsigned introduction accompanying the publication, Jewish victimhood is erased completely, yet all signs point to the Shoah in the occupied territories: "The Bagerovo ditch outside Kerch—the site of torments and the tortuous deaths of 7000 Soviet people. When our people submits its terrifying claim to Germany [...], the Bagerovo ditch will be one of the darkest reminders of the sadistic cruelty and terrifying crimes of the German invaders. [...] Listen, soldiers! The Bagerovo ditch in Kerch—it is everywhere where the German foot trod, in Kharkov, in Odessa, in Rostov and in Pyatigorsk."[242] Selvinsky kept a clipping of this indroduction in his diary.[243]

The poem's four witnesses—all of them Jews—approach the site of the then-recent mass murder:

> Под утро мы увидели долину
> Всю в пестряди какой-то. Это были
> Расползшиеся за ночь мертвецы.
> Я очень бледно это описал
> В стихотворении "Я ЭТО ВИДЕЛ!"

---

242 [Editorial introduction,] *Vpered k pobede!* 31 December 1943.
243 Reshetnikov, "Nemetskie okkupanty v Kerchi. Bagerovo" ; Sel'vinskii, "Ia eto videl!"; "Otvet Gebbel'su," *Vpered k pobede!* 31 December 1942. See also F. Reshetnikov, ed. Vishniakov, 12-14; 18-10; Reshetnikov, F[edor], http://www.maslovka.org/modules.php?name=Content&pa=showpage&pid=72, last accessed 25 December 2011.

> И больше не могу ни слова.
> Керчь...
>
> By sunrise we had come upon a valley
> All covered in some dappled cotton fabric. Those were
> The dead who had crawled out during the night.
> I have described this very hazily
> In the poem "I SAW IT"
> And I cannot add even a single word.
> Kerch....

I am especially intrigued by the line "I have described this very hazily" ("Я очень бледно это описал"). Selvinsky's "bledno" simultaneously suggests a lack of color, detail, precision, and specificity. The haziness comes in part from the devastating sight of atrocities, which precludes the witnessing poets—be it Bialik at Kishinev or Selvinsky at Kerch—from finding the right words, any words. However, Selvinsky's self-acknowledged "haziness" also stems from having attempted to straddle the historical truth and the anti-historical official rhetoric and being bewildered by this undertaking.

I find it very moving that Selvinsky admitted already in 1942, and ventured to make the admission broadly public in February 1945, the limitations of "I Saw It!"—his nationally famous poem about the Bagerovo ditch massacre. Such a sentiment concords not only with Selvinsky's stated strong dissatisfaction with the military situation in Crimea but also with his lack of enthusiasm for the works he wrote for and originally published in the army newspapers. Consider Ilya Ehrenburg's recollection in *People, Years, Life*: "Selvinsky was visiting from Kerch. He said: 'The soldiers have learned, the generals haven't,' and told about the panic, the German atrocities—herding into the catacombs first the Jews, then the POWs."[244] Consider also Selvinsky's letter to his wife, dated 20 September 1942:

> Most importantly: I don't want to write anything! [...] A shiver of disgust runs down my back. If sooner or later I

---

[244] Il'ia Erenburg, *Liudi, gody, zhizn'. Vospominaniia v trekh tomakh*, 2: 287 (Moscow: Sovetskii pisatel', 1990); cf. Erenburg, *Liudi, gody, zhizn'. Izdanie v trekh tomakh*, ed. B. Ia. Frezinskii, 2: 347 (Moscow: Tekst, 2005).

sit down to work on manuscripts (I need to eat, don't I!), it won't be before I've written two or three lyrical poems, such poems that not a single s.o.b. ["ni odna sobaka," in the original] would dare publish. [...] While working on this newspaper I've grown dumb and talentless. [...] A newspaper kills a poet. The best of what I've done during the war is either what Berezin [editor] didn't print, or what I had written before him. And, actually, I don't blame him. His superiors are even further removed from poetry than he is.[245]

In "Kerch," Selvinsky offered a less bombastic and more historicist alternative to his achievement in "I Saw It!" A Soviet photographer takes pictures of the massacre and reports (and, under censorial pressure, manipulates) the truth through images. Selvinsky and his literary brethren find themselves at a loss:

Писатель нервничает. Зажигает
Одну, другую спичку, забывая,
Что челюсти его свело от гнева,
А не от ощущенья папиросы.
"Какое зверство!" — говорит писатель,
И эхом отозвался критик: "Зверство".
Их ремесло — язык. Стихия — речь.
Они разворошили весь словарь
И выбрали одно и то же: "Зверство".

The writer seems nervous. He strikes
One match, then another, while forgetting
That his own jaws are clenched with anger—
And not from the sensation of the cigarette.
"What beastliness!" the writer slowly says.
And then the critic echoes: "Beastliness."
Language is their trade. Their element—speech.
They have rummaged through the whole dictionary
To choose the selfsame word: "Beastliness."

---

245 Sel'vinskii, "Ia eto videl (Krymskie stranitsy voennykh dnevnikov)," 84.

CHAPTER ONE

43. Ilya Selvinsky. The North-Caucasus Front. Circa autumn 1942. (Courtesy of Tatyana Selvinskaya)

The word *zverstvo* ("beastliness"; the plural, *zverstva*, usually means "atrocities") does not cut it for Selvinsky.[246] If not beastliness, then what? "Kerch,/You are the mirror, in which the abyss has been reflected" ("Керчь!/ Ты—зеркало, где отразилась бездна"), writes Selvinsky. What common or uncommon words is the poet to choose in order to both witness and describe the "abyss"?

With this question in mind, I would like to jump ahead to the Krasnodar Trial of Nazi collaborators, which Selvinsky attended on 14-18 July 1943, following the liberation of the Kuban region by the Soviet troops. Consider Arad's summary of the Krasnodar Trial: "The eleven defendants were local people who served in SS Sonderkommando 10A [of Einsatzgruppe D]. Complete proceedings of this trial were published in the Soviet press. In the whole trial record, the word 'Jew' was not mentioned. Sonderkommando 10A carried out the murder of thousands of Jews in Krasnodar, some of whom were refugees and evacuees from Ukraine and other places."[247] It was the first such war crimes trial, and Selvinsky devoted to it the poem "Sud v Krasnodare" ("The Trial in Krasnodar"). "The Trial in Krasnodar" was not published until November 1945 (also in the magazine *Banner*[248]); it was subsequently reprinted in only one of Selvinsky's numerous volumes and collections, the 1947 *Crimea, Caucasus, Kuban*. Jewish victimhood was nowhere specified in "Trial in Krasnodar," but in 1945 readers could hear the not-so-distant echoes of Selvinsky's earlier poems about the Bagerovo ditch massacre.

At the heart of the poem lies the testimony against one Ivan Rechkalov, a draft-dodging collaborator who drove a mobile gas van (*dushegubka*, in the Russian). Of particular significance is the conclusion of the poem in which, following the public hanging of the criminals, Selvinsky describes a heated exchange with N.N., presumably

---

246 Goffenshefer, in his article "Bagerovo," used the expression "bloody fascist beast."
247 Arad, "The Holocaust as Reflected in the Soviet Russian Language Newspapers in the Years 1941-1945," 213. On Sonderkommando 10A in Krasnodar, see Angrick, 572-581; 646-649.
248 As Konstantin Simonov revealed in 1971, in September 1945 he served as an outside reader for Selvinsky's "Trial in Krasnodar," and also for poems by Mark Sobol' and Iaroslav Smeliakov, all of which were under submission to *Banner*. Praising the poem and recommending publication, Simonov suggested that Selvinsky cut the scene of the execution of the Nazi collaborators and make other changes. See Simonov, "V kontse voiny", *Den' poezii* 1971 (Moscow: Sovetskii pisatel', 1971), 173-174. A detailed investigation of the archeology of Selvinsky's "Trial in Krasnodar" lies beyond the scope of this book.

a foreign correspondent also attending the Krasnodar Trial. N.N. questions the evidence presented against the accused collaborators. "Do you not feel sorry for them?" N.N. asks Selvinsky, referring to the eleven executed traitors. "No, I don't feel sorry for them," Selvinsky replies. "I don't believe you," the foreigner presses on. "Your answer is nothing more than propaganda." To this the infuriated Selvinsky replies:

> — А вы, коллега, видели в Керчи
> Семь тысяч трупов?
> — Нет, не видел. — Семь.
> Там были дети, женщины, калеки.
> Возможно, ЭТИ их и расстреляли.
> Вот тех мне было жалко […].

(—And you, colleague, have you seen in Kerch/ 7000 corpses?/ —No, I haven't.—7000./ There were children, women, invalids./ Perhaps THESE ones executed them, too./ The ones [murdered] I felt sorry for […].)[249]

"7000 corpses" is, of course, a direct quote from "I Saw It!" where the number of victims was followed by the words "Jews… Slavs…" (or, in alternative versions, "Semites… Slavs…"). This auto-reference was Selvinsky's way of signaling the Jewish losses in the occupied territories while linking them directly to an early trial of Nazi collaborators and to a broader picture of Nazi genocidal crimes in the occupied territories. The foreign correspondent N.N., who previously speculates that "perhaps /the mobile gas van [dushegubka] doesn't even exist," now admits that he can "concede" ("dopuskaiu") that Selvinsky might feel sorry for the 7000 victims of the Bagerovo massacre, yet states that "they are already dead,/ and these one [i.e. the convicted collaborators] are alive. As a Christian,/ I must feel sorry for these ones now." Selvinsky describes feeling an "unimaginable pain." His breathing having stopped for a moment, he says to the foreigner in the poem's finale: "—Leave!/ The 'Christian' [Selvinsky's quota-

---

[249] Il'ia Sel'vinskii, "Sud v Krasnodare," *Znamia* 11 (1945): 25-28; cf. "Sud v Krasnodare," in *Krym Kavkaz Kuban'. Stikhi* 147-155 (Moscow: Sovetskii pisatel', 1947).

tion marks are placed around the word "khristianin"="Christian"] was dumbfounded.—L E A V E!/ Thank god that nobody/ heard this sentence. Your hotel—/ Two blocks and on the right. Go! Now!/ I feel so sorry for your Christ." Selvinsky doubly underscored a Jewish perspective in the finale by referencing the Bagerovo ditch massacre and by showing that the foreign correspondent identifies himself as a "Christian," yet calls for mercy toward the murderers of Jews in the name of the Jew Jesus. Selvinsky thus seeks to compensate for being unable, in keeping with the proceedings of the Krasnodar Trial, to state specifically that the collaborators had participated in the annihilation of the Jewish population—participated as perpetrators in what we now call the Shoah.

Vladislav Gavrilyuk has observed that Crimea "was not only Selvinsky's actual native land, but also his spiritual and poetic native land. Crimea has entered his poetry not merely as a distinct theme [...] but as a reality that determined a way of artistic perception and depiction of the world."[250] During the war, as Selvinsky himself became a principal literary witness to the destruction of the Jewish communities of Crimea, his prewar "Crimean theme" was transformed into a longer text about the Shoah in Crimea. Prior to his troubles and punishment, as early as February 1942, Selvinsky had been contemplating a large epic work about the war, in which the Shoah in Crimea would presumably occupy an important place.[251] On 22 September 1943, Selvinsky wrote in a letter to his wife: "I must absolutely participate in the taking of Crimea. Odessa—well, I guess I could miss it. But Crimea? Simferopol, Eupatoria. Kerch.... This will have to be my epic, *Crimea*. I shall work on it after the war for five, perhaps even seven years."[252] The poet's plans for the epic never materialized.

Witnessing the Shoah in Crimea and composing poems with references to specified Jewish losses pushed Selvinsky to the utmost limits of what a Jewish-Russian poet in Soviet military uniform could

---

250 V. L. Gavriliuk, *Cherty poezii i zhizni Il'i Sel'vinskogo: k 100-letiiu so dnia rozhdeniia* (Simferopol': Krymskaia akademiia gumanitarnykh nauk, 1999), 3-4.
251 See Selvinsky, Wartime Diaries, 1 February 1942.
252 Sel'vinskii, "Na voine. Iz dnevnikov i pisem rodnym," 173; cf. Babenko, *Voina*, 49. See also R. G. Goriunova, "Epopeia v teoreticheskom osmyslenii i tvorcheskoi praktike I. L. Sel'vinskogo," in *Vestnik Krymskikh Chtenii I. L. Sel'vinskogo*, vol. 1, 38 (Simferopol: Krymskii Arkhiv, 2002).

CHAPTER ONE

say or do in the realm of official culture. In this investigation of the price that Jewish-Russian poets paid for bearing poetic witness to the Shoah, I have approached the turning point in Selvinsky's wartime biography. In the late autumn of 1943 Selvinsky was officially summoned to Moscow and brought to appear before the highest party leadership.

CHAPTER TWO

The Price of Bearing Witness to the Shoah

1. Selvinsky's Troubles of 1943-1944

In November 1943 a dramatic rupture occurred in Selvinsky's military service, resulting from his removal from the frontlines and repressions against him. As we reconstruct Selvinsky's troubles of 1943-1944, we should note that until about July 1943, things had been going relatively well in his wartime literary career. In 1941-1943 he devoted many poems, as well as song lyrics and essays, to the fighting in his native Crimea and the heroism of Soviet troops and civilians, and a number of the poems and song lyrics enjoyed mass popularity. Before the calamitous collapse of the Crimean Front, the song "Boevaia Krymskaia" ("The Crimean Battle Song," 1942; lyrics by Selvinsky and music by V. Rodin), briefly enjoyed the status of the front's official song.[1] Three collections of his poetry and his play *General Brusilov* had been published in 1942-1943. In addition to contributing numerous publications in the army newspapers of the Crimean and subsequently North-Caucasus Front, and also to the regional Krasnodar newspaper, Selvinsky was a contributor to national newspapers (*Red Star*, *Komsomolskaya Pravda*) and Moscow literary journals (*October*; *Banner*). Several of his poems and song lyrics became nationally famous.

In the summer of 1942 Selvinsky was granted a leave to recuperate from an injury and complete his work on *General Brusilov*, which drew salient historical parallels between the events of World War I and World War II. Selvinsky spent part of the leave in Chistopol, Tatarstan,

---

[1] See Selvinsky's account of Mekhlis's positive response to the song, Wartime Diaries, 27 April 1942; cf. Babenko, *Voina*, 41-42. Selvinsky also noted that "rumors had reached him that Mekhlis liked the poem 'I Saw It!'" See Selvinsky, Wartime Diaries, 2 February 1942; cf. Babenko, *Voina*, 33.

where his family had been evacuated along with other writers' families and some of the writers who were not at the front. On 13 July 1942, Selvinsky made a presentation at a meeting of the Military Commission of the Union of Soviet Writers and spoke of his Crimean frontline experiences.[2] Vera Inber (1890-1972), Selvinsky's friend and colleague since the 1920s, saw him during a brief visit to Moscow from the besieged Leningrad. In her diary, she wrote on 16 July 1942: "Selvinsky, with a cane, limping, one foot in a jackboot, the other in a night slipper, is grim (after Kerch). He is also on his way to Chistopol [...]."[3] In his first diary entry for 1943, following a long hiatus, Selvinsky summarized events dating from the retreat from Kerch and including the trip from Chistopol via Tashkent and Tbilisi back to the North-Caucasus Front (his newspaper was then based outside Sochi):

> Tbilisi. 22 March 1943. I finished my previous diary in 1942 with the Kerch tragedy. Ten months have gone by since. During this time I have been wounded in the leg, received a cerebral contusion, was sent to hospital No. 502, then to Moscow, was granted 45 days to recover, and finally visited my family in Chistopol. [They] were living with [the family of Leonid Leonov] in a little cottage [...]. I was subsequently struck by the fact that Leonov received the same decoration at the home front that I was given at the war front: Great Patriotic War, First Degree. In Chistopol at the time there lived [Nikolay] Aseev, [Boris] Pasternak, [Mikhail] Isakovsky, [Leonid] Leonov, [Konstantin] Fedin. Initially they stared at me with confusion: there was a man from the frontlines [frontovik], and they had dug in their heels at the home front. [...] Eventually they forgave me my frontline biography, and we lived simply and in a brotherly fashion.[4]

---

2   See Korshunova and Sitkovetskaia, 231-235.
3   Vera Inber, "Pochti tri goda (Leningradskii dnevnik)," in Vera Inber, *Izbrannye proizvedeniia*, 2 vols. (Moscow: Gosudarstvennoe izdatel'stvo khudozhestvennoi literatury, 1954), http://lib.mn/blog/vera_inber/142205.html, last accessed 29 January 2012. See also the entry for 24 July 1942.
4   Selvinsky, Wartime Diaries, 22 March 1943.

44. Ilya Selvinsky (center) with poets Nikolay Aseev and Boris Pasternak, during Selvinsky's leave from the front. Chistopol, Tatarstan. Circa August 1942. (Courtesy of Tatyana Selvinskaya.)

Selvinsky stood apart from some of the leading Soviet writers, who were not serving at the frontlines and thus lacked first-hand knowledge of what they wrote and published about the war.

On 12 May 1942, the day Soviet troops left Kerch for the second time, Selvinsky had composed the first version of the poem "To Russia."[5] In Selvinsky's own words, the poem was composed

> with the "blood of the heart" and the "juice of the nerves." [...] It reached all the fronts and became one of the most popular poems of the war. According to political officers, soldiers carried it on their breasts. It came out at the time of our retreat from the Don to the Volga.

---

5   Selvinsky, Wartime Diaries, 1 October 1943; cf. Babenko, *Voina*, 49.

The country was deeply disheartened—and "To Russia" comforted, cheered up, inspired one's faith in victory. [...] The significance of the poem was underscored by the enemy's assessment: the fascists issued a leaflet devoted to the poem. Well, as to be expected, again: "a Jew passing himself for a Russian patriot," etc. etc. etc.⁶

"To Russia" was originally published in May 1942 in the Krasnodar regional party newspaper. In July and August of 1942 the poem appeared twice in national periodicals, *Red Star* and *October*, thereby gaining a broad audience of soldiers and civilians.⁷ Selvinsky included the poem in two collections, *Ballads and Songs* and *War Lyrics*, both published in 1943 and "signed into print" in January and February 1943, respectively. Along with "I Saw It!," "To Russia" had been praised as one of the poet's greatest wartime works. The latter circumstance is significant to the timing of Selvinsky's troubles, which began to mount in the early summer of 1943.⁸

On its broadly familiar surface, "To Russia" is both an oath of loyalty and a confession of committment to Russia. If scrutinized through the optics of Selvinsky's identities and steeped in the context of the war and the Shoah, "To Russia" reveals a Jew's incessant imperative to vindicate his otherness by pleading passionate love for Russia:

…Опять судьба из боя в бой
Дымком затянется, как тайна.
Но в час большого испытанья
Мне крикнуть хочется: "Я твой!"

Я твой. Я сын твоей любви!
Я голос твоего народа.
Твоя волна в моей крови,
В моих костях — твоя порода!

---

6   Selvinsky, Wartime Diaries, 1 October 1943.
7   "Sel'vinskii, Il'ia L'vovich," in *Russkie sovetskie pisateli. Poety (Sovetskii period). Bibliograficheskii ukazatel'*, vol. 23: 41.
8   Selvinskii, "Rossii" ("Khokhochet, obezumev, kon'!") *Krasnaia zvezda* 15 July 1942; *Oktiabr'* 8 (1942): 81-82; *Komsomol'skaia pravda* 11 July 1943, 3; in Sel'vinskii, *Ballady i pesni*, 10-12; in Sel'vinskii, *Voennaia lirika*, 34-37. I quote from the *Komsomolskaya Pravda* version of the poem, which is the one cited in the 1943 *Izvestia* article against Selvinsky.

> Кровинкой каждою скорбя,
> Оглохший от бомбометанья,
> Люблю тебя! Люблю тебя
> До стона и до бормотанья...

(Once again [my] destiny from battle to battle/ Will be veiled in smoke, like mystery./ But in the hour of the great ordeal/ I want to shout: "I'm yours!"/ I'm yours. I am a son of your love!/ I am a voice of your people./ Your wave is in my blood,/ In my bones is your pedigree [or: breed]!/ Mourning with every little drop of blood,/ Having gone deaf from bombings,/ I love you! Love you/ To groans and to mutterings....)

Selvinsky's choice of words and his diction underscore a deep insecurity about being accepted as a native while being marked as a stranger. Note such expressions as: "I am a son of your love" (as opposed to simply "your son") or "I am a voice of your people" (rather than "I am a voice of my people" or "I am a voice of our people"). Note also the emphasis on the poet's bond with Russia, which is biological while not, strictly speaking, genetic: "Your wave is in my blood,/ In my bones is your pedigree [or: breed]!" Finally, observe the notes of desire in the (Jewish) man's confession of love for Russia. These notes adumbrate the poem's glorification of the beauty of Russia's women and of the brash craft of their love. (The latter, incidentally, is also a theme of Selvinsky's popular songs, such as "A Cossack Joke Song.")

The poet supports his opening confession of love for Russia with three tiers of evidence: his love for Russian nature and landscapes; his love for Russian women; and his love for Russian poetry. The latter is particularly intriguing for two reasons. Selvinsky fashions the Russian poetic tradition as one sustained by authors of non-native-Russian origins (Pushkin a great-grandson of an Abyssinian nobleman or perhaps of an aristocrat from another part of Africa; Pasternak a Jew of both Sephardic and Ashkenazi lineage). And Selvinsky stresses that the Russian poetic tradition transcends that which is "Russian" into that which has "universal" resonance:

Люблю великий русский стих,
Еще не понятый, однако,
И всех учителей своих
От Пушкина до Пастернака.
Для дураков они — руда,
Но умных одаряют вдвое.
Недаром "русское" всегда
Звучало в них как "мировое".

(I love the great Russian verse/ Which is still yet to be understood,/ And all my teachers/ From Pushkin to Pasternak./ To fools they are ore,/ But the smart ones— they doubly endow./ There is a reason why "Russian" always/ Sounds in them like "universal").

Unwittingly or not, Selvinsky might be leaning on Dostoevsky's remarks from his Pushkin speech of May 1880, in which Dostoevsky praised Pushkin's "capacity for universal responsiveness and complete self-transformation into geniuses of strange [foreign; alien] nations" ("sposobnost' vsemirnoi otzyvchivosti i polneishego perevoploshcheniia v genii chuzhikh natsii").[9] Selvinsky's universalist pathos of Russian poetry strikes a chord that rings quite contrary to the official expectations of Russian cultural patriotism (read: chauvinism), the expectations that go along with the overall wartime shift toward a grand-Russian Stalinist imperial culture. Terms such as "universal" were increasingly unwelcome in the Soviet authors' literary vocabulary; it would be only a matter of a few years before the word "cosmopolitan" would become a code word in the official Soviet vilification of the Jewish intelligentsia. This patriotic poem produced by this Soviet poet-soldier and widely disseminated in 1942-1943 yields a potentially liable reading when its trappings are variously examined through the lenses of Jewish history and culture.

In early 1943 Selvinsky's candidacy was submitted to the Committee for Stalin Prizes, having been nominated specifically for "To Russia" and a group of war poems.[10] On 1 March 1943, the final discussion of

---

9   F. M. Dostoevskii, *Polnoe sobranie sochinenii v tridtsati tomakh*, 26: 147 (Leningrad: Nauka, 1972-1990).
10   See Filat'ev, 72-73.

the candidates' nominations took place in the halls of the Moscow Art Theater. Selvinsky's older peer Nikolay Aseev (1889-1963), a major poet in his own right, made this recommendation to the committee:

> It seems to me that over this past year the poet Ilya Selvinsky has been working better than others and more vibrantly than others. His poems "The Kerch Ditch" and "Russia" [Aseev is referring to "I Saw It!" and "To Russia"] are truly the voice of today. [...] He has not retreated amid poetic chaos, has not attempted to alter his voice by adjusting it in haste to an urgent need of somehow expressing current developments. He had been preparing for it throughout his life in poetry and has found inner strength to address the most difficult topics, the most ominous events.[11]

In his high praise, Aseev resorted to deliberate vagueness in characterizing the "topics" and "events" described in Selvinsky's poems—perhaps fearing that specificity might hurt his candidate's chances. A Shoah-informed reading of Selvinsky's "To Russia" may be detected in the comments of the great Jewish actor and director Solomon (Shloyme) Mikhoels (1890-1948), a member of the Stalin prize committee and chairman of the Jewish Anti-Fascist Committee (JAC): "The poem 'To Russia' is monumental poetry, and also the best of what has been said about [our] country. It is striking! I had only heard it once on the radio and already remembered the phrase: 'To kill Russia—it means to take hope away from the World!' [...] I could not tear myself away when I listened, so moving it was. I support Selvinsky's candidacy!"[12] Mikhoels had the poem's finale in mind:

> Какие ж трусы и врали
> О нашей гибели судачат?
> Убить Россию — это значит
> Отнять надежду у Земли.
> Пускай рыданья и гроба

---

11 Quoted in Filat'ev, 73.
12 Quoted in Filat'ev, 73.

Чернят простор моей отчизны —
Бессмертно трепетанье жизни!
Зовуща
      русская
            труба.

(What sort of cowards and liars/ Chatter about our demise?/ To kill Russia—it means to take hope away from the World!/ Even though sobs and coffins/ Blacken the expanses of my fatherland—/ The fluttering of life is undying!/ The Russian trumpet calling.)

When the results were announced, the first-degree Stalin prizes went to the Ukrainian poet Maksym Rylsky (1895-1964) and to Mikhail Isakovsky (1900-1973), a Russian poet in the folk vein and a popular song lyricist; the second-degree Stalin prize was awarded to Margarita Aliger (1915-1992) for her 1942 long poem *Zoya*.[13] The cited poems and song lyrics by the three laureates were both patriotic and uncontroversial in their treatment of the identities of the poets and their subjects —and of the war itself. Additionally, as a token application of the Soviet nationalities' policy to culture, alongside the ethnic Russian Isakovsky the winners were a Ukrainian writing poetry in Ukrainian (Rylsky) and a Jew writing poetry in Russian (Aliger).

The two 1943 winners' writing in the Russian language were most certainly lesser poets than Selvinsky. Selvinsky was gravely disheartened by the results, probably aware of the role Stalin routinely played in cherry-picking the laureates. (In 1942 *The People Are Immortal* by Vasily Grossman had been nominated, but Stalin intervened and blocked Grossman's award; that year Ehrenburg had received the Stalin Prize for *The Fall of Paris*). On 29 January 1943 Selvinsky had sent a letter to the critic Kornely Zelinsky, an old, albeit disloyal, colleague from their days in the Literary Center of Constructivists. Selvinsky characterized what the bestowing of the Stalin Prize would have meant for him: "For me, formerly a disgraced and disfavored person ["opal'nogo cheloveka"], who had been under attack ["kotorogo bili"] for twelve

---

[13] For the complete list of winners of the Stalin prizes in the arts, see "Laureaty stalinskoi premii v oblasti literatury i iskusstva," http://ru.wikipedia.org/wiki/Лауреаты_Сталинской_премии_в_области_литературы_и_искусства, last accessed 1 July 2010.

years, for me this would be a genuine amnesty. This [would amount to] the right to creativity in the full sense of the word."[14]

On 7 June 1943 Selvinsky was in Moscow to report, now for the second time, at a meeting of the Military Commission of the Union of Soviet Writers. Once again he took the opportunity to expound upon one of his favorite questions: how should members of the artistic intelligentsia address the masses? "The front has given me the right to speak at the full height of my own voice with the biggest audience—the people. I did not claim this right immediately," Selvinsky remarked. "I served at the front, wrote some poems, but owing to my chronic malaise as a member of the intelligentsia, I could not speak to the people like a tribune. But the commanders asked me to write the poems 'To the Fighters of the Crimean Front,' 'To the Southern Slavs,' 'A Reply to Goebbels,' and I realized that in the eyes of the front I am a representative of the masses, and I am not only given the right to speak with the millions, but it is expected of me as my duty."[15] Selvinsky's comments alluded to the question of finding the right words, a question he had explored in both "I Saw It!" and "Kerch": "Under those circumstances ordinary language cannot suffice. Here from a thousand words one must chose one. And the fact that this word reaches the hearts of a wide readership speaks to the fact that I must have fulfilled my duty...."[16]

On 11 July 1943, at the height of the Kursk battle and almost a year after the poem's original publication, Selvinsky's "To Russia" was reprinted in *Komsomolskaya Pravda*. Two days later, an article titled "Undiscriminating Editors" appeared in *Izvestia*.[17] On the newspaper page, this unsigned article neighbored shorter and longer news items, also unsigned, mainly war-related news dispatches from London. The article stood out for its disrespectful, disparaging tone:

> I. Selvinsky composed a poem under the pretentious title "To Russia." In 74 lines of this literary potboiler, the author has piled up so much nonsense that the reader just cannot believe his eyes. After opening with the squealing lines [...] and an immodest declaration

---

14 Quoted in Filat'ev, 73.
15 V. Korshunova and M. Sitkovetskaia, 236.
16 V. Korshunova and M. Sitkovetskaia, 236.
17 "Nerazborchivaia redaktsiia," *Izvestia* 13 July 1943, 4; cf. Filat'ev, 76-77.

that none other than he, Selvinsky, is Russia's herald ('I am a voice of your people'), the author proceeds to confess his love for Russia thusly: "I love you! Love you/ To groans and to mutterings...." It does not take much to recognize in the opening lines how pettily and vapidly the author of these vesicles goes on about the Motherland.[18]

This was a devastating critique, not only in the substance of its attack, but in its sheer lack of any professional decorum and respect for an esteemed author. Selvinsky reflected on the *Izvestia* article in long diary entry of 10 October 1943:

> And suddenly—the abusive article [khuliganskaia zametka] in *Izvestia* on 13 July 1943, which almost literally follows the German leaflet [Selvinsky is referring to the antisemitic language of Nazi propaganda aimed at him]. It is curious that this happened over a year after the publication of "To Russia" in *Red Star*. If the poem is a potboiler and vapidness, why was *Izvestia* silent back then? Over the past year the poem had become a Soviet classic. [...]
>
> What happened? What happened? I don't understand anything. [Zoya] Kedrina told me that when this article appeared in [*Izvestia*], this caused such an indignation in literary circles that she could not recall anything like it. [...] Gurgen Boryan [Armenian poet and playwright] dedicated his poem "Stars" to me. In the Armenian edition it appeared with the dedication, and in the Russian—it was removed. A[leksandr] Yashin dedicated a poem to me. At the Molodaya Gvardiya publishing house they removed the dedication and told him in secret that there is an unspoken directive [neglasnoe rasporiazhenie] "not to praise Selvinsky's name." What happened?[19]

---

18   "Nerazborchivaia redaktsiia," *Izvestia* 13 July 1943, 4
19   Selvinsky, Wartime Diaries, 1 October 1943; cf. Babenko, *Voina*, 49-50.

The diary of the famous Soviet playwright Vsevolod Vishnevsky (1900-1951), who spent two and a half years in the besieged Leningrad, offers precious insights. Vsevolod Vishnevsky was genuinely fond of Selvinsky and corresponded with him throughout the war. On 29 April 1943 he wrote in his diary about having received a letter from Selvinsky: "He writes with warmth—I value and love Ilya. He is stubborn, valiant. Not one of those hiding behind the frontlines [ne tylovik]!"[20] On 15 July 1943 Vishnevsky reflected in his diary on various materials he read in the newspapers. He noted with horror "nightmarish evidence in the prosecutor's closing statement" at the Krasnodar Trial, at which Selvinsky was actually present as a journalist: "Annihilation of 7000 Soviet citizens, description of their execution in a hermetically sealed mobile van, by exhaust fumes from the diesel engine of a large truck. This *first* open trial related to the fascist leaders and their accomplices is noteworthy." The passage that follows in Vishnevsky's diary concerns Selvinsky: "I am reading central newspapers. In *Izvestia*—a very harsh ['rezkaia'] editorial about Selvinsky's poem 'Russia' [should be: 'To Russia']. This is a heavy blow for Selvinsky, especially in the days of the Great Patriotic War."[21]

During the siege of Leningrad, Vera Inber also stayed in the city, where she wrote her celebrated long poem *The Pulkovo Meridian* (1942). On 17 July 1943, selecting her expressions very carefully yet echoing Vishnevsky's sentiment, Inber wrote to a confidante: "[...] I read the article about Selvinsky in *Izvestia*. Tikhonov [Nikolay Tikhonov] and I

---

20   Vsevolod Vishnevskii, *Sobranie sochinenii v piati tomakh*, ed. P. P. Vershigora et al. (Moscow: Gosudarstvennoe izadatel'tvo khudozhestvennoi literatury, 1954-1961), 4: 177.
21   Vishnevskii, *Sobranie sochinenii* 4: 270; cf. Vishnevskii, V. V., "Dnevniki voennykh let (1943, 1945 gg.)" http://militera.lib.ru/db/vishnevsky_vv/07.html, last accessed 8 July 2010. Later in 1943 Vishnevsky also dispatched a friendly if somewhat cryptic warning to Selvinsky from Moscow, where he arrived from Leningrad on 11 December 1943: "You are being seriously criticized for the poems 'To Russia' and 'To whom Russia sang a lullaby...,' and for other things (some comrade-poets add). I am still not up on the current state of affairs in poetry"; see Vishnevsky, letter to Selvinsky, 17 December 1943 in Vishnevskii, *Sobranie sochinenii* 6: 561-562. Filat'ev (79) quotes from what appears to be the complete text of the same letter without giving its source; he suggests that Vishnevsky's letter had not reached Selvinsky in time. Both the editors of vol. 6 (additional) of Vishnevsky's *Works* and Filat'ev date the letter 17 December 1943. Vishnevsky opens the letter by indicating that he was writing it at Selvinsky's Moscow apartment during a visit with Selvinsky's wife and daughters. At the same time, on 18 December 1943, the following day, Vishnevsky notes in his diary: "We had dinner at the Selvinskys'. Ilya tells about the Kerch Landing Operation, the [Adzhimushzkay] catacombs, where in 1942 Soviet divisions perished"; see Vishnevskii, *Sobranie sochinenii* 4: 468. Did Vishnevsky write the letter while visiting Selvinsky and hand it to Selvinsky, so as to avoid a public conversation?

are completely dumbfounded and suspect some 'hidden mechanism,' of which we cannot be aware. What happened? [...] In any case, this painfully resonated in my heart. I feel awfully bad for Ilya. No, he must be in some sort of trouble."²²

It is a bit hard to believe that Selvinsky did not see the writing on the wall, but in his diaries and recollections he later claimed that he did not, or at least that he could not have imagined that his published wartime poems could have resulted in such great misfortunes. Selvinsky's wartime papers have preserved a clipping of the *Izvestia* article, but we do not know when Selvinsky got hold of it. According to Eduard Filatiev,

> Selvinsky's principal miscalculation was that in offering to the newspaper [*Komsomolskaya Pravda*] the poem he had written back in May 1942, Selvinsky had not taken into account how drastically, over the previous year, the situation had changed in the public consciousness of the country. [...] Now after the word "Motherland" one infallibly pronounced the name of the leader. And now, in the pages of a central newspaper, there appears a poem about the Motherland, in which the author sang everything: forests, rivers, seas, endless expanses [...] but did not ONCE mention the name of the leader! That was much too much! It sounded like a challenge, like a slap on the face. Like spitting [in the face], which cannot be left unanswered.²³

This plausible explanation of a "secret mechanism" behind Selvinsky's vilification in *Izvestia* does not account for one strange circumstance: the very fact of the poem's reprinting in the summer of 1943, in *Komsomolskaya Pravda*. Filatiev hypothesized that "the only person [to have penned the unsigned *Izvestia* article against Selvinsky] could have been Joseph Stalin himself."²⁴ Even though no documentary or archival evidence has been found to support this claim, it does seem likely that the *Izvestia* article articulated official displeasure with Selvinsky at the

---

22   Quoted in Filat'ev, 77.
23   Filat'ev, 77.
24   Filate'v, 78.

top echelon of Stalin's leadership, thus forecasting a nearing disaster.

Yet perhaps the strangest part of the story of Selvinsky's troubles of 1943-1944 has to do with his poem "Kogo baiukala Rossiia..." ("To whom Russia sang a lullaby..."). Written back in January 1943, the poem appeared in the July-August issue of *Banner*.[25] In this issue of the magazine, Selvinsky was in exceptionally strong company. Among its other contributions, it featured prose by Yuri Tynyanov, Vasily Grossman, and Viktor Shklovsky, poetry by Pavel Antokolsky and Konstantin Simonov, and criticism by Lev Ozerov. Someone with an eye for numerical representations of Jews in the pages of Soviet literature may point out that Jewish-Russian authors dominated the issue. Grossman's short story "The Old Teacher" immediately preceded Selvinsky's poem.[26] Grossman was probably the first Jewish-Russian writer of fiction to present to the Soviet reader, in the Russian language, an account of the murder of the entire Jewish population of a town, presumably in eastern Ukraine. Verging on the taboo, Grossman's story sought to open Soviet eyes to the annihilation of Jewish populations in the occupied territories. While Selvinsky's price for writing and publishing about the Shoah by bullet in Crimea had been the partial obfuscation of the fact that the Nazis singled out the Jews for annihilation, Grossman's price was the obfuscation of the extent of Ukrainian collaboration with the Nazis. The neighborhood of Grossman's "The Old Teacher" is of special significance both for the cultural context of Selvinsky's troubles and for the greater context of Soviet Shoah literature.

Not a great poem by the standards of Selvinsky's best wartime verses, "To whom Russia sang a lullaby..." is an oddball of a patriotic text. It is difficult to understand how either Selvinsky or the editors of *Banner* could not have foreseen the consequences of the poem's publication. Rereading it today, one is struck by Selvinsky's avoidance of formulaic Soviet expressions of love for one's country and of official wartime rhetoric on Russia's might and invincibility. Consider the middle part of the poem (stanzas 2-6), which, in late 1943 and early 1944, came up

---

25 Selvinskii, "Kogo baiukala Rossiia...," *Znamia* 7-8 (1943): 111; cf. "Kogo baiukala Rossiia," in Il'ia Sel'vinskii, *Izbrannye proizvedeniia*, ed. I. L. Mikhailov and N. G. Zakharenko, 210-211 (Leningrad: Sovetskii pisatel' [Biblioteka poeta], 1972).

26 About this, see Shrayer, "Bearing Witness: The War, the Shoah and the Legacy of Vasily Grossman." See Vasilii Grossman, "Staryi uchitel'," *Znamia* 7-8 (1943): 95-110; "The Old Teacher," tr. James Loeffler, in *An Anthology of Jewish-Russian Literature*, 2 vols., ed. Maxim D. Shrayer, 1: 542-560.

repeatedly in the official denunciations of Selvinsky. The phrasing and the diction here resist translation:

> Сама, как русская природа,
> Душа народа моего:
> Она пригреет и урода,
> Как птицу выходит его,
>
> Она не выкурит со света,
> Держась за придури свои—
> В ней много воздуха и света
> И много правды и любви.
>
> О Русь! Тебя не старят годы.
> Ты вся—из выси голубой.
> Не потому ли все народы
> Так очарованы тобой.
>
> Но если где какая сила,
> Грозя,
>   бряцая
>   и трубя,
> Моя теплынь, моя Россия,
> Протянет когти на тебя [...].

(Itself like Russian nature/ Is the soul of my people:/ It will shelter even a freak [the Russian "urod," a masculine noun, may be variously translated as a 'ugly person,' 'person with depravity,' or 'freak'],/ It will nurture it [or him: the freak] like a [sick] bird, || It will not erase [one] from the face of the earth/ By holding tight to its crazy ideas—/ There is lots of air and light in it,/ And lots of truth and love. || O Rus'! Years don't age you./ You are all—of the blue vault up on high./ Isn't this why all nations/ Are so enchanted by you? || But if somewhere some force,/ Threatening, brandishing, and trumpeting,/ My warmth, my Russia,/ Were to aim its claws at you [...].")

Filatiev noted that both stylistically and prosodically, "To whom Russia sang a lullaby…" came across as a sequel to Selvinsky's earlier "To Russia."[27] Furthermore, the opening line of the later poem may be read as referring not just to Russia the country but also to Selvinsky's earlier poem: not only Russia the country in general, but Russia the country or territory of his poem (the Russia of Selvinsky's "To Russia"). The poem is suffused with coded meanings, filled with metaphoric and symbolic expressions of what Selvinsky could not have said openly in print. When Selvinsky writes, of the "soul of [his, presumably Russian] people," that "it will not erase [one] from the face of the earth" ("ona ne vykurit so sveta"), might he not be speaking of the Shoah, of the annihilation of the Jews by the Nazis, and of the Russian people's refusal to do the same? The victim of the annihilation is conspicuously missing almost in defiance of Russian grammar, while a literalist interpretation of this line yields an even more provocative reading: the Russian soul will not "smoke" Jews "out of the world," with the verb "vykurivat'/vykurit'," which is habitually used in connection with *smoking* bees out of a hive. Prejudice (read: antisemitic rage), can be gleaned from Selvinsky's colloquial noun "pridur`" ("crazy ideas or behavior"): i.e., the Russian people will not succumb to collective madness. In the poem's context, the enchantment of all "nations" (peoples; ethnic groups) with Russia further brings home the notion of Russia as a place that shelters strangers—and shields Jews from Nazism and the Shoah. The latter message, incidentally, corresponds with the Jewish-and-Soviet thesis of Grossman's "The Old Teacher." There are occasional collaborators and traitors, both Grossman and Selvinsky seemed to be saying, but on the whole the internationalist Soviet people stand united in its fight against Nazism, and squarely deplore anti-Jewish atrocities and antisemitism. As Grossman puts it in the closing sentence of his story, "And it seemed to the people standing in the courtyards that in the dark smoky flame burned all that was wicked, inhuman, and vile with which the Germans polluted human souls."[28]

Note, finally, the deliberate vagueness with which Selvinsky describes the enemy: "But if somewhere some force,/ Threatening, brandishing, and trumpeting,/ My warmth, my Russia,/ Were to aim its claws at you

---

27 Filat'ev, 79.
28 Grossman, "The Old Teacher,' tr. James Loeffler, in Shrayer, *An Anthology of Jewish-Russian Literature*, 1: 560; cf. the Russian original, Vasilii Grossman, "Staryi uchitel," *Znamia* 7-8 (1943): 110.

[...]." Why does not the poet clearly identify this clawing enemy force as the Nazi invaders? In connection with the sprouting antisemitism in the country—notably in the army—one should not rule out the possibility that Selvinsky extends a salient link: from the "crazy ideas" (prejudice) to the "force(s)" threatening Russia both from without and from within as she shields her Jews from annihilation.[29]

Like a classical painter of a battle scene, Selvinsky placed himself on his poem's battlefield. In the seventh stanza, he identifies himself transparently as "Ilya" (of Murom), the legendary warrior of *byliny*, the heroic and epic poems of medieval Rus'. (Selvinsky would later write *Three Bogatyrs*, his version of the Ilya Muromets epic). Clad in a *kol`chuga*, a chain-mail body shirt, Ilya inspires the defenders of Russia to rise against the enemy force. The protector of Russia's expanses and of her lofty ideals is not the country's leader, but Ilya himself. Filatiev believes that Selvinsky was issuing a hidden warning: "I do not wish to identify my Russia with any single [person], and I am always ready to defend it with my poetic chain-mail shirt."[30]

On 28 October 1943, Colonel Dmitri Berezin, editor of *Forward for the Motherland!*, with whom Selvinsky had a difficult relationship, wrote a glowing "military reference letter" for him. Berezin named "I Saw It!" first in a short list of Selvinsky's poems that were best known and most admired "at the front."[31] As he had throughout 1941-1943, Selvinsky again volunteered to be where the military action was. This time he participated in and reported on the Kerch-Eltigen Landing Operation (November-December 1943), whereby Soviet troops initially re-conquered sections of the Kerch peninsula, but were only able to hold on to a beachhead extending south from the coast of the Azov Sea down to the north-east suburbs of Kerch.[32]

---

29 For a comprehensive documentary history of state-sponsored antisemitism in the USSR, see Gennadii Kostyrchenko, ed., *Gosudarstvennyi antisemitizm v SSSR ot nachala do kul'minatsii 1938-1953* (Moscow: Mezhdunarodnyi fond "Demokratiia"; Izdatel'stvo "Materik", 2005). Kostyrchenko does not mention Selvinsky's troubles or include the party resolutions against Selvinsky.
30 Filat'ev, 79.
31 "Voennaia kharakteristina na podpolkovnika poeta Il'iu L'vovicha Sel'vinskogo..." 28 October 1943. Ilya Selvinsky Memorial Museum.
32 See "Kerchensko-El'tigenskaka desantnaia operatsiia," http://ru.wikipedia.org/wiki/Керченско-Эльтигенская_десантная_операция, last accessed 29 January 2012. On 12 November 1943 Selvinsky contributed to *Forward for the Motherland!* an inspirational poem about the nearing takeover of Crimea by the Soviet troops; see Sel'vinskii, "Krym" ["Na karte, vsia poryvaias vpered..."), *Vpered za rodinu!* 12 November 1943. Throughout 1941-1943 Selvinsky contributed to

On or around 26 or 27 November 1943, Selvinsky was officially summoned to Moscow by radiogram.[33] At the time he was with the Soviet troops at Adzhimushkay, north-east of the city of Kerch.[34] It was at Adzhimushkay that Selvinsky apparently composed one of his best known war poems, "Adzhimushkay Quarries," dated 14-26 November 1943 and memorializing the courage and self-sacrifice of the defenders during the second Soviet retreat from the Kerch peninsula.[35] In a long undated section of his wartime diary, Selvinsky reconstructed the events of November-December 1943:

> Selvinsky summoned to Moscow. At night I flew to the mainland and reported to my superiors: summoned by Shcherbakov. Until morning I [stayed up] chatting with Kolosov [the writer Mark Kolosov, also a military journalist]. Mark tried to convince me that I was being included in a delegation that was supposedly going to the US or something of this sort: "You are fighting splendidly, writing so well, and so the government wants to recognize you. What Ehrenburg does in articles, you do in poetry."[36]

Kolosov's speculation hints, perhaps, to the trip to North America undertaken by Mikhoels and the well-known Soviet Yiddish poet Yitsik Fefer (1900-1952). Mikhoels and Fefer went on this fundraising and propaganda trip as representatives of the JAC. Kolosov, who had been at the

---

military newspapers several of such occasional poems. See, for instance, Sel'vinskii, "Na Taman'," *Vpered za rodinu!* 29 September 1943.

33 Ilya Selvinsky, Wartime Diaries, undated long entry, ca. 1943-1944. The last dated entry prior to the long entry describing Selvinsky's trip to Moscow and appearance at the Secretariat of the Central Committee is for 16 November 1943.

34 See, for instance, Selvinsky's letter to Berta Selvinskaya, dated 23 November 1943 and sent from the Adzhimushkay Quarries, in Sel'vinskii, "Ia eto videl (Krymskie stranitsy voennykh dnevnikov), 84-85.

35 In its first publication in *Forward for the Motherland!* the poem is dated 14-26 November 1943; see Sel'vinskii, "Adzhimushkaiskie kamenolomni," *Vpered za rodinu!* 2 December 1943. Yet in *Crimea, Caucasus, Kuban* the poem is dated 2-12 November 1943; see *Krym Kavkaz Kuban'*, 175. The Crimean researcher Raisa Goriunova has elucidated some of the circumstances surrounding the composition of "Adzhimushkay Quarries": Goriunova, "Sel'vinskii o tragedii Adzhimushkaia," paper delivered at 17 Krymskie mezhdunarodnye nauchnye chteniia I. L. Sel'vinskgogo "Tragicheskii opyt Velikoi Otechestvennoi voiny v istoriko-literaturnom osmyslenii," Simferopol, 15 December 2011. For details of Selvinsky's stay in the Adzhimushkay Quarries, see letter to Berta Selvinskaya of 23 November 1943, Voskresenskaya and Goriunova, "Ia eto videl," 84-85.

36 Selvinsky, Wartime Diaries.

front and may not have gotten the details correctly, did not know that Mikhoels and Fefer had already been on the road for six months and were due to return to Moscow in December 1943. However, the very possibility that Selvinsky's writings on the Shoah would make him a likely candidate for inclusion in the activities of the JAC is intriguing, and we also know that a Yiddish translation of Selvinsky's "I Saw It!" by Vladimir Elling (Ofshteyn) had already been commissioned and completed, although it does not appear to have ever been published.[37] I will return to Selvinsky's connection to the JAC in the pages to follow.

In his diary Selvinsky noted that Colonel General Ivan E. Petrov, who commanded the North-Caucasus Front (reconfigured as the Separate Maritime Army in November 1943) and was in charge of the Kerch-Eltigen Landing Operation, took a special interest in him. Selvinsky's superiors assumed that he was to be decorated.[38] "I was sent off to Moscow with fanfare [s pompoi]—a celebratory supper, toast [...]. General Petrov assigned an orderly to accompany me to Moscow."[39] Upon his arrival in Moscow, Selvinsky was initially received by Lieutenant General Nikolai Pupyshev, deputy to the powerful Aleksandr Shcherbakov, then Candidate Member of the Politburo, Secretary of the Central Committee, and First Secretary of the Moscow City Party Committee. Having replaced Mekhlis as head of the army's Main Political Department (PUR), Shcherbakov was the chief of all of the army's political officers and journalists. Selvinsky's diary records the poet's memories of his initial conversation with Pupyshev: "'What sort of things have you been up to?'—'What happened?'—'Did you write [something inappropriate]?'—'I did write. That's what a poet is for, to write.'—'Well now they'll show you poets what's what.'"[40] Pupyshev

---

37 According to Vadim Altskan, among the digital archives of the JAC, one finds very little on Selvinsky. The two principal Selvinsky-related materials apparently surviving in the JAC archives are a draft typescript and corrected typescript of a Yiddish translation of Selvinsky's "I Saw It!" by Vladimir Elling (Ofshteyn) and an essay in Yiddish by I. Borukhovich about Selvinsky's drama in verse *Reading Faust*; see the holdings of the United States Holocaust Museum, USHMM Archives, RG-22-028M, reels 180 and 132. Vadim Altskan, e-mail communication, 6 December 2011. Having done a search of *Eynikayt*, the newspaper of the JAC, Gennady Estraikh has not found any publications of Selvinsky's works in Yiddish, and one can probably assume that the translation of "I Saw It!" was never published in it. Gennady Estraikh, e-mail communication, 25 March 2012.
38 Selvinsky, Wartime Diaries; cf. Babenko, 58; for Selvinsky's recollections of General I. E. Petrov, see Babenko, *Voina*, 57-58; cf. Sel'vinskii, "Ia eto videl (Krymskie stranitsy voennykh dnevnikov)," 82-83. About General Petrov, see "Petrov, Ivan Efimovich," http://ru.wikipedia.org/wiki/Петров,_Иван_Ефимович, last accessed 8 July 2010.
39 Quoted in Babenko, *Voina*, 58.
40 Selvinsky, Wartime Diaries.

and Selvinsky went to see Shcherbakov, who received Selvinsky privately. In his recollections, Selvinsky emphasized that Shcherbakov had known him since 1934, when he "was secretary of the Union of Writers under [Maxim] Gorky" (and oversaw the Union of Writers at the Party's Central Committee) and "trusted" Selvinsky. "But he had superiors who regarded me differently [inache]," Selvinsky noted. Shcherbakov acknowledged Selvinsky's bravery in battle, yet berated him for writing "poorly" and interrogated him about the meaning of a stanza in the poem "To whom Russia sang a lullaby..."[41] Selvinsky was informed that he was to appear at a meeting of the Secretariat of the Party's Central Committee, a meeting which most likely took place on 28 November 1943.[42]

In addition to the surviving drafts and final texts of the party resolutions and internal reports by officials of the party apparatus, our principal source of information about the meeting of the Secretariat at which Selvinsky was interrogated and chastised is a long entry in Selvinsky's diary. There is reason to believe that Selvinsky wrote a summary of being summoned to Moscow and appearing at the Secretariat of the Central Committee only after some time, perhaps as many as 16 months, had elapsed. It is likely that he wrote it in the spring of 1945, when he thought the worst was over. Critics have already pointed out that while Selvinsky got a few details wrong (he erroneously refers to the Secretariat of the Central Committee as the Orgburo), his account is not "self-contradictory" (Mikhail Solomatin's expression). Some imprecision in Selvinsky's account should probably be chalked up to the great shock he had undergone. Selvinsky's account of the meeting of the Secretariat should be read and analyzed in the context both of the drafts and passed resolutions of the Central Committee and of the other relevant official documents of 1943-1944 in which Selvinsky was targeted or implicated. Archival documents published in the post-Soviet period, as well as research by historians of Soviet censorship, have added layers of complexity to the picture of Selvinsky's official troubles.

In some pages of Selvinsky's diary reconstructing the meeting of the

---

41   Selvinsky, Wartime Diaries; cf. Filat'ev who quotes selected passages (79-80).
42   In the collection *"Literaturnyi front"* D. Babichenko quotes G. Aleksandrov's on the report that G. Aleksandrov and colleagues had submitted to G. Malenkov on 26 November 1943: "Archive. The question was discussed at the Secretariat of the Central Committee with comrade Selvinsky summoned [signature illegible]." In Babichenko (104) the date is mistakenly printed as 28 July 1943, probably because the date is not easily decipherable, and "28.XI—43" looks like "28.VII—43."

Secretariat, the tone borders on irony and sarcasm, and in others on hangman's humor:

> The meeting of the Orgburo [should be: Secretariat] to which I was invited was opened by Malenkov [Georgy Malenkov, Secretary of the Central Committee]. At the table: A. A. Andreev [Secretary of the Central Committee and Politburo Member], [Vladimir] Potyomkin [Minister of Education], Shcherbakov, and [others whom I did not know]. Georgy Aleksandrov [then head of the Central Committee's Directorate of Propaganda and Agitation (UPA) and one of the Party's chief ideologists] made a presentation about me. He also started by saying that I fought well, but had been writing poorly. [...] Next to me there was a vacant armchair. At the height of [Aleksandrov's] presentation Sasha [Aleksandr] Fadeev came in—no, more like crawled into the conference room. [...] In general I noticed that Malenkov was completely in charge here—even Shcherbakov was a bit scared of him. [...] Meantime Aleksandrov had come to my main fault: "'Itself like Russian nature/ Is the soul of my people:/ It will shelter even a freak,/ It will nurture it [or him: the freak] like a [sick] bird' [this is the third quatrain of "To whom Russia sang a lullaby..."]." "Who is this freak?" Malenkov asked in a metallic voice. I attempted to explain the meaning of the quatrain, but he interrupted me: "Stop conning us [vy nam baki ne zakolachivaite, a highly colloquial Russian expression]! State directly and frankly, who is the freak? Whom in particular did you have in mind? Name?"—"I meant holy fools [iurodivykh]."—"You're not telling the truth! You knew how to steal, now you should own up to it." And then I realized that here they had Stalin in mind: his face was furrowed with pockmarks, and I had once written about it this way: "Touched with drumbeat, a rough-hewn face" [this is from an early version of *Chelyuskiniana*]. Censorship did not allow this phrase, but reported it through appropriate channels. And now

the author had allegedly gone even further: the Russian people had supposedly sheltered a Georgian freak. [...] I began to press Malenkov for an explanation of what was criminal in this stanza. Malenkov, of course, could not do that. He screamed, pounded his little foot [...]. But despite all that I sensed with some inner sensor that he liked me. Suddenly everything grew silent. From out of nowhere Stalin had somehow appeared in the room [.... H]e approached Malenkov and began to talk with him quietly about something. Insofar as I could judge, they weren't talking about me. Then Stalin moved away from Malenkov, seemingly intent on returning to his quarters, but then he glanced at me: "We should handle this man gently." He spoke with a strong Georgian accent. "Both Trotsky and Bukharin were very fond of him [ego ochen' liubili Trotskii i Bukharin]...." "So this means that you consider me a Trotskyite and a Bukharinite?" I asked. I knew I was drowning. And also Stalin was already on his way. "Comrade Stalin!" I thundered in his direction. "During the struggle against Trotskyism I wasn't a member of the Party and didn't understand anything about politics." Stalin paused and directed his piercing glance at me. Then he approached Malenkov, touched his hand with the rim of his hand and said: "Have a good talk with him: we ought to... save this man [nado... spasti cheloveka]." [...] Stalin disappeared in some invisible door, and everybody followed him with their eyes. Malenkov addressed me again [...]: "You see, how Comrade Stalin appraises [rastsenivaet] you. He considers you a totally insufficiently tempered Leninist"—"Yes, but Comrade Stalin said that I should be saved." This phrase caused such a Homeric laughter that it was now impossible to speak of my "crime" seriously. Taking advantage of the new situation, I addressed the chairman with the following words: "I'm a young Communist, only two years in the Party. Perhaps in this stanza I made some mistake, which I don't sense, but you as old Bolsheviks do. But please allow me to read another poem, which will clearly demonstrate how I see Russia and the Russian people." Shcherbakov and Fadeev, speaking in one voice, started pleading with the chairman to permit me to read my poem. [...] I read 'Russian Infantry' ['Russkaia pekhota,' a poem of 1943, one of Selvinsky's simpler war poems praising the ingenuity and strength of Russian soldiers]. As I read, Aleksandrov voraciously jotted down some observations in his notebook, but when I finished, Malenkov was so ecstatic that Aleksandrov had to "seal his lips." I have always said that bureacratism has its one good side. I returned home completely devastated: I came to the Orgburo [should be: Secretariat] a young person, and I left there a decrepit old man. My Lord! And *these* people are in charge of our culture. At home my wife and daughters surrounded me. I told them everything, except about Stalin's appearance. This I decided to conceal, since they would have been sure to share the episode with their girlfriends [...] and if so much as one sound had turned out to have been slightly distorted—this would have ruined both me and them.[43]

In this long undated entry Selvinsky inserted a horizontal line separating the above text from three additional paragraphs, which he may have added subsequently. The first of them assessed his punishment:

> About three days later they informed me of the punishment: to be dismissed from the army until the end of the war. I must confess that the punishment was prudent and sophisticated: Shcherbakov knew that I loved the war front and could not bear life at the home front, and of course it was none other than *he* who suggested this verdict, reasonably assuming that I would not rejoice at demobilization at the height of the war, but rather would find it painful. This is how it was.[44]

---

43 Selvinsky, Wartime Diaries.
44 Selvinsky, Wartime Diaries. Cf. excerpts in Babenko, *Voina*, 60; Solomatin. About Selvinsky's troubles of 1943 and punitive demobilization, see also Ozerov, "Il'ia Sel'vinskii," 8-9; Reifman.

Flying to Moscow from the Black Sea, Selvinsky could not have known that his lot had already been determined, and up for discussion was only the exact measure of the punishment. We know today that in late November 1943 Georgy Aleksandrov, the chief of Party propaganda, prepared a draft resolution of the Secretariat of the Central Committee.[45] Titled "About Errors in the Literary Works of I. Selvinsky," the draft resolution was typed on the stationery of the Secretariat of the Central Committee and stated:

> The Central Committee of the All-Union Communist Party of Bolsheviks [VKP(b)] notes that in the poems "Russia" [should be: "To Russia"], "To whom Russia sang a lullaby…," and "Episode" ["Epizod"] [46] by I. Selvinsky egregious political errors are contained. In the poem "To whom Russia sang a lullaby…" Selvinsky slanders the Russian people, asserting that, allegedly, the soul of the Russian people possesses some sort of "mad ideas" and shelters freaks. The poetic potboiler "Russia" ["To Russia"] contains nonsensically ludicrous and vapid observations about our motherland ("love you, love you to groans and to mutterings" [quoted imprecisely]. In the outrageously vapid poem "Episode," alien to the spirit of Soviet people, a slanderously perverted portrayal of the war is offered. The Central Committee of the Communist Party believes that only the absence of Selvinsky's awareness of his

---

45 Karel C. Berkhoff calls Aleksandrov "an important exponent of Russian chauvinism." Il'a Altman discusses a note that Aleksandrov submitted on 19 August 1942 to the Secretariat of the Central Committee, in which he argued that "un-Russian people (Jews predominantly)" are in charge of Soviet culture"; see Al'tman, "Glava 7: Vlast', obshchestvo i Kholokost," in Al'tman, *Kholokost i evreiskoe soprotivlenie na okkupirovannoi territorii SSSR* (Moscow: Fond "Kholokost"; Kaleidoskop, 2002), http://jhistory.nfurman.com/shoa/hfond_124.htm, last accessed 14 July 2010. Both Arlen Blium and Heinz-Dietrich Löwe have pointed to Aleksandrov's insistence on undisclosure of the specified Jewish losses and his role in censuring information about the Shoah; see, specifically, Heinz-Dietrich Löwe, "The Holocaust in the Soviet Press," in *"Zerstörer des Schweingens": Formen künstlerischer Erinnerung an die nationalsozialistische Rasse- und Vernichtungskrieg in Osteuropa*, ed. Frank Grüner et al., 40 (Cologne: Böhlau, 2006); Arlen Blium, "Otnoshenie sovetskoi tsenzury (1940-1946) k probleme Kholokosta," *Vestnik evreiskogo universiteta v Moskve* 2 (1995): 160.

46 "Episode" ("Epizod"), Selvinsky's poem of 1943, had apparently been accepted by *October* but banned from publication. It would not appear until the 1964 collection *Lirika*; see Babenko and Gavriliuk, 99-100.

responsibility and his having forgotten his duty before the Soviet people may explain the creation of such political harmful and vapid poems. The Central Committee [...] warns comrade Selvinsky that repeating such errors would place him outside of Soviet literature."[47]

In forwarding the draft resolution to Shcherbakov on 26 November 1942, Aleksandrov attached a cover note indicating that the document had been "prepared at the request of comrade Malenkov. He intended to put the matter on the agenda of the Secretariat." As early as on 1 December 1943, a party official wrote on the draft resolution: "The question has been addressed."[48] By the middle of the war, Georgy Malenkov had emerged as one Stalin's closest associates, and it is conceivable that he was pressing Selvinsky's case on Stalin's own urging.

A comparison of the text of the draft resolution with the published, anonymous attack on Selvinsky in July 1943 in *Izvestia* suggests a common source or even a common authorship, thereby lending credence to the possibility that the reprisal had originated with Stalin or his close associates. The draft resolution shares a number of words and expressions with the *Izvestia* article, including "khalturnoe proizvedenie," as compared to "khalturnoe stikhotvorenie" (potboiling literary work vs. potboiling poem); "vzdor" and "vzdorno," as compared to vzdornye [rassuzhdeniia]" (nonsense and nonsencially ludicrous vs. nonsensically ludicrous [observations]); and "poshlo" as compared to "poshleishem [stikhotvorenii]" (vapidly vs. outrageously vapid [poem]). The *Izvestia* article may have been written not by Stalin, as Filatiev has argued, but by a top official in charge of propaganda or ideology, possibly Aleksandrov. The Secretariat did not fully support Aleksandrov's initiative and opted for a more general resolution, one that would target a broader range of authors.[49] It appears that Selvinsky had an advocate in Aleksandr

---

47 Babichenko, *"Literaturnyi front,"* 81-82; cf. Babenko, Gavriuliuk, 98; cf. Arlen Blium, "Index librorum prohibitorum russkikh pisatelei," Part 4, *NLO* 62 (2003), http://magazines.russ.ru/nlo/2003/62/blum.html, last accessed 6 April 2010. See also Babenko, *Voina*, 5; Filat'ev, 79-81. Herman Ermolaev touches on the episode and the poem in his *Censorship in Soviet Literature, 1917-1991*, 72-74 (Lanham, MD: Rowman & Littlefield, 1997).
48 Babichenko, *"Literaturnyi front,"* 82, n. 3.
49 Babenko and Gavriliuk, 98. Babenko and Gavriliuk quote the text of a long note submitted to G. Malenkov by G. Aleksandrov and his associates and targeting a number of authors, among them Mikhail Zoshchenko, Andrei Platonov, Aleksandr Dovzhenko, and Valentin Kataev. The note

Shcherbakov, at least initially.⁵⁰ The change of course may have reflected internal rivalry and competition among the high Party officials in charge of propaganda and ideology, particularly between Shcherbakov and Aleksandrov.

Following the 28 November 1943 meeting of the Secretariat at which Selvinsky was brought to appear, the Secretariat of the Central Committee passed two resolutions in a row, in both of which Selvinsky was the only poet branded for chastisement, and Mikhail Zoshchenko the only fiction writer. In the resolution dated 2 December 1943 and titled "On the Control over Literary-Artistic Magazines," the Directorate of Propaganda and Agitation (UPA) was reproached for "poorly controlling the content of the magazines, especially the literary-artistic ones": "Only as a result of weak control could such politically harmful and antiartistic works as *Before the Sunrise* [*Pered voskhodom solntsa*] by Zoshchenko or Selvinsky's poem 'To whom Russia sang a lullaby…' have penetrated the pages of the magazines."⁵¹ The resolution assigned control of and responsibility for three leading Moscow monthlies, *Novy Mir*, *Banner*, and *October*, to Aleksandrov and two of his associates from the UPA. In the second resolution, dated 3 December 1943 and titled "On Raising the Responsibility of [Executive] Secretaries of Literary-Artistic Magazines," the following language was adopted: "In the magazine *October* an anti-artistic, vapid tale by Zoshchenko, *Before the Sunrise* [was published]. In *Banner* there appeared Selvinsky's politically harmful poem 'To whom Russia sang a lullaby….'"⁵² The resolution specifically warned the editors—and by implication their editorial boards—of their "personal responsibility" to the Party's Central Committee.

The scope and language of the two resolutions suggests that the Secretariat's intention was to warn the Soviet literary practitioners about deviating in any way from the official rhetoric on the war and military valor. Such a major tightening of the screws already smacked of the ensuing postwar onslaught of cultural reaction and a growing state-

---

opened with a critical discussion of Selvinsky's poems "To whom Russia sang a lullaby…" and "Episode" ("Epizod"); see Babenko and Gavriliuk, 99-100.

50   According to Tatyana Selvinskaya, Shcherbakov liked Selvinsky's poetry and took a special interest in him. Personal Interview, 15 December 2011.
51   Artizov and Naumov, 507. See also Babenko and Gavriliuk, 100; Blium, "Otnoshenie sovetskoi tsenzury (1940-1946) k probleme Kholokosta."
52   Artizov and Naumov, 508. See also Babenko and Gavriliuk, 100; Blium, "Otnoshenie sovetskoi tsenzury (1940-1946) k probleme Kholokosta."

sponsored antisemitism. Selvinsky was the only poet targeted in both resolutions, and as such became a sacrificial lamb of wartime Soviet poetry. Echoes of the attack on Selvinsky were immediately heard in official literary discussions. The label "alien ideology" was being haphazardly affixed to his poetry.[53] It is unknown why the Secretariat of the Central Committee waited until 10 February 1944 to issue a separate, and even more devastating, resolution on Selvinsky, "About I. Selvinsky's Poem 'To whom Russia sang a lullaby....'":

> It is noted that in the poem 'To whom Russia sang a lullaby..." by I. Selvinsky, published in the magazine *Banner* (nos. 7-8 for 1943), egregious political errors are contained. Selvinsky in his poem slanders the Russian people. The appearance of this poem, as well as of the politically harmful works "Russia" ["To Russia"] and "Episode" [which had not actually appeared in print—MDS] attests to serious ideological errors in the poetic work of Selvinsky, inadmissible for a Soviet writer, more so for a writer-member of the [Communist Party]. Comrade Selvinsky shall be relieved of his duties as a military journalist until comrade Selvinsky has proved with his creative work that he is capable of understanding the life and struggle of the Soviet people.[54]

All in all, the 10 February 1944 Selvinsky resolution was the only wartime resolution of the Central Committee to single out and punish one Soviet poet. The tone was much harsher than in the resolutions of 2 December 1943 and 3 December 1943, and the charges much broader.[55]

Selvinsky was stunned and dismayed by this outcome and by the severity of the official reaction to his poems. On 31 October 1944 the People's Commissar (Minister) of State Security, Vsevolod Merkulov, submitted a long report to Andrei Zhdanov, Secretary of the Central Committee and Stalin's key deputy.[56] Merkulov's report, based on surveillance in-

---

53 See Filat'ev, 80.
54 Artizov and Naumov, 510.
55 When discovered, additional archival details will create a more complete picture of Selvinsky's troubles of the autumn of 1943-winter of 1944.
56 "Informatsiia narkoma gosudarstvennoi bezopasnosti SSSR V. N. Merkulova sekretariu TsK

formation gathered by secret informers, was titled "On Writers' Political Moods and Comments" and opened with Selvinsky's name: "According to the agents' report submitted to NKGB (People's Commissariat of State Security), public discussion and criticism of the harmful works by the writers Selvinsky, Aseev, Zoshchenko, Dovzhenko, Chukovsky, and Fedin elicited a harsh [rezkuiu], largely hostile [vrazhdebnuiu] reaction from the aforementioned individuals and broad responses in the literary circles."[57] In the report, presumably gathered over a period of eight to nine months, the informant's summary of Selvinsky's remarks confirms that the poet continued to wonder why his specific poems were targeted: "The poet Selvinsky I. L. in connection with the discussion of his poem 'To whom Russia sang a lullaby...' at the Secretariat of the Central Committee of the VKP(b) stated: 'I had not expected they would summon me to Moscow for a chastisement [dlia prorabotki]. To me the poem "To whom Russia sang a lullaby..." seems to qualify [prokhodiashchee, i.e. is not inappropriate or not unfit] for publication. I had been expecting they would finally praise me, since I had been fighting pretty well. Two decorations in two years, and recommended for a third one. I was summoned to the Central Committee, scolded not too severely, and told that I was a young Communist, [which is] not so bad, I would change my ways. I think that now they will stop chastising me [prorabatyvat'], not immediately, of course, but after a period of time.... I have been terribly out of luck for 15 years now, since *Fur Trade*. One beating after another. I am not hoping for much success. Such must be my literary biography."[58]

I believe that one of the goals of the three Party resolutions (2 and 3 December 1943; 10 February 1944) was to intimidate writers into silence about Nazi crimes against the Jews and about Jewish valor. I agree with Solomatin's observation that as Selvinsky was being officially ostracized, the three poems identified in the party resolutions ("To Russia," "To whom Russia sang a lullaby...," and "Episode") were just the tip of the iceberg. The three poems were, in other words, a pretext for a harsh attack on Selvinsky. They must have been chosen as the easiest targets—as irritants in more obvious ways, which could be publicly articulated.

VKP(b) A. A. Zhdanovu o politicheskikh nastroeniiakh i vyskazyvaniiakh pisatelei," 31 October 1944, in Artizov and Naumov, 522-533; cf. *Rodina* 1 (1992), http://www.hrono.ru/dokum/194_dok/19441031merk.php, last accessed 29 June 2010.

57 Artizov and Naumov, 522.
58 Artizov and Naumov, 526; cf. Babenko and Gavriliuk, 103-104.

And even with the three poems directly implicated in the resolutions, the Stalinist leadership could not have openly attacked Selvinsky's disguised references to Russian antisemitism and the annihilation of Jews in the occupied Soviet territories. Instead, the resolutions resorted to such nonspecific formulations as "slanders the Russian people," "politically harmful works," and "ideological errors." Was the Party leadership prepared to chastise Selvinsky publicly for "I Saw It!"? This poem, with its explicit articulation of Jewish losses, had been reprinted many times in 1942-43 and admired by millions of readers at the war and home fronts. Such a public chastisement of Selvinsky would have amounted to an open admission of a party policy. A denunciation of "I Saw It!," "Kerch," or "A Trial in Krasnodar" in a party resolution would thereby have acknowledged or enunciated an official position on Jewish victimhood.

The beginning of Selvinsky's wartime troubles may be traced to the summer of 1943, when the Soviet troops went on a broad offensive and started to liberate occupied Soviet territories with sizeable prewar Jewish populations, in Ukraine and elsewhere, and came upon ubiquitous evidence of the Shoah. Indeed, the timing of Selvinsky's troubles corresponds with what is believed to have been a final shift in the official, if not publicly enunciated, Soviet attitudes to writing about both specified Jewish losses and Jewish valor. Most researchers indicate that this shift occurred between the Battle of Stalingrad and the Battle of Kursk, i.e. in the winter, spring, and summer of 1943. One of the palpable results of this shift was a systematic substitution of the unspecified "Soviet people" or "civilians" for "Jews."

In *People, Years, Life*, Ehrenburg subtly noted the shift toward Stalinist antisemitism that occurred by the summer of 1943: "I continued to write for *Red Star*, *Pravda*, military papers. However, it was becoming harder to work: something had changed. I felt it in my own case."[59] In the same section of his memoir, Ehrenburg recalled a meeting with Shcherbakov, "long and difficult for both of [them]," in which Shcherbakov asked him to tone down the discussion of Jewish military valor and to "understand the situation, 'what's on the minds of the Russian people.'[...] 'Soldiers want to hear about Suvorov [Aleksandr Suvorov (1729-1800), great Russian military leader], and you quote Heine.'"[60] Ehrenburg recalled

---

59   Erenburg, *Liudi, gody, zhizn'*, 1990, 2: 322; cf. Erenburg, *Liudi, gody, zhizn'*, 2005, 2: 389.
60   Ibid. Note the Heine epigraph in Selvinsky's "I Saw It!"

Selvinsky's troubles specifically in the context of the double silencing of Jewish losses and Jewish heroism and the beginning of a crackdown in the Soviet cultural politics: "Selvinsky wrote a good poem about Russia. He had shown personal bravery, worked for frontline newspapers, but Stalin apparently disliked some lines, and Selvinsky was chastised [...]."[61]

Vera Babenko and Eduard Filatiev, both of them students of Selvinsky's life and legacy, have investigated the poet's wartime biography on the basis of his diaries, letters, and poems, and reflections of his contemporaries. Filatiev has devoted an essay, aptly titled "The Secret of Lieutenant Colonel Selvinsky," to Selvinsky's troubles of 1943-1944, and Mikhail Solomatin subsequently revisited the subject. Filatiev's argument links Selvinsky's troubles to the official disapproval of Selvinsky's poems "To Rusia" ("Rossii," 1942) and "To Whom Russia sang a lullaby..." ("Kogo baiukala Rossiia...," 1943). Filatiev hypothesized that behind Selvinsky's official troubes was Stalin's personal displeasure over an alleged lack of praise of the leader in Selvinsky's poetry. However, as noted previously, in 1941-1942 alone Selvinsky had written and published two separate poems ("Stalin at the Microphone"; "For Motherland, for Stalin") and an article about Stalin ("Stalin's Voice"). While serving at the North-Caucasus Front in 1943, Selvinsky composed the poem "Stalin at the Microphone, 3 June 1941" ("Stalin u mikrofona 3-go iiulia 1941 g."), in whose third stanza he swore loyalty to Stalin on behalf of the fighting troops: "As enemy flocks [the Russian "stai"="flocks" here meaning "squadrons of airplanes"] are in the air./ As thunder has deafened the country—/We are everywhere with you, Stalin,/ With all the strength of our soul!"[62] The poem portrays Stalin standing over the map of the fighting country and aiming his pencil at the areas of enemy formations. There is no known record of the poem's publications in newspapers or magazines; Selvinsky subsequently included it in his 1947 volume *Lyrics and Drama*. In 1942-1943 Selvinsky also placed dithyrambic lines about Stalin in several other poems, among them "Battle for Caucasus" and "Battle at Malgobek."[63] Rather than a lack of Stalinist dithyrambs, I believe that it was Selvinsky's eyewitness imperative to report—and to continue reporting—on the Shoah that had been a major factor behind the punishment.

---

61 Erenburg, *Liudi, gody, zhizn'*, 1990, 2: 322; cf. Erenburg, *Liudi, gody, zhizn'*, 2005, 2: 390-391.
62 Filat'ev, 80-81. Sel'vinskii, "Stalin u mikrofona 3-go iiulia 1941 g.," in Sel'vinskii, *Lirika i drama*, 5-6.
63 Sel'vinskii, "Bitva za Kavkaz," in *Krym Kavkaz Kuban'*, 156-161; "Boi pod Mal'gobekom," in *Krym Kavkaz Kuban'*, 89-99.

———————————— CHAPTER TWO ————————————

There are somewhat diverging opinions among students of the Shoah in the USSR about the most accurate way of describing the official Soviet policy or perspective on presenting Jewish losses, as it had taken shape by the summer of 1943. Let us pause for a moment and consider the recent scholarship. Arguing against the notion that concealing Nazi extermination of the Jews on the occupied territories became a "policy," and instead calling it a "tendency that never became entirely consistent," Karel C. Berkhoff suggested that "[t]he scrutiny of reports on Soviet Jews well into 1942 reveals two things: Stalin's initiative, no later than January 1942, for stripping Nazi Germany's Jewish victims of their Jewishness; and a lingering inconsistency in application of this line, even among Soviet leaders."[64] Zvi Gitelman, in a study of "What Soviet People Saw of the Shoah and How It Was Reported," defined his goal as follows: "I seek to deduce Soviet policy from Soviet actions since no one has yet found written Soviet policy directives that would instruct people on how to deal with the mass murder of Jews on Soviet territory."[65] We lack sufficient data to describe the official Soviet instruments of control that were introduced with the purpose of obscuring or silencing the Shoah. In the absence of discovered written policies we must rely both on what we know factually and on what we are able to conjecture. Arlen Blium, a leading student of Jewish questions in Soviet censorship, offered this aphoristic formulation: "As soon as the turning point [was] reached and the Soviet Army [went] on the offensive (1943), then immediately there [was] a change in the general tonality of the publications, and in the attitude of the organs of control to the topic [of the Shoah]."[66] The general policy or tendency to deny the Jewish victims of Nazism their Jewishness was concomitant with a growing trend of downplaying Jewish military valor, downgrading

---

64 Berkhoff, 62; 78.
65 Zvi Gitelman, "What Soviet People Saw of the Shoah and How It Was Reported," US Holocaust Museum, Fellow Seminar, 22 March 2006, modified 11 December 2007, unpublished manuscript.
66 Blium, "Otnoshenie sovetskoi tsenzury...," 159. Note that in his study of the wartime Yiddish press, Dov-Ber Kerler demonstrated that the Soviet Yiddish press, notably the newspaper *Eynikayt* of the JAC, enjoyed a greater degree of openness and specificity in writing about the Shoah. See Dov-Ber Kerler, "The Soviet Yiddish Press: *Eynikayt* during the War, 1942-1945," in *Why Didn't They Shout? American and International Journalism during the Holocaust: A Collection of Papers Originally Presented at an Interdisciplinary Conference Sponsored by the Elia and Diana Zborowski Professorial Chair in Interdisciplinary Holocaust Studies, Yeshiva University, October 1995*, ed. Robert Moses Shapiro, 221-249 (Hoboken, NJ: Yeshiva University Press/Ktav Publishing House, 2003). Kerler's study offers a fascinating correlative to the existing studies of the Shoah in the mainstream Soviet press.

decorations and promotions for Jewish officers, and blocking Jews from high positions of military leadership, including those of senior political officers.[67] Selvinsky's punitive demobilization from the war front invites a comparison with the symbolic dismissal, also in 1943, of Major General David Ortenberg (D. Vadimov) from his influential post as editor-in-chief of *Red Star*. Ortenberg recalled a conversation with Shcherbakov that took place "several months" prior to his dismissal:

> [Shcherbakov] summoned me and said virtually this: "You have too many Jews in your editorial office.... You need to let go of [them; "nado sokratit`"]." These words coming from a Secretary of the Central Committee astonished me. I was literally dumbfounded. And then I replied: "I've already..."—"already what?"—"already let go of [them].... Special correspondents Lapin, Khatsrevin, Rozenfeld, Shuer, Vilkomir, Slutsky, Ish, Bernshtein. Killed at the front. Jews all of them. I can let go of one more—myself.' I said this and left without even saying goodbye.[68]

After Ortenberg's dismissal from *Red Star*, he was sent to the South-Western Front to head the political department of the 6th Army. The Jew Ortenberg was no longer involved in leading the Soviet military's main newspaper—and in shaping Soviet public policy at the national level.

By writing concretely and fiercely about the Nazi atrocities against the Jews, Selvinsky had exposed and publicized the very atrocities that the Soviet leadership was now increasingly reluctant to acknowledge to the public. By the summer of 1943 Selvinsky had amassed a record of

---

67 On the shift that occurred by the summer of 1943 in the official presentation of the Shoah in the Soviet media and in government documents and directives, and also on the rise of antisemitism at the war and home fronts, see Al'tman, "Glava 7: Vlast', obshchestvo i Kholokost," in Al'tman, *Kholokost*, http://jhistory.nfurman.com/shoa/hfond_124.htm, last accessed 14 July 2010; Berkhoff; Gitelman, "Politics and the Historiography of the Holocaust in the Soviet Union," in *Bitter Legacy: Confronting the Holocaust in the USSR*, ed. Zvi Gitelman, 14-42 (Bloomington: Indiana University Press, 1997); Gitelman, "The Soviet Union," in *The World Reacts to the Holocaust*, ed. David Wyman, 295-324 (Baltimore: The Johns Hopkins University Press, 1996); Gitelman, "What Soviet People Saw of the Shoah and How It Was Reported"; Arad, "The Holocaust as Reflected in the Soviet Russian Language Newspapers in the Years 1941-1945"; Löwe.
68 See David Ortenberg, "Vmesto poslesloviia," in *Sorok tretii: rasskaz-khronika* (Moscow: Politizdat, 1991), http://www.victory.mil.ru/lib/books/memo/ortenberg_di3/09.html, last accessed 14 July 2010. See also Ortenberg's letters to Stalin (1949) and Malenkov (1950) in *Gosudarstvennyi antisemitizm v SSSR ot nachala do kul'minatsii 1938-1953*, ed. Gennadii Kostyrchenko, 318-320.

publishing and republishing "I Saw It!" and other Shoah-related poems in army newspapers, regional and national civilian newspapers, literary magazines and anthologies, and also included them in his poetry collections. As his poem "A Trial in Krasnodar" demonstrated, he was prepared to continue in the same vein as a soldier-poet-eyewitness. As discussion of Nazi atrocities against the Jews in the occupied Soviet territories was becoming taboo, Selvinsky appeared undesirable to the interpreters and executioners of Stalin's will. In Ehrenburg and Grossman, the Soviet propaganda machine already had two triple-tuned—Sovietly, Russianly, and Jewishly—witnesses of history with a national reputation. As the tide of the war was turning in the summer of 1943 and the Soviet troops began to liberate large swaths of the previously occupied territories, Selvinsky and fellow Jewish-Russian literary witnesses were likely to have new opportunities to report on the aftermath of the Shoah.

In the autumn of 1943, Selvinsky cut a particularly attractive target for official repression. Then a poet of national fame, a prominent witness to the Nazi atrocities, and a political officer advancing in his military career, Selvinsky had become an ideological liability. An ambitious and outspoken poet and a nonconformist in aesthetic matters, despite his compromistic moments and flights of opportunism Selvinsky was not only suspect but downright unpredictable. In this connection, let us briefly turn to the second half of the surveillance report that Merkulov submitted to Zhdanov on 31 October 1944. Here a state security informant summarizes Selvinsky's thoughts on the "state of Soviet literature":

> Now one can only create by strictly following the commission, and one cannot do anything else.... I do not hope for a particular improvement (in terms of creative freedom) for myself after the war, as I have seen the kinds of people who direct art, and it is clear to me that they can and will only want to direct an art of sheer simplicity.[69]

A decorated military officer much admired by his military commanders and fellow officers, Lieutenant Colonel Selvinsky was thrown out of the army. A famous poet and the author of poems and song lyrics that enjoyed national acclaim, in February 1944 Selvinsky was officially

---

69   Artizov and Naumov, 526; Babenko and Gavriliuk, 104.

declared a person of no status.⁷⁰ Filatiev, who labeled Selvinsky's punitive demobilization the poet's main "secret" (*taina*), characterized Selvinsky's verdict as "unprecedented."⁷¹ Throughout his post-World War II decades, and even after Stalin's death, Selvinsky was publicly reticent about his wartime troubles, even with his family members. Tatyana Selvinskaya told me that her father had never spoken with her about the Party resolutions.⁷²

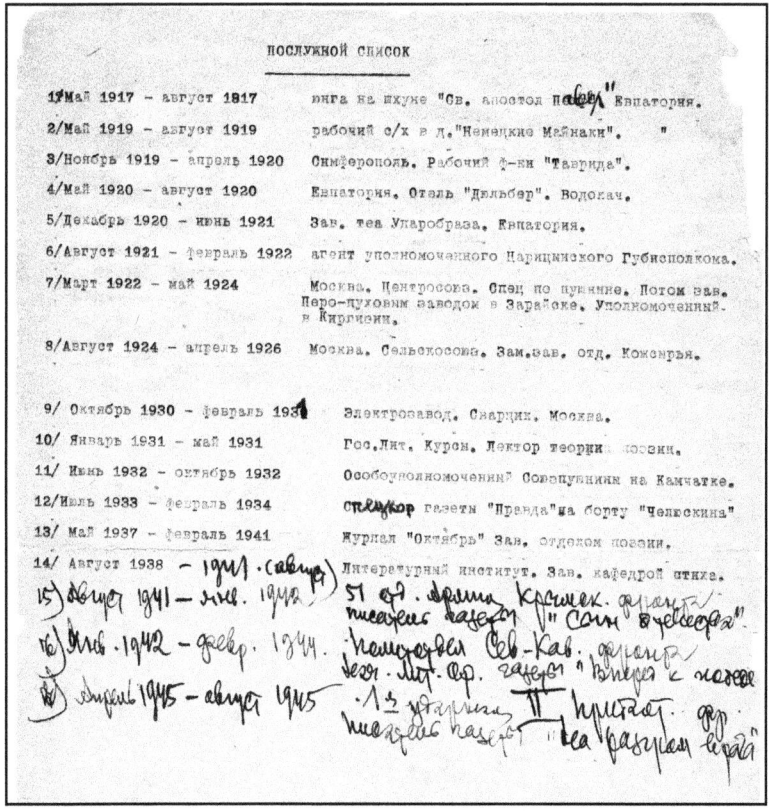

45. Ilya Selvinsky's selected list of work and service experience, 1917-1945, with corrections and the three wartime entries written in by Selvinsky. There is a gap, from February 1944 to April 1945, in Selvinsky's military service. (Courtesy of Ilya Selvinsky Memorial Museum, Simferopol).

---

70 Babenko, *Voina*, 60.
71 Filat'ev, 69.
72 Tatyana Selvinskaya, Personal Interview, 15 December 2011.

CHAPTER TWO

In his résumé, compiled after the end of the war, Selvinsky did not account for the conspicuous gap in his military service between February 1944 and April 1945, whereas his military registration card (*voennyi bilet*), issued 15 November 1948, referred to his position during this period as that of a "reservist."[73]

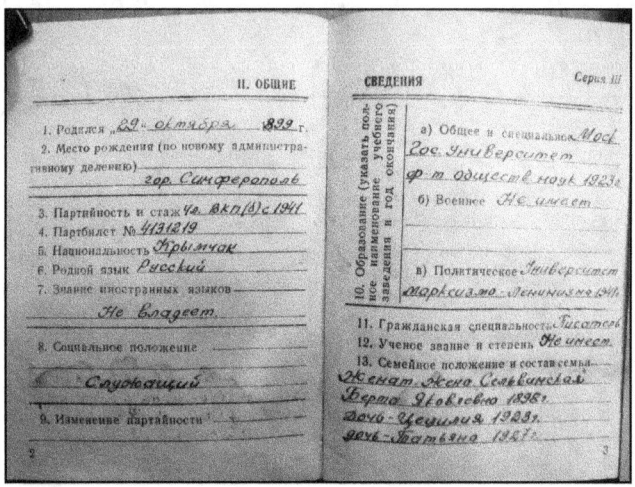

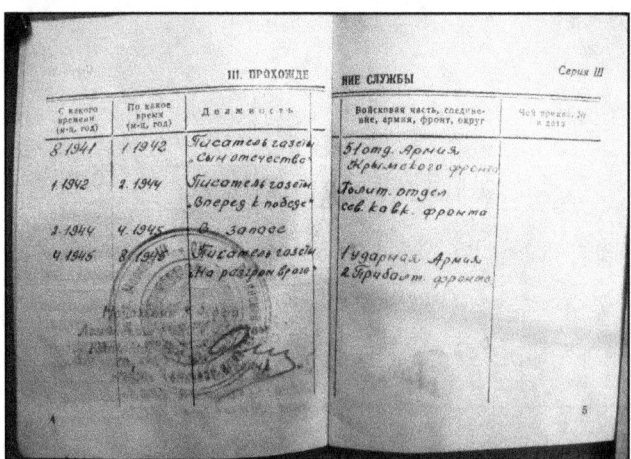

46-47. Pages 2-3 and 4-5 of Ilya Selvinsky's military registration card (*voennyi bilet*), issued on 15 November 1948. Pages 2-3 list Selvinsky's nationality as "Krymchak" and his native language as "Russian." Pages 4-5 refer to the period from February 1944 to April 1945 as being "a reservist." (Courtesy of the Ilya Selvinsky Memorial Museum, Simferopol.)

---

73   Selvinsky's biographer Reznik referred to this conspicuous gap as "being a reservist for a period of time"; see Reznik, 223.

2. In the Moscow Exile

At a time when a return home from the war front promised a respite and a semblance of a peaceful existence, Selvinsky found himself a discharged officer and restless exile to wartime Moscow. Denunciations of the poem "To whom Russia sang a lullaby...," which would not be reprinted until 1971, continued to resonate in the official discussions of 1944-1945.

On 23 February 1944, Dmitry Polikarpov, Aleksandrov's deputy chief at the Directorate of Propaganda and Agitation (UPA), chairman of the State Radio Committee and a senior functionary at the Union of Soviet Writers, reported to Malenkov and Shcherbakov about the recent plenum of the governing body of the Union of Soviet Writers (5-9 February 1944). According to Polikarpov's note, one of the negative features of the plenum was that it did not sufficiently denounce the "slandering moves" by "Selvinsky, [Nikolay] Aseev, [Aleksandr] Dovzhenko [...]."[74] Also of interest is a note that Aleksandrov and his two deputies, Fedoseev and Polikarpov, submitted to Malenkov on 7 August 1944.[75] The note carried an extended negative appraisal of the magazine *Banner* and proposed an overhaul of its editorial board and apparatus. Among other targeted contributors, almost all of whom were Jews, the Party bureaucrats harshly criticized the noted critic Lidia Poliak (1899-1992), author of several prewar textbooks of literature. They attacked an essay by Poliak, "On 'Lyrical Epic' of the Great Patriotic War," published in the double issue of September-October 1943. Polyak had surveyed a broad cross-section of wartime Soviet poetry, saving her highest praise for Antokolsky's long poem *Son*. Selvinsky, whom she criticized for one poem and praised for "I Saw It!," was in no way the main focus of Poliak's essay. "The same article by Poliak praises Selvinsky as a poet who found 'new, but simple, genuine, fullproof words,'"[76] Aleksandrov and his associates commented on the critic's discussion of Selvinsky "I Saw It": "This was written already after the Central Committee condemned both I. Selvinsky's mistakes and those of the editorial board of the magazine, which had published I.

---

74 See Reifman.
75 See "Dokladnaia zapiska upravleniia propagandy i agitatsii TsK VKP(b) sekretariu TsK VKP(b) G. M. Malenkovu o zhurnale 'Znamia,'" 7 August 1944, in Artizov and Naumov, 518-521.
76 Artizov and Naumov, 520; the note quotes L. Poliak, "O 'liricheskom epose' Velikoi Otechestvennoi voiny," *Znamia* 9-10 (1943): 298.

Selvinsky's politically harmful poem 'To whom Russia sang a lullaby...'"[77] The eager authors of the note made an error: Poliak's article had been created and appeared before the resolutions of December 1943 and February 1944 on Selvinsky. The note communicated an expectation that critics would follow the party line by avoiding praise of Selvinsky's work, and a ban on acknowledging Selvinsky's contributions remained in effect throughout the rest of the war.

A retrospective glance at Selvinsky's troubles helps account for the fact that he did not participate in the work of *The Black Book* project, originally led by Ehrenburg and conducted under the aegis of the JAC. Seven reports, testimonies, and essays about the Shoah in Crimea were collected in *The Black Book*, in the section on the Russian Federation. Two Crimea-related contributions were prepared by the Yiddish poet Leib Kvitko (1890-1952), three by the prose writer and scholar Abram Derman (1880-1952), one by Ehrenburg himself, and one by the Russian prose writer and playwright of Tatar origin Lidia Seifullina (1889-1954).[78] Among the Crimea-related materials in *The Black Book* one finds "The Story of Iosif Vaingertner, a Fisherman from Kerch." This account by a survivor of the Bagerovo ditch massacre, prepared for *The Black Book* by Kvitko, partly overlaps with an earlier testimony by the same person, which had appeared in 1943 alongside Selvinsky's "I Saw It!" in the volume *Atrocities of the German Fascists in Kerch*. Furthermore, the circumstances of the fisherman's survival (he fell into the ditch next to his murdered wife) may have been a source for the image of a survivor of the Bagerovo massacre in Selvinsky's "Kerch."[79]

Given his background and wartime experience, and his literary acclaim, Selvinsky would have been a logical choice to work on *The Black Book*'s Crimean materials. Moreover, Ehrenburg and his colleagues engaged a number of Jewish-Russian poets in the project, among them

---

77 Artizov and Naumov, 520.
78 See Ehrenburg and Grossman, eds., *The Complete Black Book of Russian Jewry*, 223-236; 427-430.
79 See "The Story of Iosif Vaingertner, a Fisherman from Kerch," ed. Leib Kvitko, in *The Complete Black Book of Russian Jewry*, ed. Ilya Ehrenburg and Vassily Grossman, [English] tr. and ed. David Patterson, 223-226 (New Brunswick, NJ: Transaction Publishers, 2002); cf. I. Vaingardten, "Nikogda ne zabudu," in *Zverstva nemetskikh fashistov v Krymu*, 45-50. The 1943 volume lists the survivor's name as Vaingardten, not Vaingertner; Vol'fson (35) calls him I. S. Vaingardt, "worker of the fish cannery"; Gubenko (*Kniga pechali*, 23) identifies him as "Iosif Solomonovich Vaingardten." In October 1942 Kvitko had written in Yiddish about the atrocities at Kerch in the newspaper *Eynikayt*.

Pavel Antokolsky, Vera Inber, Lev Ozerov, and Margarita Aliger, and Selvinsky's glaring absence from the list of contributors immediately catches one's eye. Was Selvinsky not asked to participate because of the notoriety he had gained through his official misfortunes? What stood behind Selvinsky's absence from the *The Black Book* project may have had less to do with a degree of dissonance between Selvinsky and Ehrenburg dating to the prewar years[80] and more to do with a reluctance of the literary commission of the JAC to engage Selvinsky after his troubles and dismissal from the army. In the spring 1944, when Crimea was liberated and work on *The Black Book* project was already going at fast clip, Selvinsky's position remained uncertain.

On 2 December 1943, Selvinsky's newspaper printed his poem "Adzhiushkay Quarries" which he had composed just before being summoned to Moscow.[81] Following his last known publication of 1943 (12 December 1943, in the Krasnodar *Bolshevik*, where Selvinsky had regularly contributed poetry), no works by Selvinsky appeared in army or civilian newspapers and magazines for three months during the winter of 1943-1944—compared to the almost weekly rate of Selvinsky's pub-

---

80 According to Boris Frezinsky, Ehrenburg and Selvinsky had known each other since the 1920s, but "never enjoyed any degree of closeness"; see Frezinskii, ed., *Pochta Il'i Erenburga. Ia slyshu vse...*, 215. In his commentary to the 2000 edition of Ehrenburg's poems, Frezinsky analyzes Selvinsky's mixed—and in places harsh—reader's report on the manuscript of Ehrenburg's collection *Vernost'* (*Loyalty*, 1941), which took Ehrenburg to task for an alleged disparity between his public positions as stated in his essays and journalism and his private views as expressed in his poetry; see Erenburg, *Stikhotvoreniia i poemy*, ed. B. Ia. Frezinskii, 720-721(St. Petersburg: Akademicheskii proekt [Novaia biblioteka poeta, Bol'shaia seriia], 2000). Frezinsky did not state whether or not Ehrenburg knew of Selvinsky's report, but implied that he did; see also Aleksandr Rubashkin, *Il'ia Erenburg: put' pisatelia*, 278-280 (Leningrad: Sovetskii pisatel', 1990). Other evidence indicates that Selvinsky did not consider Ehrenburg a master of the poetic craft. See, for instance, Boris Slutsky's recollection of an episode he claims to have witnessed at the Central House of Writers in Moscow, in which Sel'vinskii and Lilia Brik made remarks about the insufficient quality of rhyming in Ehrenburg's collection *Derevo* (*Tree*); Slutskii, *O drugikh i o sebe*, 234 (Moscow: Vagrius, 2005). At the same time, Selvinsky clearly sought contact with Ehrenburg, as may be inferred from the fact that on 20 February 1944, after the 10 February 1944 Party resolution against Selvinsky, he sent Ehrenburg a copy of his *War Lyrics* with the inscription "To dear Ilya Grigorievich with the respect of a colleague and admiration of a frontliner." See B. Frezinsky's commentary in Erenburg, *Liudi, gody, zhizn'* 2005, 2: 555; cf. Frezinskii, ed., *Pochta Il'I Erenburga. Ia slyshu vse...1916-1967*, 215. Also, on 1 May 1944 Selvinsky sent Ehrenburg a congratulatory telegram on the occasion of the award of the Order of Lenin, on 20 June 1945 Selvinsky sought Ehrenburg's assistance in helping the family of a university friend, and on 5 February 1949 Selvinsky sent Ehrenburg a telegram expressing support. See Frezinskii, ed., *Pochta Il'I Erenburga. Ia slyshu vse...1916-1967*, 152; 215; 247-248.

81 Sel'vinskii, "Adzhimushkaiskie kamenolomni," *Vpered za rodinu!* 2 December 1943.

lications in the preceding 2.5 years of the war.[82] It is, of course, possible that one or two poems may have slipped through the censorial cracks and appeared in the army press. Bibliographers have identified a total of four publications of Selvinsky's poetry and one of his prose in 1944, of which only two were in national periodicals. One of the remaining three pieces was in a collective volume, and two were in army and navy newspapers. Selvinsky and his family lived on the earnings generated by the continuing production of Selvinsky's play *General Brusilov* in theaters across the country, among them theaters in the liberated Kiev and Lvov, and also in Erevan, Tbilisi, Tashkent, Yaroslavl, Saratov, and Penza, although, apparently, not in Moscow or Leningrad.[83] Selvinsky also worked with poetry students at the Literary Institute, albeit in a more limited capacity than before the war.[84] Tatyana Selvinskaya recalled that there was an unspoken recognition among the intelligentsia that Selvinsky was having a rough time, and friends and colleagues offered support. A student of painting, in late 1943 Selvinskaya resumed taking art lessons with the distinguished painter Robert Falk (1886-1958), who had returned to Moscow from Central Asia. Prior to the war Falk, to whom Selvinsky had personally attached his daughter, had charged them for the lessons. In 1943-1944 Falk, who experienced need himself, refused to charge Selvinsky's daughter. In the eyes of those even vaguely aware of the facts of Selvinsky's fate, the official punishment seemed absolutely incongruous. In 1944-1945 Selvinsky remained, along with Pasternak, one of the heroes of the Soviet artistic intelligentsia, which included a significant proportion of Jews. At the same time, the intelligentsia tended to look down upon Aleksandr Tvardovsky, Konstantin Simonov, and Aleksey Surkov, whose poetry the Stalinist cultural apparatus actively cultivated

---

82   See "Sel'vinskii, Il'ia L'vovich," in *Russkie sovetskie pisateli. Poety (Sovetskii period)*, vol. 23: 43; 51.
83   Tatiana Selvinskaya, Personal Interview, 15 December 2011. In 1943-1944 Selvinsky's *General Brusilov* was staged at least in 8 theaters in the capitals of Soviet republics and in major provincial (oblast) capitals. See "Il'ia L'vovich Sel'vinskii," in *Russkie sovetskie pisateli. Poety (Sovetskii period)*, vol. 23: 163-164. See also Selvinsky, Wartime Diaries, 16 October 1943; cf. Babenko, *Voina*, 50-51.
84   The Literary Institute was on the verge of being closed in the summer of 1944, and it apparently only survived because of K. Simonov's lobbying and Stalin's interference. Among the charges advanced by Central Committee's Directorate of Agitation and Propaganda (UPA) were accusations that a group of "anti-Soviet minded" students based their aesthetic, which was deemed alternative to socialist realism and to the poets whom the regime actively championed, on the aesthetic of Ilya Selvinsky and other former constructivists. See Gennadii Kostyrchenko, *Stalin protiv "kosmopolitov". Vlast' i evreiskaia intelligentsia v SSSR*, 106-108 (Moscow: Rosspen, 2009).

during the war as models of Soviet Russocentric popular art.[85]

Selvinsky's rehabilitation was gradual: he appeared first in a regional navy newspaper *Forpost Baltiki* (*Forepost of the Baltic,* 8 March 1944), and then in the main newspaper of the Soviet air force, *Sokol Rodiny* (*Falcon of the Motherland*, 26 March 1944).[86] It was not until the late summer and autumn of 1944 that his work made it back to print in a national magazine (*October*) and a national newspaper (*Literary Gazette*). The latter two publications are especially significant in light of the December 1943 resolutions of the Central Committee, which emphasized control over literary magazines and targeted Selvinsky. Let us examine both publications with an eye toward Selvinsky's continuing resistance to the silencing of Jewish suffering and Jewish military valor.

To the magazine *October*, Selvinsky contributed "The Ballad of Laar" ("Ballada o Laare").[87] This ballad commemorates Iosif Laar (1905-1943), an ethnic Estonian from the Stavropol region of Russia.[88] On 7 August 1943, in a battle in the Krasnodar Region, Sergeant Laar threw himself at the embrasure of an enemy machine gun. He was posthumously awarded the title of Hero of the Soviet Union. Laar repeated the act of glory which had been propelled into collective Soviet memory by the example of Aleksandr Matrosov, who was reported to have covered a Nazi machine gun with his body on 27 February 1943.[89] Matrosov's act of glory ("podvig Matrosova," as it is still commonly known in Russian), had been previously committed by other Soviet servicemen, including a Jewish soldier, Abram Levin, who perished on 22 February 1942 but

---

85 See, for instance, the recollections of Naum Korzhavin about coming to Moscow in April 1944 and encountering a former acquaintance, now a student at the Literary Institute, who told Korzhavin that in her circle "it was accepted to love Pasternak and Selvinsky, and to despise Tvardovsky and Simonov." See Naum Korzhavin, "'Vikhri vrazhdebnye' i inye (Litinstitut v aprele sorok chetvertogo)," *Novyi mir. Iz portfelia redaktsii* 2012, http://magazines.russ.ru/novyi_mi/redkol/kor/mosk402.html, accessed 29 January 2012.

86 See also an article by V. Goffenshefer published in *Son of Fatherland*, commemorating the Bagerovo ditch massacre and describing Selvinsky witnessing the aftermath in January 1944; Goffenshefer, "Ne gasi ego, pamiat'!" *Syn otechestva* 16 March 1944, and an excerpt from "I Saw It!" reprinted in *Son of Fatherland*, probably without Selvinsky's consent, Sel'vinskii, "Tol'ko ognem..." *Syn otechestva* 7 April 1944. Both clippings survived in Selvinsky's wartime diary.

87 Sel'vinskii, "Ballada o Laare," *Bolshevik* [Krasnodar], 31 August 1943; *Oktiabr'* 7-8 (1944): 130. I am quoting from the *October* publication as I have not examined the *Bolshevik* publication *de visu*.

88 See "Laar, Iosif Iosifovich," http://www.warheroes.ru/hero/hero.asp?Hero_id=4002, last accessed 16 July 2010.

89 See, for instance, "Matrosov, Aleksandr Matveevich," http://ru.wikipedia.org/wiki/Матросов,_Александр_Матвеевич, last accessed 16 July 2010; commentary in Sel'vinskii, *Izbrannye proizvedeniia*, 1972, 902.

was not posthumously named Hero of the Soviet Union and remained largely unknown.[90] Selvinsky's wartime papers have preserved a clipping from *Forward for the Motherland!* for 27 October 1943 with an article about three heroic soldiers, one of whom was Laar.[91] Having previously published "The Ballad of Laar" in a Krasnodar-based regional newspaper, Selvinsky now used it as a vehicle for reentering the Soviet literary mainstream. The ballad is structured as a question and answer session with the hero followed by a eulogy. Laar responds to the question "What had you known of life, comrade Laar?" with the words: "I knew the seashore./ I knew the seashore and the screams of loons,/ Which rang with longing./ Of this, from a young age,/ I had been reading books/ (I was not in the country of my forefathers),/ But each of my nerves hummed like metal,/ Hearing the call of the Motherland." When the poet asks Laar, "What did you want from life, Laar?" the hero replies: "I did not want much:/ Only that the young and old/ Would not foreswear their lot,/ That all races and lands/ Would not know need or evil,/ And with them would flourish/ My Estonia!"[92]

In the context of Selvinsky's repressions, several things clamor for attention. The very choice of hero, an ethnic Estonian born and raised in Russia and fighting for her, is remarkable in terms of both the wartime mythology of Soviet brotherhood of nations and the rhetoric of grand-Russian heroism that was being actively encouraged at the time. In Laar's (Selvinsky's) diction, the words "all races and lands" ("vse rasy i vse kraia") sound eerily intentional, as if it is meant to alert the Soviet reader not only to the poison of Nazi racial hatred but also to the hydra of prejudice raising its head at home. Granted, the soldier's double sacrifice for the (Soviet) "motherland" and "[his] Estonia" is supposed to buttress the idea of a Soviet Estonia, and not the Estonia which had been annexed by the USSR in 1940 and then welcomed the Nazis in 1941. Only a few months separated the publication of the poem in *October* in the summer of 1944, from the recapturing of Estonia by Soviet troops in the autumn of 1944. Selvinsky is not innocent of propaganda, but in the same breath,

---

90 See Aleksandr Kats, "Evrei—geroi sovetskogo soziuza i geroi Rossiii," http://politiky.net/content/евреи-герои-советского-союза-и-герои-россии, last accessed 16 July 2010; "Statistika o evreiiakh v sovetskoi armii vo 2MV," http://www.jewniverse.ru/biher/AShulman/30.htm, last accessed 16 July 2010; Mikhail Bronshtein, "A. Matrosov i matrosovtsy," *Zapad Vostok* (2 May 2007), http://www.westeast.us/06/article/641.html, last accessed 16 July 2010.

91 Malin, A. "Nosov, Primak, Laar," *Vpered za rodinu!* 27 October 1943.

92 Sel'vinskii, *Izvrannye proizvedeniia*, 1972, 218-219.

in the same stanzas, he does not fail to register his (unwanted) Jewish perspective. As a member of a minority, as someone not raised "in the country of my forefathers" ("v strane ottsov"), Iosif [Joseph] Laar, whose first name is missing in the text of the poem, stands for the ethnic or religious other—and therefore also for Jewish heroes of the Great Patriotic War. Coupled with his first name, of Hebrew origin, which was also Stalin's first name, the trappings of Laar's biography oddly resemble those Jewish heroes whose valor and sacrifice were being systematically and increasingly silenced.

Selvinsky's second appearance in the national press, following his demobilization and literary quarantine, occurred in December 1944, when he published a tribute to another slain Joseph, this time the Jewish-Russian poet Iosif Utkin (1903-1944). Utkin, whose poems and song lyrics enjoyed wide popularity in the prewar Soviet Union, was best known for *The Tale of Red-Headed Motele, Mr. Inspector, Rabbi Isaiah, and Commissar Blokh*. Set in Kishinev, Bialik's "city of slaughter," and originally published in 1925, Utkin's poem offered one of the most ambitious and politically opportunistic treatments of Jewish topics in Soviet Russian-language poetry of the time. Composed and published during the years of a ferocious battle against Judaism and traditional Jewish life (and a national antireligious campaign), Utkin's *Tale of Red-Headed Motele* was a hit with the Jews of his generation who had made a transition from the Pale to large Russian cities in the late 1910s and early 1920s, receiving higher education, rapidly assimilating, and remaining hopeful about Jewish prospects in the USSR. Utkin volunteered for military duty right after the Nazi invasion and was seriously wounded in the fall of 1941. While returning from Chistopol to the Black Sea coast during the summer of 1942, Selvinsky had seen Utkin in Tashkent, where Utkin had been recuperating after the injury. "In Tashkent I ran into Utkin, who had four fingers of his right hand torn off at the front," Selvinsky noted in his diary.[93] Utkin returned to the army in the summer of 1942 as a frontline correspondent and died in an airplane crash in November 1944. Like many, perhaps the majority, of the Jewish-Russian poets who witnessed the aftermath of the Shoah, Utkin resorted to the nondescript pathos of Soviet patriotism. Following in Selvinsky's footsteps, Utkin

---

93 Selvinsky, Wartime Diaries, 22 March 1943.

titled a short 1942 poem "I Saw It Myself!" ("Ia videl sam!").⁹⁴ In it he spoke of the "beasts" that killed "innocent" little children with bayonets and burned their mothers, but did not even attempt to signal that he was witnessing genocide of Jews.⁹⁵ In the poem "Poplars of Kiev" ("Topolia Kieva," 1943) Utkin called for vengeance on the "executioners," yet said nothing specific about Babi Yar.⁹⁶

In his tribute to Utkin, Selvinsky partly wrote about the death of a colleague, partly about Jewishness as a category in Soviet culture, and partly about himself and other Jewish-Russian poets as soldiers and witnesses. Through resonant references and through silence and omission, Selvinsky also alluded to the destruction and disappearance of the traditional world of Jewish life. This is vintage Selvinsky, who never gave up speaking Jewishly even at the worst of times, and who mixed historical truth and historical fiction as a Soviet literary method and as a Soviet means of survival. A reassessment of Utkin's *The Tale of Red-Headed Motele* offered Selvinsky a chance to remember life in the Pale of Settlement:

> [...] this long poem, playing on Jewish intonations, bravely and fearlessly introduced us to that little world of Jewish small-town daily living ["mirok mestechkovogo byta"] which was considered something utterly antipoetic. We knew this world from the stories of Sholem Aleichem and the canvasses of Marc Chagall. Both the millennial longing of exile which had suffused the heart of the great writer and the Hasidic fantasy ["khasidskaia fantastika"] of the remarkable Parisian painter had lifted this meager theme to the level of high art. Utkin had accomplished the same, but via different means. He was helped by the great internationalism of the revolution. Deeply saturated with the feeling of the peoples' brotherhood, *The Tale of Red-Headed Motele* happily es-

---

94 See Ozerov, *Biografiia stikhotvoreniia*, 47.
95 Iosif Utkin, "Ia videl sam!" *Literatura i iskusstvo* 18 April 1942; Cf. Iosif Utkin, *Stikhotvoreniia i poemy*, ed. A. A. Saakiants, 220 (Leningrad: Sovetskii pisatel', 1966). About Utkin, see Shrayer, "Iosif Utkin," in Shrayer, *An Anthology*, 1: 319-320. In connection with nonspecific responses of many Jewish-Russian poets to the Shoah, consider also the career of Mikhail Svetlov (b. Sheinkman, 1903-1964) and a selection of his wartime poems in Svetlov, *Stikhotvoreniia i poemy*, ed. E. P. Liubareva (Leningrad: Sovetskii pisatel', 1966).
96 Utkin, *Stikhovoreniia i poemy*, 240.

caped the danger of turning its storyline into a "Jewish anecdote."[97]

In keeping with the stock Soviet rhetoric of Jewish revolutionary liberation, which had found expression not only in Utkin's charmingly middlebrow poems but in the poetry of the illustrious Bagritsky, Selvinsky ritually distanced himself from the "little world" of the Pale. In writing in the collective "we," Selvinsky outwardly sought to fashion himself not as a Jew of his generation raised before the 1917 revolutions but as a statistically average Soviet reader who might indeed have learned about Jewish life in the Pale by reading Sholem Aleichem in Russian translation. At the same time, one should observe how in this short paragraph Selvinsky used the word "Jewish" twice while referencing the Jewish exile (in the Russian, "izgnanie" contextually stands for the Hebrew *galut*) and enlisting the word "Hasidic" without any disparaging antireligious commentary. Furthermore, by calling Chagall not a Jewish or Russian artist but a Parisian one, Selvinsky circumvented Chagall's questionable status in the USSR, yet emphasized the unity and continuity of Jewish culture across time and national borders. Finally, the comment about Jewish-themed art deteriorating into a "Jewish anecdote" (or a "Jewish joke") cut both ways. On the one hand, Selvinsky was in effect saying that the ideology of Soviet internationalism showed Utkin and other Soviet Jews of their generation a path from parochial (and supposedly laughable) Jewish national interests to a Soviet construction of identity. On the other hand, through the notion of a Jewish (perhaps anti-Jewish) anecdote or joke Selvinsky could not but allude to the legacy of prejudice, a legacy which had been laced with renewed, virulent antisemitism during the occupation of the former Pale of Settlement by the Nazis and their allies. The topic was, of course, taboo in the Soviet press, and yet the news from the liberated Kiev troubled Selvinsky in Moscow, as it also troubled Ehrenburg, Grossman, and many other Jewish writers and Jewish soldiers.[98]

Selvinsky's memorial essay about Utkin made for a generous tribute, but it was not free of critical comments about the literary quality of Utkin's popular poems. The essay culminated in the discussion of Utkin

---

97 Sel'vinskii, "Poeziia Iosifa Utkina," *Literaturnaia gazeta* 2 December 1944, 4.
98 For an assessment, with a particular focus on Kiev, see Victoria Khiterer, "We Did Not Recognize Our Country: The Rise of Anti-Semitism in Ukraine before and after World War II (1937-1947)," forthcoming in *Polin: Studies in Polish Jewry*, 26.

as a poet-soldier: "Utkin entered a new, mature period of his creative work, and his participation in World War II played a huge role in this process [of transformation]." Here Selvinsky spoke of his own career as much as he memorialized Utkin, and in doing so he deliberately referenced "I Saw It!"—his most famous wartime poem. He did it not only by leaning on his own rhetoric in "I Saw It!" in order to express the collective desire of "poets, artists, musicians" that art be "materialized in metal": "So that it would be able to destroy! To blow up! Like a trumpet, to raise armies to attack!" Selvinsky also alluded to himself through a summary of Utkin's wartime career: "At the front Iosif Utkin wrote marching and glorifying songs, went on long treks with the Red Army soldiers, participated in battles alongside them. His poems call for vengeance ('On the Dnieper'; 'Oath'), sear a brand of infamy on the fascist army of murderers ["kleimiat pozorom fashistskuiu armiiu ubiits"] ('I Saw It Myself!'; 'Listen to Me'; 'I Saw a Murdered Girl') [....]." Here it would be difficult to miss the deliberate reference to Selvinsky's "I Saw It!" in both the characterization of Utkin's poems and the title. Yet, as Selvinsky knew well—and as a reading of Utkin's wartime poetry reveals—Utkin never spoke of Jewish victimhood in specific terms or fashioned himself as a witness to the Shoah. By omission, Selvinsky adroitly made this point.

"[Utkin's] death was accidental and therefore senseless. This death has not completed anything. On the contrary, it interrupted the poet's path at the very time of an upheaval," wrote Selvinsky in the closing paragraph. He concluded the tribute in a way both predictable and rhetorically advantageous for the occasion. Utkin was only forty-two at the time of his death; Selvinsky was forty-five at the time of the writing. The death of a poet, a cardinal motif in Russian poetry since its Golden Age, here reverberated with personal, generational self-reflection by a fellow poet-soldier who had survived in the war because of a combination of bravery and luck, and in part, parodoxically, because of his punitive demobilization and repressions against him. Even after the resolutions of 1943-1944 and throughout his Moscow exile, Selvinsky could not steer clear of controversy as he sought to rehabilitate himself and regain his military rank and position.[99]

---

99 The Crimean scholar Raisa Goriunova used the expression "house arrest" to describe Selvinsky's punishment. See R. G. Goriunova, "Epopeia v teoreticheskom osmyslenii i tvorcheskoi praktike I. L. Sel'vinskogo," in *Vestnik Krymskikh Chtenii I. L. Sel'vinskogo*, vol. 1: 38 (Simferopol: Krymskii Arkhiv, 2002). Tatiana Selvinskaya objects to this formulation as overstated and inaccurate.

3. (Re)reading Stalin

Looking back at his Moscow exile with a mix of self-importance and double irony, Selvinsky thus summarized his life and work during 1944 and early 1945:

> On 28 February 1944 I was demobilized. I completed *The Livonian War*, revised the ending of *Babek* [another epic],[100] practically rewrote the youthful *Lynx*, perfected the collection of war lyrics *Crimea, Caucasus, Kuban*. Lived beside wife and daughters, ate well, enjoyed comfort, went to the theater, in the evenings played "66" in a house robe. Spring came. One could go to the *dacha*, to Peredelkino. Is that a bad life? The government, in the end, treats me well, and how much distress have I caused it. If [Konstantin] Simonov or [Sergei] Mikhalkov had allowed themselves even one hundredth of what I allow myself....[101]

Some time in 1944 Selvinsky composed the poem "Reading Stalin" ("Chitaia Stalina"). He included "Reading Stalin" in the retrospective collection of war lyrics *Crimea, Caucasus, Kuban*, which, as he later reminisced, was approved for publication by Aleksandr Shcherbakov himself during a meeting with Selvinsky in November 1944.[102] (When the collection finally appeared in early 1947, it also included several poems written in the spring of 1945 and Selvinsky's literary translations of poems by frontline comrades.)

Additionally, "Reading Stalin" would be featured in Selvinsky's volume *Lyrics and Drama*, also to be published in 1947. Along with Selvinsky's other Stalinist dithyrambs, it was excluded from all post-Stalinist editions of Selvinsky's works. According to Filatiev, the poet composed "Reading Stalin" in order to earn back his status: "In it was everything that was expected of the poet: the recognition of the leader's primacy in all matters, accomplishments, victories and even in

---

100 See Sel'vinskii, *Babek. Tragediia* (Moscow: Sovetskii pisatel', 1946); *Livonskaia voina. Tragediia.* (Moscow: Iskusstvo, 1946).
101 Selvinsky, Wartime Diaries.
102 Filat'ev, 81.

the private life of every Soviet person."[103]

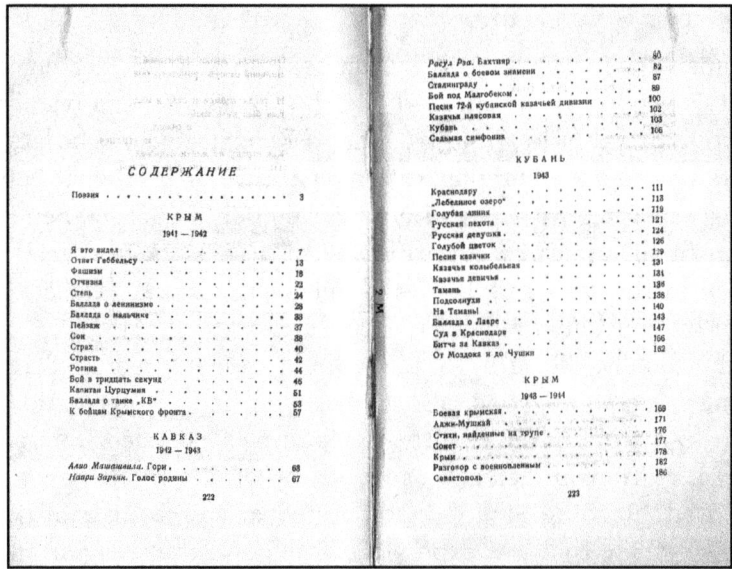

48-49. Title page and first two pages of the table of contents of Ilya Selvinsky's *Crimea, Caucasus, Kuban*. Moscow, 1947.

---

103 Filat'ev, 81.

"Reading Stalin" was not only the longest of Selvinsky's wartime poems about the Soviet dictator, but also the most unabashedly formulaic in its glorification of him, signifying Selvinsky's desperate act of writing his way out of the Moscow exile. No matter how one looks at this spasm of survival, Selvinsky's wartime Stalin poems are an artistic low point and a self-betrayal, especially to a reader steeped in his entire poetic oeuvre. Toward the end of the war the cult of Stalin's personality had reached epic proportions, and one feels from the opening of Selvinsky's dithyramb that its author makes no mistake about it. When Selvinsky praised Stalin, a bit timidly, in the short essay "The Voice of Stalin," printed in the *Literary Gazette* in the early days of the Nazi invasion, he used as an epigraph verses from his own poem "Stalin at the Microphone." In "Reading Stalin" Selvinsky opted for a non-literary epigraph: "Everything will be as Stalin said (from soldiers' conversations)." The epigraph mythologized Stalin as an oracular, visionary leader whose words resonate with providential power. This motif gained momentum in the opening stanza, where Selvinsky, employing the "we" mode, wrote: "Like our own life, we read a collection/ Of your military orders, Stalin."[104] Thence followed a sweeping summary of Nazi conquests and a picture of whole countries disappearing from the map of Europe, a map that kept shrinking until Stalin stood over the frontlines and Stalin's "science of victory" "prophetically pronounced death to fascism" ("gibel' fashizmu proizrekla"). The poem's thesis replicated that of Selvinsky's "Stalin at the Microphone, 3 June 1941" (1943) while multiplying two- or threefold the glorification of the leader in the earlier poem. "Reading Stalin" abounded in the kinds of cultist stock phrases about Stalin as leader and warrior that Soviet readers consumed on a daily basis in wartime newspapers and magazines and also read in Soviet literary works of the day. In the poem, voices of Russia's greatest military leaders, Generalissimo Suvorov and Field Marshal Kutuzov, lined up behind Stalin as he conceived of the victorious plan. (Stalin would be named Generalissumus of the Soviet Union already after the victory over Nazi Germany.) Paraphrasing Selvinsky's dithyramb in translation gives one the impression of something both more embarrassing and less embarrassing than the Russian original

---

104 Sel'vinskii, "Chitaia Stalina," in Sel'vinskii, *Krym, Kavkaz, Kuban'*, 196-200 (Moscow: Sovetskii pisatel', 1947).

CHAPTER TWO

of the poem, from which Selvinsky did not even attempt to weed out blatant clichés ("But Stalin's voice stood over [Hitler's and Mussolini's propaganda]/ Like a mountain range in a spring rain storm"). The adjective "great" ("velikii") and the noun "prophesy" ("prorochestvo") are applied to Stalin and his ideas, while the poem's crowning image features regiments marching "like the mighty thoughts [...] of the leader." In its inferior literary quality, "Reading Stalin" was no match even to some of Selvinsky's previous dithyrambs, in which poetic language and technique still mattered.

Perhaps the only noteworthy aspect of the poem had to do with Selvinsky's choice of historical evidence to support his thesis about Stalin's military genius. Before his narrative of the war approaches the battle of Stalingrad as a turning point, Selvinsky twice refers to Soviet troops retreating from Kerch—that is, for the second time during the war, not in November 1941 but in May 1942. This is the only salient aspect of "Reading Stalin" that calls attention to Selvinsky's destiny and the literary and civic choices he made in 1942-1943 as a Jewish-Russian poet bearing witness to the murder of Jews in Crimea. Selvinsky could not shake the memory of what he had seen at the Bagerovo ditch outside Kerch, and even in this Stalinist dithyramb written on spec he continued to claim the topic of the Shoah in Crimea as his own.

Feeling immensely out of place in Moscow as the war entered its final year and then its final months, Selvinsky petitioned the authorities to allow him to return to the frontlines.[105] In his wartime diary, in the paragraph concluding the long undated summary of his appearance at the Secretariat of the Central Committee in late November 1943, Selvinsky mentions rather casually and in passing that "several months later [sic]" he "wrote a letter to the Central Committee, requesting to be restored in the army [...]. The letter, as I understand, made a very good impression. They quickly recommissioned me, without lowering my rank or taking away my decorations."[106] Selvinsky does not mention "Reading Stalin" in this diary entry. His formal petition to the "Central Committee" was apparently submitted in March 1945, quite a bit longer than "several months" after Selvinsky's return to Moscow in November 1943. In April 1945 Lieutenant Colonel Selvinsky finally put

---

105 See Babenko, 64-65.
106 Selvinsky, Wartime Diaries.

his uniform back on, donning as well a *kubanka*, a Cossack-style round astrakhan hat, which stands out among the regular officers' peaked caps in photographs from April and May of 1945. Had "Reading Stalin" been Selvinsky's ticket out of the cul-de-sac of living as an ostracized poet and punitively dismissed senior officer? The answer should probably be a qualified "yes." While I doubt that the pardoning of Selvinsky hinged solely on this extensive dithyramb, the poem paved the way for the restoration of Selvinsky's rank and position.

In the same long diary entry describing a brief conversation with Stalin at the Secretariat of the Central Committee and ending with Selvinsky's punishment and subsequent restoration, the poet offers a masterful sketch of the Soviet dictator: "The color of Stalin's face is yellow with a patina of greenness. In his speech one hears the sound of an elongated tooth. A smile does not become him: with it his face somehow gloats with malice, robber-like [razboinichim]."[107] These are not words of a slavish Stalinist. Like Selvinsky's other diary entries about Stalin, the comments reflect the poet's being conflicted about Stalin's role in history and about writing poetry devoted to him.

There is a fascinating postscript to this diary entry. Titled "N.B.," this passage speaks directly to Selvinsky's anxiety over Stalin's view of his work, an anxiety here fueled by Selvinsky's perennial distaste for the poetry of Aleksandr Tvardovsky (1910-1971). From the time *Vasily Terkin* (1941-1945) was being published serially—and throughout his postwar decades—Selvinsky regarded Tvardovsky's narrative poem about a soldier's adventures as an example of imitative, cheap, and folkish literature, simple and created for lowbrow consumption.[108] He considered Tvardovsky's verse to be of pedestrian quality, envied Tvardovsky's success, and could not comprehend why Stalin championed it:

> During the meeting with Shcherbakov I actually asked him: "Why is *Vasily Terkin* being so blown out of proportion? Is this not a soldier from 1925, and not [today's]

---

107 Selvinsky, Wartime Diaries.
108 See, for instance, the recollections of David Shrayer-Petrov in "Karaimskie pirozhki," 277; see also Selvinsky's letter to Ehrenburg of 25 November 1956, in which he critiques Tvardovsky and argues that his *Vasily Terkin* never acts like a "Soviet man." See Boris Frezinskii, ed., *Pochta Il'i Erenburga. Ia slyshu vse...1916-1967*, 331-334 (Moscow: Agraf, 2006).

Red Army fighter?" "Comrades Zhdanov and Andreev have both asked Stalin this question," Shcherbakov replied. "Zhdanov even called Terkin a Carpathian soldier. "And what did Stalin reply?" "Stalin replied, as always succinctly and wisely: Now it serves us well. Have we not opened the churches, even though we are atheists?[109]

---

109 Selvinsky, Wartime Diaries.

CHAPTER THREE

The Victory and Beyond

1. *Selvinsky and Jewish-Russian Shoah Poetry in 1944-1945*

The years 1944-1945 are remarkable for our understanding of the history of both Jewish-Russian poetry and Shoah memory in the Soviet Union.¹ Although as early as 1942-1943 Jewish-Russian writers, most explicitly Selvinsky in poetry and Grossman and Ehrenburg in prose, decried atrocities committed against the Jews in the occupied Soviet territories, a new stage in witnessing and documenting the Shoah opened in the summer of 1944, when Soviet troops began to liberate Nazi camps. Just how much of a shock the sight of the Nazi camps must have been to even the best-informed of the writers and journalists can be gleaned from Ehrenburg's panoramic memoir *People, Years, Life*, published mostly in 1960-1965. In the words of Shimon Markish, *People, Years, Life* "had a major role in maintaining and increasing Jewish consciousness, despite all the concessions to the censor, all the subterfuges, ruses, omissions, fictions, and attempts at self-justification of which Ehrenburg has been accused and to which he himself admitted, at least to some degree."² Ehrenburg included an account of visiting the site of the Maly Trostenets (Trostinets) camp in Belarus in July 1944, and this account was not deleted by Soviet censors:

> […] I saw Trostenets. There Hitlerites buried Jews in the ground—Jews of Minsk and Jews brought from Prague,

---

1   About this, see Shrayer, "Jewish-Russian Poets Bearing Witness to the Shoah, 1941-1946: Textual Evidence and Preliminary Conclusions."
2   Shimon Markish, "The Role of Officially Published Russian Literature in the Reawakening of Jewish National Consciousness (1953-1970), in *Jewish Culture and Identity in the Soviet Union*, ed. Yaacov Ro'i and Avi Becker, 222 (New York: New York University Press, 1991).

Vienna. The doomed ones were brought here in mobile gas chambers [...]. I saw charred women's bodies, a little girl, hundreds of corpses. [...] Then I did not yet know about Majdanek, Treblinka, or Auschwitz. I stood there, unable to move [....] It is hard to write about this—no words.³

Seeking and being unable to find words to document the aftermath of the Shoah was a leitmotif in works by writer-witnesses, pointing back to Selvinsky's poems of 1942 about the Bagerovo ditch.

Military journalists and writers traveled with the advancing Soviet troops, first beyond the pre-1941 Soviet borders and then beyond the pre-1939 Soviet borders. In July 1944 the Soviet troops came to Majdanek, which the Nazis had attempted to demolish in haste, leaving the gas chambers standing.⁴ In the summer of 1944 the Soviet troops also came to the *Aktion Reinhard* death camps, Bełżec, Sobibor, and Treblinka, all three of which had been nearly dismantled in 1943. Grossman was with the Soviet troops in August 1944 when they came upon the fields of powdered bones on the site of the Treblinka death camp. In November 1944 Grossman's documentary tale "The Hell of Treblinka" appeared in *Banner*, publicizing the truth about the Nazi genocide of the Jews.⁵ In his article "To Remember!" published in *Pravda* on 17 December 1944, Ehrenburg put forth an accurate number, almost 6 million, for the Jews murdered in the Shoah. He presented the murder of Jews in the occupied Soviet territories and in the death camps in occupied Poland as part of the same genocidal Nazi plan.⁶ In January 1945, with the liberation of Auschwitz-Birkenau, Soviet troops and the writers traveling with them encountered all-encompassing evidence of the Nazi extermination industry and the so-called "Final Solution." After Auschwitz-Birkenau

---

3   Erenburg, *Liudi, gody, zhizn'*, 1990, 2: 337; cf. Erenburg, *Liudi, gody, zhizn'*, 2005, 2: 408; cf. Erenburg, *Liudi, gody, zhizn'*, in Erenburg, *Sobranie sochinenii v deviati tomakh*, 9: 394 (Moscow: Khudozhestvennaia literatura, 1967). In the essay "Enough!" published in *Pravda* in April 1945, Ehrenburg gave a short list of sites of mass executions and death camps whose very names speak louder than commentary: "I do not have the words to remind the world once again of what the Germans have done with my land. Perhaps it would be better to repeat the names alone: Babi Yar, Trostenets, Kerch, Ponary, Bełżec"; Erenburg, "Khvatit!" *Pravda* 9 April 1945.
4   For a brief overview, see "Liberation of Nazi Camps," http://www.ushmm.org/wlc/en/article.php?ModuleId=10005131, last accessed 1 March 2011.
5   Vasilii Grossman, "Treblinskii ad," *Znamia* 11 (1944): 121-144.
6   Il'ia Erenburg, "Pomnit'," *Pravda* 17 December 1944.

came the other death and concentration camps in Poland, the Baltic lands, and Germany.

In 1944-1945 Ilya Ehrenburg, Lev Ozerov, and Pavel Antokolsky wrote their key poems about the Shoah while Selvinsky returned to the cultural mainstream with more poems on the subject. These poems were originally published in 1945-46 in three leading Moscow-based magazines. By the wartime standards—in fact by any standards—their official print runs (circulations) were sizeable: 30,000 for *Novy Mir* in January 1945, when Ehrenburg's cycle of six poems about Babi Yar, memory, loss, and response to catastrophe appeared there; 60,000 for *Banner* in 1945-1946, when Selvinsky's "Kerch" and "The Trial in Krasnodar" and Antokolsky's "Death Camp" and "No Memory Eternal" were published there; 60,000 for *October* in 1946, when Selvinsky's *Kandava* and Ozerov's *Babi Yar* appeared there.[7] Opening the eyes of a huge and diverse audience of Soviet readers, these works owed their publication mainly to the historical context of the war moving beyond the Soviet borders in 1944-45 and the liberation of the Nazi death camps, and, to some extent, to a brief season of cultural liberalization in 1945 and early 1946. The entire publishing window of opportunity lasted from the autumn of 1944 until the late summer of 1946. *Zhdanovshchina*, the onslaught of ideological and cultural reaction so known after the party's secretary for ideology Andrei Zhdanov, began in August 1946, to be followed in 1948 by the onset of the so-called anticosmopolitan campaign. The interlude of publishing about the Shoah came to a halt by 1947, with the steamrolling of the publication of the Ehrenburg-Grossman *Black Book*.

In 1945 the Moscow magazine *Banner* was the principal venue for Selvinsky's poems about the Shoah. In August 1944, after the Central Committee had issued a critical resolution on *Banner*,[8] Vsevolod Vishnevsky, now Moscow-based, was appointed the magazine's editor-in-chief. Vishnevsky had not shunned his friend Selvinsky even after the repressions against him, personally overseeing the publication of

---

7 Il'ia Sel'vinskii, "Kerch'," *Znamia* 2 (1945): 78-79; Pavel Antokol'skii, "Lager' unichtozheniia," *Znamia* 10 (1945): 34; Sel'vinskii, "Sud v Krasnodare," *Znamia* 11 (1945): 25-28; Antokol'skii, "Ne vechnaia pamiat'," *Znamia* 7 (1946): 64-65; Sel'vinskii, *Kandava*, *Oktiabr'* 1-2 (1946): 3-6; Lev Ozerov, *Babii Iar*, *Oktiabr'* 3/4 (1946): 160-163.

8 See Artizov and Naumov, 521.

Selvinsky's "Kerch" in the February 1945 issue of *Banner*.⁹ In the spring of 1945, "Kerch" having just been published in *Banner* and "I Saw It!" still well known and remembered, Selvinsky knew that he held the distinction of being the first Soviet poet to speak in print of the Nazi annihilation of Jews in the occupied Soviet territories. After Kerch, Selvinsky also witnessed the aftermath of atrocities perpetrated by the Nazis and their collaborators around the Krasnodar region.

Crimea was a personal wound for Selvinsky, just as Kiev was a personal wound for both Ehrenburg and Ozerov, and Berdichev a personal wound for Grossman. Kerch continued to lacerate, even as Selvinsky may have tried to close the page on the recent past. What Selvinsky observed on the Kerch peninsula in 1942, and also to some extent in the North Caucasus and Kuban in 1942-43, would continue to inform his poems written in 1944 during the Moscow exile and also those composed at the Baltic fronts during the victorious spring of 1945. Very revealing are the three poems Selvinsky wrote in 1944-1945 to commemorate the liberation of his native Crimea, which the Soviet troops had completed in May 1944.¹⁰

In the poem "Krym" ("Crimea"), written in 1944 but not published until March 1946, when it appeared in *Novy mir* and was also included in *Crimea, Caucasus, Kuban*, Selvinsky placed at least two apparent references to the Jewish and Judaic presence in Crimea. He rendered the sounds eagles make as "Khazarian crowing" ("khazarski[i] kar[k]").¹¹ In conjuring up an image of his Krymchak grandfather, Selvinsky describes him as a devout old man frowning upon leisurely seaside activities and blowing beach sand off the pages of his Tanakh. The Shoah in Crimea enters the text of the poem in one of the final stanzas:

> Крым! Золотой ты мой, задушевный,
>   Наш отвоеванный кровью Крым…
> Что из того, что твои деревни
>   Тлеют пеплом седым?

---

9   See Vishnevsky's diary entry for 13 January 1945; Vishnevskii, *Sobranie sochinenii* 4: 706.
10 See Babenko, 60.
11 Sel'vinskii, "Krym," *Novyi mir* 3 (1946): 42-43.

("Crimea! My golden, cherished one,/ Our Crimea won back with blood,/ What of your villages where/ Gray ashes linger?"

There is something uncharacteristically shifty in the diction of these lines. Was Selvinsky searching for a way of leaving behind his eyewitness memories of the Nazi atrocities as he suggested that the landscape, atmosphere, and lore of ancient Crimea were still there? As I read the poem through the prism of Selvinsky's wartime experience, I imagine the poet choking back unwanted tears: "And if we want happiness really badly/ You and I will go to Crimea!"

The second example is Selvinsky's long poem *Sebastopol*, written in 1944 and published in the double January-February 1946 issue of the journal *Leningrad*, which was soon to be pogromized and closed. Composed in blank iambic pentameter, *Sebastopol* recalled the versification of "Kerch" and anticipated the versification of *Kandava* (1945), Selvinsky's last poetic act of bearing witness to the Shoah. As he marked the liberation of Sebastopol, which the Soviet troops had left in July 1942 after a 250-day siege and retook in May 1944, Selvinsky reminisced about the Civil War and paid tribute to his literary youth, to Constructivism and to Bagritsky, while also mourning the destruction of Jewish life in his native Crimea.[12] A remarkable text for the evocativeness of its descriptions of the Sebastopol of Selvinsky's youth, it made allusions to Selvinsky's punitive stay in Moscow.

Selvinsky opened the poem with a recollection of a double anecdote. Detained, presumably during the Civil War, the nineteen-year-old lyrical hero is kept in a Sebastopol jail. Upon his release from detention, he chances upon a gorgeous young woman who initially takes him for a beggar and offers him money, but then comforts him with tenderness. Selvinsky had been in Sebastopol in October 1941, and he superimposes memories of the visit, which he also describes in his wartime diaries, upon an imagined scene of the city's liberation. Imagined, because the Moscow-exiled Selvinsky then fast-forwards, from the Civil War

---

12 To my knowledge, David Shrayer-Petrov was the first to observe strong parallels between Bagritsky's long poem *Fevral'* (*February*, 1933-34; pub. 1936) and Selvinsky's *Sebastopol*; see Shraer-Petrov, "Karaimskie pirozhki," in *Vodka s pirozhnymi: roman s pisateliami*, 272-282 (St. Petersburg: Akademicheskii proekt, 2007). Written in the 1980s in the United States, the memoir originally appeared in the New York-based magazine *Novyi zhurnal* (*The New Review*) in 1991.

to the spring of 1944, when the Soviet offensive liberated Sebastopol. Wistfully, Selvinsky sees himself entering the city-port, now lying in the ruins. Selvinsky's protagonist recognizes the remains of the city's sites and buildings which he had known in his youth. He also recognizes a raven with blue eyes that used to perch on the window sill of a little house he passed as he roamed around Sebastopol in 1919 upon his release from jail. Is this the raven of E. A. Poe's famous poem, previously domesticated by several Russian-language poets, among them Konstantin Balmont, Vladimir (Ze'ev) Jabotinsky and Valery Bryusov? Selvinsky's raven is said to be a hundred years old, a witness to a bygone era. As Selvinsky's hero envisions himself standing with the victorious Soviet troops in the liberated Sebastopol, he experiences a fusion of the personal and the historical, a fusion which is supposed to communicate a lyrical pathos of patriotism but instead sounds a strained, dispirited note:

> […] И тут я понял,
> Что лирика и родина — одно.
> Ты помнишь, ворон, девушку мою?
> Как я сейчас хотел бы разрыдаться!
> Но это больше невозможно: стар.

([…] And then I understood,/ That lyric and motherland—are the same./ Do you remember, raven, my girl?/ O how I wish I could burst into tears!/ But this is no longer possible: I'm old).[13]

A poem marking the liberation of Sebastopol warranted a dose of victorious Soviet rhetoric, but Selvinsky was unable to muster it. When contrasted with Selvinsky's Stalinist dithyrambs, especially "Reading Stalin," which was also written in 1944, *Sebastopol* ultimately shows that Selvinsky was not capable of marring his good poems, especially

---

13 In the post-1950s editions, including the 1972 Poet's Library volume, Selvinsky restored or added several lines in several places in the poem, including the finale, where after "That lyric and motherland—are the same" and before "Do you remember, raven, my girl?" he placed these lines: "That motherland is also a book,/Which we write for ourselves/ With a cherished light feather [or quill pen] of memories,/ Crossing out prose [meaning both prose as opposed to poetry and prose as the quotidian realm] and wordy places,/ And keeping sun and love" (Sel'vinskii, 1972, 230).

those about his Crimean motherland and about the Shoah, with edgy notes of allegiance.

This finally brings us to the poem "There are regions which centuries cannot stir..." ("Byvaiut kraia, chto nedvizhny vekami..."), which Selvinsky wrote in 1945 but did not publish until 1964. In the extensive Poet's Library edition of 1972, which posthumously incorporated some of Selvinsky's wishes, "Crimea" from 1944 was grouped together with the eponymous poem of 1945 into a two-part cycle, also titled "Crimea." Once again, in trying to gauge the ideological currents of the victorious year 1945, Selvinsky sought, not very successfully, to fabricate a rhetoric that would allow him to move beyond the poems about the Shoah in Crimea.[14] In light of escalating official antisemitism, Selvinsky's poem about the liberated Crimea simultaneously denounces Nazi racial anthropology and pays lip service to the rhetoric of Soviet peoplehood. Selvinsky began with an overview of Crimean premodern history, in which different tribes and civilizations vied for domination of the peninsula. The opening offered but a very pale echo of Selvinsky's summation, in *Bar-Kokhba*, of the various ethnic groups and nations whose soldiers served Rome and came to Judea in order to crush the rebellion, and of some pages of *Fur Trade*. In Selvinsky's presentation Scythians oust Cimmerians; Goths and then Huns pillage the region; Khazars and Tatars hold the steppes while Greeks colonize the coast; and Venetian mercenaries fight Genovese mercenaries. "Customs, gods, wives got mixed,/ nations poured into nations,"[15] wrote Selvinsky. The term "race" ("rasa") enters the poem as Selvinsky speaks of traces of different races in the modern-day inhabitants of Crimea. Here we can see what Selvinsky is after: "Here it's not just a Crimean chronicle,/ Here's its whole soul./ Recognize in the semicircular eyebrows of a Karaite/ A Polovtsian from Sivash,/ Find in the reddish Crimean Jew/ A Goth, who had rotted here,—/ And you will come to understand that which one can in the wisest fasion,/ Term changeability." Of course Selvinsky knew that the Nazis annihilated both Crimea's Ashkenazi Jews and the

---

14 Although in her article "The 'Crimean People' and the 'Crimean Culture' in I. Selvinsky's Perception" A. A. Bachinskaia does not discuss Selvinsky's poems about the Shoah in Crimea, her observations about Selvinsky's view of Crimea's polyethnicity are relevant to the topic. See Bachinskaia "'Krymskii narod' i 'krymskaia kul'tura' v osmyslenii I. Sel'vinskogo," in *I. L. Sel'vinskii i literaturnyi protsess XX veka. V Mezhdunarodnaia nauchnaia konferentsiia, posviashchennaia 100-letiiu I. L. Sel'vinskogo*, 108-11 (Simferopol: Krymskii arkhiv, 2000).

15 Selvinskii, "Byvaiut kraia, chto nedvizhny vekami....," in Selvinskii, 1972, 233-236.

Krymchaks during the occupation, whereas the Crimean Karaites had largely survived. Selvinsky's forced advocacy of a rhetoric of assimilation of different ethnic groups into a *Homo sovieticus* serves to displace the subject of Jewish victimhood during the Shoah. In the context of Selvinsky's record as a literary witness to the destruction of Jewish communities in Crimea, his abstract critique of racial or national exceptionalism sounds barren and unconvincing: "That races will not be able to preserve/ A fence around their heritage./ That even behind its armored arrogance/ A nation is not insular,/ And the destiny of a nation is not in the shape of the nose,/ Not in the curve of the mouth." Selvinsky even slapped on a passage about German communists fighting the Nazis under Soviet banners.

One could, I suppose, offer an apologetic view of the poem by suggesting that Selvinsky exposed the absurdity of Nazi racial anthropology, especially when it was applied to a region such as Crimea where, as Selvinsky sought to argue, so many disparate racial and ethnic features have been enmeshed, preserved, and obliterated. Half-baked renditions of the Soviet rhetoric on nationalities express the poet's desperation: "Let some have slanted eyelids,/ And the others—straight,/ But one affinity has fused forever,/ Their proud souls:/ It [the affinity] gives birth to a new race,/ To the sounds of a wild racist roar,/ We are those who pave with labor a road/ To the world where there will be no slaves." These are lines composed by a Soviet poet in a state of aesthetic and ideological shock, by a Jew trying to put memory away.

As we seek to contextualize Selvinsky's return to print in the late 1944 and 1945 and the restoration of his military rank and status, we should keep in mind that as a poetic witness Selvinsky stood apart from Ehrenburg, Antokolsky, and Ozerov, the other three cardinal Jewish-Russian poetic voices of the Shoah, in three fundamental ways. Selvinsky was among a very small group of Soviet literary professionals—and perhaps the only published poet in this group—to have witnessed the aftermath of the Shoah by bullet in the first months of 1942. In this sense, Selvinsky had "seen it" and described it in verse about two years earlier than did the other Jewish-Russian poets who wrote poems about the Shoah in 1944-1945. At the same time, following the fighting in Kuban and liberation of Krasnodar in 1943, Selvinsky stayed in the Black Sea region until his punitive dismissal from the army. From the late autumn of 1943 up until April of 1945 he was in Moscow and could not be with the troops liberating the occupied Soviet territories; he could not and did not visit the sites of the massacres such as Drobitski Yar in Kharkov and Babi Yar in Kiev. Furthermore, Selvinsky did not have the opportunity to see the Nazi death camps as they were being liberated by Soviet troops in the summer and autumn of 1944 and winter of 1945.

2. Kandava/Kandau

"Well now, once again I am a Red Army officer," Selvinsky wrote on 7 April 1945. "A month ago I submitted a petition to Malenkov about being restored in the army and sent to the front. The Central Committee approved my request and instructed PUR to dispatch me to a military newspaper at one of the active fronts. PUR, acting on this instruction, is sending me [...] to an army newspaper at the only inactive front: the Second Baltic Front (at the Kurland [Courland] peninsula). So it started all over again. Shcherbakov is sick and I have nowhere to turn."[16]

According to the poet's recollections, Selvinsky was not too happy with the assignment and told PUR's chief of staff, Lieutenant General Nikolai Pupyshev, that "at this front I will not see that which is necessary to me as a writer." "You asked to be assigned to the army? [...] So your request has been satisfied. The rest should not be of concern to you," the general replied.[17] Selvinsky wanted to be in Berlin to witness the triumph of the victors. But still, as he noted in the diary, "I am leaving with an easy feeling. The editor [of the army newspaper], whom I already met (he was in Moscow) [...] is a very nice person. Perhaps we won't get into a fight. Besides, sooner or later Shcherbakov will recuperate—I will be able to write him—he will help out."[18] An alcoholic, Shcherbakov would die on the night of 9 May 1945 from a myocardial infarction.[19] Selvinsky was leaving for the front on the wings of the recent success of his historical verse epic *The Livonian War* (pub. 1946), which was enthusiastically received by leading Soviet poets, among them Antokolsky, who was then at the zenith of his official Soviet acclaim.

---

16 Selvinsky, Wartime Diaries, 7 April 1945; cf. Babenko, *Voina*, 65.
17 Babenko, *Voina*, 65.
18 Selvinsky, Wartime Diaries, 7 April 1945.
19 See "Shcherbakov, Aleksandr Sergeevich," http://ru.wikipedia.org/wiki/Щербаков,_Александр_Сергеевич, last accessed 30 January 2011.

CHAPTER THREE

Also on Selvinsky's mind was the recent controversy he had created. In several public literary discussions in the spring of 1945, Selvinsky had suggested that socialist *symbolism*, rather than socialist realism, was a much more suitable method for Soviet art. Selvinsky also spoke of a "crisis in contemporary Soviet dramaturgy."[20] As Selvinsky described it in his wartime dairies, "[Dmitry] Polikarpov raised a scream at a party meeting of the Literary Institute, that I was a revisionist of the Party line in literature." After the Soviet victory over Nazism, on 20 May 1945, Selvinsky would comment on what he saw as the ills of Soviet society and cultural life: "In our public [v nashei obshchestvennosti] I am dismayed by the immobility of error, if this error is made by somebody on instruction from above."[21] Selvinsky used as examples two public ostracisms, one from the 1920s after the publication of *Fur Trade*, another from the spring of 1945: "The same happened with the term 'soc[ialist] symbolism.' At the presidium [of the Union of Soviet Writers] they were trying to prove to me that it was a terrifying lack of literacy [on Selvinsky's part—MDS] from the point of view of politics etc. etc. etc.—and when I pulled out an article printed in *Literary Gazette* on 10 March 1940, where Molotov says, why cannot we do creative work in the mode of soc[ialist] symbolism, nobody dared [to say anything] and they continued to insist on [my] error as though M[olotov] had never said anything [like this]."[22] Even after all the recent troubles Selvinsky could not conform to the official line as he tried again to forecast the winds of cultural politics.

Prompted by thoughts about his new tragedy, *The Livonian War*, and the location of his service, the Baltics, in the spring of 1945, Selvinsky also recorded these painful lines about a poet's immortality and Stalin's role in history:

> A poet's immortality is decided not by the years to come, but by the present time. [...] If my *Livonian War* had appeared already back [when it was set], in the sixteenth

---

20 See the report by Egolin to Malenkov, "Dokladnaia zapiska zamestitelia nachal'nika Upravleniia Propagandy i Agitatsii VKP(b) A. M. Egolina sekretariu TsK VKP(b) G. M. Malenkovu o polozhenii v literature," 3 August 1945, Artizov and Naumov, 534; cf. Babichenko, "*Literaturnyi Front*," 161-162.
21 Selvinsky, Wartime Diaries, 20 May 1945.
22 Selvinsky, Wartime Diaries, 20 May 1945. I was unable to verify the information about Molotov's speech of 1940. Naum Korzhavin comments on Selvinsky's use of "socialist symbolism" in "'Vikhri vrazhdebnye' i inye."

century, it would have become immortal. But of what importance is it today? A creation of crafty hands. Yet nevertheless I am torturously, wildly jealous of the poet who will write about Stalin in 70-100-150 years! What a huge horizon will have opened before him, what depths of ideas, times, evaluations. [...] Since never before in history had there been a greater horror than the Soviet-Fascist war, then the clash of two symbols—light and darkness—STALIN and Hitler. [...] Revealing Stalin's image will help understand the world.[23]

Selvinsky arrived at the front on 15 April 1945. "I was thrown across from the Black Sea to the Baltic Sea [...]. I found myself at the Kurland turf [kurliandskii piatachok]," Selvinsky reminisced in 1967, in a diary entry, "where *real war* was no longer happening."[24] "This is why, despite the fact that [...] by virtue of both my personal biography and the nature of my creativity I was, as it were, made for a war epic, I could give the reader nothing more than frontline lyrics," the poet wrote. "This immediately became clear to me, and with this emotional trauma I arrived at the First Shock Army."[25] Selvinsky remained in the Baltic region until August 1945, when he was demobilized again, this time with an honorable dismissal, and returned to Moscow. In his accounts Selvinsky greatly overstated the "quietness" of the Second Baltic Front, perhaps because his experience in Kurland differed vastly from that of his days of battle in Crimea, North Caucasus, and Kuban.[26] On the Kurland (Courland) peninsula, troops of the First Shock Army blockaded Germany's Army Group 3 (later renamed Army Group Courland).[27] Selvinsky contributed to the newspaper of the First Shock Army *Na razgrom vraga* (*For the Defeat of the Enemy*) and to the newspaper *Suvorovets* (*Suvorovite*) of the Second Baltic Front.[28]

---

23 Selvinsky, Wartime Diaries, April 1945.
24 Quoted in Khelemskii, "Kurliandskaia vesna," 136.
25 Quoted in Khelemskii, "Kurliandskaia vesna," 168.
26 See "Vtoroi Pribaltiiskii front," http://ru.wikipedia.org/wiki/2-й_Прибалтийский_фронт, last accessed 8 March 2011; "1-aia udarnaia armiia," http://ru.wikipedia.org/wiki/1-я_ударная_армия, last accessed 8 March 2011; "Courland Pocket," http://en.wikipedia.org/wiki/Courland_Pocket, last accessed 8 March 2011.
27 See "Pervaia udarnaia armiia," http://ru.wikipedia.org/wiki/1-я_ударная_армия, last accessed 12 March 2011.
28 Khelemskii, "Kurliandskaia vesna," 128.

CHAPTER THREE

50. Ilya Selvinsky (first on left) with Yakov Khelemsky (center), their fellow officers and a driver. 2nd Baltic Front. May 1945. (Courtesy of Tatyana Selvinskaya).

The editorial office of *Suvorovite*, to which Selvinsky was attached with the task of mentoring younger writers working on the newspaper staff, was located in the town of Viekšniai in the northwestern corner of Lithuania near the Latvian border. While stationed in the Baltic region, Selvinsky gave readings from his works before audiences of soldiers and officers, and at least in the army was treated as a living classic of Soviet poetry.[29] The poet Yakov Khelemsky (1914-2003), who got to know Selvinsky during their service at the Second Baltic Front in 1945, reminisced that he and the other military journalists "knew by heart 'I Saw It!,' 'Ballad about Leninism,' and 'Taman.'"[30] On 23 May 1945

---

29 Khelemskii, "Kurliandskaia vesna," 127-128; 134-135.
30 Khelemskii, "Kurliandskaia vesna," 131.

Suvorovite reported on one of Selvinsky's readings: "On 21 May the House of the Red Army [of the Second Baltic Front] hosted an evening with one of the most prominent [odnogo iz krupneishikh] Soviet poets, Ilya Selvinsky. [...] During the evening Ilya Selvinsky spoke of his work during the days of the war and his creative plans. [...] Ilya Selvinsky read [...] his widely-known poems 'I Saw It!' 'Ballad about Leninism,' '[To] Russia,' as well as new lyrical poems."[31] Directly after the fall of Berlin and Germany's capitulation, Selvinsky was placed in charge of a group of officer-journalists sent by way of the Lithuanian coast, via Klaipeda, "across E[ast] Prussia to Königsberg. They gave us a powerful truck, two canisters of gasoline and ten officers of different nationalities (Russians, Ukrainians, Jews, Uzbeks, Kazakhs). Goal: to bring thoughts from there. To tell, to summarize the impressions, to share forecasts, since our front is the only front remaining on our soil, and the people want to know what goes on over there."[32] Selvinsky pondered the sources of Nazism as he stood on the soil of East Prussia. "Goethe, Schiller, Novalis ... Kant, Fichte, Hegel ... Bach, Mozart, Beethoven! What heights, what loftiness! I simply have a hard time believing that *this* nation could have created such geniuses. A scary, dumb nation with a one-track mind (if it thinks at all)," Selvinsky wrote down on 2 June 1945.[33] Yakov Khelemsky, a staff writer for *Suvorovite* who was with Selvinsky on the trip, recalled how en route to Königsberg Selvinsky helped the family of an injured German girl by bringing them food and flowers. Later, when they were already in Königsberg, a member of their delegation confronted Selvinsky:

> "Wasn't it a bit much, Comrade Lieutenant Colonel? Well, you helped them out with some food from your personal ration—that's fine. But what were the flowers for? What did they do with our children! Should we be pouring gifts onto theirs?"
>
> Selvinsky turned crimson. "Comrade Captain, you forget that we're liberating from fascism not only our land, but also Germany. [...] The ditch outside Kerch still

---

31 "Tvorcheskii vecher Il'i Sel'vinskogo," *Suvorovets* 23 May 1945, 3.
32 Selvinsky, Wartime Diaries, 20 May 1945.
33 Selvinsky, Wartime Diaries, 2 June 1945.

haunts me in my dreams. So does this mean that I should respond to it with a Königsberg ditch?"[34]

After explaining to his colleagues that "here today is not the right place and time for vengeance. Especially when we're talking about old people, women, children," Selvinsky suggested that the Soviet officers look for the grave of Immanuel Kant. The principal journalistic output of Selvinsky's trip to East Prussia was the fatigued essay "Königsberg Today (Travel Notes)," which speaks with about an equal passion of Kant and of the Soviet victory.[35] "Soldatskaia pesnia" ("A Soldier's Song"), which Selvinsky also composed during the trip to East Prussia, reads like a faint echo of Selvinsky's fabulous song lyrics from 1942-1943. Selvinsky again has a hard time praising Stalin with verve and conviction: "And [the wave of heroic warriors] speaks with holiness/ Of military events—/Of the young falcon-solider/ And of Stalin-eagle."[36]

During the Moscow exile, as Selvinsky's daughter Tatyana Selvinskaya recalled, Selvinsky would pace back and forth in his study and "talk to Stalin all the time. He was proving to him that he was loyal.... He was constantly proving something to [Stalin]."[37] In his Kurland diary entries for early May 1945, Selvinsky writes at times with astonishing self-awareness, at other times with self-delusion, and sometimes also with the kind of political loyalism that he could never muster up in his literary works. On 2 May 1945 Selvinsky jots down: "Today Berlin fell. And again, as I often have in recent times, I am thinking of Russia, of the astonishing destiny of this incomparable country."[38] Eventually he comes to the subject of Nazism and fascism and of the initial success of the German invasion:

> Those were days of horror because everything incomprehensible horrifies. Incomprehensibility was the strength of fascism. Where was it coming from? Why are the people symbolizing evil, openly saying in the face of ev-

---

34 Khelemskii, "Kurliandskaia vesna," 146-147. In a letter to his wife of 30 May 1945, Selvinsky describes the trip and touches on the encounter with a little German girl and her family. See Sel'vinskii, "Na voine. Iz dnevnikov i pisem rodnym," 174-175.
35 Sel'vinskii, "Kenigsberg segodnia (Putevye zametki)," *Na razgrom vraga* 1 June 1945.
36 Sel'vinskii, "Soldatskaia pesnia," in *Krym Kavkaz Kuban'*, 218-219.
37 Tatyana Selvinskaya, Personal Interview, 15 December 2011.
38 Selvinsky, Wartime Diaries, 2 May 1945.

ery nation [or people] that they despise it and will make it their slave—why were these people so strong, that actually for a period of time they had managed to enslave Europe? "If fascists live in this world, then there is no god ...," one old woman said [this is in fact a direct quote from "I Saw It!"—MDS]. But god will not take offense at this statement, and to prove his existence he will not punish the Germans, and the fascists will not become weaker from this. And suddenly "the miracle on the Volga."

Thoughts of Stalingrad—and inevitably of his own years at the war fronts in the Black Sea region—summon Stalin's image in the poet's mind:

> And again, as always, appearing before me and striking my consciousness, is Stalin's image. There is a person at whose pedestal all my skepticism evaporates. Believing in Stalin I become taller. Stronger. With this faith my life becomes easier. Every person has his Stalin, just as every person has his god. Perhaps this is why it would be hard for me to see Stalin in daily life [v bytu], to talk to him. [...] I have written twice about Stalin: in *Arctic* (part III, ch. I [Selvinsky is referring to *Chelyuskiniana*, the prewar version of would eventually become *Arctic*] and in the poem "Reading Stalin" [Selvinsky omits several other wartime poems and an article]. This is the best of what the poets have written about Stalin. But it is too little not only for Stalin's image, but also in comparison with what I could and should say about him. But I cannot write for the "desk drawer." This would kill the quality of a contemporary in me. [...] I want to write about Stalin.[39]

While in the Baltics Selvinsky reflected at length on what had become, in his mind, a nexus of historical and literary anxieties: the war and the horrors he had personally witnessed, the price of survival and victory, Soviet history, Stalin.

---

39 Selvinsky, Wartime Diaries, 2 May 1945.

CHAPTER THREE

Was Selvinsky thinking of Latvia and the nearby Lithuania as lands where the Nazis and the local murderers had annihilated the Jewish communities? Was he seeing parallels between the Shoah in his native Crimea and the Shoah in the Baltic lands? It is unclear whether in April-May 1945 Selvinsky saw Libava (Liepāja) or Ventpils, the sites of mass executions of Latvian Jews in 1941, or stopped at the killing sites and mass graves in the villages and small towns which he passed through or was stationed in, or made the point of visiting the Dondangen (Dundaga) concentration camp. We know that the map of his travels in the north of Lithuania included Viekšniai, Mažeikiai, and Žagarė, whose ancient Litvak communities had been massacred in the summer and autumn of 1941. Selvinsky also visited Kretinga, Palanga, and Klaipeda on Lithuania's coast. Finally, we know that in early June he was stationed outside Riga, although we do not know whether he saw the site of the Rumbala massacre, in which about 25,000 Jews of Riga were murdered in late November and early December 1941, the same weeks as the Jews of Kerch were being massacred at the Bagerovo anti-tank ditch. He did not write poems about the devastation of Latvia's and Lithuania's Jewish communities.[40] One possible explanation behind Selvinsky's poetic silence about the devastation of Latvia's and Lithuania's Jewish communities is that in the spring of 1945 he could not have written—could not feel that his knowledge of the scene qualified him to write—poems of bearing witness in the vein of "I Saw It!" and "Kerch." But there are other, more speculative and politically motivated explanations as well. In Selvinsky's Baltic diaries from the spring and summer of 1945 one finds no information on the area's Jewish past, no reflections on the Shoah in Latvia and Lithuania.

At the same time, we know that Selvinsky continued to reflect on his first-hand experiences of the Nazi atrocities against the Jews going back to his military service in 1941-43. The proof is Selvinsky's long poem *Kandava* (1945), which was in fact composed outside Riga in June

---

40 Yakov Khelemsky's cycle of poems "Gulf of Riga" includes the poem "On the outskirts of Riga a ghetto died out..." (October 1944), in which the poet writes: "Here every stone was the Wailing Wall" and describes the trucks carrying victims to the execution site in the Biķernieki Forest, but does not identify the victims as Jews. The cycle was published in Khelemsky's collection *On the Road* (1948), which featured other poems with circumspect Shoah allusions. See Iakov Khelemskii, "V predmest'iakh Rigi vymershee getto...." in *V puti*, 77-78 (Moscow: Sovetskii pisatel', 1948). Khelemsky was not the first Jewish-Russian author to resort to the image of the Wailing (Western) Wall in wartime writing so as to signal Jewish suffering.

1945[41] and marked with the place of its composition, "Dzintari," an area of the resort of Jūrmala. The poem *Kandava* is especially important in Selvinsky's career as a Jewish-Russian poetic witness to the Shoah because it bridges what he saw and witnessed in Crimea, North Caucasus, and Kuban in 1941-1943 and what he learned about the Nazi camps in the spring of 1945. In *Kandava* Selvinsky deliberately linked the murder of Jews in Crimea in 1941-42 with the murder of Jews in the death camps in Poland, thus bringing together the Shoah by bullet and the so-called "Final Solution" into a single history.

When Selvinsky's *Kandava* appeared in the January-February 1946 issue of *October*, it was printed as part of "Vesna 1945 goda" ("Spring of 1945"), a selection of four poems composed in the Baltic area in the spring of 1945. Selvinsky would include these poems in *Crimea, Caucasus, Kuban* (1947), the first book he published after the 1943-1944 party resolutions. In *October* Selvinsky's selection immediately preceded three texts by Mikhail Isakovsky, inviting a comparison. The magazine version of *Kandava* was shorter than the one published in *Crimea, Caucasus, Kuban*, where Selvinsky added one long passage and one short passage to the poem and also made a number of smaller changes. At the heart of the narrative lies a fusion of Selvinsky's recorded nightmare with his firsthand account of the surrender of a Nazi division at Kandava (Kandau).

Selvinsky's diary offers invaluable material toward a reconstruction of the poet's artistic laboratory during the "Kurland spring"; it is indispensable for the understanding of how the personal and the historical, the Soviet and the Jewish, the witnessed and the imagined, coalesced in the poet's psyche. On 5 May 1945, Selvinsky wrote down the contents of a nightmare which has, among its literary sources, Vasily Grossman's "The Hell of Treblinka" and also, perhaps, Joseph Conrad's *Heart of Darkness*:

> Today I had a dream that Berta [Selvinsky's wife] and I found ourselves at a death factory [na fabrike smerti] in Majdanek or Treblinka. We walked side by side with the other victims along an asphalted path, and on both side, forming two lines, there stood the Germans and looked at us with the eyes of people who are entertained by the sight of those condemned to die now walking

---

41   See Khelemskii, "Kurliandskaia vesna," 159-160.

toward their execution. [...] The most terrifying thing in my nightmare consisted not in the fear of dying, but in the fact that I had a whole lot of time to picture it in my mind. I walked with B[erta] for a long time and thought of *where* I was going and *what* exactly awaits us there? What tools of execution? What devices?[42]

Selvinsky writes of seeing lines of German soldiers who were his "enemies" and who "stared with curiosity at him in anticipation of his execution." He wakes up from his nightmare "no longer feeling anything but horror, horror, horror." Then comes the poet's interpretation of the dream, in which his experience as a witness to the Shoah finds cogent expression—as do also his two earlier poems, "I Saw It!" and "Kerch":

I woke up. That is, I passed from one state of being into another the way one passes from life into death. Unfortunately, I don't believe in disintegration—and therefore I dare not make conclusions. But here is the thing: we judge a person on the basis of what his life was like. We say: a person's character is defined by the fact that they had murdered his three children, his wife hanged herself, and he was kept rotting in jail for five years. Or something of the sort. Yes? Clear. This is biography. An occurrence which one simply cannot disregard. But what about a life of [night] dreams? Do we not have, besides our official biography, a second one? One of dream-visions? In my life, the sight of 7000 corpses in the Bagerovo ditch at Kerch in 1942 played a huge role. Those who would want to study my character would need to take this into account. I experienced through that what victims of Majdanek and Treblinka experienced. I could describe this in bright colors and with all the details. My nervous system is oblivious to the fact that this did not happen with comrade Ilya-Karl Lvovich S., 45 years of age, white-collar worker, party member, never sentenced, never tried, never this and that. With him

---

42   Selvinsky, Wartime Diaries, 5 May 1945.

this never happened, but with *them*, with all of you it did happen! Therefore it also happened with him. [...] Was I in Treblinka? If you ask my memory—no. If you pose this question to my nerves—undoubtedly yes I was.[43]

For days Selvinsky remained under the spell of his nightmare. On 7 May 1945, as a follow-up to his previous diary entry, he recorded that "in early childhood [he] used have a dream about a cart harnessed with a white horse, and on the cart—my father's corpse. [...] This was in 1906, after a Jewish pogrom. My father died seventeen years after that, when I was already a fourth-year [university] student. [...] And yet this dream, which I subsequently had two more times—in Odessa (1910) and in Eupatoria (1911)—stayed in my consciousness like a trauma."[44]

On 12 May 1945, on the heels of his harrowing dream, Selvinsky wrote down the following account of events:

> General Vasiliev (Commander of the 1 Corps [Lieutenant General Ivan Vasiliev, who in 1944 had distinguished himself during the liberation of Crimea]) and commander of the 306 Division [Major General Mikhail] Kucheryavenko drove to the Germans to accept the capitulation of a division. I went with them. It was somewhere beyond the town of Kandava. [...] We drove into some sort of a clearing beside a forest—the division's *platz*. The generals disappeared into some little house, to which the German *obersts* [literally "colonels," but Selvinsky probably uses it to mean "top commanders"], who had been expecting them, had driven up; I stayed outside. Before me, formed into a tetrangle, there stood a division, about 4000 or 5000 people. [...] These SS [men] [...]—everything I had seen on the screen, in photos and also on posters—all of this was real. I was drawn, with irresistible force, to stride before this formation. *It was that very nightmare of 5 May, which had struck me literally five days ago*.... I walked on a stomped-out path ... and 10,000 eyes that belonged

---

43 Selvinsky, Wartime Diaries, 5 May 1945.
44 Selvinsky, Wartime Diaries, 7 May 1945.

to the vilest enemies of my people (both Russian and Jewish) stared at me from the formation. [...] Miracles! O miracles.... 5000 fascists, who had carried out that which cannot be erased from memory, the museum of horror in Majdanek and Treblinka, do not dare touch with a finger a Jew who strolls before them.[45]

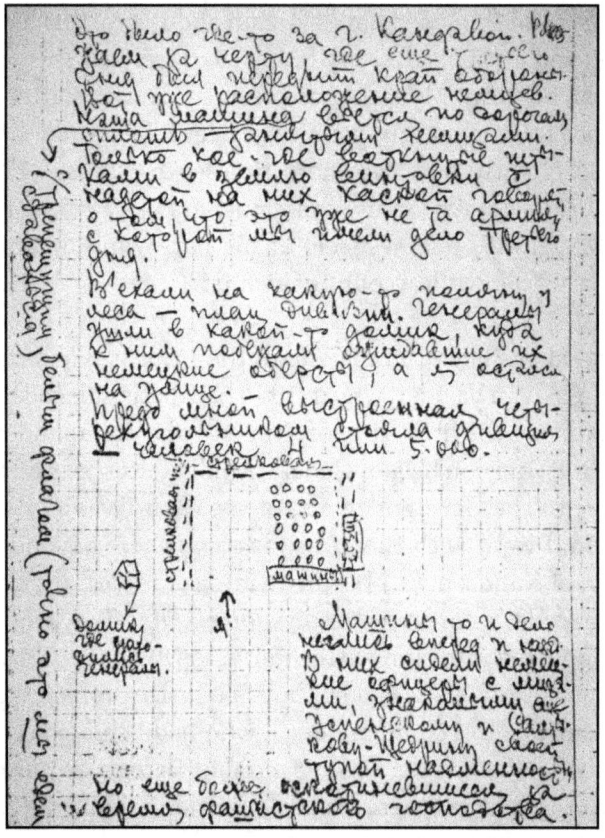

51. Page of Ilya Selvinsky's wartime diary entry for 12 May 1945, with a description and a sketch of the capitulation of a Nazi division at Kandava. (Courtesy of Ilya Selvinsky Memorial Museum, Simferopol.)

In the structure of the resulting poem, *Kandava*, Selvinsky's recollected, personal nightmare occasions a lengthy documentary-like

---

45 Selvinsky, Wartime Diaries, 12 May 1945.

description of the surrender of Nazi troops. The description, in turn, prompts an opportunity to imagine a Nazi officer's nightmare of revenge by Soviet soldiers and by Jewish voices of the Nazis' victims.

Selvinsky opens the poem with a nightmarish dream transformed into the lyrical hero's recollection:

> мне снился накануне сон: иду
> с женою рядом где-то в Освенциме
> или в Майданеке. Иду пред строем
> фашистских серо-голубых солдат,
> и тысячи оледенелых глаз,
> презрительных, насмешливых, злорадных,
> а то и просто любопытных, смотрят
> на то, как мы идем на гибель.

> (I had a dream just on the eve: I walk/ with my wife somewhere in Auschwitz/ or Majdanek. I walk before a formation/ of fascist grey-blue soldiers/ and thousands of icy eyes,/ contemptuous, mocking, vicious,/ or just plain curious, looking/ at us walking to our death[46]).

Soon thereafter the mode shifts from oneiric vision to reconstructed reality, and the tone changes accordingly as Selvinsky describes being in a group with a Soviet general and seven Soviet officers as they accept the surrender of a Nazi division. As Selvinsky's eyes scan the rows of soldiers and officers, his thoughts drift to his recent nightmare about being murdered, alongside his wife, at a Nazi concentration camp:

> [...] мне вспомнился вчерашний мой кошмар...
> Вот! Вот они, те самые глаза,
> что на меня со спутницей глядели,
> когда мы шли на гибель. Я узнал
> вот этого! И вон того! И тех,

---

46 Sel'vinskii, *Kandava*, *Oktiabr'* 1-2 (1946): 3-6. I am deliberately quoting from the shorter, magazine version of *Kandava* as it appeared in *Oktiabr'* as part of the selection of Selvinsky's poems titled "Vesna 1945 goda" ("Spring of 1945"). A longer version of the poem appeared in *Krym Kavkaz Kuban'* (209-217) and in subsequent editions. However, in the longer version Selvinsky left intact all the references to Nazi atrocities and the Shoah.

что во второй... что во второй шеренге...
Скажите им: "Майданек", "Освенцим",
"Треблинка" или "Керчь". Они поймут.
Они оттуда! [...].

([...] I recalled my yesterday's nightmare.../There! There they are, those same eyes,/ which started at me and my beloved. I recognized/ This one! And that one! And those,/ The ones... the ones standing in the second row.../Were I to say to them: 'Majdanek,' 'Auschwitz,'/ 'Treblinka,' or 'Kerch,' they would understand./ They are from there! [...]).[47]

Yakov Khelemsky, a native of Kiev like his childhood friend Lev Ozerov, devoted a long memoir to Selvinsky, which reads as a novella in its own right. Penned in 1980 and titled *Kurland Spring*, Khelemsky's memoir fleshed out some of the details of the events that inspired and informed Selvinsky's *Kandava*. Khelemsky unearthed Selvinsky's previously unpublished letter to his wife, dated 10 May 1945, in which he described the nightmarish dream he would later capture in *Kandava*:

> [...] I never got to see the very torments of death because I finally managed to wake up, but one odd sensation has stayed with me: "two lines of Germans, and between them down a paved path you and I are walking alongside the other condemned ones [...]." Yesterday I saw the very same sight. And all the while, as I walked behind the general, I felt your presence beside me—and this awareness that it's the *day of our wedding anniversary*, and precisely on this day Kandava, and not Majdanek, defines our life together, made me absolutely giddy with happiness.[48]

---

47 In "Conversation with a POW," a poem of 1944, Selvinsky argues that a German soldier has no right to say that he was forced to fight after having walked "across cities,/ Disregarding ditches filled with corpses [Nevziraia na rvy v trupakh],/ From mass executions and mobile killing vans." See Sel'vinskii, "Razgovor s voennoplennym," in *Krym Kavkaz Kuban'*, 183.

48 Selvinsky, letter to Berta Selvinskaya, 10 May 1945, quoted in Khelemskii, "Kurliandskaia vesna," 158.

Having previously written and published two key poems about the Shoah in Crimea ("I Saw It!" and "Kerch"), Selvinsky placed the Bagerovo massacre in the same category as three Nazi death camps in Poland, Auschwitz-Birkenau, Majdanek, and Treblinka. But the poem did not stop with the surrender of the Nazi troops and Selvinsky's superimposed nightmare of dying in a camp. In a particularly powerful, cinematic twist of imagination (or was this, too, a factual reconstruction?), Selvinsky describes how he noticed that a Nazi captain wore a brass emblem of the Crimean peninsula, Selvinsky's homeland. Such "Crimean shields" were given to the German participants of the Crimean campaign from 21 September 1941 to 4 July 1942[49]:

> Я разглядел чеканку очертаний
> расстрелянного Крыма. Боже мой!
> На нем оттиснут пунктом: Симферополь...
> (Я там родился.) Севастополь! (Здесь
> я обучался воинскому долгу.)
> Евпаторийский берег — берег муз,
> где занялась любовь моя и песня.
> Я сам не помню, как это случилось...
> Я, как лунатик, подошел к нему
> и посмотрел в глаза. Готов поклясться,
> что я их видел. Видел накануне
> в Майданеке. И спутница моя,
> наверное, узнала б их мгновенно.

> (I made out the stamped shape/ of the executed Crimea. O god!/ On it, incised was the dot of Simferopol.../ (I was born there.) Sebastopol! (Here/ I learned military duty.)/ The coast of Eupatoria—coast of Muses./ Where my love and song had taken root./ I don't remember myself, how this all happened.../ Like a somnambulist, I approached him/ And looked him in the eyes. I swear/ That I had seen them. Just seen them/ in Majdanek. And my beloved, too,/ Would have probably recognized them right away.)

---

49 A photograph is reproduced in O[leg] V. Roman'ko, *Krym pod piatoi Gitlera*. A copy of the shield is on display at the Ilya Selvinsky Memorial Museum, Simferopol.

In the longer version of the poem, Selvinsky added the city of Kerch to the landmarks of Crimea incised on the Nazi "Crimean shield": "And finally, gray from ancient age,/ overwhelmed with ashes like Pompeii,/ splattered over with blood and brains,/ the peak of all my torments— 'Kerch'!"[50]

In the lyrical notes taking the poet back to his youth and to the Judaic and Graeco-Roman roots in Crimea, and also to his wartime years of personal bravery and eyewitnessing, Selvinsky repeats some of the phrases from "Kerch" (1942).[51] Selvinsky describes himself as moving "как лунатик" ("like a somnambulist")—exactly the way a survivor of the Bagerovo ditch execution is said to amble in the text of "Kerch." The versification of *Kandava*, its blank iambic pentameter, also points to Selvinsky's earlier masterpiece. In reflecting on the unity of Selvinsky's wartime poetry, Khelemsky, a Jewish-Russian poet from the younger generation who spoke guardedly of the Shoah in poems published in the late 1940s, proposed that a number of Selvinsky's wartime poems, including "I Saw It!" and "Kerch," formed a cycle of epic proportions.[52] "[…]t turns out," Khelemsky wrote in 1980, that "Kerch" and *Kandava*, similar in their texture of verse and also forming an internal dialogue, apparently frame [Selvinsky's extensive epic] narrative."[53] In the Soviet (Jewish) game of understatement and code-speaking, Khelemsky gave the reader a number of clues that a principal unifying factors of Selvinsky's wartime poetry was the recurrent subject of the Shoah in Crimea.

To return to the narrative of *Kandava*, Selvinsky ends up coming up to the SS officer and ripping the brass Crimean emblem off the captain's uniform. This gives him a feeling of "bliss" ("blazhenstvo") of a kind he "had never experienced before." But what is more, now Selvinsky reads in the terrified eyes of the Nazi captain another nightmarish fantasy: eight Soviet prisoners are walking before a Nazi formation in Auschwitz, and one of the Soviet prisoners suddenly comes up to the captain and rips off from his chest—"с него — эсэсовца, арийца —/ эмблему покоренья Крыма" ("from him, an SS member, an Aryan,/

---

50 *Krym Kavkaz Kuban'*, 216.
51 Khelemsky was, I believe, the first to note a philological kinship of "Kerch" and *Kandava*; see Khelemskii, "Kurlianskaia vesna," 172.
52 Khelemskii, "Kurliandskaia vesna," 170.
53 Khelemskii, "Kurliandskaia vesna," 172.

the emblem of the subjugation of the Crimea"). The phrase "покоренья Крыма" ("[of] the subjugation of Crimea"; exactly in the genitive singular) echoes a famous line from *Woe of Wit* (1824), Aleksandr Griboedov's play in verse, where the protagonist, Chatsky, says in Act 2, Scene 5:

> А судьи кто? — За древностию лет
> К свободной жизни их вражда непримирима.
> Сужденья черпают из забытых газет
> Времен Очаковских и покоренья Крыма.

> (And who are the judges?—In their ancient age/ Their enmity toward free life has no end,/ They draw their judgments from forgotten papers/ From the times of [the siege of] Ochakov and the subjugation of Crimea).

In *Kandava* Selvinsky emphasized his deep grounding in not only Russian modernism, but also the Golden Age of Russian poetry. The reference to the outspoken intellectual Chatsky of *Woe of Wit* cut both ways. On the one hand, it alluded to both the time when Crimea and parts of the Black Sea coast became part of the Russian Empire (in the course of two Russo-Turkish wars) and the then-recent Nazi occupation of Crimea. On the other hand, it hinted at Selvinsky's own Soviet "judges" and at the poet's refusal to let go of the topic of the Nazi atrocities in his native Crimea. In fact, "forgotten papers" point to Selvinsky's dismissal of "newspaper columns" in favor of the poet-witness's first-hand knowledge of Nazi atrocities in "I Saw It!"—yet another way of linking *Kandava* and Selvinsky's Shoah poems of 1942-1943.

In reality, as opposed to the dream within the poem's reality, the surrendering SS captain stands silently, "paralyzed by the law of collapse,/ crushed by the downfall of *Vaterland*." In his "furious silence" ("iarostnom molchan'e") Selvinsky hears:

> [...] шум красноармейских стягов,
> браваду труб и грохот барабанов
> и ликованье тысяч голосов
> из пепла, из поэм, из сновидений!"

([...] the hum of Red Army unfurled banners,/ the bravado of trumpets and the thunder of drums/ and the jubilation of thousands of voices/ from ashes, from poems, from night visions!)

This motif of victims of the Shoah mourned, remembered, and memorialized through poetry unites Selvinsky's finale with the conclusions of Shoah poems by Ehrenburg, Ozerov, and Antokolsky. This, in turn, gives further validity to the idea that in 1944-1945 the historical context of the Shoah elicited something of a concordant response from the different poetic sensibilities of the poet-witnesses.[54]

3. Selvinsky during zhdanovshchina and the Anticosmopolitan Campaign

Notes of bitterness, disappointment, and unrealized hopes and ambitions can be heard in Selvinsky's diary entry of 5 June 1945:

> The war is over. There is nothing left for me to do here [...] soon I will probably be demobilized. But what will I write about the war? I have seen nothing but the bad: retreat, defeat, corpses of civilians. I did not get to see the victory. I am sitting inside "a blind-ended tube" ["slepaia kishka"]—thank god, they have spared my life. But is this why I had appealed to the Central Committee to be restored [recommissioned] in the army? I walked in the footsteps of victory in E[ast] Prussia. This offers precious little.[55]

In Selvinsky's rueful comments one can glean not only a longing for the glory of a Soviet soldier-poet come to the vanquished Berlin, but also a realization that in the earlier days of the war he had witnessed and written about events that were becoming more and more peripheral

---

54 I discuss the issue in "Jewish-Russian Poets Bearing Witness to the Shoah, 1941-1946: Textual Evidence and Preliminary Conclusions."
55 Selvinsky, Wartime Diaries, 5 June 1945; cf. Babenko, 66.

to the official rhetoric of victory over Nazism and to the growing body of Soviet war literature. In Tatyana Selvinskaya's assessment, her father "believed that he had not seen the victory [...] and [because of that] he did not write an epic work about the war. That's what he said."[56]

If a poet's diary is ever a blueprint of his or her thoughts, the entry from Selvinsky's diary dated 8 June 1945 is remarkable for the risk Selvinsky was taking in recording some of his thoughts about the Soviet regime just one month after the capitulation of Nazi Germany:

> Peace. But what lies ahead? Demobilization, home sweet home, wife, children, beloved work. And that's all? Not too much. After all that we have endured, after all that we have shouldered—this is really very little! What will happen in our domestic politics? Further construction of socialism? Yes, of course, but by which methods? Seven million people are trapped in prisons....
>
> The main contradiction of our Soviet life consists in that along with the presence of social freedom (and this we have, undeniably) there is individual slavery of each and every one. Just one and only one person has a right to think. [...] The people are brainwashed into believing they are happy. Children thank Stalin for a happy childhood. He who does not feel this way is a counter-revolutionary and belongs behind bars. [...]
>
> The only people who flourish here are the ones with gifts that have nothing to do with philosophy ["ne sviazany s filosofiei"] [...]. Composers, painters, architects, and especially writers have it bad. They will be given money, they will not starve, but let them forget that they themselves can represent something. [...] Even for these lines, if they end up in the hands of a scoundrel, I could be arrested or in the very least deprived of the right to write. [...]
>
> Will the victory give us something?
> Will we be able to spread our shoulders?[57]

---

56 Tatyana Selvinskaya, Personal Interview, 15 December 1945.
57 Selvinsky, Wartime Diaries; cf. Babenko, 66-67.

CHAPTER THREE

As a Jew and an avant-gardist, Selvinsky saw little room for himself in the cultural climate of postwar Stalinism.[58] Echoes of the official punishment would continue to trouble the poet throughout the postwar years until Stalin's death and the beginning of the Thaw. Selvinsky's record as a poetic witness to the murder of Jews in the occupied Crimea could never be erased. No Stalinist dithyrambs or rhetorical contortions would protect Selvinsky, in whose collections of 1942-1953 opportunistic texts continued to neighbor Shoah poems.

52. Ilya Selvinsky. 1940s. (Courtesy of Tatyana Selvinskaya.)

---

58 For an overview of Stalinist antisemitic politics and policies in the postwar years, see Timothy Snyder, "Stalinist Anti-Semitism," in *Bloodlands: Europe between Hitler and Stalin*, 339-377 (New York: Basic Books, 2010).

When *zhdanovshchina* was being launched in the summer of 1946, Malenkov admonished Leningrad's literary journals: "You've made it cozy for Selvinsky! [Sel'vinskogo prigreli]."⁵⁹ In a report dated 7 August 1946 and submitted to Zhdanov by officials of the Directorate of Propaganda and Agitation (UPA) concerning the "unsatisfactory state of the magazines *Star* and *Leningrad*," Selvinsky's *Sebastopol* was criticized along with other works about the Great Patriotic War published in *Leningrad*, which were deemed "poor from the artistic point of view and ideologically corrupt." Of Selvinsky's *Sebastopol* the report offered the following judgment: "[...] I. Selvinsky describes his impressions of visiting the heroic city after its liberation by the Red Army. But the poet says nothing of the courageous defenders of the city; he only recalls running into a young woman in the street [...] The young woman's appearance is described vapidly [...]."⁶⁰

An uncorrected stenographic record of the 9 August 1946 expanded meeting of the Orgburo of the Central Committee has preserved an exchange between Stalin and the poet Boris Likharev, editor of *Leningrad* and executive secretary of Leningrad's branch of the Union of Writers during the years of the Great Patriotic War. Stalin pressured Likharev to respond to the criticism of the Leningrad–based journals, and Likharev minced words: "Likharev: In Selvinsky's *Sebastopol* there is a conclusion, he recalls his youth in Sebastopol, remembers a young woman whom he saw there, who called him darling. This he remembered for the rest of his life. Here is his poem. Stalin: This is a trick ["ulovka"; could also mean "subterfuge"]."⁶¹ Speaking with damning sarcasm, Stalin issued a laconic verdict on Selvinsky's *Sebastopol* at another discussion in advance of the notorious 14 August 1946 party resolution on the magazines *Star* and *Leningrad*: "Zhdanov: 'The magazine *Leningrad* publishes weak contents. Here the poet Selvinsky sees in the burned-down Sebastopol nothing [...] but one woman [...]. Stalin: 'As if there is not enough material for him.'"⁶² "Luckily for Selvinsky," Solomatin notes, "his name did not figure in the summing-up resolution [...] of 14 August

---

59 See Ozerov, "Il'ia Sel'vinskii," 9.
60 Artizov and Naumov, 563-564.
61 Artizov and Naumov, 568.
62 Quoted in Ozerov, "Il'ia Sel'vinskii," 9; cf. A. Ezhelev, "Dushnoe leto 46-go. Kak prinimalos' Postanovlenie o zhurnalakh 'Zvezda' i 'Leningrad'," *Izvestiia* 21 May 1988.

[1946]," the resolution which [...] vilified Akhmatova and Zoshchenko.⁶³ Yet the ostracism of Selvinsky continued throughout *zhdanovshchina*. In October 1946 Aleksandr Fadeev, then Secretary General of the Union of Soviet Writers and thus the principal of Soviet literature, addressed a meeting of Moscow poets. His speech developed the main points of the party documents aimed at the magazines *Star* and *Leningrad* and applied them left and right. Fadeev charged not only Selvinsky's prewar poetry but also some of his wartime poems with being under the influence of "Nietzschean-Bergsonian" views which, as Fadeev reminded his audience, were alien to the Soviet vision of the world.⁶⁴ In February 1947 Fadeev delivered a long address at the Institute of World Literature in Moscow. He subsequently read the latter address at the XIth Plenary Meeting of the Secretariat of the Union of Soviet Writers in June 1947; in 1947-1948 it appeared several times in print, in both abridged and complete form, ultimately as "Goals of Literary Theory and Criticism." One section of Fadeev's lengthy address targeted both Pasternak and Selvinsky as examples of writers who had not broken with their past "prejudices."⁶⁵ The attack on Selvinsky felt half-hearted and strained when coming from the same writer who at an official meeting in May 1939 had ranked Selvinsky most highly, including him in a selected list of leading Soviet poets: "The founder of our poetry is Mayakovsky; there had not been such a poet [in any country] in the twentieth century [...]. In the camp of our adversaries either in Western Europe or in America there are no poets of such caliber as Bagritsky, Aseev, Marshak, Selvinsky, Tikhonov, Tvardovsky, Bazhan, Tychyna, Samed Vurgun."⁶⁶ Nearly eight years later, in 1947, Fadeev stated this about Selvinsky:

---

63   Solomatin; cf. the text of the 14 August 1946 resolution in Artizov and Naumov, 857-591.
64   In a letter sent to the editors of *Literary Gazette* on 16 October 1946, Fadeev then disputed the accuracy of the report on the meeting as published in the newspaper on 12 October 1946. He claimed that he did not criticize Selvinsky's writings as a whole and that "both before the war and during the war [the poet] had composed useful Soviet works demonstrating great talent." See Fadeev, "V redaktsiiu 'Literaturnoi gazety,'" in A. Fadeev, *Sobranie sochinenii v piati tomakh*, ed. E. F. Knipovich et al. 5: 354-355 (Moscow: Gosudarstvennoe izdatel'stvo khudozhestvennoi literatury, 1959-1961).
65   See Aleksandr Fadeev, "Zadachi literaturnoi teorii i kritiki," in *Problemy sotsialisticheskogo realizma: sbornik statei*, ed. B. I. Bialik et al., 37-40 (Leningrad, Sovetskii pisatel', 1948). In the text, already revised after Stalin's death, Fadeev toned down or omitted some of the comments, but the thrust of the attack remained the same: "Zadachi literaturnoi teorii i kritiki," in A. Fadeev, *Sobranie sochinenii piati tomakh*, 4: 433-435; commentary 4: 731.
66   Fadeev, "Pisatel' i kritik," in A. Fadeev, *Sobranie sochinenii v piati tomakh*, 4: 254-260.

[...] before the war and especially during the war Selvinsky wrote a number of good Soviet poems. [...] Selvinsky is also a member of the Communist Party, that is a person who, it would seem, shares its ideas and positions. And suddenly, already after the passing of the resolution of the Central Committee he had the daring to publish a volume of *Selected Works*, in which he included the majority of his previous creations. There is nothing in all of Soviet poetry that is as alien in its spirit and even hostile to the very essence of our attitude to life: cult of the biological, animalistic elements in the human being, extreme individualism, preaching of decadence in art, never mind the egregious political ignorance in the treatment of the New Economic Policy in *The Lay of Ulyalaev*. [...] Yet Selvinsky imagines that everything is permitted to him. In fact, if one analyzes the formal aspects of Selvinsky's previous poetry, his command of poetic language is on the poor side; he lacks a sense of measure: there is so much tastelessness and so much pretentious, cheap provincialism. What use do we have of this small-town Nietzscheism?[67]

In this address and another essay of 1947 in which he attacked Selvinsky, Fadeev circumvented his poems about the murder of Jews in Crimea and avoided being specific about Selvinsky's wartime poetry.[68]

The pressure Selvinsky was under may also be inferred through a close comparison of two volumes of his poetry published in 1947. Selvinsky had prepared *Crimea, Caucasus, Kuban* in the fall of 1944, and subsequently added to it a section based on his experience in the Baltic in the spring of 1945. The volume became a retrospective of all of Selvinsky's wartime poetry, its structure corresponding with the years and places of his service: Crimea 1941-1942; Caucasus 1942-1943; Kuban 1943; Crimea 1943-1944; Spring of 1945 [Kurland; East Prussia]. By reading the book and examining the dates and places of the

---

[67] Fadeev, "Zadachi literaturnoi teorii i kritiki," in *Problemy sotsialisticheskogo realizma*, 39; cf. "Zadachi literaturnoi teorii i kritiki," in *Sobranie sochinenii piati tomakhi*, 4: 434.
[68] See "Zadachi sovetskoi literatury," in A. Fadeev, *Sobranie sochinenii v piati tomakh*, 4: 469-470.

poems' composition, one would not even know that Selvinsky had been confined to Moscow for a year and a half. Officially signed into print on 4 January 1947, as the door was shutting on Jewish self-expression in the USSR, *Crimea, Caucasus, Kuban* featured all of Selvinsky's poems about the Shoah in Crimea with the exception of "Kerch," which would remain conspicuously absent from print for four decades; the volume also featured *Kandava*. Selvinsky's second volume of 1947, *Lyrics and Drama*, showcased not one but two Stalinist dithyrambs and already bore the stamp of the brewing anticosmopolitan campaign in its thinned-out selection of wartime poems. Still, "I Saw It!," *Sebastopol*, and *Kandava* were reprinted, and Selvinsky would succeed in including "I Saw It!" and *Kandava* in two of his three books printed in 1948-1953, and *Sebastopol* in all three books.

53. Ilya Selvinsky in his study, with a bust of Voltaire. Moscow. 1940s. (Courtesy of Tatyana Selvinskaya.)

During the Stalin years, Selvinsky's last significant discussion of the Shoah occurred in his review essay of Lev Ozerov's collection *Downpour* (*Liven'*), published in 1947 under the editorship of Pavel Antokolsky. In assessing Ozerov's talent and artistry, Selvinsky managed to make profound observations about the transformation of the younger poet's sensibility after Babi Yar, and also about the challenge of resorting to the "tried and true literary devices" before the face of Babi Yar's tragedy.[69] Ozerov, whom Selvinsky had known but had not mentored before the war, was the only Jewish-Russian poet of his generation to publish an explicit poem about the Shoah, *Babi Yar*, and to publish it, first in a magazine and then in a collection, right on the cusp of the darkest years for Soviet Jewry. Selvinsky deemed Ozerov's *Babi Yar* his "most imperfect" creation, yet also his "strongest and most inspired" poem.[70] But he also found excessive saccharine sweetness in the tone Ozerov employed in describing the scene of mass execution and of little children's last words—the very stanzas that belong to the most gut-wrenching pages in all of Shoah poetry:

> Девочка, снизу: — Не сыпьте землю в глаза мне... —
> Мальчик: — Чулочки тоже снимать?—
> И замер,
> В последний раз обнимая мать.

> A girl, from below:—Don't throw dirt in my eyes—
> A boy:—Do I have to take off my socks, too?—
> Then he grew still,
> Embracing his mother for the last time.[71]

> (Tr. Richard Sheldon)

Selvinsky stressed a lack of epic vision or "dramatic fire" in Ozerov's *Babi Yar*. Without being "overspecific" (as Vladimir Nabokov might put it in reference to one's cherished, hidden knowledge), Selvinsky spoke of

---

69 Sel'vinskii, "Poeziia L. Ozerova" [Rev. of Lev Ozerov, *Liven'*, Moscow, 1947]," *Oktiabr'* 8 (1947): 179.
70 Sel'vinskii, "Poeziia L. Ozerova," 179.
71 Ozerov, *Babii Iar, Oktiabr'* 3/4 (1946): 160-163; cf. *Babii Iar*, in Ozerov, *Liven'*, ed. P. Antokol'skii, 25-32; (Moscow: Molodaia gvardiia, 1947; Ozerov, *Babi Yar*, tr. Richad Sheldon, in Shrayer, *An Anthology of Jewish-Russian Literature*, 1: 575-579.

Ozerov but had his own poetry in mind. In writing of Ozerov the way a demanding teacher might speak about a student who no longer wishes to be one (or never was one), Selvinsky implied, rightly or wrongly, that bearing witness to Babi Yar in 1944 and writing a poem about it may not be the same as standing over the corpses of Jews murdered at Kerch in January 1942 and immediately responding with "I Saw It!"

Selvinsky's review was printed in August 1947 in *October*, as dark clouds once again gathered over his head. On 31 December 1947 the critic Vladimir Shcherbina, then a rising theoretician of socialist-realist aesthetics, reviewed two recently published books by Selvinsky, *Crimea, Caucasus, Kuban* and *Lyrics and Drama*, in *Kul'tura i zhizn'* (*Culture and Life*), the newspaper of the Directorate of Propaganda and Agitation (UPA). Titled "False Direction," Shcherbina's article charged Selvinsky with "contempt for the spiritual life of the people" and "rejection of realism."[72] Most of Selvinsky's war lyrics were harshly dismissed. "External relevance here only covers up the internal stasis of the poetry," wrote Shcherbina. "But such literature does not have a long life."

In 1949, in the pages of the same newspaper, Selvinsky's poetry was declared "cosmopolitan" and "anti-party," the latter being a particularly grave charge. Tatyana Selvinskaya told me that her parents "feared nighttime rings of the doorbell and every night prepared themselves that somebody would come for them.... Feared they would arrest him. He expected it every night."[73] Tatyana Selvinskaya believes that her father owed his survival to a measure of Stalin's patronage. As was typical of the cultural policies of the day, Selvinsky's blacklisting was not complete: two volumes of his poetry did appear, in 1948 and 1950 respectively, and so did a volume of his tragedies in 1952. Yet only a handful of Selvinsky's poems were printed in Soviet periodicals between 1947 and Stalin's death in 1953, and no essays between 1948 and 1952.

The historian John D. Klier characterized the place of the Shoah in the postwar Stalin years as follows:

> In contrast to the period at the end of the war, when writers spoke openly of the special suffering of Jews at

---

72 V[ladimir] Shcherbina, "Lozhnoe napravlenie," *Kul'tura i zhizn'* 31 December 1947, 3.
73 Tatyana Selvinskaya, Personal Interview, 15 December 2011. Also see Ozerov, "Il'ia Sel'vinskii, ego trudy i dni," 9.

the hands of the Nazis, the Shoah was never specifically acknowledged by the Soviet state. Instead, the fate of the Jews was submerged in the category of the twenty million victims of Fascism. Efforts to recall or commemorate the special victimization of the Jews were discouraged or condemned as a manifestation of "bourgeois nationalism."[74]

In January 1950, at the height of the campaign against the "bourgeois nationalist" and "cosmopolitan" trends in Soviet culture—which also amounted to a near-complete liquidation of Yiddish culture in the Soviet Union—Anatoly Tarasenkov published the article "On National Traditions and Bourgeois Cosmopolitanism" in *Banner*.[75] This was the same Tarasenkov who as an editor had worked closely with a number of major Russian poets, including Pasternak, and who was listed as the editor of record for Selvinsky's 1947 *Crimea, Caucasus, Kuban*. The main targets of Tarasenkov's attack were poets Bagritsky and Selvinsky, both of whom were Russian Jews, and the fiction writer Aleksandr Grin (1880-1932), who was not (or at least was not commonly treated as one). In his menacing critique, Tarasenkov contrasted Bagritsky and Selvinsky with Vladimir Mayakovsky, claiming that "neither Bagritsky nor Selvinsky could, or had any political right to, take Mayakovsky's place, to say nothing of the fact that they bear no comparison to the great poet of the revolution."[76] Building on Zhdanov's speeches and Party documents of August 1946—and on Fadeev's noted essay of 1946—Tarasenkov sought to show that from his earlier works about the revolution and the Civil War (e.g. *The Lay of Ulyalayev*) all the way to his wartime poems, Selvinsky was and remained a "bourgeois cosmopolitan." Perhaps the most disparaging aspect of Tarasenkov's essay was his critique of Selvinsky's poem "To Russia," a critique that rooted the postwar defamation of the poet in his officially denounced wartime

---

74 John D. Klier, "Outline of Jewish-Russian History Part II: 1954-2001," in *An Anthology of Jewish-Russian Literature*, ed. Shrayer, 2: 1201.
75 Anatolii Tarasenkov, "O natsional'nykh traditsiiakh i burzhuaznom kosmopolitizme. Stat'ia pervaia," *Znamia* 1 (1950): 152-164. See also Boris Solov'ev's attack on "formalist" trends in poetry, "O novatorstve i traditsiiakh," *Znamia* 3 (1950): 141-167. In a section titled "II. Poeziia ili geometricheskie uprazhneniia?" (147-149), Solov'ev targets both Selvinsky and Ozerov in connection with Selvinsky's review of Ozerov's collection.
76 Tarasenkov, 159.

poems. Furthermore, Tarasenkov argued that despite the fact that on a number of occasions the Party had "sharply and severely" criticized Selvinsky's "interpretation of Russian [sic] history" and "egregious political errors," Selvinsky "repeated his mistakes over and over again."[77] Since both Bagritsky and Grin, Tarasenkov's other targets in the essay, were dead, the attack could only threaten their legacy. Selvinsky was alive and very vulnerable.

4. The Ashes and Bones of Crimea

As we leave behind the postwar years of late Stalinism, let us pause and draw some preliminary conclusions about Ilya Selvinsky's path as a Shoah poet. By bearing witness to the immediate aftermath of the murder of Jews by Nazis and their accomplices in the occupied Soviet territories, Selvinsky simultaneously committed acts of civic courage and Jewish zealotry. Selvinsky's contribution to Shoah literature is all the more more significant because his poems appeared in the Soviet mainstream during and immediately after the Great Patriotic War and were available in print during the most destructive years for Soviet Jewish culture.

With changes and emendations, after 1942 Selvinsky's "I Saw It!" kept reappearing in various editions of his works and in collective volumes and anthologies, except for Selvinsky's books published in 1950 and 1953.[78] "I Saw It!" became one of his best known texts (even giving its title to a volume of his poetry published in 1985 in Moscow). In contrast to "I Saw It!" the poem "Kerch," after its publication in 1945, was not reprinted in the Soviet Union until 1984. Causal explanations based on Soviet official taboos and censorial demands, on the ideological climate, on spoken and unspoken policies toward the Jews, as well as on the poet's instinct of self-preservation, fail to do justice to the history of the creation and publication of Selvinsky's Shoah poems.

As we reflect on the price Selvinsky and other Jewish-Russian poets paid for bearing witness to the Shoah, we should first consider the

---

77 Tarasenkov, 161.
78 See, for instance, the reprinting of "I Saw It!" in the major post-Stalinist anthology of Russian-language Soviet poetry: "Ia eto videl!" in *Antologiia russkoi sovetskoi poezii*, ed. L. O. Belov et al., 1: 448-451.

cultural and ideological contexts of the Stalin era. Selvinsky's 1943 collection *Ballads and Songs* featured "I Saw It!" and opened with "Stalin at the Microphone," and this dithyrambic text was reprinted in his volume *Wartime Lyric* (1943), where "I Saw It!" also appeared. At the same time, in Selvinsky's wartime notebook one comes across a handwritten table of contents for a projected short collection of selected poems, the majority of them drawn from the wartime lyrics. It opens with "I Saw It!" and "A Reply to Goebbels" and also includes "To Russia" and "Episode," both of which had been condemned in party resolutions. The table of contents does not list any poems about Stalin, and in the notebook it is directly preceded by Selvinsky's notes for a poem or dramatic monologue titled "God of Poetry" ("Bog poezii"). "The government does not love me. And the people/ does not know me. ... I am the god of poetry. I am the ruler of reveries," so opens the poem, which apparently remained unfinished.

What do Selvinsky's Stalinist dithyrambs tell us about the literary and ideological cost of bearing witness to the Shoah? Was praising the dictator through poetry the price that Selvinsky and other Jewish-Russian poets paid for being able to mourn the victims of the Shoah—to mourn them as Soviets, as Russians, and as Jews?

The Jewish upheaval that Selvinsky, Antokolsky, Ozerov, and other Jewish-Russian poets experienced during the war and the Shoah might be described as the effect of "the ashes of Klaas" ("pepel Klaasa," in the Russian). In fact, as early as 1942 Soviet authors and polemicists invoked "the ashes of Klaas" to describe the Soviet people's response to Nazi atrocities in the occupied territories.[79] The expression comes from *The Legend of Thyl Ulenspiegel and Lamme Goedzak* (1867), a novel by the Belgian writer Charles de Coster (1827-1879), which became very popular in Russia and the USSR, and which was further popularized by its 1976 screen adaptation by Aleksandr Alov and Vladimir Naumov. The novel's protagonist, the young Flemish man Thyl Ulenspiegel, becomes a fighter against the Spanish invaders during the Dutch War of Independence, after the inquisition burns his father, Klaas, as a heretic. Following the auto da fé, Thyl and his mother take a bit of ashes from the execution site; the widowed mother sews a small sachet, puts the ashes into it, and hangs it on Thyl's neck to serve as a reminder of his father's death and of his mission as an avenger. As he fights for the free-

---

79 See, for instance, the *Red Star* editorial "Svora ubiits i grabitelei," *Krasnaia zvezda* 8 January 1942.

dom of Flanders, Thyl keeps repeating to himself: "The ashes of Klaas are knocking at my heart."[80] The bones and ashes of the murdered Jews of his native Crimea knocked at Selvinsky's heart as he bore poetic witness to the Shoah in 1942-1945. Throughout those years Selvinsky continued to howl about the annihilation of Jews even though the Soviet leadership discouraged such activity ever more forcefully. Not even during the Thaw, when the ideological conditions were generally more favorable and the risk of official punishment lower, would Selvinsky behave so bravely or write new poems based on his wartime experience as a witness to the Shoah.

In contextualizing the place of Selvinsky's poems about the Shoah in Crimea in the postwar Soviet society, one would benefit from considering one more circumstance. In the words of the historian Jonathan Dekel-Chen, "After liberation, the Jewish community [of Crimea] began anew, but with far fewer farmers; the Soviet regime had abolished the Jewish autonomous districts and non-Jews had occupied the colonies. In 1959, Jews constituted 2.2 percent (or 26,374 persons [as compared to the prewar 5.8 percent or 65,452 Jews]) of the total population, almost all in the cities."[81] The Shoah had wiped out what had been built in the 1920s and 1930s under the aegis of the Jews on land program. As Selvinsky mourned the victims of the Shoah in the occupied Crimea, he also implicitly took stock not only of the total loss of life, but specifically of the irrevocable damage done to Jewish life in Crimea.

By 1949, in the USSR Crimea had become something of a dirty word as a result of the fabricated charges against the disbanded JAC. In what became known as the "Crimean affair," the JAC's former members were accused of conspiring with foreign Jewish organizations to establish a Jewish enclave in the liberated Crimea, take over the peninsula, and break away from the USSR. The Crimean affair was one of the leitmotifs during the interrogations and trial of the thirteen JAC members, including five leading Yiddish writers, who were executed in 1952.[82] As

---

80 "Pepel Klaasa stuchit v moem serdtse," in Vadim Serov, *Entisklopedicheskii slovar' krylatykh slov i vyrazhenii*, http://www.bibliotekar.ru/encSlov/15/19.htm, last accessed 14 February 2011.
81 Dekel-Chen, "Crimea."
82 For details, see Joshua Rubenstein and Vladimir P. Naumov, eds., *Stalin's Secret Pogrom: The Postwar Inquisition of the Jewish Anti-Fascist Committee*, tr. Laura Esther Wolfson (New Haven: Yale University Press, 2001), esp. 17-22; Shimon Redlikh and Gennadii Kostyrchenko, eds., *Evreiskii antifashistskii komitet v SSSR 1941-1948* (Moscow: Mezhdunarodnye otnosheniia), 95-98; 136-139; Kostyrchenko, *Stalin protiv "kosmopolitov,"* 300-328. For a brief assessment of the "Crimean

Dekel-Chen observed, "although the regime refuted the 'plot' in the late 1950s and gradually rehabilitated its victims, the concocted image of Crimea as a potential American Jewish bridgehead has persisted."[83] Selvinsky, of course, knew and understood the Crimean Jewish context and recognized the further danger of coupling Jewish and Crimean themes under the shadow of the "Crimean affair." His insistence on reprinting the Crimean Shoah poems in the late 1940s and early 1950s constituted a further act of Jewish valor and ought to be acknowledged as such.

---

affair" in the context of postwar Soviet foreign affairs and nationalities politics, see S. M. Plokhy, *Yalta: The Price of Peace* (New York: Viking, 2010), 60-61.

83   Deckel-Chen, "Crimea."

CHAPTER FOUR

SELVINSKY'S LEGACY AND SOVIET SHOAH POETRY

1. The Anxiety of Noninfluence: Ozerov, Slutsky, Samoilov

In an interview conducted in 2009 on the occasion of the 110th anniversary of Ilya Selvinsky's birth, Tatiana Selvinskaya bemoaned the state of affairs with her father's legacy:

> I believe that father is underappreciated as a poet. They often reproach him for the poem against Pasternak [...] in which there were the lines that Pasternak had muddled the source that had been so pure. The most terrible thing lies in this phrase. I cannot understand why they cannot forgive father this line, even though it could not have harmed Pasternak in any serious way. And Pasternak has been forgiven the telephone conversation with Stalin about the fate of Mandelstam. [...] Yes, this was one of the worst acts my father committed, but he had other acts, too, of the directly opposite sort. He said it himself that by the age of forty he had been broken.[1]

Selvinsky showed his greatest courage as a poet and a witness to history during the most dangerous of times, the years of Stalinism, World War II, and the Shoah, yet faltered during the Thaw and the Pasternak affair—when little threatened his well-being, career, status, and family.

---

1 Mikhail Boiko, "K soroka godam ego slomali [interview with Tatiana Sel'vinskaia]," *Ex Libris NG* 23 April 2009, http://exlibris.ng.ru/tendenc/2009-04-23/6_selvinsky.html, last accessed 17 March 2011.

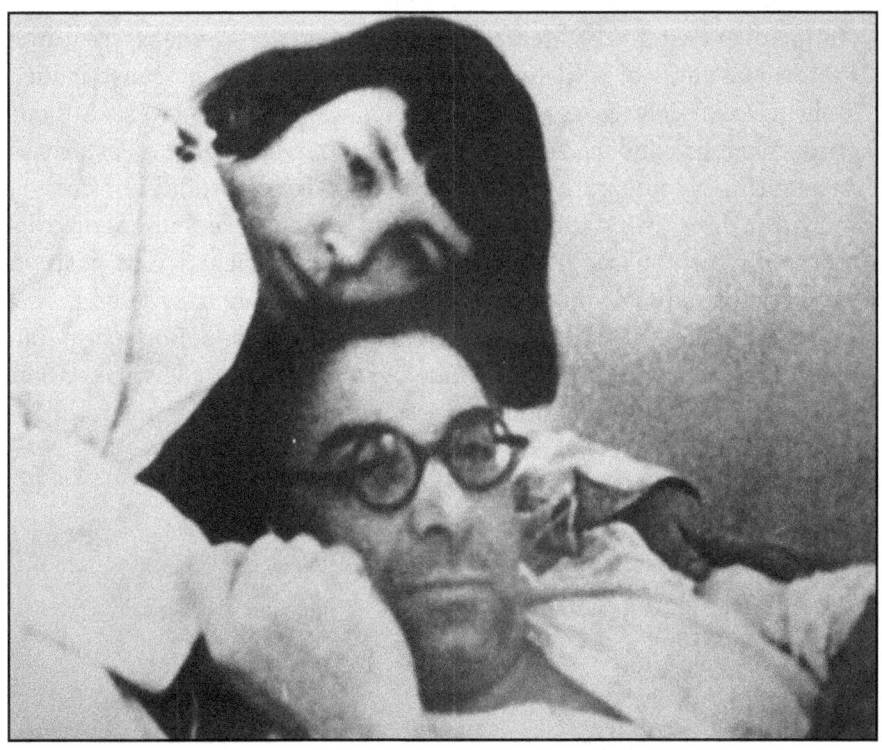

54. Ilya Selvinsky with Tatyana Selvinskaya. 1949. (Courtesy of Tatyana Selvinskaya.)

Why did Selvinsky join some other talented—and many worthless—Soviet writers of many backgrounds, identities, and literary languages in voicing uncharitable comments about Pasternak in 1958-1959?[2] Was

---

2   About Selvinsky's conduct following the announcement of Boris Pasternak's Nobel Prize for Literature, see, for instance, Olga Ivinskaia, "My poimenno vspomnikm vsekh, kto podnial ruku," in Ivinskaia, *Gody blizosti s Pasternakom: v plenu vremeni* (Moscow: Libris, 1992), http://www.sakharov-center.ru/asfcd/auth/auth_booka14f.html?id=84901&aid=170, last accessed 17 March 2011; Benedikt Benedikt, "Bednyi Len. Iz vospominanii o V. B. Shklovskom," *Lekhaim* 5 (2008), http://www.lechaim.ru/ARHIV/193/sarnov.htm, last accessed 17 March 2011. Two principal claims are usually levelled against Selvinsky. On 31 October 1958 Selvinsky, Viktor Shklovsky, and two other littérateurs published a denunciation of Pasternak's Nobel Prize in the Yalta-based *Kurortnaia gazeta* (*Vacational Gazette*). In the poem "Fathers, don't irritate your progeny..." ("Ottsy, ne razdrazhaite vashikh chad..."), published in the magazine *Little Flame* in 1959, Selvinsky criticized Pasternak without identifying him by name. See Sel'vinskii, "Iz novykh stikhov," *Ogonek* 11 (1959): 25. While decrying Selvinsky's poem about Pasternak, Korzhavin offers a nuanced perspective on Selvinsky's public conduct during the scandal over Pasternak's Nobel Prize; see Korzhavin, "'Vikhri vrazhdebnye' i inye."

CHAPTER FOUR

Selvinsky's reaction to Pasternak's Nobel Prize a way of venting his frustration over Pasternak's literary laurels? Should one, perhaps, scrutinize Pasternak's views of Jewishness and the Shoah, expressed most deliberately in *Doctor Zhivago*, as a possible explanation of other Jewish-Russian writers' public conduct during the Soviet campaign against Pasternak? Attempting a comparative ethics of writers' conduct does not do very much for our understanding of Selvinsky's discursive and poetic comments directed at Pasternak. Apologetics, either negative or positive, would do little to advance our understanding of Selvinsky's decision to repudiate Pasternak in public comments and in a poem. Both the public conduct and the poem should be weighed on the scale of Selvinsky's own previous acts of civic and literary valor, especially his wartime record as a poet-warrior and a witness to the Shoah.

55. Ilya Selvinsky. 1950s. (Courtesy of Tatyana Selvinskaya.)

When exactly was Ilya Selvinsky "broken"? Corresponding with the rise of Stalinism in Soviet culture, this gradual process began with the dismantling of the Literary Center of Constructivism in 1930, continued with the three waves of Selvinsky's official ostracism during the late 1930s, and culminated in 1943-1944. The wartime troubles, the aftershocks of which Selvinsky continued to experience until Stalin's death, depleted his stock of both Jewish and Soviet historical optimism. Mikhail Solomatin, who values Selvinsky as "perhaps the most vibrant poet of the Soviet epoch," made this comment in his recent reconsideration of Selvinsky's troubles: "What force bent these people? Nobody would answer. Nobody would confess to fearing *them*, their leaders, more than fascists."[3] Indeed, it is difficult to imagine how Selvinsky's official chastisement in 1943-1944, and its second spiral in 1946-1950, could not have rendered him a crushed person. But there is, perhaps, another aspect to his wartime devastation: had he not overexerted himself—and I mean this both literally and figuratively—when he witnessed the Shoah in his beloved Crimea?

Kandava was Selvinsky's last major text bearing poetic witness to the Shoah. After 1945-1946, he did not return to the topic until the peak years of the post-Stalinist Thaw. In 1960 he wrote and published "Strashnyi sud," an anguished poem about commemorating the victims of the Shoah. The original Russian title should be rendered in English as "Last Judgment," yet gains more from a literal translation, "Terrible Judgment." Selvinsky dedicated it to Boris Slutsky, a poet of the younger generation who had fought in the war, had a very distinctive poetic voice, and was at the time rapidly gaining a national literary reputation. After this poem, Selvinsky only hinted at his experience as a poetic witness to the Nazi atrocities in 1966, in a published polemic with Lev Ozerov. In both instances, Selvinsky's immediate addressees were poets of the very generation that took the torch from his hands and those of the other older Soviet poets in the years immediately preceding the Great Patriotic War. This was the generation of poets who in their twenties were shaped by the war and came to dominate the literary scene in the mid- to late 1950s. To finish the story about the price Selvinsky paid for bearing witness to the Shoah, let us turn to a consideration of Selvinsky's relationship with the poets of Slutsky's and Ozerov's literary generation.

---

3   Solomatin, "My eto videli."

56. Ilya Selvinsky. Portrait by Tatyana Selvinskaya. (Courtesy of Tatyana Selvinskaya.)

Selvinsky's poem "Terrible Judgment" originally appeared in the Tajikistan-based Russian-language magazine *Guliston* in 1960 and was reprinted in 1962 and 1964, and then posthumously in 1972.[4] In constructing a scene of a synagogue service, presumably taking place in the vicinity of a former Nazi death camp, Selvinsky's poem mourns the victims and strikes, at least on the surface of it, an antireligious note: "That day in the synagogue/ Few thought about god./ Here they cried, wept,/ Ripped the collar at the neck [...]." (After the Soviet fashion, Selvinsky did not capitalize God.) The Jewish mourners come out of the synagogue "no longer writhing in grief: Now from the torment/ Only a quiet exhaustion remained."[5] The procession, which is said to include "empty caskets" ("pustye groby"), moves in the direction of a former "Death camp" ("k byvshemu 'Lageriu smerti'")[6], so as "to submit the

---

[4] Here and hereafter I quote from Sel'vinskii, "Strashnyi sud," *Guliston* 3 (July-September 1960): 5-7; cf. Sel'vinskii, 1962, 125; Sel'vinskii, 1972, 310-313.

[5] Perhaps inadvertently, Selvinsky paraphrases Mayakovsky's line about Lenin's death from the long poem *Vladimir Ilych Lenin* (1924): "[...] the acute longing/ has become a clear, conscious pain."

[6] Selvinsky places the words "Death camp" in quotation marks and capitalizes the first word.

murdered ones to the Firmament ['Tverdi']." The mourners (and the poem's narrator) ask: "But where are the corpses? [...] Where are the ashes, at least? The grave?" The gazes of the Jews fall on "molten layers of austere soap/ Shining in vast vats." At this point the mourners accuse the old rabbi leading the service of being unable to offer them any words of comfort or wisdom and ultimately of lying that "all earthly is in god's power." The mourners have rejected the rabbi, yet the poem's finale presents a blending of miracle and politics. First "an archangel with a broken wing" and then a "swarm of cherubs" fall from the sky, "losing feathers in the air." Consider the last six lines:

А тучу в небе размыло —
И пал
        оттуда
            на слом
Средь блеска душистого мыла
Архангел с разбитым крылом...
За ним херувимов рой,
Теряющих в воздухе перья,
И прахом,
        пухом,
            пургой
Взрывались псалмы и поверья!
А выше, на газ нажимая,
Рыча, самолеты летели,
Не ждавшие в месяце мае
Такой сумасшедшей метели.

(And with dust [and ashes], down feathers, snow flurry,/ Psalms and legends exploded,/ And above, pressing on the gas,/ Roaring,/ Airplanes were flying,/ Not having expected in the month of May/ Such an insane snow storm.)

By implication the poem rejected religion and pronounced it defunct in a world where such apparent evil as the Nazi death camps had been allowed to happen. Yet Selvinsky's poem cited Leviticus in a Russiantransliterated (if mistranslated) Hebrew,[7] and made references, some of them incorrect, to Jewish religious customs and rituals. Even so, its debatable rhetoric aside, Selvinsky's poem was highly anomalous for the Soviet cultural mainstream of the day, in both its discussion of the Shoah and its invocation of Judaic rites and traditions. The poem referenced Nazi experiments in making soap from human bodies, which, Selvinsky most certainly knew, the Soviet side described at the Nuremberg Military Tribunal of 1946,[8] and which became part of what most Soviets knew about Nazism. While the poem seemed to suggest that the memorial service was taking place in an undisclosed postwar year in Poland, it is not unlikely that Selvinsky also had in mind some of the commemorations of the victims of the Shoah that occurred in the USSR. In the words of Mordechai Altshuler, "Although the [Soviet] authorities vehemently opposed outdoor memorial assemblies for Shoah victims, in the last phases of the war they authorized and even encouraged such assemblies in synagogue."[9] The most famous of these officially sanctioned services was the one at the Moscow Choral Synagogue on 14 March 1945. Furthermore, Selvinsky may have known that both outdoor commemorative events and memorial services took place in his native Crimea, in Simferopol and elsewhere, in 1945-1946.[10] Thus "Terrible Judgment" could be seen as a composite text based on what Selvinsky knew and imagined of various commemorative activities in the post-Shoah USSR and Eastern Europe.[11]

---

7   See Grinberg, "*I am to be read not from left to right but in Jewish: from right to left*": *The Poetics of Boris Slutsky* (Boston: Academic Studies Press, 2011), 336.
8   See the Soviet presentation of evidence, "Sixty-Second Day, Tuesday 19 February 1946," http://avalon.law.yale.edu/imt/02-19-46.asp, last accessed 22 February 2012.
9   Altshuler, "Jewish Holocaust Commemoration Activity in the USSR under Stalin," http://www1.yadvashem.org/odot_pdf/Microsoft%20Word%20-%205422.pdf, last accessed 20 February 2012.
10 I am grateful to Boris Berlin for sharing with me two archival reference letters which were issued in 2002-2003 by the State Archive of the Autonomous Republic of Crimea (GAARK) to the Charitable Jewish Center Khesed Shimon (Simferopol). The two reference letters (*spravki*) refer to a commemorative rally (*torzhestvennyi miting*) organized by the "leaders of the Jewish religious community" on 13 May 1945, and also to a religious rite-memorial service (*obriad bogosluzheniia-panikhida*) carried out on 6 August 1946 by "the observant members of the Simferopol Jewish community" to commemorate "the Jews executed by the Germans [sic] during the occupation of Crimea with a group trip to the site where the execution had taken place [...]." About this, also see Tiaglyi, *Mesta massovogo unichtozheniia*, 68.
11 In an overview of Soviet Shoah commemoration, Altshuler discusses some of the postwar activities and memorial services; he does not discuss Crimea. See his "Jewish Holocaust Commemoration Activity in the USSR under Stalin," http://www1.yadvashem.org/odot_pdf/Microsoft%20

57. Ilya Selvinsky. Circa 1964. (Courtesy of Tatyana Selvinskaya.)

A more detailed analysis of the poem goes beyond the scope of this investigation, and Marat Grinberg recently examined it in connection with the dialogue between Slutsky and Selvinsky.[12] Suffice it to say that Selvinsky's dedication of his only post-1945 poem about the Shoah to Slutsky constituted a poignant gesture. In Grinberg's view, "[Selvinsky] strongly and clearly identifies Slutsky as his Jewish interlocutor, the

---

Word%20-%205422.pdf, last accessed 20 February 2012.

12 See Marat Grinberg, "'Leader and Mentor': Il'ia Sel'vinskii," in Grinberg, *"I am to be read..."* 324-354. In a Russian-language article about Slutsky's dialogue with his contemporaries, Grinberg offers a harsher assessment of Sel'vinsky's "Terrible Judgment"; see Grinberg, "Vychityvaia Slutskogo," *Kreshchatik* 3 (2008), http://magazines.russ.ru/kreschatik/2008/3/gr23.html, last accessed 17 March 2010. Benjamin Pinkus briefly touched on "Terrible Judgment" in *The Soviet Government and the Jews. 1948-1967. A Documentary Study*, 400.

only figure capable of recognizing the value of his project and unraveling it."¹³ Concordantly, Selvinsky also identified Slutsky as a poet who was profoundly influenced by Selvinsky's poems about the Shoah.

To contextualize both Selvinsky's dedication and Slutsky's responses, we should recall at least the following pertinent facts of Slutsky's career: in the late 1930s, Slutsky joined Selvinsky's seminar at the Moscow Literary Institute and became a leading member of a circle of young poets that included Semyon Gudzenko, Pavel Kogan, Mikhail Kulchitsky, Sergey Narovchatov, and David Samoilov (Kogan and Kulchitsky would both perish in battle).¹⁴ In 1941 a poem by Slutsky appeared in *October*, with Selvinsky's help, in a selection of poems by five "Moscow students," Anisim Krongauz, Kulchitsky, Boris Slutsky, Narovchatov, and Samoilov.¹⁵ Slutsky apparently waited twelve years for his next publication of poetry. Some of Slutsky's earliest poems (1938–40) have most likely been lost, but the surviving ones reveal that the poet's self-consciously Jewish response to Nazism and the brewing catastrophe of European Jewry dated to 1938. Slutsky volunteered immediately upon the Nazi invasion and spent 1942–44 at the southern fronts; in 1943 he learned of the murder of his family members in the occupied Ukraine. He wrote virtually no poetry during his frontline years. Slutsky completed a book of documentary prose about his experiences in 1944–45 as a Soviet military officer in Romania, Bulgaria, Yugoslavia, Hungary, and Austria. In the chapter "The Jews," Slutsky interspersed authorial observations with survivors' testimony. This book remained unpublished until the post-Soviet years. In 1956 Slutsky became an icon of the Thaw; a Jew, a war veteran, a Party member, and an heir to the 1920s Left Art, he remained a conspicuous Soviet literary figure until the late 1970s. Having seen the immediate aftermath of the Shoah in 1944–45 and written nonfiction about it, Slutsky returned to poetry as the anticosmopolitan campaign gained speed in 1947-1948. Memories of the destruction of European Jewry became enmeshed in his acutely political imagination with the antisemitic crimes of late Stalinism, giving rise to a conflation of Jewish questions that he put into verse in the 1950s and 1960s (and

---

13   Grinberg, *"I am to be read...,"* 335.
14   See Shrayer, "Boris Slutsky," in *An Anthology of Jewish-Russian Literature*, ed. Shrayer, 2: 639-642; 794.
15   Boris Slutskii, "Maiakovskii na tribune," *Oktiabr'* 3 (1941): 114. See "Poeziia studentov Moskvy," *Oktiabr'* 3 (1941): 112-115. In 1937-1941 Selvinsky served as poetry editor at *October* magazine.

later revisited in the 1970s). The most daring and revealing of Slutsky's poems about the Shoah and antisemitism did not appear in the USSR until the final, reform years, although several circulated in samizdat and were smuggled to and published in the West. Four of his poems addressing Jewish topics appeared in Soviet magazines as Khrushchev's Thaw peaked and entered its downward spiral.[16] This brings us up to 1960, the time of Selvinsky's dedication of this postwar Shoah poem to Slutsky. In the 1950s–1970s Slutsky steered into Russian-language print more poems in which the Shoah was memorialized, the Jewish question was explicitly debated, and the word "Jew" was unabashedly used than did any of his Soviet contemporaries. Slutsky returned to the themes of the Shoah and antisemitism in the late 1960s and early 1970s. In February 1977, following his wife's death, severe depression set in. He wrote no poetry for the rest of his life and died in 1986.

In his first study of Slutsky's poetics, Grinberg suggested that in the Shoah poems from the 1970s Slutsky entered into dialogue with Selvinsky's *Kandava* and "Terrible Judgment."[17] In characterizing the Slutsky-Selvinsky dynamic, Grinberg has argued that "[...] whenever Selvinsky [...] touched at his end of the chain, Slutsky reverberated at his and vice versa."[18] Indeed, on several occasions, in poems written in the late 1960s and early 1970s but not printed until the reform or post-Soviet years, Slutsky spoke of Selvinsky as a teacher and mentor. But even Slutsky's lines of appreciation betray a motion toward displacing Selvinsky and relegating him to a relic of the pre-World War II Soviet past.[19] In other places, Slutsky expressed a subtle apprehension less through fact than through tone, or else suggested that Selvinsky might be jealous of him. To minimize the effect of poetic ambiguity, here we shall pay more attention to what Slutsky said about Selvinsky not through both rhyme and reason combined but through reason alone, in the discursive works that he clearly composed for the desk drawer. What role had Selvinsky's wartime poems played in the creation of Soviet Shoah

---

16   See Shrayer, "Boris Slutsky."
17   See Grinberg, "I am to be read...," 330-331; 338.
18   See Grinberg, "I am to be read...," 334.
19   The two most telling examples of Slutsky's poetic displacement of Selvinsky are the poems "Sel'vinskii, broshennaia zona… ("Selvinsky—and abandoned zone…," circa late 1960s; pub. 1989) and "Zalistannyi, zachitannyi…" ("Thoroughly leafed through, thoroughly read through…," circa 1971, pub. 1991); see Slutskii, *Sobranie sochinenii*, 3 vols., ed. Iu. Boldyrev, 2: 207-208; 371; commentary 547; 554. (Moscow: Khudozhestvennaia literatura, 1991).

literature? What was the real meaning of Slutsky's response to Selvinsky in the 1960s and 1970s? Finally, did Slutsky and other Jewish-Russian poets of his generation fully appreciate Selvinsky's contribution?

To answer these questions, I would like to turn to a volume of reminiscences and tributes published in 1982 and coedited by the poet's stepdaughter, Tsetsilia Voskresenskaya. As was often the case with such memorial volumes published in the Soviet Union, *About Selvinsky* took a number of years to materialize. Selvinsky's widow, Berta Selvinskaya, who had been instrumental in putting it together, did not live to see its publication. Among the volume's thirty-four contributors, notable Soviet authors of Selvinsky's generation were represented by Kornely Zelinsky and Evgeny Gabrilovich, both Selvinsky's former Constructivist colleagues, Pavel Antokolsky, and the poet Nikolay Ushakov. The next generation made a poorer showing, both overall and specifically with regard to Selvinsky's prewar mentees. Absent, glaringly, were contributions by Boris Slutsky and David Samoilov, both of them former participants in Selvinsky's seminar and his protégés, both of them Jews and leading figures on the post-Stalinist literary scene. And yet in the 1970s, prior to the publication of the memorial volume, both Samoilov and Slutsky had penned reminiscences of Selvinsky and his poetry seminar.[20]

The longest memoir in the volume belongs to Yakov Khelemsky, who had served alongside Selvinsky in Kurland in the spring of 1945 and had published, originally in the late 1940s, poems with references to the Shoah. Sergey Narovchatov (1919-1981), a former member of Selvinsky's poetry seminar, a military journalist during the war, the editor of *Novy mir* in 1974-1981, and an important functionary at the Union of Soviet Writers, contributed an appreciation of Selvinsky which steered clear of politics while carefully adding gold leaves to Selvinsky's

---

20   In 1974 Samoilov wrote "V masterskoi stikha" ("In the Master Workshop of Poetry") as part of a projected book of memoiristic essays, which appeared posthumously in 1995, edited by Samoilov's widow Galina Medvedeva; see Samoilov, *Pamiatnye zapiski*, ed. G. I. Medvedeva, 177-181 (Moscow: Mezhdunarodnye otnosheniia, 1995). See also Samoilov, "Nash uchitel'" ("Our Teacher"), which offered a much more critical assessment of Selvinsky, in *Novyi mir* 6 (2010), http://magazines.russ.ru/novyi_mi/2010/6/sa11.html, last accessed 10 February 2011. Finally, in an essay dated 1982, Samoilov sketched a visit to Selvinsky by a group of young poets from the Moscow Institute of Philosophy, Literature and History (MIFLI); see *Pamiatnye zapiski*, 118-121. Written in the 1970s prior to 1978, Slutsky's recollections of Selvinsky were part of a series of essays critically reflecting on Slutsky's teachers and senior contemporaries. See Slutsky, "Seminar Sel'vinskogo," in Slutskii, *O drugikh i o sebe*, ed. Petr Gorelik, 232-235 (Moscow: Vagrius, 2005); see also Slutskii, *O drugikh i o sebe*, 217-219.

Soviet laurels. Ozerov contributed the second-longest essay to the volume, which was also the essay most significant for understanding Selvinsky's poetry and personality.

58. Lev Ozerov. Circa early 1960s. Lev Ozerov, *Lirika*, Moscow, 1964. Copy autographed to David Shrayer-Petrov. (Courtesy of D. Shrayer-Petrov).

In order to contextualize Ozerov's writings about Selvinsky we should recall that he was born Lev Goldberg in Kiev in 1914 and studied philology at the Moscow Institute of Philosophy, Literature, and History (MIFLI) in 1934–39.[21] As we noted previously, Ozerov had been profes-

---

21 See Maxim D. Shrayer, "Lev Ozerov"; for an extensive, albeit not exhaustive bibliography of works by and about Ozerov, see "Lev Adol'fovich Ozerov," in *Russkie pisateli. Poety (Sovetskii period)*, vol. 16: 89-179 (St. Petersburg: Rossiiskaia natsional'naia biblioteka, 1994).

sionally acquainted with Selvinsky since 1936, but he was not among his prewar disciples and mentees. Peers identified Ozerov's aesthetics of the time with the Lake School of English romanticism (*ozernaia shkola*), hence his flight in 1935 to the non-Jewish pseudonym Ozerov (literally "of the lakes"). During the war, Ozerov contributed to the newspaper *Victory Shall Be Ours* (*Pobeda za nami*) and to the radio broadcasts of the political department of the Separate Mechanized Brigade for Special Tasks (OMSBON), as well as to the national civilian newspapers *Literature and Art*, *Labor* (*Trud*), and others. Recalled to Moscow in 1943 to defend his candidate's dissertation in literary studies, Ozerov stayed on to teach creative writing at the Literary Institute.

Ozerov apparently visited his native Kiev soon after its liberation in November 1943.[22] His article "Kiev, Babi Yar," based on collected eyewitness testimony and other documents, opened Part 1 ("Ukraine") of the Ehrenburg–Grossman (derailed) *Black Book*.[23] To recap, Ozerov held the record on writing about the Shoah for his entire generation, as the author of *Babi Yar* (1944-1945), the longest Russian-language Shoah poem written and published in Stalin's time. Originally published in the April-May 1946 issue of *October*, where Ozerov served as poetry editor in 1946-1948, *Babi Yar* was reprinted in Ozerov's collection *Downpour*, which Selvinsky reviewed favorably but not uncritically. Reprinted for the first time twenty years later in Ozerov's 1966 *Lyric: Selected Poems* (and again in 1974, 1978, and 1986), Ozerov's poem endured as the most historically reliable and extensive treatment of Babi Yar in all of Soviet poetry.[24] In the postwar decades Ozerov did not explicitly write about the Shoah or explore Jewish themes and subjects. He was a key figure on the Russian literary translation scene, a learned critic and professor of creative writing, although his poetic reputation was more modest than either Slutsky's or Samoilov's. *Babi Yar* had been not only

---

22 Beyond what follows from Ozerov's contribution to *The Black Book*, I am not aware of Ozerov's own discursive accounts of visiting Babi Yar immediately after Kiev's liberation; see, for instance, Sel'vinskii, "Poeziia L. Ozerova [rev. of *Liven'* by Lev Ozerov]," 178.

23 See Ozerov, "Kiev: Babi Yar," in Ehrenburg and Grossman, *The Complete Black Book of Russian Jewry*, 3-12.

24 Ozerov, "Babi Iar," *Oktiabr'* 3/4 (1946): 160-163; "Babii Iar," in Lev Ozerov, *Liven'*, ed. P. Antokol'skii, 25-32 (Moscow: Molodaia gvardiia, 1947); "Babii Iar," in Ozerov, *Lirika: 1931-1966*, 57-62 (Moscow: Sovetskii pisatel', 1966); "Babii Iar," in Ozerov, *Izbrannye stikhotvoreniia*, 449-45 (Moscow: Khudozhestvennaia literatura, 1974); "Babii Iar," in Ozerov, *Stikhotvoreniia*, 45-55 (Moscow: Khudozhestvennaia literatura, 1978); "Babii Iar," in Ozerov, *Istochnik sveta. Perevody i stikhotvoreniia*, 80-84 (Alma-Ata: Zhazushy, 1986).

Ozerov's most significant literary achievement but his greatest act of civic courage and Jewish self-expression.

While Ozerov's own poetry showed little Selvinskian influence, Ozerov became Selvinsky's keenest Soviet reader and a dedicated keeper of Selvinsky's legacy. It bears remembering that during the war Ozerov had not only written about Selvinsky with great perception on at least two occasions in 1942, but deliberately lauded him in print for the poems about the Shoah in Crimea. In the 1970s and 1980s Ozerov wrote several essays and memoirs about Selvinsky. In his 1981 book *A Poem's Biography*, a brief anthology of six exemplary poems from the nineteenth and twentieth centuries furnished with extensive commentary, Ozerov included a chapter on Selvinsky's "I Saw It!"[25] He highlighted a direct link between "I Saw It!" which had remained in print, and "Kerch," which at the time had not been reprinted since 1945. While the chapter had its roots in Ozerov's wartime articles about Selvinsky, in the 1981 commentary Ozerov made two essential points about Selvinsky's "I Saw It!"—naturally without resorting to the terminology a Western or Israeli student of Shoah literature might have employed at the time. The first point grew out of Ozerov's succinct analysis of the relationship between "I Saw It!" and "Kerch": "As regards the self-characterization ('I have described this very hazily'), it should be correlated with the overwhelming tragedy of the people, which had entered [the poet's life] on 11 January 1942 near the Bagerovo ditch. What he had seen and experienced was for him deeper and more painful than what he was able to convey in verses."[26] The code expression here is "tragedy of the people [or nation]" ("tragediia naroda"), which in the context of Selvinsky's poems refers to the Shoah; the absence of the word "Soviet" before "people" further underscores Ozerov's reason for being deliberately vague. Here the tragedy of *the people* refers to the *Jewish* people (or nation), and not just to the tragedy of the Soviet people. Ozerov's second point is about Selvinsky's insufficiently acknowledged influence on Soviet literature about World War II. "The title of the poem, 'I Saw It!' has gained a broader meaning," wrote Ozerov. "After Selvinsky others bore witness, as participants [kak uchastniki], to what they had seen, there appeared: 'I Saw It Myself!" by Iosif Utkin, the short novel *I Was Killed near Kharkov* by Fyodor Kandyba,

---

25 Ozerov, "'Ia eto videl!'" In Ozerov. *Biografiia stikhotvoreniia*, 40-48.
26 Ozerov, "'Ia eto videl!'" in Ozerov. *Biografiia stikhotvoreniia*, 47.

Aleksandr Tvardovsky's poem 'I Was Killed near Rzhev,' Boris Slutsky's 'The Pit of Cologne,' and the long poem *Babi Yar* by the one writing these lines."[27] The selection of the four poems in Ozerov's list speaks loudly for itself. Of these poems, which grew out of their authors' wartime experiences, only one, "I Was Killed near Rzhev" (1945-1946) by Selvinsky's antagonist Tvardovsky, is not directly about the murder of Jews by Nazis.[28] The other three, Utkin's "I Saw It Myself" (1942), Ozerov's *Babi Yar* (1944-1945; pub. 1946), and Slutsky's "The Pit of Cologne" (ca. 1944; pub. 1956), are poems by Jewish-Russian authors who followed in the footsteps of Selvinsky's "I Saw It!" by speaking in Soviet print of the genocide of the Jews. The degree of openness and clarity in these and other Soviet poems about the Shoah varied significantly, Ozerov's own explicit articulation of Jewish losses being the exception, and Utkin's referential opaqueness being rather the norm of presenting murdered Jews as generalized Soviet citizens. Ozerov not only stated that Jewish-Russian poets writing about the Shoah in the 1940s relied on the achievement of Selvinsky's "I Saw It!," he also implied that much of the Soviet poetry about Nazi atrocities and the victimhood of the Soviet people were actually veiled poems about the murders of Jews—about the Shoah. I believe Selvinsky understood this point all too well, and this knowledge caused him much anxiety in the postwar decades.

To the 1982 memorial volume *About Selvinsky*, Ozerov contributed the essay "A Glass of Ocean," so titled after "stakan okeana," the last two words in Selvinsky's poem "Velikii okean" ("Great [or Pacific] Ocean," 1932). Ozerov started with the premise that "Selvinsky had not been published in full and therefore was not fully appreciated. A lot of rubbish ['vzdora'] has been said about him and has not dispersed. Imprecise versions of his life and oeuvre keep multiplying. The reader, in short, still has an impossible time getting to the truth."[29] When Ozerov wrote his reflection, the wave of the Jewish emigration from the Soviet Union was about to crest, and the domestic climate was particularly hostile for Jewish self-expression. Careful not to step on ideological landmines,

---

27 Ozerov, "'Ia eto videl!'" in Ozerov, *Biografiia stikhotvoreniia*, 47.
28 In a 1975 article published in a Czech scholarly journal, Elvira Olonova briefly discussed Selvinsky's "I Saw It!" She suggested that "I Saw It!" held a special place among other wartime poems (with examples from Aleksei Surkov, Konstantin Simonov, Margarita Aliger, and Pavel Antokolsky) that also exhibit a documentary imperative and seek to bear witness to the events described. See Olonova, "Lirika na voine," *Československá rusistika* 20.2 (1975): 59-60.
29 Ozerov, "'Stakan okeana,'" 367.

Ozerov made no mention of Selvinsky's poems about the Nazi atrocities or Selvinsky's wartime or postwar troubles. Yet in what was hardly a favorable atmosphere, Ozerov devoted a whole passage to Selvinsky's origins and Jewish-Crimean ancestors. He did not embellish Selvinsky's legacy when he reminisced about his jealousy of Pasternak's literary legend and enduring popularity with lovers of poetry. Finally, and perhaps most pertinently to Selvinsky's tattered Soviet mantle as a Shoah poet, Ozerov mentioned his own disagreements with Selvinsky, notably their polemics about immortality, which I will now briefly revisit.

On 12 August 1966 Ozerov published an essay in the Moscow weekly *Literaturnaia Rossiia* (*Literary Russia*). Titled "Should One Dream of Immortality?," it carried the subtitle "An Open Letter to Ilya Selvinsky."[30] Ozerov introduced his essay as having been occasioned by rereading Selvinsky's poems. Specifically, behind the title of Ozerov's essay stood Selvinsky's cycle of philosophical poems "Davaite pomechtaem o bessmert'e" ("Let Us Dream about Immortality," 1964-1966). Ozerov identified "death and immortality" as one of Selvinsky's recurrent themes. In Ozerov's understanding, as both a "poet-materialist" (Ozerov refers to Selvinsky's philosophical orientation) and as one who has looked death in the eye on many occasions, Selvinsky refused to believe in death as either the termination of consciousness or a metaphysical transformation. Ozerov argued that, having rejected traditional religious explanations of an afterlife, Selvinsky resorted to modern scientific advances of cybernetics, believing, as it were, in an electronic survival of consciousness. Which was all well and good, except that Ozerov admitted to being unable to reconcile the survival of literary memory in the poet's consciousness with the prospect of (digitally) living on in an electronic otherworld (more nebulous then than now). That an essay of this nature was allowed to appear in a Soviet periodical was in and of itself a remarkable occurence. But even more astonishing was the publication, on 23 September 1966, of Selvinsky's punchy "Reply to Lev Ozerov."[31]

---

30 Ozerov, "Mechtat' li o bessmertii? Otkrytoe pis'mo Il'e Sel'vinskomu," *Literaturnaia Rossiia* 12 August 1966, 16-17.
31 Sel'vinskii, "Otvet L'vu Ozerovu," *Literaturnaia Rossiia*, 23 September 1966, 9; here and hereafter quoted from this source. For a younger contemporary's brief assessment of Selvinsky's views of immortality, see David Petrov [David Shrayer-Petrov], *Poeziia i nauka*, 45-47 (Moscow: Znanie, 1974).

Selvinsky started with a Mayakovskian testament: "If there is on our wonderful planet something nauseatingly repugnant, it is, undoubtedly, death." (Subsequently he paraphrased Mayakovsky's 1924 "Iubileinoe" ["Anniversary Poem"] once again: "I adore life and detest death"). Selvinsky framed his response with references to his continuing heart troubles: "After the second myocardial infarction, convinced that I would not survive a third one, I started psychologically preparing myself for death." The poet also acknowledged his philosophical debt to modern science, specifically to Albert Einstein, Norbert Wiener (founder of cybernetics), but also to Konstantin Tsiolkovsky, a Russian visionary of astronautics. And Selvinsky countered his science-inspired thinking about survival of consciousness after death with the discourse of traditional world religions, "Judaism, Christianity, Islam." In answering his own question about the endurance of religions, Selvinsky stated:

> What is the foundation of religion? Is it merely ignorance, which Marx called a "demonic force"? No, not only that. Religion CONSOLES. But with each new scientific discovery this kind of consolation grows more and more faint, and especially so when one comes face to face with life's monstrous [chudovishchnymi] occurrences. "If fascists live in this world/ Then there is no god!" said one elderly lady, who had for all the seventy years of her life believed in "the father, the son, and the holy spirit" [Selvinsky did not capitalize members of the Holy Trinity]. The eyes of the people open wider and wider to reality. Religious consolation is having an increasingly difficult time.

A careful reader of Selvinsky (and Selvinsky's direct addressee was the discerning and prudent Ozerov) would immediately recognize that both the "elderly lady" and her words of despair leapt onto the pages of *Literary Russia* directly from Selvinsky's "I Saw It!"—just as she had previously leapt from the poem to the pages of Selvinsky's discursive writings. The elderly lady, portrayed as an Orthodox Christian lying with the other victims in the Bagerovo ditch, rejected the possibility of believing in a benevolent and omnipotent divine power. The rejection occured in view of the Nazi atrocities, the atrocities which neither divine powers nor Soviet troops had prevented from happening. Obviously, Selvinsky could not and would not openly resuscitate, in a 1966 newspaper polemic about immortality and poetry, his painful legacy as a literary witness to the Shoah. Nor could he even speak of death and postmortem survival of consciousness with the nakedness of his diary entry for 5 May 1945, in which he had recounted a recent nightmare of walking to his death in "Majdanek or Treblinka." And yet, the auto-reference served as more than another piece of evidence in Selvinsky's argument against the very possibility of religious faith in the post-Shoah world. In the shimmering logic of Selvinsky's argument, the horror of what he had seen at the Bagerovo ditch reaffirmed his own faith in science and in Marxism-Leninism—and not in religious explanations of mortality and immortality. "Future is Communism," Selvinsky stated. "But what will life be under Communism—neither Marx, not Lenin liked to talk about this." According to his daughter, Selvinsky said privately that in the Soviet Union "Communists had gone underground [kommunisty ushli v podpol'e]."[32] As an aging Jewish man and a veteran Soviet poet, the Selvinsky of the 1960s still trumpeted public notes of Marxist allegiance even as he evoked the massacres at Kerch while publicly addressing a fellow Jew and a fellow poetic witness to the Shoah.

The 1966 polemical exchange, in which Ozerov came out as an outdated romantic idealist as compared to Selvinsky's electronic-age materialist, could have alienated Ozerov, but it did not. Ozerov subsequently contributed an introduction to the two-volume edition of Selvinsky's works published in 1989.[33] A paler version of "A Glass of Ocean," Ozerov's perestroika-era essay forgot all about his polemical confrontation with Selvinsky. Ozerov filled some historical and biographical gaps, included a section about official attacks on Selvinsky both in 1943-1944 and during the postwar Stalin years, and mentioned "I Saw It!" in the context of Selvinsky's troubles.

Ozerov's memoirs of Selvinsky painted a fundamentally accurate picture of a major poet whose legacy called for a thorough reexamination. Ozerov died in 1996, outliving most of his contemporaries, including Slutsky and Samoilov, and in 1999 his unfinished book of versified memoirs, *Portraits without Frames*, appeared posthumously. The volume

---

32 Tatyana Selvinskaya, Personal Interview, 15 December 2011.
33 Ozerov, "Il'ia Sel'vinskii, ego trudy i dni."

included a touching poetic memoir of Selvinsky in the 1960s, when the poet suffered from severe cardiac illness. Ozerov concluded his tribute to Selvinsky this way: "I consider myself immeasurably rich,/ Having had the gift of the mighty poet's friendship./ He called me his younger brother/ And did acts of goodness [delal dobro]/ Without remembering he did so."[34] Ozerov understood the price Selvinsky had paid for his poems about the Shoah in the occupied territories. This takes us back to the vexing problem of Selvinsky's reception by his former mentees, disciples and protégés. To restate some of the main facts: neither Samoilov nor Slutsky were among the contributors to the 1982 volume of memoirs and appreciations, yet in the 1970s both had written separate memoirs about Selvinsky and had also reminisced about him in connection with other writers and subjects.[35] Their memoirs of Selvinsky would remain unpublished until the post-Soviet years.

According to Tatyana Selvinskaya, who was shocked to learn about Slutsky's memoiristic accounts of her father, Slutsky "adored papa. He wept at the funeral.... Slutsky was beside papa to the end."[36] Slutsky left a separate memoir of Selvinsky, "Selvinsky's Seminar." In reading it one senses an apprehension similar to the one expressed in Slutsky's poems about Selvinsky. This is not a fond or grateful recollection of a mentor, and here the problem does not lie in the tone alone. Slutsky mentions that Selvinsky "did not connect with [his prewar] poetry ("stikhi moi emu ne byli blizki").[37] As is often the case in such memoirs, the harshest verdict appeared in a displaced and particularly alien context, not in the essay about Selvinsky himself but in Slutsky's piece about Aleksandr Tvardovsky. Selvinsky openly despised Tvardovsky, refusing to appreciate him both on artistic grounds and on the basis of Tvardovsky's record of wartime valor, which Selvinsky thought to be paltry. (In the 1950s and 1960s Tvardovsky paid Selvinsky in kind by not publishing him in *Novy mir* during both of his tenures as the journal's editor).[38] Slutsky

---

34 Ozerov, "Sel'vinskii," in Lev Ozerov, *Portrety bez ram*, ed. A. Ozerova and S. Kugel', 165-169 (Moscow: Academia, 1999).
35 See Slutskii, "Seminar Sel'vinskogo"; "Tvardovskii" in Slutskii, *O drugikh i o sebe*, ed. Petr Gorelik (Moscow: Vagrius, 2005), 232-235; 215-221. See Samoilov, "V masterskoi stikha"; Samoilov, "Iz prozaicheskikh tetradei," ed. Galina Medvedeva, *Novyi mir* 6 (2010), http://magazines.russ.ru/novyi_mi/2010/6/sa11-pr.html, last accessed 1 July 2010.
36 Tatyana Selvinskaya, Personal Interview, 15 December 2011.
37 Slutskii, "Seminar Sel'vinskogo," 233.
38 See Slutskii, "Tvardovskii," 218-219; see Shraer-Petrov, "Karaimskie pirozhki," 277-278.

writes: "The war ended, having cancelled special discounts and wartime allowances. One had to write the full truth about it [the war], and upon returning from the war I discovered that in [Mikhail] Isakovsky's "The enemies burned the native hut..." ("Vragi sozhgli rodnuiu khatu...") and in [Aleksandr] Tvardovsky's new long poem this truth was present, and in the work of my teachers, Selvinsky in particular, it was absent."[39] Here Slutsky adds insult to injury by preferring not only Tvardovsky, an important literary figure, but also Isakovsky, author of catchy lyrics to songs of national fame who had made no original contribution to the Russian poetic tradition.

59. Boris Slutsky. Circa middle 1970s. (Boris Slutsky, *Neokonchennye spory*, Moscow, 1978.)

---

39   Slutskii, "Tvardovskii," 217.

Slutsky's comments also betray another festering wound going back to the years immediately following Stalin's death, when Slutsky almost instantaneously rose to the top of the Soviet literary pantheon, and to a polemic about "national" poetry that Slutsky's poems ignited. On 8 July 1956, some four months after the 20th Congress of the Communist Party at which Stalin's cult of personality was denounced in Nikita Khrushchev's "secret speech," Ehrenburg lauded Slutsky's poetry in *Literary Gazette*, helping forge Slutsky's fame. Ehrenburg praised much in Slutsky's poetry, employing the overloaded term *narodnost'* and its cognates and arguing that Slutsky was endowed with traits of a poet with a national voice.[40] A polemic ensued, both publically and privately in literary circles, in which Ehrenburg and Slutsky were both attacked and both defended, and this polemic only buttressed Slutsky's popularity. On 18 October 1956 Selvinsky responded with a long article in *Literary Gazette*, titled "Nationhood and Poetry." Selvinsky argued, resorting to Marx and Engels, to the then-recent dismantling of Stalinism, and to examples drawn from Russian classical literature, painting, classical ballet, and key figures of Soviet prose and drama, that the notion of *narodnost'* could not and should not be applied to Soviet art and letters: "Thus, in the life of a socialist society there cannot be a division of public activity into national and un-national [na narodnuiu i nenarodnuiu]. Just as we cannot have a national and an un-national ministry, so unthinkable is an art divided into national and un-national."[41] In a private letter to Selvinsky that followed this article, Ehrenburg expressed his dislike of both the article and the position. On 25 November 1956 Selvinsky responded with a long missive that provides important evidence for the understanding of the dynamics of the Jewish question in postwar Soviet letters, and may also shed concrete light on the aspersions Slutsky would subsequently cast on Selvinsky. In justifying and explaining his polemical response to Ehrenburg's article about Slutsky, Selvinsky suggested that "without suspecting it, [Ehrenburg has] played the hand of one very reactionary and very strong group in our poetry."[42] He continued:

---

40   See Erenburg, "O stikhakh Borisa Slutskogo," *Literaturnaia gazeta* 8 July 1956.
41   Sel'vinskii, "Narodnost' i poeziia," *Literaturnaia gazeta* 18 October 1956.
42   See Selvinsky, Letter to Ehrenburg, 25 November 1956 in Frezinskii, ed., *Pochta Il'i Erenburga. Ia slyshu vse...1916-1967*, 331-334. Hereafter this source of the letter is quoted.

By hook or by crook, the grand imperial Slavophiles [velikoderzhavnye slavianovily] are pushing for the acceptance by our public of the notion that only one national line [narodnaia liniia] exists in Soviet poetry—the line of Tvardovsky. [...] By declaring Boris Slutsky a national [poet] in your article, you as much as concede that there are also un-national Soviet poets. This is exactly what the chauvinists are waiting for and what, out of cautiousness, they had not dared to say out loud. [...] Do you know, by the way, that in the [editorial portfolio of *Literary Gazette*] there is an article, wherein the author polemicizing with you writes that "in poetry, in order for it to become national, it matters not only *what* is written, not only *how* it is written, but also *who* wrote the work." Clear? With my article, in which I seek to prove the impossibility of dividing our art into national and un-national Soviet trends, I have thus far forestalled the danger that your article created.[43]

Selvinsky, not surprisingly in the context of the Thaw, went on to say to Ehrenburg that the "present goal of the critic" is not to "juxtapose Slutsky to the style *à la russe* but [to juxtapose] things Communist to things anti-Communist [...] or else our entire culture will irrevocably begin to slide back. No matter how beastly the crimes committed by Stalin, not matter how egregious the mistakes committed by our Party, communism remains a sacred idea of human history." He stated that he saw his "civic duty" in trying to repair a crack in the people's faith in Communism and prevent "a flood of all the conservative, reactionary, and counterrevolutionary forces of dark Russia [...]." It is not easy to read these words today, but it is even worse to hide them or to hide from them. Yes, Selvinsky must have taken personal offense—from Slutsky, Ehrenburg, and the whole situation. Selvinsky must have been incensed that he, who had placed young Slutsky on the map of Soviet poetry back in March 1941, was not asked to be his herald during the Thaw. But the other, greater part of Selvinsky's motivation was a tacit

---

43 Selvinsky, Letter to Ehrenburg, 25 November 1956 in Frezinskii, ed., *Pochta Il'i Erenburga. Ia slyshu vse...1916-1967*, 331-334.

recognition that World War II and postwar Stalinism had washed away the hopes for an internationalist, cosmopolitan, intelligentsia-driven Soviet culture. Neither in a published article nor in a private letter could Selvinsky articulate his bitterness over a crisis of aspirations, both aesthetic and ideological, both Soviet and Jewish, however misplaced these aspirations may appear today. For the Selvinsky of 1956, a critique of the notion of *narodnost'* (sense of nationhood or peoplehood) was not only a response of a "Communist gone underground" but a viscerally Jewish response couched in Soviet internationalist rhetoric.[44]

Let us now return to Slutsky's memoiristic notes about Selvinsky. In introducing Slutsky's memoirs, his dedicated friend and executor Pyotr Gorelik drew on the poet's view of the genre: to be "passionate and unfair."[45] I would describe Slutsky's reflections on and recollections of Selvinsky as calculatedly unfair, and this goes not only for the maudlin pleasure of a student dancing on his teacher's grave, which one hears in Slutsky's remarks. What absence, and of what "truth," was Slutsky talking about? How could Slutsky say this after Selvinsky's wartime record of bearing witness to the Shoah and writing about Jewish victimhood? Could Slutsky possibly mean that in his wartime poems like "I Saw It!" "Kerch," or *Kandava*, Selvinsky made concessions in order to speak at least part of the truth about the Shoah?

What is especially intriguing and disturbing is that, *mutatis mutandis*, Boris Slutsky's discursive comments about Selvinsky concorded with the reflections penned within the same decade by David Samoilov, a poet of a very different fate and talent, and with a different relationship with his Jewish identity. Samoilov was born David Kaufman in 1920 in Moscow.[46] Before the Great Patriotic War, Samoilov attended the Moscow Institute of Philosophy, Literature and History (MIFLI) and participated in Selvinsky's seminar at the Literary Institute. He debuted under his birth name in March 1941 in *October*, in an issue for which Selvinsky facilitated a collective publication of poems by five student

---

44 Elsewhere Selvinsky even managed to decry chauvinism and nationalism, both Russian and Ukrainian, in print, under thin disguises. For instance, in an article on the seventieth anniversary of Pavlo Tychyna's birth, Selvinsky used the word "otechestvennyi" (domestic; homegrown) to refer very clearly to Ukrainian nationalists. See Sel'vinskii, "Sila poeta."
45 Slutskii, *O drugikh i o sebe*, 248.
46 Useful information is found in "David Samuilovich Samoilov," in *Russkie pisateli. Poety (Sovetskii period). Bibliograficheskii ukazatel'*, vol. 22: 170-257 (St. Petersburg, Rossiiskaia natsional'naia biblioteka, 1999).

poets,[47] and subsequently adopted the penname "Samoilov," derived from his patronymic "Samuilovich."

60. David Samoilov. Circa 1980s. (David Samoilov. *Pamiatnye zapiski*. Moscow, 1995).

Samoilov spent 1942-1945 at the war fronts, starting as a private and ending the war a junior lieutenant; with the Soviet troops Samoilov went through Poland and Germany all the way to Berlin. Samoilov's first collection of poetry, *Nearby Countries*, did not appear until 1958. While in some of his poems Samoilov reflected on wartime experiences, he did not touch on Jewish victimhood and subsequently circumvented the subject of the Shoah in his discursive works. In the mid-1970s he

---

47 "Poeziia studentov Moskvy," *Oktiabr'* 3 (1941): 112-115.

———————————— CHAPTER FOUR ————————————

told the writer David Shrayer-Petrov that he had neither poems about Jews nor Jewish self-awareness.[48] Indeed, a few tired attributes and images aside, Samoilov's poetry was virtually free of Jewish motifs, the only exception being the long poem *Solomonchik the Tailor. A Brief Life Story*. Grinberg has deemed this long poem, which did not surface in print until 2005, Samoilov's "single full-blooded Jewish text."[49] Samoilov apparently composed it in the late 1940s or early 1950s.[50] In Grinberg's summary, "[t]he poem, paying tribute to the stereotypes of Jewish characters gathered from Babel, Bagritsky, Utkin, and Ehrenburg's *The Stormy Life of Laz[ik] Roitshvantz*, tells a story of a simple tailor from Odessa, who had unlearned his Yiddish burr [misrolled Russian r's—MDS], having become Russia's Soviet son."[51] In its poetic intonation, *Solomonchik the Tailor* borrowed widely from Soviet Russian poetry of the 1920s-1940s, from Mikhail Svetlov to Konstantin Simonov. A past participant in the Civil War and therefore a Soviet Jew from the generation that preceded Samoilov's (i.e. the generation of Selvinsky and Ehrenburg), the fictional Solomonchik volunteers in 1941 following the Nazi invasion. He meets his death on the battlefield by covering with his body an enemy machine gun and committing an act of ultimate sacrifice (see above the discussion of Aleksandr Matrosov and his Jewish and non-Jewish antecedents and successors). As Grinberg observes, the poem's lines which immediately follow the description of Solomonchik's death, "No Palestine/ Is needed for him," carry a "possible allusion to the creation of the State of Israel in 1948."[52] Samoilov's Jewish-Russian everyman dies for Russia like a Russian—Soviet—soldier, and is buried in the middle of the vast country. Of his life and destiny Samoilov wrote: "He was a small drop of blood/ Amid a sea of different bloods,/ He was a small drop of man-

---

48 See David Shraer-Petrov, "Tezka. David Samoilov" in Shraer-Petrov, *Vodka s pirozhnymi*, 289.
49 See Samoilov, "Solomonchik portnoi. Kratkoe zhizneopisanie" in David Samoilov, *Poemy*, ed. Galina Medvedeva and Andrei Nemzer, 334-341 (Moscow: Vremia, 2005) and Grinberg, "I am to be read..." 311. I did not discover *Solomonchik the Tailor* until after the publication of *An Anthology of Jewish-Russian Literature* (2007), and I suspect I was not the only student of Jewish-Russian literature to have been disappointed by Samoilov's reliquary long poem.
50 See commentary in Samoilov, *Poemy*, 379-380.
51 Grinberg, "I am to be read..." 309. In a chapter on Samoilov and Slutsky, Grinberg offers a detailed consideration of Samoilov's Jewish background and of Samoilov's reflections on Jewish history and culture, Judaism, and the Shoah; see "Blindness and No Insight: David Samoilov," in Grinberg, 285-323.
52 Grinberg, 309.

hood,/ Amid a sea of men...."⁵³ Samoilov's articulation of Solomonchik's dissolution in Russian history stands directly in line with Samoilov's self-awareness as a Soviet Jew becoming a Russian poet by burying his own Jewishness. Perhaps the hardest thing to come to terms with in *Solomonchik the Tailor* is the poem's intonation. Coupled with the story Samoilov tells, the pathos teeters between the heroic and the mock-heroic. In the context of the postwar and post-Shoah Soviet years, such a teetering may be indicative of Samoilov's indecision about his Jewish poem's intended Soviet message.

One of the most admired Russian poets and literary translators of the post-Thaw Soviet decades, Samoilov was especially lionized by members of the Jewish-Russian intelligentsia who deluded themselves into believing that the Jewish presence in Russia would only survive via total assimilation and Russianization. In his life Samoilov displayed an affinity with Orthodox Christianity and an indifference to Jewish history and culture. He also exhibited a visceral sensitivity to Jews who wrote in Russian about their dual identity or sought to emigrate from the USSR.⁵⁴ Samoilov reminisced about Selvinsky on two principal occasions. His book *Memorial Notes*, published posthumously, features the essay "In the Master Workshop of Poetry," written in 1974. This memorial essay painted a portrait of Selvinsky as a famous poet of the prewar years, passionate and dedicated to his students and to the cause of poetry, generous and giving, inspiring and edifying. "[Selvinsky] taught us to judge poetry according to the Hamburg reckoning," wrote Samoilov, evoking Viktor Shklovsky's expression. "We trusted him and in many ways are indebted to him. He possessed a remarkable intuition for and understanding of talent. Everyone whom he singled out became a poet."⁵⁵ With a few expurgations, "In the Master Workshop of Poetry" would have been suitable for publication in the Soviet 1970s and 1980s, and perhaps Samoilov did not originally write it for the proverbial desk drawer. However, in the 1970s Samoilov also penned a second piece about Selvinsky. Titled "Our Teacher," not without caustic wit, this vignette was recently extracted from Samoilov's papers and published by his widow, Galina Medvedeva, with a selection of other

---

53 Samoilov, "Somonchik portnoi," 341.
54 See David Shraer-Petrov, "Tezka. David Samoilov," 283-297.
55 Samoilov, "V masterskoi stikha," 178.

notes and vignettes. Medvedeva acknowledged that while some of the details "inevitably repeat themselves," this is a "more personal, partial" view, which "perhaps does not strive for objectivity [...]."[56] The contrast between Samoilov's two memoirs of Selvinsky is not just a matter of authorial voice and angle of vision, but also one of principal disparities in the two assessments of Selvinsky. Consider Samoilov's appraisal of Selvinsky in the prewar literary context:

> He had started writing poetry when everything was possible, and throughout his entire life knew how to reject that which was *not possible* [*ne mozhno*; this could also mean "not permitted"], because he did not want and feared that which was *not possible*. With that he ruined himself. The most unspiritual poet of Russia, the greatest of the unspiritual ones—our teacher Ilya Selvinsky. Who else would have undertaken to mentor us, in the prewar epoch, when Akhmatova lingered in long isolation, when Pasternak in his tragic well-being dug out metaphors in the kitchen garden of his Peredelkino dacha, scared of his disciples' spreading themselves across poetry [...]. Thank god, the teacher was he, who alone wanted and could be our teacher, Ilya Selvinsky.
>
> It was our happy fortune that Selvinsky was our teacher. And he had chosen us. Whatever else one can say about Selvinsky, he is our teacher. And I wish that the disciples, who have eclipsed us, would repay us with the same eternal love—and there is no transient love in poetry—as we, only those very few of us still alive, have for him, would repay us and remember and forgive us.
>
> I recently reread Selvinsky's volume of poetry in the Poet's Library [...] [Selvinsky] is all completely made up, from period to period. From character to biography, from feelings to thoughts, from love to hate, from friends to enemies.[57]

---

56   David Samoilov, "Iz prozaicheskikh tetradei," ed. Galina Medvedeva, *Novyi mir* 6 (2010), http://magazines.russ.ru/novyi_mi/2010/6/sa11-pr.html, last accessed 1 July 2010.
57   Samoilov, "Iz prozaicheskikh tetradei."

Selvinsky's poetry and biography refute Samoilov's characterization. Like some other leading Soviet modernists of his generation, Selvinsky worked hard to create a larger-than-life mythology of the self, especially in his epic poems and historical dramas. At the same time, Selvinsky's life and art, and especially the years of World War II, the Shoah, and late Stalinism, offer overwhelming evidence that his enemies were not "made up." They were quite real and came from the ranks of fascists and antisemities of all colors and stripes, both foreign and domestic. It is unthinkable that Samoilov did not understand this.

Why, then, were both Samoilov and Slutsky, Selvinsky's former students, so unfair in the judgments they put forth in the 1970s? Are we dealing with two sides of the same issue of Soviet memory of the Shoah? Was Samoilov putting down Selvinsky because he was ashamed of his own silence about the Shoah? By the same token, did Slutsky feel a need to obfuscate Selvinsky's role as a poet-soldier-witness in order to inflate his own place in the canons of both Soviet and Jewish literature? Selvinsky's own gestures in the direction of Slutsky and his other former mentees exhibit a response, both preemptive and reactive, that can be described as an anxiety of noninfluence—a variation on Harold Bloom's classic model.[58] At the same time, the former students' cannibalism of their teacher's memory represents a particularly Soviet variety of the anxiety of influence, here riddled with issues of Soviet Shoah memory.

Both Slutsky and Samoilov, different poets and different Jews as they were, disparaged Selvinsky's contribution. Their discursive comments about Selvinsky, which appeared in the cultural mainstream in the 1990s and 2000s, amounted to a sad epitaph to the story of Selvinsky's legacy.

2. Selvinsky Agonistes

In the postwar decades, Selvinsky's glory as a poetic witness to the Shoah in the occupied Soviet territories was overshadowed not just by Boris Slutsky's edifice but also by the writings of younger, non-Jewish

---

58 Harold Bloom, *The Anxiety of Influence: A Theory of Poetry* (London: Oxford University Press, 1973). I originally used the notion of the anxiety of noninfluence in order to describe the Bunin side of the Ivan Bunin-Vladimir Nabokov relationship. See Shrayer, *The World of Nabokov's Stories*, 292 (Austin and London: University of Texas Press, 1998).

poets who were children during the war. Their poetic protests against the Soviet non-commemoration of the Shoah originally entered the public sphere during the latter years of Khrushchev's rule. Selvinsky lived to see the publication of "Babi Yar" (1961) by Yevgeny Evtushenko (b. 1933), a *cause célèbre* of the Thaw which immediately gained a worldwide audience. However, Selvinsky did not live to see the publication of *Ditch* (1985-1986) by Andrei Voznesensky (1933-2010), a work specifically devoted to the remembrance of the Shoah in Crimea. Composed between December 1985 and May 1986, Voznesensky's *Ditch*, a cycle of interconnected poems interspersed with discursive prose and commentary, is a case in point. An early version of *Ditch* was published in the July 1986 issue of the popular Moscow literary monthly *Iunost'* (*Youth*).[59] Just as the Soviet Union was finally testing the limits of what could openly be said about its history—and as the subject of the Shoah was inching its way into the national public discourse—Voznesensky revised *Ditch*, and it was published as a centerpiece of his 1987 volume of poetry and prose, which was also titled *Ditch*.[60] The subtitle of Voznesenky's *Ditch* is "Spiritual Trial," and in broadening the text of the original version, which in a draft form had been titled *Greed*, Voznesensky's principal authorial decision was to append to it excerpts from the readers' letters written in response to the original magazine publication.

The discursive frame of *Ditch* described the poet's visit, in July 1986, to the site where, in the late autumn of 1941, between 12,000 and 14,000 Ashkenazi Jews and Krymchaks were murdered by the Nazis.[61]

By the time he saw the site of the Simferopol massacre in July 1986, Voznesensky had apparently already composed a number of poetic sections of *Ditch*. Driving from Simferopol on the Simferopol-Feodosia Highway, Voznesensky and his companions came upon a freshly dug section of the wartime anti-tank ditch outside Simferopol. This, in turn, led to the shocking discovery that local scavenger-gravediggers (*grobokopateli*) were continuing to prey on the remains of the victims by opening the ditch, removing and breaking up the skulls, and extracting gold teeth and crowns. Voznesensky's visit to the site of the Simferopol mass execution came fast on the heels of a trial of a Crimean band of scavengers

---

59 See Andrei Voznesenskii, "Rov," *Iunost'* 7 (1986): 6-15.
60 See A. Voznesenskii, "Rov. Dukhovnyi protsess," in *Rov. Stikhi. Proza* (Moscow: Sovetskii pisatel', 1987), 80-138.
61 On the murder of the Jews of Simferopol, see Tiaglyi, *Mesta massovogo unichtozheniia*, 60-68.

61. The anti-tank ditch at the 10th km. of the Simferopol-Feodosia Highway. 14 December 2011. Photo by Maxim D. Shrayer.

who systematically pillaged the Simferopol ditch and sold the extracted precious metal to jewelry businesses for meltdown. Standing over the unearthed remains of the Shoah victims, Voznesensky witnessed both the past Nazi genocide and the unabashed, recent Soviet desecration of the victims' memory. Both Voznesenky's posture in the poetic parts of *Ditch* and his authorial perspective in the work's discursive passages revealed a reliance on three principal textual sources in addition to the poet's own observations, conversations with local residents, and wrathful reflections. Voznesensky's sources included proceedings of the then-recent trial of scavengers in Simferopol, archival materials, and wartime literary texts written by authors of Selvinsky's generation and published during the war. Specifically, Voznesensky quoted from the essay "Utselel odin" ("One Survived") by Selvinsky's senior contemporary Lidia Seifullina. In this essay, which Seifullina contributed to *The Black Book* (in 1986-1987 still unpublished in the Soviet Union), she reported on the December 1941 mass murder of Jews outside Simferopol.[62]

---

62 See Voznesenskii, "Rov. Dukhovnyi protsess," 135; cf. Seifullina, "One Survived: The Story of Evsey Efimovich Gopshtein," in Ehrenburg and Grossman, *The Complete Black Book of Russian Jewry*, 427-430.

―――――― CHAPTER FOUR ――――――

Voznesensky failed to acknowledge Selvinsky's contribution as his predecessor and as the first poetic witness to the Shoah in Crimea, and yet several sections of *Ditch* breathe with a poetic knowledge of "I Saw It!" Voznesensky even mentioned Kerch in one of the poems. In an admiring review of *Ditch*, the critic Anatoly Pikach was quick to remind Voznesensky of the apparent trace of Selvinsky's "I Saw It!": "He saw it all himself. I do not know whether Voznesensky remembered Selvinsky's poem, written in 1942 in Kerch (not even so far from Simferopol), but this is how those verses from a while ago were echoed [in Voznesensky's long poem]." And Pikach went on to quote the opening of "I Saw It!"[63]

```
              Уважаемый товарищ!                    Народный артист РСФСР, композитор
    МОСКОВСКАЯ ПИСАТЕЛЬСКАЯ ОРГАНИЗАЦИЯ                       М. И. БЛАНТЕР
         СОЮЗА ПИСАТЕЛЕЙ РСФСР                       Народный артист РСФСР
      И ЦЕНТРАЛЬНЫЙ ДОМ ЛИТЕРАТОРОВ                         П. И. ВИШНЯКОВ
         ПРИГЛАШАЮТ ВАС В ПЯТНИЦУ,
           24 ОКТЯБРЯ 1969 г. НА                    Заслуженный артист РСФСР
                  ВЕЧЕР                                    А. ГОНЧАРОВ
    посвященный 70-летию со дня рождения            Артистка Московской Государственной
                                                    филармонии
              Ильи Львовича                                А. КУЗНЕЦОВА
              СЕЛЬВИНСКОГО
                (1899—1968)                         Солистка Всесоюзного радио
     Председатель — С. И. КИРСАНОВ                  и телевидения
     Слово о поэте — О. С. РЕЗНИК                          Л. СИМОНОВА
    ВЫСТУПАЮТ:                                              ВЫСТАВКА
         П. Г. АНТОКОЛЬСКИЙ                         посвященная жизни и творчеству
         К. Л. ЗЕЛИНСКИЙ                                  И. Л. СЕЛЬВИНСКОГО
         Л. С. СОБОЛЕВ
         Л. А. ОЗЕРОВ                               (из фондов библиотеки ЦДЛ, Гос. архива
         Ю. И. ОКУНЕВ                                 литературы и искусства и семьи)
         Д. С. САМОЙЛОВ                                Начало в 19 часов
    Народная артистка РСФСР                                (ул. Герцена, 53)
         Ц. Л. МАНСУРОВА
```

62. Front and back of the invitation to an evening commemorating the 70th anniversary of Ilya Selvinsky's birth at the Central Writers' House in Moscow. 24 October 1969. The participants include poets Semyon Kirsanov, Pavel Antokolsky, Lev Ozerov, and David Samoilov. (Collection of Maxim D. Shrayer.)

---

63 A[natolii] Pikach, "Kogda prozrevaet dusha" [Rev. of Andrei Voznesenskii, "Rov"], *Literaturnoe obozrenie* 1 (1987): 61-62; 64.

Selvinsky's Shoah poems, "I Saw It!" first and foremost, had remained in print and in libraries throughout the postwar Soviet decades. At the same time, downplaying or disregarding Selvinsky's wartime contribution had become a pattern in postwar Soviet literary culture, even when its leading makers, such as Voznesensky, rallied against unremembrance.

Ilya Lvovich Selvinsky, of blessed memory, died on 22 March 1968 in Moscow of multiple heart-related ailments.[64] He did not live to see his recognition, either at home or abroad, as a major Jewish poet and an early and steadfast poetic witness to the Shoah. When the Western public became aware of Soviet Shoah writing, first in the 1960s and then more so in the 1970s and 1980s, the recognition was largely limited to Evgeny Evtushenko and Boris Slutsky in poetry, Vasily Grossman and Anatoly Rybakov in fiction, and Ilya Ehrenburg and Vasily Grossman in nonfiction. Until the last three or four years of the country's existence, the terms "Holocaust," "Shoah," and "Catastrophe" of European Jewry remained taboo in the Soviet Union, and so did, a few exceptions aside, the possibility of Soviet writing about Jewish victimhood. In post-Soviet Russia and in Selvinsky's native Crimea, now an autonomous republic within the independent Ukraine, the critics' resistance to open discussion of Selvinsky's contribution to Shoah literature goes hand in hand with the continuing disinclination of the general public to consider Jewish wartime losses apart from the generalized war losses.[65]

Tatyana Selvinskaya, who said of her father that he "was not a Zionist but loved [Jewish] culture," and "felt himself to be a Jew [...] but was nevertheless a cosmopolitan," recalled her father's private "rapture" (vostorg) upon the founding of Israel in 1948 and again upon Israel's victory in the Six-Day War of 1967.[66] In 1960 the ailing Selvinsky published

---

64 The obituary, published in *Literary Gazette* and signed by the governing body (*pravlenie*) the Union of Soviet Writers, the Union of Writers of the Russian Federation, and the Moscow Branch of the Union of Writers, characterized Selvinsky as "one of the most distinguished masters of Soviet literature of the older generation" and a "poet-Communist"; see "I. L. Sel'vinskii [obituary]," *Literaturnaia gazeta* 27 March 1968, 2. Three writers who knew Selvinsky well offered reflections on the same page of the newspaper: Semyon Kirsanov, Rasul Rza, and Kornely Zelinsky; see "Pamiati tovarishcha," *Literaturnaia gazeta* 27 March 1968, 2. The obituary and the writers' reflections made no mention of Selvinsky's contribution to the literature about World War II or his poems about Nazi atrocities.

65 See, for instance, a recent essay by the young Simferopol-based author Viktoria Anfimova (b. 1977), "Kak ia uvidela voinu glazami I. Sel'vinskogo (stikhotvorenie 'Ia eto videl!')," in "Raboty konkursa 'Mir bez voiny i nasiliia,' Obshchestvo imeni I. K. Aivazovskogo," http://www.aivazovskydb.com/topic.php?id=10307, last accessed 29 February 2012.

66 Tatyana Selvinskya, Personal Interview, 15 December 2011.

a selection of lyrical poems in *Little Flame*, where a number of his other poems appeared in the late 1950s and 1960s. The selection included the poem "Evreiskaia melodiia," which can literally be translated as "Jewish Melody." The title invariably dialogues with Byron's "Hebrew Melodies," which in 1836 Mikhail Lermontov had acculturated for the Russian poetic tradition.[67] Selvinsky's Jewish—Hebrew—melody has not appeared in many of his books and is conspicuously missing from the 1972 Poet's Library edition of his work, along with "Kerch," another of the poet's key Jewish texts, and *Bar-Kokhba*.

63. Ilya Selvinsky with grandson Kirill. July 1963. (Courtesy of Tatyana Selvinskaya.)

---

67 By turning to the subject of the biblical Samson, Selvinsky might also—and not for the first time—be deferring to Jabotinsky, this time not as a poet or translator but as the author of the novel *Samson the Nazarite* (*Samson Nazorei*, 1927).

Илья СЕЛЬВИНСКИЙ

Гёте и Маргарита

О, этот мир, где лучшие предметы
Осуждены на худшую судьбу.
                      Шекспир.

Пролетели золотые годы,
Серебрятся новые года...
«Фауста» закончив, едет Гёте
Сквозь леса неведомо куда.

По дороге заглянул в корчму,
Хорошо в углу на табуретке.
Только вдруг почудилась ему
В кельнерше голубоглазой Гретхен.

И застрял он, как медведь в берлоге,
Никуда он больше не пойдет.
Гёте ей читает монологи,
Гёте мадригалы ей поет.

Вот уж этот неказистый дом
Песней на вселенную помножен!
Но великий позабыл о том,
Что он не ведь чертом омоложен.

Но Марго об этом не забыла,
Хоть и знает пиво лишь да квас:
— Раз уж я капрала полюбила,
Не разменивать же на вас!

Зависть

Что мне в даровании поэта,
Если ты к поэзии глуха,
Если для тебя культура эта
Что-то вроде школьного греха!

Что мне в озарении поэта,
Если ты для быта создана:
Ни к чему тебе, что в гулах где-то
Горная дымится седина!

Что мне в сердцеведенье поэта,
Что мне этот всемогущий лист,
Если в лузу, как из пистолета,
Бьет без промаха биллиардист!

Тигр

Обдымленный, но избежавший казни,
Дыша боками, вышел из тайги.
Зеленой гривой он повел шагн,
Заиндевевший. Жесткий. Медно-красный.

Угрюмо горбясь, огибает падь,
Всем телом западая меж лопаток,
Взлетает без разбега на распадок
И в чащу возвращается опять.

Он забирает запахи до плеч,
Рычит —
        не отзывается тигрица...
И снова в путь. Быть может, под картечь,
Теперь уж незачем ему таиться.

Вокруг поблескивание слюды,
Пунцовой клюквы жуткие накрапы.
И вдруг — следы... Тигриные следы...
Такие дорогие сердцу лапы...

Они вдоль гривы огибают падь,
И словно здесь для всех один порядок,
Взлетают без разбега на распадок
И в чащу возвращаются опять.

А он — по ним! Гигантскими прыжками!
Веселый, молодой не по летам!
Но неведом летящему, как пламя,
Что он несется по своим следам.

Молдавская песня

У коня дыханье, как у девушки.
Только что мне от такого проку?
Расступитесь, дубушки-деревушки,
Дайте непутевому дорогу!

Но не сыщешь тропку ту заветную,
Голубкам не ворковать на ветке...
Все равно ты гордою, запретною
Для меня останешься навеки.

И зачем живу на белом свете я,
За версту твой хутор объезжая?
Эх, кабы моложе на столетия
Были мы с тобой, моя чужая!..

Я б не стал над арчаком сутулиться,
Знать не знал вот этой дикой боли:
Подхватил бы я тебя на улице,
Кинул на седло — и ветер в поле!

Пусть тогда с легавыми да гончими
Вся меня округа бы сковала,
Пусть хотя бы пулею прикончили —
Ты по мне на крик бы тосковала...

Еврейская мелодия

Спасибо за тяжелый сон,
Который ты мне подарила:
Как обессиленный Самсон,
Лежал я пред тобой, Далила.

А впрочем, что мне в сказке сей?
Разве я хоть двенадцать дюжин,
Тебе к попросту не нужен
Со всею силою своей.

И все же ты сыграла роль
Далилинскую отчасти...
Благодарю тебя за счастье,
Хоть это счастье — только боль.

Стихотворцу-неудачнику

В стихах не Пушкин ты, а Пущин,
Но не спеши несчастным быть:
Талант не всякому отпущен,
Но каждому дано любить.

Любовь же — это вдохновенье,
Дурманящее, словно дым,
Как солнце, льющееся в вены
Бродящим хмелем золотым.

И занеможешь ты... И ты
Раскроешь сонные ресницы

И так почувствуешь цветы,
Как и поэтам не приснится.

А что слова? Не суесловь!
Влюблен? Так, значит, нет проблемы!
Меняю все свои поэмы
На шалости твои, Любовь.

         * * *
                      Б. Я. С.
Мечта моей ты юности,
Легенда моей старости...

Но как не пригорюниться
В извечной думе-наросте
О том, что юность временна,
А старость долго тянется,
И кажется, совсем она
При мне теперь останется!

Но ты со мной, любимая!
И как судьба ни взбесится,
В который раз из дыма я
Прорежусь новым месяцем
И стану плыть в безлунности
Сиянием для паруса.

Мечта моей ты юности,
Легенда моей старости!

Береза

Березка в розоватой коже
Стоит, сережками струясь,
А на березке — темный глаз,
На око девичье похожий.

Однажды, перейдя межу,
Я шел по молодому лугу,
Но увидел. Но подскочу —
И мы глядим в глаза друг другу.

Она как будто вся горит,
Как бы испытывает: струшу?
Заглядывает прямо в душу
И... только что не говорит.

И — черт возьми! — не знаю сам,
Но я подпал под обаянье
Простого дерева. Глазам
Березы этой изваянье
Предстало, точно древний рок!

Так женственно сияло тело,
Так горестно она глядела,
И был в зрачке такой упрек,
Что я смутился и пойти
Решил не лугом, а деревней,
Как будто встретился в пути
С завороженною царевной.

         * * *

Пускай не все решены задачи
И далеко не закончен бой —
Бывает такое чувство удачи,
Звериности сил, упоенья собой,
Такая стихия сродни загулу,
В каждой кровинке такой магнит,
Что прикажи вот этому стулу:
«Взлететь!» — и он удивленно... взлетит.

64. Ilya Selvinsky. A selection of poems published in *Ogonek* (*Little Flame*) 60 (1960), with "Jewish Melody" in the central column.

Еврейская мелодия

Спасибо за тяжелый сон,
Который ты мне подарила:
Как обессиленный Самсон,
Лежал я пред тобой, Далила.

А впрочем, что мне в сказке сей?
Развей я хоть двенадцать дюжин,
Тебе я попросту не нужен
Со всею силою свой.

И все же ты сыграла роль
Далилианскую отчасти...
Благодарю тебя за счастье,
Хоть это счастье — только боль.[68]

(Thank you for the [gift of] heavy sleep,/ Which you have given me:/ Like Samson rendered weak,/ I lay before you, Dalilah. || But actually, what is this fairy tale to me?/ Even if I dispersed twelve dozens/ You simply would not need me,/ With all my might. || And yet you have played a role/ Which was partly Delilahesque.../ I thank you for the happiness,/ Even though this happiness—is but pain.)

It is hardly surprising that Selvinsky envisions himself as Samson the warrior and avenger in the Book of Judges, a mighty Jew who was rendered devoid of his powers by a combination of Delilah's charms and perfidy, and was thus defenseless before the Philistines. But who is Selvinsky's Delilah? It could not possibly be his devoted Jewish wife Berta Selvinskaya, to whom he had dedicated a poem originally published alongside "Jewish Melody": "Dream of my youth you are,/ Legend of my old age...."[69] Is it Alisa (Alicia Z.), a young Polish student at the

---

[68] Sel'vinskii, "Evreiskaia melodiia," *Ogonek* 28 (1960): 19; cf. *O vremeni, o sud'bakh, o sebe* (Moscow: Sovetskii pisatel', 1962), 125.

[69] Sel'vinskii, "Mechta moei ty starosti...," *Ogonek* 28 (1960): 10. Tatyana Selvinskaya agrees that "Jewish Melody" could not have been written for her mother. In connection with Selvinsky's

Literary Institute, whom Selvinsky admired in Moscow after the war and later made the heroine and addressee of his cycle "Alisa" (1951)?[70] Or, perhaps, could it be "Katya, Katya, Katerina," the unforgettable "black-eyed Cossack woman" in the lyrics of Selvinsky's most popular song "Kazach'ia shutochnaia" ("A Cossack Joke Song") which Matvey Blanter, also a Russian Jew, so luminously set to music in 1943, and which is still frequently performed across the former USSR?[71]

Is the addressee of this Jewish melody Russia herself, she who tempted Selvinsky, drained him of his might by censoring him, and left him a broken and unneeded warrior? In Judges 16, acting on the Philistines' behest and having thrice failed to extract from Samson the secret of his prowess, Delilah says to him: "How can you say you love me, when you don't confide in me? This makes three times that you've deceived me and haven't told me what makes you so strong."[72] Samson finally revealed the secret, and Delilah "cut off seven locks of his head" which have never previously been cut. "The Philistines seized him and gouged his eyes. They brought him down to Gaza and shackled him with bronze fetters, and he became a mill slave in the prison."

Selvinsky alluded to his self-awareness as a Shoah poet who was literally and figuratively deprived of being able to speak, both for his people and of his people's suffering. By taking on the voice and lyrical persona of Samson, Selvinsky was also tipping his hat to Milton, as a poet of Samson's agony. In *Samson Agonistes*, Milton pointedly connects

---

poetic fantasies of an older Jewish man's desire for a non-Jewish woman (and for greater acceptance), we should consider another Jewish poem from the 1960s. Titled "A Little Song about a Woman's Heart," it appeared in Banner in 1962 and was subsequently reprinted; see Sel'vinskii, "Pesenka o zhesnkom serdtse," *Znamia* 6 (1962): 17; "Pesenka o zhesnkom serdtse," in *Izbrannye proizvedeniia*, 1972, 316; commentary 908. In this poem of four quatrains freely re-envisioning Heinrich Heine's poem "Die Jahre kommen und gehen..." ("The years come and go...") from the cycle "Die Heimkehr" ("The Homecoming," 1823), Selvinsky imagines an (aging) Heine "whispering" to a young woman (probably a courtesan) in French, "O, madame, je vous adore!" (O, madame, I adore you!) only to hear back the following answer: "You, poor thing, are a little old man,/ And beside that also a Jew." Selvinsky's poem goes back to his early Gymnasium poems, which included two translations "from Heine"; see Sel'vinskii, "Sklonias' ukhodiat pokolen'ia," in *Rannii Sel'vinskii*, 11. In Heine's original German, the older Jew speaks the words, "Madam, ich liebe sie!" in German, and not French.

70 See "Ona byla pol'ka, a zvali ee Alisoi....," *Solnechnyi veter*, http://vilavi.ru/raz/alisa/0.shtml, last accessed 17 March 2011.
71 The song is better known as "Chernoglazaia kazachka" ("The Black-Eyed Cossack Woman"); see http://a-pesni.golosa.info/drugije/tchernkazatchka.htm, last accessed 17 March 2011.
72 Here and hereafter, all quotations from Judges 16 are from *Tanakh: A New Translation of the Holy Scriptures*, 405-40.

Samson's loss of might and the warrior's subsequent pain not only to desire, but also to infidelity to the Lord. Says Milton's Samson:

> I yielded, and unlocked her all my heart,
> Who with a grain of manhood well resolved
> Might easily have shook off all her snares:
> But foul effeminacy held me yoked
> Her bond-slave. O indignity, O blot
> To honor and religion! Servile mind
> Rewarded well with servile punishment!

In Judges 16, Samson's story (which Selvinsky calls "skazka" ["fairy tale"] in his "Jewish Melody") ends with his regaining some of his strength as his hair grows back. "Then Samson called to the LORD, 'O Lord God! Please remember me, and give me strength just this once, O God, to take revenge of the Philistines, if only for one of my two eyes." Samson mustered up all his remaining might, embraced two pillars of his captors' temple, and brought it crashing down. The Hebrew biblical poet says of Samson's death and legacy, "Those who were slain by him as he died outnumbered those who had been slain by him when he lived. || His brothers and all his father's household came down and carried him up and buried him in the tomb of his father Manoah, between Zorah and Eshtaol. He had led Israel for twenty years."

Is the Delilah of Selvinsky's life indeed the poet's Russia—she who cut and censured his poetic prowess and rendered him powerless to change the course of Jewish-Russian history, first during the Shoah and then during the postwar Soviet years? If Selvinsky imagines himself as a Jewish-Russian Samson fighting to defend his country's Jews from annihilation, then Selvinsky's "Hebrew" or "Jewish" melody is a darkly ironic valediction. The Soviet unremembrance of what Selvinsky witnessed and described in 1942-1945 may well have been the poet's greatest pain and sorrow in the last decades of his life.

Appendix: Two Shoah Poems by Ilya Selvinsky:
Russian originals and English translations

Я это видел!

> *Германия! Саван тебе мы соткем!*
> *В него мы тройное проклятье вплетем!*
> Гейне[1]

Можно не слушать народных сказаний,
Не верить газетным столбцам.
Но я это видел! Своими глазами!
Понимаете? Видел! Сам!
Вот тут — дорога. А там вон — взгорье.
Меж ними вот этак — ров.
Из этого рва подымается горе,
Горе — без берегов.
Нет! Об этом нельзя словами...
Тут надо рыдать! Рычать!
7000 расстрелянных в волчьей яме,
Заржавленной, как руда.
Кто эти люди? Бойцы? Нисколько.
Может быть, партизаны? Нет!
Вот лежит курносый Колька —
Ему 11 лет;
Тут вся родня его, хутор "Веселый",
Весь "Самострой" — 120 дворов.
Милые... Страшные... Как новоселы
Их тела заселили ров.
Лежат, сидят, сползают на бруствер,
У каждого — жест удивительно свой.

---

1 Перевод П. Лаврова (Translated by P. Lavrov).

Зима в мертвеце заморозила чувство,
С которым смерть принимал живой.
И трупы бродят, грозят, ненавидят...
Как митинг, шумит эта мертвая тишь!
В каком бы их ни свалило виде —
Глазами, оскалом, шеей, плечами
Они пререкаются с палачами,
Они восклицают: "Не победишь!"
Вот у обрыва повис хромоножка,
А все-таки черный костыль торчит!
Вот ястребок, покивав немножко,
Вспрыгнул на груди — и труп ворчит.
Бабка. У этой монашье отребье.
В левой орбите застыл сургуч.
Но правое око — глубоко в небо
Между разрывами туч.
А горло таким насыщено карком,
Такие в нем клокочут слова,
Что тронь — и рванется с хрипением жарким
Отреченье от божества!
Значит, и в этой дремучей, мшистой,
Вороньей мистике вспыхнул свет.
"Коли на свете живут фашисты —
Стало быть, бога нет!.."
Рядом истерзанная еврейка.
Тут же — детеныш. Совсем как во сне:
С какой заботой детская шейка
Повязана маминым серым кашне.
О материнская, древняя сила!
Идя на расстрел! Под пулю идя!
За час! За полчаса до могилы
Мать от простуды спасала дитя.
Но даже и смерть для них не разлука!
Не властны теперь над ними враги:
И рыжая струйка из детского уха
Стекает в горсть материнской руки.
Иди же! Клейми! Ты стоял над бойней!
Ты за руку их поймал — уличил!

Ты видишь, как пулею бронебойной
Дробили нас палачи.
Так загреми же, как Дант, как
         Овидий!
Пусть зарыдает природа сама —
Если
     все это
          сам ты
              видел,
И не сошел с ума!
Но молча стою я над страшной
                могилой.

Что слова? Истлели слова.
Было время, писал я о милой,
О чмоканьи соловья...
Казалось бы — что в этой теме такого?
Правда? А между тем,
Попробуй найти настоящее слово
Даже для этих тем.
А тут? Да ведь тут же нервы, как луки!
Но струны... глуше вареных вязиг.
Нет. Для этой чудовищной муки
Не создан еще язык.
Для этого нужно созвать бы вече
Из всех племен, от древка до древка,
И взять от каждого все человечье,
Все оплаканное за века —
И если бы каждое в этом хоре
Давало по слову, близкому всем,
То уж великое русское горе
Могло бы добавить семь!
Да нет такого еще языка...
Пусть окровавленный ваш закат
Не мог я оплакать в неслыханных строфах,
Но есть у нас и такая речь,
Которая всяких слов горячее:
Картавя, сыплет ее картечь!
Гаркает ею гортань батареи!

Вы слышите грохот на рубежах?
Она отомстит! Бледнеют громилы!
Но некуда будет им убежать
От вашей кровавой могилы.
Ослабьте же мышцы. Прикройте веки.
Травою взойдите у этих высот.
Кто вас увидел — отныне навеки
Все ваши раны в душе унесет.
Ров... Поэмой ли скажешь о нем?
7000 трупов... Евреи... Славяне...
Да! Об этом нельзя словами:
Огнем! Только огнем!

1942

I Saw It

Germany, now we weave you a shroud,
And into it we weave a threefold scourge.[2]

Heine, "The Silesian Weavers"

One may choose to dismiss people's tales
Or disbelieve printed columns of news.
But I saw it! With my own eyes.
Do you understand? I saw it. Myself.
Here—the road. Over there—a higher plain.
Between them, just so—a ditch.
From the ditch rises boundless pain

---

2 Deutschland, wir weben dein Leichentuch,/ Wir weben hinein den dreifachen Fluch (Heinrich Heine, "Die schlesischen Weber," 1844).

And sorrow—without end.
No! About this one cannot—with words...
One must sob. Roar.
7000 murdered ones—in a wolf's hollow,
A hollow rusty like ore...
Who are these people? Soldiers? Hardly.
Perhaps partisans? No.
Here lies the pug-nosed Kolka—
He's eleven years old.
His kin is all here, Merriment Homestead,
All the Samostroy houses—120 of them,
So dear ... so scary.... Like new residents,
Their bodies have moved into the ditch.
Lying, sitting, sliding onto the breastwork,
Each one—his own inimitable pose.
Winter froze in the dead ones
What the living felt at their death.
And corpses wander, menacing, abhorring...
Like a rally, this dead silence rumbles.
No matter how they looked when they had fallen—
With eyes, bared teeth, shoulders, necks—
They wrangle with their executioners,
They cry out "You will not triumph!"
Over the gully there dangles a cripple,
His black crutch still juts out.
A young hawk bows his little curved beak,
Then jumps on the chest—and the corpse groans.
An old woman in a tattered nun's habit.
The wax has hardened, sealing her left eye.
But her right one gazes deep into the heavens
Through clefts in this cloudy sky.
And such crow-calls fill her gullet,
Such words rage in her throat cavity,
Just touch it—and out, with seething sounds,
A disavowal of divinity.
This means: through this ancient, mossy, overgrown
Black-crow mysticism—light has burst,
"If fascists live in this world,

Then there is no god...."
Nearby, a mauled Jewish woman,
And a small child with her. Is he awake?
The mother's grey shawl is wrapped with such care
Around the babe's neck.
O maternal, o ancient strength!
Walking to the execution, just before she was killed,
An hour, half an hour, before the grave,
Mother was saving child from a chill.
And even death has not pried them apart.
Over them the enemies have no power.
An auburn trickle from the child's ear
Seeps into the mother's cupped palm.
Go now. Brand them! You have seen the blood bath.
You have caught them red-handed—an eyewitness.
You see how with armor-piercing bullets
The executioners decimate us.
So thunder now, like Dante, like Ovid,
Let nature itself weep and moan,
If
        you
                saw
                          all of this,
And have not gone mad.
But silent I stand over the burial pit.
What words? The words have turned to rot.
There was a time: I wooed a sweetheart,
I praised a nightingale's chant.
One might have thought—so what?
Same old tune. And yet,
Try finding the right word,
Even for a familiar event.
And here? Here the nerves are like taut bows,
But the strings ... are deafer than boiled sturgeon sinews.
No, for this unbearable torment
No language has been devised.
To do this, one would have to call a council
Of all tribes, flagpole to flagpole,

And from each one take all that is personal—
Over the centuries everything bewailed—
And if all tribes were to give to this chorus
One word each, one word we all shared,
Then the great Russian sorrow
To each word would add seven.
But no such language has been devised.
Even if in unheard-of stanzas
I have failed to mourn your blood-soaked sunset,
We do have just the kind of speech,
More scorching than any verbal artistry:
Canister shots, *r*'s misrolled, keep
Rattling the larynx of the battery.
Can you hear this blast at the boundary?
The avenging fire... Murderers grow pale!
But they will have nowhere to flee
From your blood-soaked burial.
Now relax your muscles. Lower your eyelids,
Rise like grass over these heights.
He who saw you, henceforth forever
Shall carry your wounds in his heart.
The ditch... Tell about it in meter?
7000 corpses... Jews... Slavs...
No! About this one cannot—with words:
Fire! Only with fire.

1942

Translated, from the Russian, by Maxim D. Shrayer

Керчь

У нас в гимназии делили Крым
На эллинский и дикий. Все приморье
От Евпатории и до Керчи
Звалось Элладой. Если же случалось,
Перевалив за горную преграду,
Спуститься в степь, то называлось это —
"Поехать в Скифию". Хотя и в шутку,
Мы называли наши города
По-гречески, как это было древле.
Об этом я давно уж позабыл.
И вдруг, когда десантные войска,
Форсировав пролив, обосновались
На Крымском берегу, и я увидел
Невдалеке перед собою Керчь, —
Мой голос прошептал: "Пантикапея..."

В лиловом и оранжевом тумане
Над морем воспарил амфитеатр
Пленительного города. Гора
С каким-то белым и высоким храмом
Курилась облаками. Дальний мыс
Чернел над хризолитовым заливом.
А очертанья зданий на заре
Подсказывали портики, колонны
И статуи на форуме. Эллада
Дышала сном. Один туман, как грезы,
Описывал громады парусов,
Орду козлов или толпу сатиров, —
И я был старше на пять тысяч лет.
Объятый полудремою веков,
Я мысленно по площади бродил,
Где эллины, как птицы, торговались,
А в виде серебра ходила рыба;
Здесь хлеб и сыр меняли на ставридки.
Здесь медный щит, наполненный макрелью,

Считался платой за стихотворенье;
А если звонким осетром платили
За девушку такого же объема,
Того же водяного блеска, той же
Плавучей обтекаемости линий,
То это не обидно осетру.
(Обидно ль девушке, об этом
Не думали в ту грубую эпоху.
Ужасный век!) И вдруг на этот город,
Как фурии по мановенью Зевса, —
Аэропланы! И когда из дыма
Опять он появился над заливом
И танки с красным флагом потянулись
По набережной, а увидя ров,
Ушли сквозь стену банка в переулок, —
У берега уже лежала Керчь.
Так за один лишь день я увидал
Два лика города. Но мне война
Готовила еще и третий.

   Ночью,
В армейскую газету, очень тихо
И как-то лунатически, как будто
Одно и то же неотступно видя
И об одном задумавшись навеки,
Вошел не бледный, нет, а просто белый,
Невероятный чем-то человек.
Далеким голосом (таким далеким,
Что нам казалось, будто бы не он,
А кто-то за него) — он нам поведал
Пещерным слогом каменного века,
Рубя на точках:
   «В десяти верстах
Тут Багерово есть. Одно село.
Не доходя, направо будет ров.
Противотанковый. Они туда
Семь тысяч граждан. И меня.
   Но я
Нарочно рухнул на секунду раньше.

Я даже не ушибся. На меня
Упала мать. Ей голову. Потом...
Потом жена. А после — обе дочки.
Одна еще вздыхала. Я прорылся
И на руках принес было. Да зря.
Она пока в колодце. Каждый раз
Я под водою различаю глазки.
И ротик. Взбаламутится вода —
И дочка вроде плавает...
        Дык это...
Про што я с вами говорил?
Ага, про Багерово. Значит, так:
Не доходя сажон двухсот и вправо".
Мы тут же и пошли. Писатель Ромм,
Фотограф, я и критик Гоффеншефер.
Под утро мы увидели долину
Всю в пестряди какой-то. Это были
Расползшиеся за ночь мертвецы.
Я очень бледно это описал
В стихотворении "Я ЭТО ВИДЕЛ!"
И больше не могу ни слова.
Керчь...
Есть города, значение которых
Не в их пейзаже, не в культуре их,
Не в ореоле их бессмертной славы,
А в той молниеносной вспышке правды,
Когда дымящаяся тайна века
Вдруг прояснится, как в тумане ров.
Кем были мы до нашей встречи, Керчь?

Писатель нервничает. Зажигает
Одну, другую спичку, забывая,
Что челюсти его свело от гнева,
А не от ощущенья папиросы.
"Какое зверство!" — говорит писатель,
И эхом отозвался критик: "Зверство".
Их ремесло — язык. Стихия — речь.
Они разворошили весь словарь

И выбрали одно и то же: "Зверство".
Но звери подходили по ночам
К огромному до горизонта моргу
И всем чутьем звериным ощущали
В безмолвии стоящий перед ними
Стихийный ужас.
       Галки и вороны,
Взлетая друг над другом, не решались
Перемахнуть за линию холмов.
Лисица-караганка, пробегая
По заячьей тропинке за оврагом,
Вдруг увильнула в сторону от следа
И понеслась, отбрехиваясь так,
Как будто бы за ней гремела свора.
И даже волчья тень меж мертвецов
Тревожно закружилась... Замерла...
Потом рысцой вернулась на курган,
Оттуда обернулась угнетенно,
Помедлила и тихо скрылась.
Керчь!
Ты — зеркало, где отразилась бездна.

1942

Kerch

In high school we divided the Crimea
Into Hellenic and Wild. The coast
From Eupatoria down and all the way to Kerch
Was called Hellas. And then, if one should happen
To steal across the mountains and descend
Onto the steppe, we used to call this:
"Going to Scythia," although in jest
We called our towns and cities
By their Greek names, as in days of yore.
I had long forgotten all about this.
But suddenly when our landing forces
Traversed the strait and took their position
On the Crimean shore, when I saw
Not far ahead of me the city of Kerch,
My voice then whispered "Panticapaeum."

In lilac and orange fog, above the sea
An amphitheater of a resplendent city
Soared, while some white and lofty temple
Rose from a mountain into the sky
Amid smoking clouds. A distant cape
Shone black over the bay of chrysolite.
And silhouettes of buildings at daybreak
Suggested porticoes and columns
And statues in the forum, while Hellas
Breathed in her deep slumber. Only the fog,
Like reveries, encircled colossal sails,
A horde of billy goats or a crowd of satyrs,
And I was older by five thousand years.
Enveloped by the dozing centuries,
In my thoughts I roamed the square,
Where the Hellenes bargained like old birds
And fish scales passed locally for silver.
Here bread and cheese were traded for horse mackerel;
A copper shield filled to the brim with mullet,

Was an apposite payment for an ode;
And if with a spindly sturgeon they paid
For a young lady of matching shape and form—
The same aqueous sheen, the very same
Body contours and flowing curves,
The sturgeon wouldn't be offended.
(And what about the young lady? Of her offence
They hardly thought in those ruffian days.
A terrible age!) And suddenly upon this city,
Like Furies dispatched by Zeus,
Airplanes! And when out of the smoke
The city once again appeared over the bay,
And tanks with red flags rolled in, one after another
Along the embankment, then encountered a ditch
And drove through a bank's façade into a side street—
By now Kerch was lying there by the shore.
Thus, in one day I got to see two faces
Of the same city. But the war
Held a third one in store for me. That night
To the office of the army newspaper, very quietly—
Like a somnambulist, as though before him
The same vision stood incessantly, forever
Stuck on the same unceasing thought—
Came someone not pale, but simply white,
A man who was in some ways unimaginable.
In a faraway voice (so faraway
That we felt it wasn't he who spoke,
But someone else spoke for him)—he told us
In caveman's speech of Stone Age intonations,
Incising the full stops: "Six miles from here.
There's Bagerovo. A small town.
Before you get there, to the right there's a ditch.
Anti-tank. They took over there
Seven thousand folks. Myself included. But I
On purpose threw myself down a second earlier.
I didn't even get hurt. On top of me
Mother fell. They—in the head. Then....
Then wife. And after that—both my daughters....

One was still moaning. I dug myself out
And carried her in my arms. But in vain.
She's in the well, for now. Each time
I see her little eyes beneath the water.
Her little mouth. When the water surges,
It looks like my daughter's swimming....
                                      So then....
What was it I was telling you about?
Oh right, about Bagerovo. So then:
About five hundred yards before you get there, turn right."

We set out right away. The writer Romm.
The photographer, myself, and the critic Goffenshefer.
By sunrise we had come upon a valley
All covered in some dappled cotton fabric. Those were
The dead who had crawled out during the night.
I have described this very hazily
In the poem "I SAW IT"
And I cannot add even a single word.
Kerch...
There are cities whose significance lies
Not in their landscape, nor in their culture,
Nor in the aura of their everlasting glory,
But in that lightning bolt of verity,
When the smoldering mystery of the epoch
Would suddenly be revealed, like a ditch in morning fog.
Who were we before our meeting, Kerch?

The writer seems nervous. He strikes
One match, then another, while forgetting
That his own jaws are clenched with anger—
And not from the sensation of the cigarette.
"What beastliness!" the writer slowly says.
And then the critic echoes: "Beastliness."
Language is their trade. Their element—speech.
They have rummaged through the whole dictionary
To choose the selfsame word: "Beastliness."
But wild beasts under cover of night approached

The morgue so vast it covered the horizon,
And felt with all the senses of wild beasts
The elemental horror standing silently
Before them. Magpies and crows
Taking off, flying over each other, wouldn't dare
Cross over that line of hillocks.
The karagan fox, though following the scent
Along the rabbit tracks beyond the deep ravine,
All of a sudden veered off the path,
Scurried away, yelping and howling in terror,
As if a thunderous pack of hounds were chasing her.
And even the shadow of a wolf amongst the dead
Whirled around anxiously.... Then froze....
And trotted back to his remote barrow,
From there the wolf's shadow turned despondently,
Lingered, then quietly vanished from sight.
Kerch,
You are the mirror, in which the abyss has been reflected.

1942

Translated, from the Russian, by Maxim D. Shrayer

Russian originals copyright © The Estate of Ilya Selvinsky. English translations copyright © Maxim D. Shrayer.

Works Cited

Abramov, Vsevolod. *Kerchenskaia katastrofa 1942*. Mocow: Iauza; Eksmo, 2006. http://militera.lib.ru/h/abramov_vv/index.html. Last accessed 9 June 2010.

Agamben, Giorgio. *Remnants of Auschwitz: The Witness and the Archive*, translated by Daniel Heller-Roazen. New York: Zone Books, 1999.

Akhiezer, Golda. "Karaites." In *The YIVO Encyclopedia of Jews in Eastern Europe*, 2 vol., edited by Gershon David Hundert, 1: 860-862. New Haven: Yale University Press, 2008.

Angrick, Andrej. *Besatzungspolitik und Massenmord. Die Einsatzgruppe D in der südlichen Sowjetunion 1941-1943*. Hamburg: Hamburger Edition, 2003.

Al'tman, Il'ia [Ilya Altman], ed. *Russkaia literatura o Kholokoste. Khrestomatiia dlia uchashchikhsia*. Moscow: Nauchno-prosvetitel'skii tsentr "Kholokost," 1997.

Al'tman, I[l'ia]. *Kholokost i evreiskoe soprotivlenie na okkupirovannoi territorii SSSR*. Moscow: Fond "Kholokost"; Kaleidoskop, 2002. http://jhistory.nfurman.com/shoa/hfond_100.htm. Last acccessed 15 July 2010.

---. *Zhertvy nenavisti: Kholokost v SSSR. 1941-1945*. Moscow: Fond "Kovcheg," 2002.

---. "Memorializatisia Kholokhosta v Rossii: istoriia, sovremennost', perspektivy." *Neprikosnovennyi zapas* 2-3 (2005). http://magazines.russ.ru/nz/2005/2/alt28.html. Last accessed 8 April 2010.

---, ed. *Kholokost na territorii SSSR. Entsiklopediia*, 2nd ed. Moscow: Rosspen, 2011.

Al'tman, M[ariia]. "Poeziia." In *Kholokost na territorii SSSR. Entsiklopediia*, 2nd ed., edited by I. A. Al'tman, 788-790. Moscow: Rosspen, 2011.

Altshuler, Mordechai. "Jewish Holocaust Commemoration Activity in the USSR under Stalin." Shoah Resource Center, The International School for Holocaust Studies. http://www1.yadvashem.org/odot_pdf/Microsoft%20Word%20-%205422.pdf. Last accessed 20 February 2012.

---. "The Holocaust in the Soviet Mass Media during the War and in the

First Postwar Years Re-examined." *Yad Vashem Studies* 39.2 (2011): 121-163.

Androsov, S[ergei]. A. "Arkhivy Kryma v gody Velikoi Otechestvennoi voiny (1941-1945)." *Istoricheskoe nasledie Kryma. Zhurnal* 8 (2004). http://old.commonuments.crimea-portal.gov.ua/rus/index.php?v=1&tek=87&art=324. Last accessed 12 January 2012.

Anfimova, Viktoriia. "Kak ia uvidela voinu glazami I. Sel'vinskogo (stikhotvorenie 'Ia eto videl!') Raboty konkursa Mir bez voiny i nasiliia." Obshchestvo imeni I. K. Aivazovskogo. http://www.aivazovskydb.com/topic.php?id=10307. Last accessed 29 February 2012.

Antokol'skii, Pavel [Pavel Antokolsky]. "Lager' unichtozheniia." *Znamia* 10 (1945): 34.

---. "Lager' unichtozheniia." In Pavel Antokol'skii, *Izbrannoe*, 174-75. Moscow: Molodaia gvardiia, 1946.

---. "Lager' unichtozheniia." In Pavel Antokol'skii, *Tret'ia kniga voiny*, 38-40. Moscow: Sovetski pisatel', 1946.

---. "Ne vechnaia pamiat'." *Znamia* 7 (1946): 64-65.

---. "Nevechnaia pamiat'." In Pavel Antokol'skii, *Izbrannoe*, 2 vols., 2: 170-174. Moscow: Khudozhestvennia literatura, 1966 [here "nevechnaia" is spelled as one word].

---. "Il'ia Sel'vinskii." In *O Sel'vinskom: vospominaniia*, edited by Ts. A. Voskresenskaia and I. P. Sirotinskaia, 4-12. Moscow: Sovetskii pisatel', 1982.

---. *Izbrannoe*. Moscow: Molodaia gvardiia, 1946.

---. *Tret'ia kniga voiny*. Moscow: Sovetski pisatel', 1946.

Antselovich, I[zrail']. "Fashistskie ubiitsy." *Kerchenskii rabochii* 12 January 1941: 1.

---. "Gnusnye ubiitsy." *Ogonek* 8 March 1942: 7.

---. "Zverstva fashistov v Kerchi." In *Ne zabudem, ne prostim* [*Zverstva fashistov v Kerchi*]. Moscow: Goskinoizdat. Moscow: Goskinoizdat, 1942 [booklet-poster].

Antselovich, I[zrail], I[zrail'] Ozerskii, and D[mitrii] Bal'termants [phot]. "Zlodeiianiia gitlerovtsev v Kerchi." *Ogonek* 8 (March 1942): 6-7.

Arad, Yitzhak. "The Holocaust as Reflected in Soviet Russian Language Newspapers in the Years 1941-1945." In *Why Didn't They Shout? American and International Journalism during the Holocaust: A Collection of Papers Originally Presented at an Interdisciplinary Conference Sponsored by the Elia and Diana Zborowski Professorial Chair* in *Interdisciplinary Holocaust Studies, Yeshiva University, October 1995*, ed. Robert Moses Shapiro, 199-220. Hoboken, NJ: Yeshiva University Press/Ktav Publishing House, 2003.

---. *The Holocaust in the Soviet Union*. Lincoln: University of Nebraska Press; Jerusalem: Yad Vashem, 2009.

Arkharova, M[aria] F. "Vmeste s nami shli v nastuplenie stikhi Sel'vinskogo." In *O Sel'vinskom: vospominaniia*, edited by Ts. A. Voskresenskaia and I. P. Sirotinskaia, 106-112. Moscow: Sovetskii pisatel', 1982.

Artizov, Andrei, and Oleg Naumov, eds. *Vlast' i khudozhestvennaia intelligentsia: dokumenty TsK RKP(b)-VKP(b), VChK-OGPU-NKVD o kul'turnoi politike, 1917-1953 gg*. Moscow: Mezhdunarodnyi fond "Demokratiia," 1999.

"Avtory 'Boevoi Krymskoi.'" *Literaturnaia gazeta*, 6 May 1970: 5 [collation of interviews].

Az Nevtelen. "Dnevniki imperatritsy. Romanovy v Krymu v opisanii Vol'fsona." http://ru-history.livejournal.com/3272322.html. Accessed 7 January 2012.

Babenko, V[era]. S. *Voina glazami poeta: Krymskie stranitsy iz dnevnikov i pisem I. L. Sel'vinskogo*. Simferopol': Krymskaia akademiia gumanitarnykh nauk; Dom-muzei I. L. Sel'vinskogo, 1994.

---. "Vmesto poslesloviia." In *Gor'kaia pamiat' viony. Krym v Velikoi Otechestvennoi*, edited by V. K. Garagulia et al., 41-42. Simferopol': Krymskaia akademiia gumanitarnykh nauk, 1995.

Babenko, Vera, and Gavriliuk, Vladislav. "'Net, ia ne legkoi zhizn'iu zhil....'" *Krymskie penaty* 2 (1996): 88-107.

Babichenko, D. L. *"Literaturnyi front." Istoriia politicheskoi tsenzury 1932-1946 gg. Sbornik dokumentov*. Moscow: Entsiklopediia rossiiskikh dereven', 1994.

Bachinskaia, A. A. "'Krymskii narod' i 'krymskaia kul'tura' v osmyslenii I. Sel'vinskogo." In *I. L. Sel'vinskii i literaturnyi protsess XX veka. V Mezhdunarodnaia nauchnaia konferentsiia, posviashchennaia 100-letiiu I. L. Sel'vinskogo*, 108-113. Simferopol': Krymskii arkhiv, 2000.

"Bagerovskii rov g. Kerch" [electronic forum]. http://forum.j-roots.info/viewtopic.php?f=26&t=144. Last accessed 7 April 2010.

"Bagerovskii rov." http://sarafanews.ru/Bagerovskij-rov.html. Last accessed 27 January 2012.

"Bagerovskii rov." *Murzik Media*. 29 November 2011. http://murzik-media.blogspot.com/2011/11/blog-post.html. Last accessed 27 January 2012.

Belotserkovskaia, R[aisa]. "Budem mstit' fashistam. Pis'mo zheny krasnoarmeitsa R. Belotserkovskoi." *Krasnaia zvezda* 17 January 1942.

---. "Pis'mo zheny krasnoarmeitsa R. Belotserkovskoi." In *Dokumenty obviniaiut. Sbornik dokumentov o chudovishchnykh zlodeistvakh germanskikh vlastei na vremenno zakhvachennykh imi sovetskikh territoriiakh*, vol. 1, 192-194. Moscow: Gosudarstvennoe izdatel'stvo politicheskoi literatury, 1943.

---. "Istrebliaite fashistov!" *Syn otechestva* 7 April 1944.

Berlin, Boris. "Kholokost v Krymu." Paper delivered at 17 Krymskie mezhdunarodnye nauchnye chteniia I. L. Sel'vinskgogo "Tragicheskii opyt Velikoi Otechestvennoi voiny v istoriko-literaturnom osmyslenii." Simferopol. Ilya Selvinsky Memorial Museum. 16 December 2011.

Berezin, D. "Oruzhiem stikha." In *O Sel'vinskom: vospominaniia*, edited by Ts. A. Voskresenskaia and I. P. Sirotinskaia, 101-105. Moscow: Sovetskii pisatel', 1982.

Berkhoff, Karel C. "'Total Annihilation of the Jewish Population': The Holocaust in the Soviet Media, 1941-45." *Kritika: Explorations in Russian and Eurasian History* 10.1 (Winter 2009): 61-105.

Bialik, Hayim Nahman. "Be Ir HaHariga." http://benyehuda.org/bialik/beir.html. Last accessed 4 November 2011.

Bialik, Kh. N. [Hayim Nahman Bialik]. *Skazanie o pogrome*. In Bialik, Kh. N., *Pesni i Poemy*, translated by Vl. Zhabotinskii, 3rd ed., 167-177. St. Petersburg: S. D. Zaltsman, 1914.

---. *Songs from Bialik*. Edited and translated by Atar Hadari. Syracuse: Syracuse University Press, 2000.

Blium, Arlen. "Otnoshenie sovetskoi tsenzury (1940-1946) k probleme Kholokosta." *Vestnik Evreiskogo universiteta v Moskve* 2 (1995): 156-167.

---. "Index librorum prohibitorum russkikh pisatelei." Part 4. *NLO* 62 (2003). http://magazines.russ.ru/nlo/2003/62/blum.html. Last accessed 6 April 2010.

Bloom, Harold. *The Anxiety of Influence: A Theory of Poetry*. London: Oxford University Press, 1973.

Boiko, Mikhail. "K soroka godam ego slomali [Interview with Tat'iana Sel'vinskaia]." *Ex Libris NG* 23 April 2009. http://exlibris.ng.ru/ten-

denc/2009-04-23/6_selvinsky.html. Last accessed 17 March 2011.
Borodulin, Lev. "O Dmitrii Bal'termantse." http://www.sem40.ru/famous2/m736.shtml. Last accessed 27 January 2012.
Bronshtein, Mikhail. "A. Matrosov i matrosovtsy." *Zapad Vostok* (2 May 2007). http://www.westeast.us/06/article/641.html. Last accessed 16 July 2010.

Chursin, P. A. and R. M. Vul', eds. *Nemetskie varvary v Krymu*. Simferopol': Krasnyi Krym, 1944.
"Courland Pocket." http://en.wikipedia.org/wiki/Courland_Pocket. Last accessed 8 March 2011.
Czerny, Boris. "Babij Jar. La mémoire de l'histoire," in *Génocides: lieux (et non-lieux) de mémoire*, ed. Georges Bensoussan, 61-77 (Paris: Centre de Documentation Juive Contemporaine, 2004).

Daineko, L[iudmila].I. "Sel'vinskii i Kerch. Noiabr', 1941-mai, 1942." In *Vestnik Krymskikh Chtenii I. L. Sel'vinskogo*, vol. 1, 63-71. Simferopol': Krymskii arkhiv, 2002.
Dekel-Chen, Jonathan. "Crimea." In *The YIVO Encyclopedia of Jews in Eastern Europe*, 2 vol., edited by Gershon David Hundert, 1: 363-364. New Haven: Yale University Press, 2008.
Desbois, Father Patrick. *The Holocaust by Bullets: A Priest's Journey to Uncover the Truth Behind the Murder of 1.5 Million Jews*. New York: Palgrave Macmillan, 2009.
Dobrenko, Evgenii. *Formovka sovetskogo pisatelia: Sotsial'nye i esteticheskie istoki sovetskoi literaturnoi kul'tury*. St. Petersburg: Akademicheskii proekt, 1999.
Dobrovol'skaia, I. A. *"Eshche moi brig ne trogalsia s prichala...": O iunosti poeta Il'i Sel'vinskogo*. Simferopol': Krymskaia akademiia gumanitarnykh nauk, 1999.
Dokumenty obviniaiut. Sbornik dokumentov o chudovishchnykh zlodeistvakh germanskikh vlastei na vremenno zakhvachennykh imi sovetskikh territoriiakh. Vol. 1. Moscow: Gosudarstvennoe izdatel'stvo politicheskoi literatury, 1943.
Domil', Valentin. "Zvezdy i ternii Il'ii Sel'vinskogo. Evreiskii vopros 'korolia poetov'." *Sekretnyi portal. Zhurnal Vladimira Pletinskogo* 16 April

2010. http://velelens.livejournal.com/45472.html. Last accessed 29 January 2012.

Dostoevskii, F. M. *Polnoe sobranie sochinenii v tridtsati tomakh*, 30 vols. Leningrad: Nauka, 1972-1990.

Dubrovna, V. "Grabiteli." In *Zverstva nemetskikh fashistov v Kerchi. Sbornik rasskazov postradavshikh i ochevidtsev*, 69-70. Sukhumi: Krasnyi Krym, 1943.

Emel'ianova, Tetiana, ed. *Ukraina i Druga Svitova viina. Kinolitopys. Anotovanyi katalog kinozhurnaliv, dokumenalnykh fil'miv, kinosiuzhetiv, spetsvypuskiv (1939-1945)*. Kyiv: Derzhavnyi komitet arkhiviv Ukrainy; Tsentral'nyi derzhavnyi kinofotofonoarkhiv Ukrainy imeni G. S. Pshenichnogo, 2005.

Erenburg, Il'ia [Ilya Ehrenburg]. "Evreiskomu narodu." In *Ia zhivu*, 51-52. St. Petersburg: n.p., 1911.

---. "Evreiiam." *Izvestiia* 26 August 1941.

---. "Evreiiam." In Il'ia Erenburg, *Staryi skorniak i drugie proizvedeniia*, 2 vols., edited by M. Vainshtein, 2: 251-252. Jerusalem: n.p., 1983.

---. "Kogda volk nachinaet bleiat'...." *Krasnaia zvezda* 6 January 1942.

---. "Znaki otlichiia." *Krasnaia zvezda* 27 February 1942: 3.

---. "Narodoubiitsy." *Znamia* 1-2 (1944): 185-186.

---. "Pomnit'" *Pravda* 17 December 1944.

---. "Stikhi." *Novyi mir* 1 (1945): 16 [cycle of 6 untitled poems, numbered 1-6].

---. "Khvatit!" *Pravda* 9 April 1945.

---. "O stikhakh Borisa Slutskogo." *Literaturnaia gazeta* 8 July 1956.

---. *Derevo. Stikhi 1938-1945 gg*. Moscow: Sovetskii pisatel', 1946.

---. *Letopis' muzhestva. Publitsisticheskie stat'i voennykh let*. Ed. L. Lazarev. 2nd ed. Moscow: Sovetskii pisatel', 1983.

---. *Sobranie sochinenii v deviati tomakh*, 9 vols. Moscow: Khudozhestvennaia literatura, 1962-1967.

---. *Liudi, gody, zhizn'. Vospominaniia v trekh tomakh*. Moscow: Sovetskii pisatel', 1990.

---. *Liudi, gody, zhizn'. Izdanie v trekh tomakh*, 3 vols., edited by B. Ia. Frezinskii. Moscow: Tekst, 2005.

---. *Pis'ma*. 1908-1967, 2 vols., edited by B. Ia. Frezinskii. Moscow: Agraf, 2004. [Vol. 1: *Dai oglianuts'a...Pis'ma 1908-1930*. Vol. 2: *Na tsokole istoii... Pis'ma 1931-1967]*.

Erenburg, Il'ia, and Vasilii Grossman, eds. *Chernaia kniga: O zlodeiskom povsemestnom ubiistve evreev nemetsko-fashistskimi zakhvatchikami vo vremenno-okkupirovannykh raionakh Sovetskogo Soiuza i v lageriakh unichtozheniia Pol'shi vo vremia voiny 1941-1945 gg*. Jerusalem: Tarbut, 1980.

Erenburg, Il'ia, and Vasilii Grossman, eds. *Chernaia kniga: O zlodeiskom povsemestnom ubiistve evreev nemetsko-fashistskimi zakhvatchikami vo vremenno-okkupirovannykh raionakh Sovetskogo Soiuza i v lageriakh unichtozheniia Pol'shi vo vremia voiny 1941-1945 gg*. Kiev: MIP "Oberig," 1991.

Ehrenburg, Ilya, and Vassily Grossman, eds. *The Complete Black Book of Russian Jewry*. Edited and translated by David Patterson. New Brunswick, NJ: Transaction Publishers, 2002.

Ermolaev, Herman. *Censorship in Soviet Literature, 1917-1991*. Lanham, MD: Rowman & Littlefield, 1997.

Eshanov, Aleksandr. "V preddverii zamysla." *Alef* 991 (2009). http://www.alefmagazine.com/pub1917.html. Accessed 29 January 2012.

Evtushenko, Evgenii. "Nesostoiavshiisia velikii. Il'ia Sel'vinskii." *Novye izvestiia* 24 March 2006. http://www.newizv.ru/culture/2006-03-24/43038-nesostojavshijsja-velikij.html. Last accessed 10 April 2011.

Ezhelev, A. "Dushnoe leto 46-go. Kak prinimalos' Postanovlenie o zhurnalakh 'Zvezda' i 'Leningrad'." *Izvestiia* 21 May 1988. 3.

F., V. "Pisateli-chernomortsy." *Literatura i iskusstvo* 13 June 1942 [article is signed with the initials V.F.].

Fadeev, A[leksandr]. "Pisatel' i kritik." In A. Fadeev, *Sobranie sochinenii v piati tomakh*, edited by E. F. Knipovich et al. 4: 254-260. Moscow: Gosudarstvennoe izdatel'stvo khudozhestvennoi literatury, 1959-1961.

---. "V redaktsiiu 'Literaturnoi gazety.'" In A. Fadeev, *Sobranie sochinenii v piati tomakh*, edited by E. F. Knipovich et al. 5: 354-355. Moscow: Gosudarstvennoe izdatel'stvo khudozhestvennoi literatury, 1959-1961.

---. "Zadachi literaturnoi teorii i kritiki." In *Problemy sotsialisticheskogo realizma. Sbornik statei*, edited by B. I. Bialik et al. 7-48. Leningrad: Sovetskii pisatel', 1948.

---. "Zadachi literaturnoi teorii i kritiki." In A. Fadeev, *Sobranie sochinenii v piati tomakhi*, edited by E. F. Knipovich et al., 4: 403-460. Moscow: Gosudarstvennoe izdatel'stvo khudozhestvennoi literatury, 1959-1961.

---. "Zadachi sovetskoi literatury." In A. Fadeev, *Sobranie sochinenii v piati tomakh*, edited by E. F. Knipovich et al., 4: 461-473. Moscow: Gosudarstvennoe izdatel'stvo khudozhestvennoi literatury, 1959-1961.

Feferman, Kiril. "Nazi Germany and the Karaites in 1938-1944: Between Racial Theory and *Realpolitik*." *Nationalities Papers* 39.2 (March 2011): 277-294.

Filat'ev, Eduard. "Taina podpolkovnika Sel'vinskogo." In Babenko, V. S., *Voina glazami poeta: Krymskie stranitsy iz dnevnikov i pisem I. L. Sel'vinskogo*, 69-82. Simferopol': Krymskaia akademiia gumanitarnykh nauk; Dom-muzei I. L. Sel'vinskogo, 1994.

Fleishman, Lazar'. *Boris Pasternak v tridtsatye gody*. Jerusalem: Magnes Press/Hebrew University, 1984.

Frank, Siuzanna [Susanne Frank]. "Teplaia Arktika: k istorii odnogo starogo literaturnogo motiva." Translated from the German by Tatiana Lastovka. *NLO* 108 (2011). http://magazines.russ.ru/nlo/2011/108/fr7.html. Last accessed 29 January 2012.

Frezinskii, B[oris]. Ia, ed. *Pochta Il'ia Erenburga. Ia slyshu vse... 1916-1967*. Moscow: Agraf, 2006.

Garrard, John, and Carol Garrard. *The Bones of Berdichev: The Life and Fate of Vasily Grossman*. New York: Free Press, 1996.

Gasparov, Mikhail. "Aleksandr Romm. Stikhi 1927-28 gg." *Toronto Slavic Quarterly* 2 (Fall 2002). http://www.utoronto.ca/tsq/02/romm.shtml. Last accessed 8 April 2010.

Gavriliuk, V[ladislav]. L. *Cherty poezii i zhizni Il'i Sel'vinskogo: k 100-letiiu so dnia rozhdeniia*. Simferopol': Krymskaia akademiia gumanitarnykh nauk, 1999.

Gitelman, Zvi. "Soviet Reactions to the Holocaust, 1945-1991." In *The Holocaust in the Soviet Union: Studies and Sources on the Destruction of Jews in the Nazi-Occupied Territories of the USSR, 1941-1945*, edited by Lucjan Dobroszycki and Jeffrey S. Gurock, 3-27. Armonk, NY: M.E. Sharpe, 1993.

---. "The Soviet Union." In *The World Reacts to the Holocaust*, edited by David Wyman, 295-324. Baltimore: The Johns Hopkins University Press, 1996.

---. "Politics and Historiography of the Holocaust in the Soviet Union." In *Bitter Legacy: Confronting the Holocaust in the USSR*, edited by Zvi Gitelman, 14-42. Bloomington: Indiana University Press, 1997.

---. "What Soviet People Saw of the Shoah and How It Was Reported." US Holocaust Museum, Fellow Seminar, 22 March 2006; modified 11 December 2007 [manuscript].

"Gnev naroda." *Kerchenskii rabochii* 10 January 1942, 1.

Gofman, Iosif. *Niurnberg predosteregaet. Vospominaniia telokhranitelia glavnogo obvinitelia ot SSSR R. A. Rudenko o Niurnbergskom sudebnom protsesse*, 2nd ed. Poltava: n.p. 2007.

Gol'dina, O. I., et al., "Chudovishchnye zverstva fashistov v Kerchi (pis'mo vrachei goroda Kerchi)." *Komsomol'skaia pravda* 8 January 1942, 1

Goffenshefer, V[eniamin]. "Bagerovo." *Syn otechestva* 29 January 1942.

---. "Ne gasi ego, pamiat'!" *Syn otechestva* 16 March 1944.

Gol'd, Z. "Palachi." In *Zverstva nemetskikh fashistov v Kerchi. Sbornik rasskazov postradavshikh i ochevidtsev*, 99-102. Sukhumi: Krasnyi Krym, 1943.

Gol'dshtein, Aleksandr. "O Sel'vinskom." *Zerkalo* 15-16 (2000). http://magazines.russ.ru/zerkalo/2000/15/14selv.html. Last accessed 20 February 2012.

Goriunova, R. G. "Epopeia v teoreticheskom osmyslenii i tvorcheskoi praktike I. L. Sel'vinskogo." In *Vestnik Krymskikh Chtenii I. L. Sel'vinskogo*, vol. 1, 33-39. Simferopol: Krymskii arkhiv, 2002.

---. "Sel'vinskii o tragedii Adzhimushkaia." Paper delivered at 17 Krymskie mezhdunarodnye nauchnye chteniia I. L. Sel'vinskgogo "Tragicheskii opyt Velikoi otechestvennoi voiny v istoriko-literaturnom osmyslenii." Simferopol. Ilya Selvinsky Memorial Museum. 15 December 2011.

Grinberg, Marat. "Vychityvaia Slutskogo." *Kreshchatik* 3 (2008). http://magazines.russ.ru/kreschatik/2008/3/gr23.html. Last accessed 17 March 2010.

---. *"I am to be read not from left to right but in Jewish: from right to left": The Poetics of Boris Slutsky*. Boston: Academic Studies Press, 2011.

Grishin, Aleksandr. "…Etot fil'm o voine tak i ne byl sniat." *Krymskie izvestiia* 19 February 2011. http://www-ki-old.rada.crimea.ua/nomera/2011/031/this.html. Last accessed 22 February 2012.

Grossman, Vasilii [Vasily Grossman]. "Staryi uchitel'." *Znamia* 7-8 (1943): 95-110.

---. "The Old Teacher." Translated by James Loeffler. In *An Anthology of Jewish-Russian Literature: Two Centuries of Dual Identity in Prose and Poetry, 1801-2001*, 2 vols., edited by Maxim D. Shrayer, 1: 542-560. Armonk, NY: M. E. Sharpe, 2007.

---. "Treblinskii ad." *Znamia* 11 (1944): 121-144.

---. Grübel, Rainer. "Genij-Geije. Zur Struktur und zur Strukturbildenen Funktion eines Reims in dem Gedicht 'Evreiskij vopros' von Il'ja Sel'vinskij." *Die Welt der Slaven* 18 (1973): 163-189.

---. *Gody Voiny*. Moscow: Pravda, 1989.

Gubenko, Gitel'. *Kniga pechali*. Simferopol: Redotdel Krymskogo upravleniia po pechati, 1991.

Gurkovich, V. N. "Istoricheskii kommentarii k stikhotvereniiu I. L. Sel'vinskogo 'Ia eto videl!'" In *Vestnik Krymskikh chtenii I. L. Sel'vinskogo,* vol. 2, 89-95. Simferopol: Krymskii arkhiv, 2003.

---. "K voprosu o rasstrelakh mirnogo naseleniia v Bagerovskom rvu v 1941 godu." In *Kerch voennaia. Sbornik statei. 60-letiiu osvobozhdeniia goroda posviashchaetsia*, 27-31. Kerch: Kerchenskii gosudarstvennyi istoriko-kul'turnyi zapovednik, 2004.

Gutman, Il'ia. [dir.]. *Niurnberg: 40 let spustia*. Moscow, 1986. http://films.academic.ru/film.nsf/9268/Нюрнберг%3A+40+лет+спустя. Last accessed 20 February 2012.

Hicks, Jeremy. "From Atrocity to Action: How Soviet Cinema Initiated the Holocaust Film: Imagining the Unimaginable in the Soviet Context." In *Justice, Politics and Memory in Europe after the Second World War. Landscape after Battle*, vol. 2, edited by Suzanne Bardgett, David Cesarini et al., 249-266. London: Vallentine Mitchell, 2011.

Hirszowicz, Lukasz. "The Holocaust in the Soviet Mirror." In *The Holocaust in the Soviet Union: Studies and Sources on the Destruction of Jews in the Nazi-Occupied Territories of the USSR, 1941-1945*, edited by Lucjan Dobroszycki and Jeffrey S. Gurock, 29-59. Armonk, NY: M.E. Sharpe, 1993.

Iablonskii, L[eonid]. ["Photo of Nazi atrocities"]. *Kerchenskii rabochii* 14 January 1942.

"Iablonskii Leonid Isaakovich." In "Крымовед: Personalia." http://www.krimoved-library.ru/books/evrei-kryma14.html. Last accessed 27 January 2012.

Iakovlev, V[asilii]. *Prestupleniia. Bor'ba. Vozmezdie.* Simferopol: Krymizdat, 1961.

Inber, Vera. "Pochti tri goda (Leningradskii dnevnik)." *Izbrannye proizvedeniia*, 2 vols. Moscow: Gosudarstvennoe izdatel'stvo khudozhestvennoi literatury, 1954. http://lib.mn/blog/vera_inber/142205.html. Last accessed 29 January 2012.

"Informatsiia narkoma gosudarstvennoi bezopasnosti SSSR V. N. Merkulova sekretariu TsK VKP(b) A. A. Zhdanovu o politicheskikh nastroeniiakh i vyskazyvaniiakh pisatelei," 31 October 1944." *Rodina* 1 (1992): http://www.hrono.ru/dokum/194_dok/19441031merk.php. Last accessed 29 June 2010.

Ish, Lev. "Krovavye zverstva fashistov v Kerchi." *Krasnyi Krym* 29 January 1942, 2. *Izvestiia* 1 January-1 March 1942.

Ivinskaia, Ol'ga. "My poimenno vspomnim vsekh, kto podnial ruku." In *Gody blizosti s Pasternakom: v plenu vremeni*. Moscow: Libris, 1992. http://www.sakharov-center.ru/asfcd/auth/auth_booka14f.html?id=84901&aid=170. Last accessed 17 March 2011.

"Iz pis'ma vrachei goroda Kerchi v redaktsiiu gazety 'Komsomol'skaia pravda' ot 8/I 1942." *Dokumenty obviniaiut. Sbornik dokumentov o chudovishchnykh zlodeistvakh germanskikh vlastei na vremenno zakhvachennykh imi sovetskikh territoriiakh*, vol. 1, 191-192. Moscow: Gosudarstvennoe izdatel'stvo politicheskoi literatury, 1943.

Kalinin, A[natolii], and B[oris] Vakulin. "Kak byli vziaty Kerch' i Feodosiia." *Komsomol'skaia pravda* 3 January 1942, 2.

---. "Boi v Krymu." *Komsomol'skaia pravda* 6 January 1942, 2.

Kandel', Feliks. "Ocherk shest'desiat chetvertyi. 'Chernaia kniga'. Deiateli kul'tury i Katastrofa." In *Kniga vremen i sobytii. Vol. 5. Istoriia evreev Sovetskogo Soiuza, 1939-1945.* http://felixkandel.org/index.php/books/295.html. Last accessed 28 January 2012.

Karmen, R[oman]. "Mertvye obviniaut." *Izvestiia* 20 February 1946.

Katina, Vera. "'Kazhdyi chelovek imeet pravo na tumannyi ugolok dushi' (evreiskaia tema v zhizni i tvorchestve Il'i Sel'vinskoogo)." In *Dolia evreis'kykh gromad tsentral'noi ta skhidnoi Evropy v pershii polovyne XX stolittia. Materialy konferentsii 6-28 serpnia 2003 r., Kyiv.* http://www.judaica.kiev.ua/Conference/Conf2003/46.htm. Last accessed 26 February 2011.

Kats, Aleksandr. "Evrei—geroi sovetskogo soziuza i geroi Rossiii." http://politiky.net/content/евреи-герои-советского-союза-и-герои-россии. Last accessed 16 July 2010.

Katsap, Izia. "Ia eto videl svoimi glazami. Ia eto sam perezhil." *Forum: Evreiskaia gazeta na russkom iazyke dlia semeinogo chteniia* 22-28 April 2010, 15.

Katsis, Leonid. "'Doktor Zhivago' B. Pasternaka: ot M. Gershenzona do Ben-Guriona." *Evreiskii knigonosha* 8 (2005): http://echo.oranim.ac.il/main.php?p=news&id_news=47&id_personal=9. Last accessed 24 February 2011.

"Kerchenskie evrei otmetili godovshchinu Kholokosta." http://www.kerch.com.ua/articleview.aspx?id=10066. Last accessed 7 April 2010.

"Kerchensko-El'tigenskaia desantnaia operatsiia." http://ru.wikipedia.org/wiki/Керченско-Эльтигенская_десантная_операция. Last accessed 29 January 2012.

"Kerch v gody Velikoi otechestvennoi voiny." In *Forum vypusknikov Bagerovskoi srednei shkoly.* http://bagerovo-school.ru/phpBB3/viewtopic.php?f=27&t=1371. Last accessed 20 October 2011.

Kerler, Dov-Ber. "The Soviet Yiddish Press: *Eynikayt* during the War, 1942-1945." In *Why Didn't They Shout? American and International Journalism during the Holocaust: A Collection of Papers Originally Presented at an Interdisciplinary Conference Sponsored by the Elia and Diana Zborowski Professorial Chair in Interdisciplinary Holocaust Studies, Yeshiva University, October 1995*, edited by Robert Moses Shapiro, 221-249. Hoboken, NJ: Yeshiva University Press/Ktav Publishing House, 2003.

Khelemskii, Iakov. *V puti*. Moscow: Sovetskii pisatel', 1948.

---. "Kurliandskaia vesna." In *O Sel'vinskom: vospominaniia*, edited by Ts. A. Voskresenskaia and I. P. Sirotinskaia, 125-175. Moscow: Sovetskii pisatel', 1982.

Khiterer, Victoria. "We Did Not Recognize Our Country: The Rise of Anti-Semitism in Ukraine Before and After World War II (1937-1947)." *Polin: Studies in Polish Jewry*, 26 (forthcoming, 2012).

Kirsanov, Semen. "Pamiati tovarishcha." *Literaturnaia gazeta* 27 March 1968, 2.

Klier, John D. "Outline of Jewish-Russian History. Part II: 1954-2001." In *An Anthology of Jewish-Russian Literature: Two Centuries of Dual Identity in Prose and Poetry, 1801-2001*, 2 vols., edited by Maxim D. Shrayer, 2: 1199-1205. Armonk, NY: M. E. Sharpe, 2007.

"Kniga, Vasilii Ivanovich." http://ru.wikipedia.org/wiki/Книга,_Василий_Иванович. Accessed 24 January 2012.

Komsomol'skaia pravda 3 January-1 March 1942.

Kornilov, Vladimir. "Dvoe. Kniazhii vnuk i vnuchka prachki." http://www.chukfamily.ru/Lidia/Biblio/kornilov_dvoe.htm. 29 January 2012.

Korotkova G. V. "Okkupatsionnyi rezhim v Kerchi v period Velikoi Otechestvennoi voiny i ego posledtviia." In *Kerch voennaia. Sbornik statei. 60-letiiu osvobozhdeniia goroda posviashchaetsia*, 304-339. Kerch: Kerchenskii gosudarstvennyi istoriko-kul'turnyi zapovednik, 2004.

---. "K voprosu o rabote chrezvychainykh komissii v Kerchi (1944 g.). In *Na kerchenskom platsdarme. K 60-letiiu osvobozhdeniia Kerchi. Sbornik nauchnykh statei*, 166-183. Kerch: Kerchenski gosudarstvennyi istoriko-kul'turnyi zapovednik, 2004.

---, ed., "Dnevnik I. A. Kozlova iz fondov Kerchenskogo zapovednika." In *Nauchnyi sbornik Kerchenskogo zapovednika*, 2: 484-536. Kerch: Kerchenskii istoriko-kul'turnyi zapovednik, 2008.

Korshunova, V., and M. Sitkovetskaia, M., pub. "O voine, o literature, o sebe....Vystupleniia A. Tvardovskogo, I. Sel'vinskogo, I. Erenburga." *Voprosy literatury* 5 (1975): 225-241.

Korzhavin, Naum. "'Vikhri vrazhdebnye' i inye (Litinstitut v aprele sorok chetvertogo)." *Novyi mir. Iz portfelia redaktsii* 2012. http://magazines.russ.ru/novyi_mi/redkol/kor/mosk402.html. Accessed 29 January 2012.

Kostyrchenko, Gennadii, ed. *Gosudarstvennyi antisemitizm v SSSR ot nachala do kul'minatsii 1938-1953*. Moscow: Mezhdunarodnyi fond "Demokratiia"; Izdatel'stvo "Materik," 2005.

---. *Stalin protiv "kosmopolitov". Vlast' i evreiskaia intelligentsia v SSSR*. Moscow: Rosspen, 2009.

Kotel', M. "Gorod mertvykh." In *Zverstva nemetskikh fashistov v Kerchi. Sbornik rasskazov postradavshikh i ochevidtsev*, 75-78. Sukhumi: Krasnyi Krym, 1943.

Kotel'nikov, P[etr]. *Kerch 1935-1945 (Vospominaniia ochevidtsa).* Simferopol': n.p., 2007.
Kozyrev, F. "Nashi chasti tesniat vraga." *Pravda* 5 January 1942: 1.
Krasnaia zvezda. 1 January-1 March 1942.
"Krovavye zverstva nemtsev v Kerchi." *Pravda* 5 January 1942: 2.
Kucherenko, G. N. et al., eds. *Krym. Atlas turista.* Kiev: Kartografiia, 2011.
Kuptsov, Anatolii and Liubov' Semenova. "O morskoi baze, desante, pervom osvobozhdenii goroda." *Kerchenskii rabochii* 14 January 2012, http://www.krab.crimea.ua/?p=3687. Accessed 12 February 2012.

"Laar, Iosif Iosifovich." http://www.warheroes.ru/hero/hero.asp?Hero_id=4002. Last accessed 16 July 2010.
"Laureaty stalinskoi premii v oblasti literatury i iskusstva." http://ru.wikipedia.org/wiki/Лауреаты_Сталинской_премии_в_области_литературы_и_искусства. Last accessed 1 July 2010.
"Liberation of Nazi Camps." http://www.ushmm.org/wlc/en/article.php?ModuleId=10005131. Last accessed 1 March 2011.
Lidin, Vl[adimir]. "Plevely." *Izvestiia* 31 January 1942: 2.
Löwe, Heinz-Dietrich. "The Holocaust in the Soviet Press." In *"Zerstörer des Schweingens": Formen künstlerischer Erinnerung an die nationalsozialistische Rasse- und Vernichtungskrieg in Osteuropa*, edited by Frank Grüner et al., 34-55. Cologne: Böhlau, 2006.
Lower, Wendy. *Nazi Empire-Building and the Holocaust in Ukraine.* Chapel Hill, NC: The University of North Carolina Press, 2007.
Luppol, I. K., M. M. Rozental', and S. M. Tret'akov, eds. *Pervyi vsesoiuznyi s"ezd sovetskikh pisatelei. 1934. Stenograficheskii otchet*, reprint. Moscow: Gosudarstvennoe izdatel'stvo "Khudozhestvennaia literatura," 1934. Moscow: Sovetskii pisatel', 1990.

Machavriani V. "Stikhi o liubvi k Rodine i nenavisti k vragam" [Rev. of *Ballady, plakaty i pesni* by Il'ia Sel'vinskii]. *Vpered k pobede!* 15 July 1942.
Malin, A. "Nosov, Primak, Laar." *Vpered za rodinu!* 27 October 1943.
Markish, Shimon. "The Role of Officially Published Russian Literature in the Reawakening of Jewish National Consciousness (1953-1970).

In *Jewish Culture and Identity in the Soviet Union*, edited by Yaacov Ro'i and Avi Becker, 208-231. New York: New York University Press, 1991.

"Massacre by Germans in Kerch." *The Evening Post* [Wellington, New Zealand], 6 January 1942, 6.

"Matrosov, Aleksandr Matveevich." http://ru.wikipedia.org/wiki/Матросов,_Александр_Матвеевич. Last accessed 16 July 2010.

Mekhlis, L[ev]. "[Zapiska] Molotovu, Kaganovichu, Zhdanovu o poeme Sel'vinskogo 'Cheliuskiniana.' 28 December 1937." Fond Aleksandra N. Iakovleva website, http://www.alexanderyakovlev.org/fond/issues-doc/1015940. Accessed 29 Januaru 2012.

Melkov, Leonid. *Kerch'. Povest'-khronika v dokumentakh, vospominanikah i pis'makh uchastnikov geroicheskoi zashchity i osvobozhdeniia goroda v 1941-1944 godakh*. Moscow: Izdatel'stvo politicheskoi literatury, 1981.

Merzhanov, M. "Zversvta gestapovtsev." *Pravda* 10 January 1942, 2.

Militsyn, Boris. "Tatarstanskie stranichki iz zhizni sem'i Il'i Sel'vinskogo." *Kazanskie istorii* 5 February 2011. http://history-kazan.ru/2011/02/татарстанские-странички-из-жизни-сем/. Last accessed 3 October 2011.

Mitrofanov, Vl[adimir]. "Krym pered ob"ektivom." *Literatura i iskusstvo* 21 March 1942, 3.

"Molotoff [sic] Accused Nazi of Atrocities—Note Detailing 'Crimes' Handed to All Foreign Diplomats." *The New York Times* 7 January 1942, 8.

"More Nazi Crimes Listed by Soviet; Molotoff Note to All Friendly Countries Charges Germany Orders Terrorism—Vast Looting Is Alleged Attacks on Women and Girls Said to Be Part of Program—Mass Murders Described." *The New York Times* 8 January 1942, 7.

Mukhat, M., et al. "Akt o fashistskikh zverstvakh. 30/XII-41 g." *Kerchenskii rabochii* 7 January 1942, 1.

Murav, Harriet. *Music from a Speeding Train: Jewish Literature in Post-Revolutionary Russia*. Stanford: Stanford University Press, 2011.

"My ne prostim!" [editorial]. *Krasnyi Krym* 24 January 1942, 1.

"My eto videli. Rasskazy ochevidtsev o zverstvakh nemtsev v Krymu." *Syn otechestva* 7 April 1944.

"Nasha pobeda v Krymu [editorial]. *Pravda* 31 December 1941, 1.

Nekrasova, E. A. "Voennaia zhurnalistika Il'i Sel'vinskogo." In *Vestnik*

Krymskikh chtenii I. L. Sel'vinskogo, vol. 2, 76-84. Simferopol: Krymskii arkhiv, 2003.

Nepomniashchii, A. A. "Istoriia nauki v Krymu. Nerealizovanye krymovedcheskie proekty 1930-kh godov: deistvuiushchie litsa." *Istoricheskoe nasledie Kryma. Zhurnal* 20 (2007). http://old.com-monuments.crimea-portal.gov.ua/rus/index.php?v=1&tek=105&par=74&l=&art=613. Accessed 7 January 2012.

"Nerazborchivaia redaktsiia." *Izvestiia* 13 July 1943, 4.

Lebedeva, N. S., et al., eds. *Niurnbergskii protsess. Prestupleniia protiv chelovechestva*, vol. 5. Moscow: Iuridicheskaia literatura, 1991. http://lib.ru/MEMUARY/1939-1945/NURNBERG/np5.txt. Last accessed 5 October 2011.

"Nota Narodnogo komissara inostrannykh del tov. V. M. Molotova o povsemestnykh grabezhakh, razorenii naseleniia i chudovishchnykh zverstvakh germanskikh vlastei na zakhvachennykh imi sovetskikh territoriiakh." *Pravda* 7 January 1942, 1-2.

"Nota Narodnogo komissara inostrannykh del tov. V. M. Molotova o povsemestnykh grabezhakh, razorenii naseleniia i chudovishchnykh zverstvakh germanskikh vlastei na zakhvachennykh imi sovetskikh territoriiakh." *Izvestiia* 7 January 1942, 1-2.

"Nota Narodnogo komissara inostrannykh del tov. V. M. Molotova o povsemestnykh grabezhakh, razorenii naseleniia i chudovishchnykh zverstvakh germanskikh vlastei na zakhvachennykh imi sovetskikh territoriiakh." *Krasnaia zvezda* 7 January 1942, 1-2.

"Nota Narodnogo komissara inostrannykh del tov. V. M. Molotova o povsemestnykh grabezhakh, razorenii naseleniia i chudovishchnykh zverstvakh germanskikh vlastei na zakhvachennykh imi sovetskikh territoriiakh." *Komsomol'skaia pravda* 7 January 1942, 1-2.

"Nota Narodnogo komissara inostrannykh del tov. V. M. Molotova o povsemestnykh grabezhakh, razorenii naseleniia i chudovischnykh zverstvakh germanskikh vlastei na zakhvachennykh imi sovetskikh territoriiakh, 6 ianvaria 1942 g." In *Dokumenty obviniaiut. Sbornik dokumentov o chudovishchykh zverstvskh germanskikh vlastei na vremenno zakhvachennykh imi sovetskikh territoriiakh*, vol. 1, 33-45. Moscow: Gosudarstvennoe izdatel'stvo politicheskoi literatury, 1943.

"Nota Narodnogo komissara Inostrannykh del tov. V. M. Molotova o chudovishchnykh zlodeianiiakh, zverstvakh i nasiliiakh nemetsko-fashistskikh zakhvatchikov v okkupirovannykh sovetskikh raionakh i ob otvetstvennosti germanskogo pravitel'stva i komandovaniia za eti prestupleniia. 27 aprelia 1942 g." In *Dokumenty obviniaiut. Sbornik dokumentov o chudovishchnykh zverstvakh germanskikh vlastei na vremenno zakhvachennykh imi sovetskikh territoriiakh*, vol. 1, 9-32. Moscow: Gosudarstvennoe izdatel'stvo politicheskoi literatury, 1943.

"Note on German Atrocities in Occupied Soviet Territory." http://www.ibiblio.org/pha/policy/1942/420106b.html. Last accessed 7 April 2010.

Novikova, M. A. "Zagadki biografii Il'ii Sel'vinskgoo (nekotorye novye metody eksursionnoi raboty)." In *Vestnik Krymskikh chtenii I. L. Sel'vinskogo,* vol. 2, 95-101. Simferopol: Krymskii arkhiv, 2003.

"Nuremberg Trial Proceedings. Vol. 7. Sixtieth Day. Friday, 15 February 1946." [The Avalon Project.] http://avalon.law.yale.edu/imt/02-15-46.asp. Accessed 20 February 2012.

"Nuremberg Trial Proceedings. Vol. 7. Sixty-Second Day. Tuesday, 19 February 1946." [The Avalon Project.] http://avalon.law.yale.edu/imt/02-19-46.asp. Accessed 20 February 2012.

Olonova, El'vira. "Lirika na voine." *Československá rusistika* 20.2 (1975): 55-60.

Ol'shanskaia, Evdokiia. "Mne zhizn' podarila vstrechi s poetom." *Zerkalo nedeli* (1998). http://www.litera.ru/stixiya/articles/397.html. Last accessed 7 April 2010.

"Ona byla pol'ka, a zvali ee Alisoi...." *Solnechnyi veter.* http://vilavi.ru/raz/alisa/0.shtml. Last accessed 17 March 2011.

Ortenberg, D[avid]. I. *God 1942. Rasskaz-khronika*. Moscow: Izdatel'stvo politicheskoi literatury, 1988.

---. *Sorok tretii. Rasskaz-khronika*. Moscow: Politizdat, 1991. http://www.victory.mil.ru/lib/books/memo/ortenberg_di3. Last accessed 14 July 2011.

---. "Vmesto poslesloviia." In *Sorok tretii: rasskaz-khronika*. Moscow: Politizdat, 1991: http://www.victory.mil.ru/lib/books/memo/ortenberg_di3/09.html. Last accessed 14 July 2010.

"Otomstim!" *Fotogazeta Glavnogo politicheskogo upravleniia Krasnoi Armii* 19 (February 1942): 1.

Ozerov, Lev. "Voennaia lirika Il'ii Sel'vinskogo." *Literatura i iskusstvo* 25 July 1942, 3.

---. "Sila slova." *Moskovskii bol'shevik*. 11 December 1942, 3.

---. "Babii Iar." *Oktiabr'* 3/4 (1946): 160-163.

---. "Babii Iar." In *Liven'*, edited by Pavel Antokol'skii, 25-32. Moscow: Molodaia gvardiia, 1947.

---. *Babi Yar*, translated by Richad Sheldon, in *An Anthology of Jewish-Russian Literature: Two Centuries of Dual Identity in Prose and Poetry, 1801-2001,* 2 vols., edited by Maxim D. Shrayer, 1: 575-579. Armonk, NY: M. E. Sharpe, 2007.

---. "Mechtat' li o bessmertii? Otkrytoe pis'mo Il'e Sel'vinskomu." *Literaturnaia Rossiia* 12 August 1966, 16-17.

---. "'Stakan okeana." In *O Sel'vinskom: vospominaniia*, edited by Ts. A. Voskresenskaia and I. P. Sirotinskaia, 366-396. Moscow: Sovetskii pisatel', 1982.

---. "Il'ia Sel'vinskii, ego trudy i dni." In Il'ia Sel'vinskii, *Izbrannye proizvedeniia v dvukh tomakh*, 2 vols., edited by Ts. Voskresenskaia, 1: 5-20. Moscow: Khudozhestvennaia literatura, 1989.

---. "'Ia eto videl!'" In *Biografiia stikhotvoreniia*. 40-48. Moscow: Znanie, 1981.

---. "Sel'vinskii." In his *Portrety bez ram*, edited by A. Ozerova and S. Kugel', 165-169. Moscow: Academia, 1999.

---. *Liven'*, edited by Pavel Antokol'skii. Moscow: Molodaia gvardiia, 1947.

---. *Lirika: 1931-1966*. Moscow: Sovetskii pisatel', 1966.

---. *Portrety bez ram*, edited by A. Ozerova and S. Kugel'. Moscow: Academia, 1999.

"Pamiati tovarishcha" [Reflections on I. Selvinsky's death by S. Kirsanov. R. Rza, K. Zelinskii]. *Literaturnaia gazeta* 27 March 1968, 2.

"Peredaem soderzhanie noty Narodnogo komissara inostrannykh Del tov. V. N. Molotova." *Kerchenskii rabochii* 8 January 1942, 1.

"Pervaia udarnaia armiia." http://ru.wikipedia.org/wiki/1-я_ударная_армия. Last accessed 12 March 2011.

"Petrov, Ivan Efimovich." http://ru.wikipedia.org/wiki/Петров,_Иван_Ефимович. Last accessed 8 July 2010.

"Pepel Klaasa stuchit v moem serdtse." In Vadim Serov, *Entisklopedicheskii slovar' krylatykh slov i vyrazhenii*. http://www.bibliotekar.ru/encSlov/15/19.htm. Last accessed 14 February 2011.

Pikach, Anatolii. "Kogda prozrevaet dusha" [Rev. of Andrei Voznesenskii, "Rov"]. *Literaturnoe obozrenie* 1 (1987), 61-64.

Pinkus, Benjamin. *The Soviet Government and the Jews, 1948-1967: A Documentary Study*. Cambridge: Cambridge University Press, 1984.

Plokhy, S. M. *Yalta: The Price of Peace*. New York: Viking, 2010.

"Poeziia studentov Moskvy." *Oktiabr'* 3 (1941), 112-115 [a selection of poems by 4 poets].

Poliak, L[idiia]. "O 'liricheskom epose' Velikoi Otechestvennoi voiny." *Znamia* 9-10 (1943): 292-299.

Polonskii, Viasheslav. *Ocherki literaturnogo dvizheniia revoliutsionnoi epokhi*, 2nd ed. Moscow: Gosudarstvennoe izdatel'stvo, 1929.

Polonsky, Antony. *The Jews in Poland and Russia*, 3 vols. Oxford: Littman Library of Jewish Civilization, 2010-2012.

Pravda 1 January-1 March 1942.

Redkin, Mark [phot.]. "Fashisty poplatiatsia za eto golovami! Otomstim za krov' bezvinnykh zhertv. Fotodokumenty o zverstvakh nemtsev v Kerchi." *Komsomol'skaia pravda* 20 January 1942.

---. "Strashnye prestupleniia gitlerovskikh palachei." *Ogonek* 4 February 1942, 4.

Redlikh, Shimon, and Gennadii Kostyrchenko, eds. *Evreiskii antifashistskii komitet v SSSR 1941-1948*. Moscow: Mezhdunarodnye otnosheniia, 1996.

Reifman, P. S. "Glava piataia: Vtoraia mirovaia. Chast' vtoraia." In P. S. Reifman, *Iz istorii russkoi, sovetskoi i postsovetskoi tsenzury*. http://www.gumer.info/bibliotek_Buks/History/reifm/16.php. Last accessed 6 April 2010.

Reshetnikov, F[edor]. "Nemetskie okkupanty v Kerchi. Bagerovo." *Vpered k pobede!* 31 December 1942.

Reshetnikov, Fedor. [*Works*], edited by B. V. Vishniakov. Moscow: Izobrazitel'noe iskusstvo, 1982.

Reshetnikov, F[edor]. http://www.maslovka.org/modules.php?name=Content&pa=showpage&pid=72. Accessed 25 December 2011.

Revich, Aleksandr. "Sedoe s detstva pokoleni'e." In Il'ia Sel'vinskii, *Iz pepla, iz poem, iz snovidenii*, edited by A. M. Revich. 5-20. Moscow: Vremia, 2004.

Reznik, Osip. *Zhizn' v poezii: Tvorchestvo I. Sel'vinskogo*. Moscow: Sovetskii pisatel', 1981.

Roman'ko, O[leg]. V. *Krym pod piatoi Gitlera. Nemetskaia okkupatsionnaia politika v Krymu, 1941-1944 gg.* Moscow: Veche, 2011.

Romm, Aleksandr. "Nadiusha." *Kerchenskii rabochii* 15 January 1942.

---. "Pisatel'-voin." *Literatura i iskusstvo* 4 July 1942.

"Romm, Aleksandr Il'ich." http://ru.wikipedia.org/wiki/Ромм,_Александр_Ильич. Last accessed 8 April 2010.

Roskies, David G. *Against the Apocalypse: Responses to Catastrophe in Modern Jewish Culture*. Cambridge, MA: Harvard University Press, 1984.

Rubashkin, Aleksandr. *Il'ia Erenburg: put' pisatelia*. Leningrad: Sovetskii pisatel', 1990.

Rubenstein, Joshua, and Vladimir Naumov, eds. *Stalin's Secret Pogrom: The Postwar Inquisition of the Jewish Anti-Fascist Committee*. Translated by Laura Esther Wolfson. New Haven: Yale University Press, 2001.

Rubenstein, Joshua, and Ilya Altman, eds. *The Unknown Black Book: The Holocaust in the German-Occupied Soviet Territories*. Bloomington: Indiana University Press, 2008.

Rustemova, L[iudmila] A. "Krymskii 'kontekst' I. Sel'vinskogo." In *I. L. Sel'vinskii i literaturnyi protsess XX veka. V mezhdunarodnaia nauchnaia konferentsiia, posviashchennaia 100-letiiu I. L. Sel'vinskogo. Materialy*, 73-80. Simferopol': Krymskii arkhiv, 2000.

Samarianov, Vladimir. *Prervannoe detstvo*. http://www.proza.ru/2011/03/27/1786. Accessed 28 December 2011.

Samoilov, David. "Okhota na mamonta." *Oktiabr'* 3 (1941): 115 [signed D. Kaufman].

---. "V masterskoi stikha." In his *Pamiatnye zapiski*, edited by G. I. Medvedeva, 177-181. Moscow: Mezhdunarodnye otnosheniia, 1995.

---. "Iz prozaicheskikh tetradei." Pub. G. I. Medvedeva. *Novyi mir* 6 (2010). http://magazines.russ.ru/novyi_mi/2010/6/sa11.html. Last accessed 10 February 2011.

---. "Solomonchik portnoi. Kratkoe zhizneopisanie." In his, *Poemy*, edited by Andrei Nemzer and Galina Medvedeva, 334-341, Moscow: Vremia, 2005.

---. *Pamiatnye zapiski*, edited by G. I. Medvedeva. Moscow: Mezhdunarodnye otnosheniia, 1995.

---. *Poemy*, edited by Andrei Nemzer and Galina Medvedeva. Moscow: Vremia, 2005.

---. *Stikhotvoreniia*, edited by V. I. Tumarkin and A. S. Nemzer. St. Petersburg: Akademicheskii proekt, 2006.

"David Samuilovich Samoilov." In *Russkie pisateli. Poety (Sovetskii period). Bibliograficheskii ukazatel'*, vol. 22, 170-257. St. Petersburg: Rossiiskaia natsional'naia biblioteka, 1999.

Sanzharovets, V. F. "Antropotoponimy kerchenskogo poluostrova: proiskhozhdenie nekotorykh istoricheskikh i sovremennykh oikonimov (opyr istoriko-toponimicheskogo issledovaniia)." *Nauchnyi sbornik kerchenskogo zapovednika* 3 (2011): 389-411.

Sarnov, Benedikt. "Bednyi Len. Iz vospominanii o V. B. Shklovskom." *Lekhaim* 5 (2008). http://www.lechaim.ru/ARHIV/193/sarnov.htm. Last accessed 17 March 2011.

Seifullina, Liudmila. "One Survived: The Story of Evsey Efimovich Gopshtein." In Ilya Ehrenburg and Vasily Grossman, *The Complete Black Book of Russian Jewry*, tr. and ed. David Patterson, 427-430. New Brunswick: Transaction Publishers, 2003.

Sel'vinskaia, T. I. "Roditeli." *Krymskie penaty. Al'manakh literaturnykh muzeev* 6 (2010): 126-129.

Sel'vinskii, Il'ia. "Adzhimushkaiskie kamenolomni." *Vpered za rodinu!* 2 December 1943.

---. "Antisemity." In *Izbrannye proizvedeniia*, 2 vols., 1: 155. Moscow: Goslitidat, 1956.

---. "Antisemity." *O vremeni, o sud'bakh, o liubvi*, 69. Moscow: Sovetskii pisatel', 1962.

---. "Ballada o Laare." *Oktiabr'* 7-8 (1944): 130.

---. "Ballada o leninizme." *Bolshevik* [Krasnodar]. 27 January 1942, 2.

---. "Ballada o leninizme," *Krasnaia zvezda* 13 February 1942, 3.

---. "Ballada o tanke 'KV'." In *Krym Kavkaz Kuban'. Stikhi*, 53-56. Moscow: Sovetskii pisatel', 1947.

---. "Byvaiut kraia, chto nedvizhny vekami..." In *Izbrannye proizvedeniia*, edited by I. L. Mikhailov and N. G. Zakharenko, 233-236. Sovetskii pisatel' [Biblioteka poeta], 1972. [Part 2 of a two-part cycle titled "Krym."]

---, and Matvei Blanter [music]. "Chernoglazaia kazachka." http://a-pesni.golosa.info/drugije/tchernkazatchka.htm. Last accessed 17 March 2011.

---. "Bitva za Kavkaz." In *Krym Kavkaz Kuban'. Stikhi*, 156-161. Moscow: Sovetskii pisatel', 1947.

---. "Boi pod Mal'gobekom." In *Krym Kavkaz Kuban'. Stikhi*, 89-99. Moscow: Sovetskii pisatel', 1947.

---. "Chitaia Stalina." In *Krym Kavkaz Kuban'. Stikhi*, 196-200. Moscow: Sovetskii pisatel', 1947.

---. "Chitaia Stalina." In *Lirika i dramy*, 98-101. Moscow: Gosudarstvennoe izdatel'stvo khudozhestvennoi literatury, 1947.

---. "Eshche o zverstvakh gitlerovtsev." *Boevoi natisk* 24 February 1942.

---. "Evreiskaia melodiia." *Ogonek* 28 (1960): 19.

---. "Evreiskaia melodiia." In *O vremeni, o sud'bakh, o sebe*, 125. Moscow: Sovetskii pisatel', 1962.

---. "Evreiskii vopros." In *Izbrannye proizvedeniia*, 2 vols., 1: 156. Moscow: Goslitidat, 1956.

---. "Evreiskii vopros." In *O vremeni, o sud'bakh, o sebe*, 69-70. Moscow: Sovetskii pisatel', 1962.

---. "Evreiskomu narodu." In *Ballady, plakaty i pesni*, 21-23. Krasnodar: Kraevoe izdatel'stvo, 1942.

---. "Evreiskomu narodu." In *Voennaia lirika*, 41-43. Tashkent: Gosudarstvennoe izdatel'stvo UzSSR, 1943.

---. "Fashisty—o blagodarnost' sud'be..." *Syn otechestva* 20 October 1941.

---. "Golos Stalina." *Literaturnaia gazeta* 6 July 1941.

---. "Ia eto videl!" *Krasnaia zvezda* 27 February 1942, 3.

---. "Ia eto videl!" [with editorial intro]. *Vpered k pobede!* 31 December 1942.

---. "Ia eto videl!" *Oktiabr'* 1-2 (1942): 65-66.

---. "Ia eto videl!" In *Ballady, plakaty i pesni*, 87-92. Krasnodar: Kraevoe izdatel'stvo, 1942.

---. "Ia eto videl." In *Ne zabudem, ne prostim* [*Zverstva fashistov v Kerchi*], Moscow: Goskinoizdat, 1942 [booklet-poster].

---. "Ia eto videl!" In *Zverstva nemetskikh fashistov v Kerchi. Sbornik rasskazov postradavshikh i ochevidtsev*, 33-38. Sukhumi: Krasnyi Krym, 1943.

---. "Ia eto videl!" In *Voennaia lirika*, 18-22. Tashkent: Gosudarstvennoe izdatel'stvo UzSSR, 1943.

---. "Ia eto videl!" In *Sbornik stikhov*, edited by V[asilii] Kazin and V[iktor] Pertsov, 373-375. Moscow: Gosudarstvennoe izdatel'stvo khudozhestvennoi literatury, 1943.

---. "Ia eto videl!" In *Ballady i pesni*, 42-45. Moscow: Goslitizdat, 1943.

---. "Ia eto videl!" In *Krym Kavkaz Kuban'. Stikhi*, 7-12. Moscow: Sovetskii pisatel', 1947.
---. "Ia eto videl!" In *Lirika i dramy*, 51-55. Moscow: Gosudarstvennoe izdatel'stvo khudozhestvennoi literatury, 1947.
---. "Ia eto videl!" In *Izbrannye proizvedeniia*, 2 vols., 1: 162-165. Moscow: Gosudarstvennoe izdatel'stvo khudozhestvennoi literatury, 1956.
---. "Ia eto videl!" In *Antologiia russkoi sovetskoi poezii*, 2 vols., edited by L. O. Belov et al., 1: 448-451. Moscow: Gosudarstvennoe izdatel'stvo khudozhestvennoi literatury, 1957.
---. "Ia eto videl!" In *Lirika*, 249-253. Moscow: Khudozhestvennaia literatura, 1964.
---. "Ia eto videl!" In *Vo ves' golos. Soviet Poetry*, edited by Vladimir Ognev, 133-138. Moscow: Progress Publishers, n.d. [ca. 1965].
---. "Ia eto videl!" In *Sobranie sochinenii v shesti tomakh*. Vol. 1. *Stikhotvoreniia*, 352-355. Moscow: Khudozhestvennaia literatura, 1971.
---. "Ia eto videl!" In *Izbrannye proizvedeniia*, edited by I. L. Mikhailov and N. G. Zakharenko, 206-209. Leningrad: Sovetskii pisatel' [Biblioteka poeta], 1972.
---. "Ia eto videl!" In Lev Ozerov, *Biografiia stikhotvoreniia*. 41-44. Moscow: Znanie, 1981.
---. "Ia eto videl!" In *Stikhotvoreniia. Tsarevna-lebed': tragediia*, edited by Ts. Voskresenskaia, 111-114. Moscow: Khudozhestvennaia literatura, 1984.
---. "Ia eto videl!" In *Ia eto videl! Stikhotvoreniia i poemy*, edited by Vladimir Ognev, 96-100. Moscow: Sovetskaia Rossiia, 1985.
---. "Ia eto videl!" In *Izbrannye proizvedeniia v dvukh tomakh*, 2 vols., edited by Ts. Voskresenskaia, 1:176-179. Moscow: Khudozhestvennaia literatura, 1989.
---. "Ia eto videl!" In *Menora. Evreiskie motivy v russkoi poezii*, edited by Ada Kolganova, 130-134. Moscow-Jerusalem: Evreiskii universitet v Moskve, 1993.
---. "Ia eto videl!" In his *Iz pepla, iz poem, iz snovidenii*, edited by A. M. Revich, 139-144. Moscow: Vremia, 2004.
---. "Ia eto videl (Krymskie stranitsy voennykh dnevnikov)." In *Krym-90. Al'manakh*, edited by Ts. A. Voskresenskaia and R. M. Goriunova, 77-83. Simferopol: Tavriia, 1990.
---. "I Saw It!" translated by Denis Johnson & IWP. In *Twentieth-Century Russian Poetry*, edited by John Glad and Daniel Weissbort, 178-182.

Iowa City: University of Iowa Press, 1992.
---. "Iz novykh stikhov..." *Ogonek* 11 (1959): 25.
---. "Kandava." *Oktiabr'* 1-2 (1946): 3-6.
---. "Kandava." In *Krym Kavkaz Kuban'. Stikhi*, 209-217. Moscow: Sovetskii pisatel', 1947.
---. "Kandava." In *Lirika i dramy*, 106-112. Moscow: Gosudarstvennoe izdatel'stvo khudozhestvennoi literatury, 1947.
---. "Kandava." In *Izbrannye proizvedeniia*, edited by I. L. Mikhailov and N. G. Zakharenko, 236-243. Leningrad: Sovetskii pisatel' [Biblioteka poeta], 1972.
---. "Kandava." In *Ia eto videl! Stikhotvoreniia i poemy*, edited by Vladimir Ognev, 118-125. Moscow: Sovetskaia Rossiia, 1985.
---. "Kandava." In *Izbrannye proizvedeniia v dvukh tomakh*, 2 vols., edited by Ts. Voskresenskaia, 139-145. Moscow: Khudozhestvennaia literatura, 1989.
---. "K boitsam Krymskogo Fronta." In *Krym Kavkaz Kuban'. Stikhi*, 57-60. Moscow: Sovetskii pisatel', 1947.
---. "Kenigsberg segodnia (Putevye zametki)." *Na razgrom vraga* 1 June 1945.
---. "Kerch'." *Znamia* 2 (1945): 78-79.
---. "Kerch'." In *Stikhotvoreniia. Tsarevna-lebed': tragediia*, edited by Ts. Voskresenskaia, 108-111. Moscow: Khudozhestvennaia literatura, 1984.
---. "Kerch'." In *Izbrannye proizvedeniia v dvukh tomakh*, 2 vols., edited by Ts. Voskresenskaia, 1: 193-196. Moscow: Khudozhestvennaia literatura, 1989.
---. "Kerch'." In his *Iz pepla, iz poem, iz snovidenii*, edited by A. M. Revich, 150-154. Moscow: Vremia, 2004.
---. "Kogo baiukala Rossiia...." *Znamia* 7-8 (1943): 111.
---. "Kogo baiukala Rossiia." In *Izbrannye proizvedeniia*, edited by I. L. Mikhailov and N. G. Zakharenko, 210-211. Leningrad: Sovetskii pisatel' [Biblioteka poeta], 1972.
---. "Koga baiukala Rossiia." In *Izbrannye proizvedeniia v dvukh tomakh*, 2 vols., edited by Ts. Voskresenskaia, 197-198. Moscow: Khudozhestvennaia literatura, 1989.
---. "Krym" ["Na karte, vsia poryvaias' vpered..."]. *Vpered za rodinu!* 12 November 1943.
---. "Krym" ["Kak boi barabana, kak golos kartechi..."]. *Novyi mir* 3 (1946): 43-43.

---. "Krym" ["Kak boi barabana, kak golos kartechi..."]. In *Krym Kavkaz Kuban'. Stikhi*, 178-181. Moscow: Sovetskii pisatel', 1947.
---. "Krym" ["Kak boi barabana, kak golos kartechi..."]. In *Izbrannye proizvedeniia*, edited by I. L. Mikhailov and N. G. Zakharenko, 231-232. Leningrad: Sovetskii [Biblioteka poeta], 1972 [part 1 of a two-part cycle "Krym"].
---. "Krym" ["Byvaiut kraia, chto nedvizhny vekami...]." In *Lirika*, 318-322. Moscow: Khudozhestvennaia literatura, 1964.
---. "Krym." In *Izbrannye proizvedeniia*, edited by I. L. Mikhailov and N. G. Zakharenko, 233-236. Leningrad: Sovetskii pisatel' [Biblioteka poeta], 1972. [A cycle of 2 poems, "Kak boi barabana, kak golos kartechi..." and "Byvaiut kraia, chto nedvizhny vekami...."]
---. "Mechta moei ty starosti...." *Ogonek* 28 (1960): 19.
---. "Shest' dokumentov." *Boevoi natisk* 22 February 1942: 2.
---. "Na chetyrekh iazykakh. O gazete Severo-Kavkazskogo fronta 'Vpered k pobede'." In *Literaturnoe nasledstvo. Sovetskie pisateli na frontakh Velikoi Otechestvennoi voiny*, vol. 1: 520-523. Moscow: Nauka, 1966.
---. "Na voine. Iz dnevnikov i pisem rodnym." Edited by Ts. Voskresenskaia. *Novyi mir* 12 (1984): 163-175.
---. "Narodnost' i poeziia." *Literaturnaia gazeta* 18 October 1956, 3.
---. "Na Taman'," *Vpered za rodinu!* 29 September 1943.
---. "Otsy, ne razdrazhaite vashikh chad!..." *Ogonek* 11 (1959): 25.
---. "Otvet Gebbel'su." *Vpered k pobede!* 31 January 1942.
---. "Otvet Gebbel'su." *Bol'shevik* [Krasnodar] 1 January 1943.
---. "Otvet Gebbel'su." In *Krym Kavkaz Kuban'. Stikhi*, 13-17. Moscow: Sovetskii pisatel', 1947.
---. "Otvet L'vu Ozerovu." *Literaturnaia Rossiia* 23 September 1966, 9.
---. "Pesenka o zhesnkom serdtse." *Znamia* 6 (1962): 17.
---. "Pesenka o zhesnkom serdtse." In *Izbrannye proizvedeniia*, edited by I. L. Mikhailov and N. G. Zakharenko, 316. Leningrad: Sovetskii pisatel' [Biblioteka poeta], 1972.
---. "Pesn' 72-i Kubanskoi Kazachei Divizii." In *Krym Kavkaz Kuban'. Stikhi*, 100-101. Moscow: Sovetskii pisatel', 1947.
---. "Poezia Iosifa Utkina." *Literaturnaia gazeta* 2 December 1944.
---. "Poeziia L. Ozerova" [Rev. of Lev Ozerov, *Liven'*, Moscow, 1947]." *Oktiabr'* 8 (1947): 175-179.
---. "Razgovor s voennoplennym." In *Krym Kavkaz Kuban'. Stikhi*, 182-

185. Moscow: Sovetskii pisatel', 1947.
---. "Rossii." *Krasnaia zvezda* 15 July 1942.
---. "Rossii." *Oktiabr'* 8 (1942): 81-82.
---. "Rossii." *Komsomol'skaia pravda* 11 July 1943, 3.
---. "Rossii." In *Ballady i pesni*, 10-12. Moscow: Goslitizdat, 1943.
---. "Rossii." In *Voennaia lirika*, 34-37. Tashkent: Gosudarstvennoe izdatel'stvo UzSSR, 1943.
---. "Russkaia pekhota." *Suvorovets* 23 May 1945, 3.
---. "Sevastopol'." *Leningrad* 1-2 (1946): 17.
---. "Sevastopol'." In *Krym Kavkaz Kuban'. Stikhi*, 186-191. Moscow: Sovetskii pisatel', 1947.
---. "Sevastopol'." In *Lirika i dramy*, 68-72. Moscow: Gosudarstvennoe izdatel'stvo khudozhestvennoi literatury, 1947.
---. "Sila poeta." *Literaturnaia gazeta* 28 January 1961.
---. "Soldatskaia pesnia." In *Krym Kavkaz Kuban'. Stikhi*, 218-219. Moscow: Sovetskii pisatel', 1947.
---. "Stalin u mikrofona." *Oktiabr'* 12 (1942): 3.
---. "Stalin u mikrofona." In *Ballady, plakaty i pesni*, 6-7. Krasnodar: Kraevoe izdatel'stvo, 1942.
---. "Stalin u mikrofona." In *Ballady i pesni*, 3. Moscow: Goslitizdat, 1943.
---. "Stalin u mikrofona." In *Voennaia lirika*, 4-5. Tashkent: Gosudarstvennoe izdatel'stvo UzSSR, 1943.
---. "Stalin u mikrofona 3-go iiulia 1941 g." In *Lirika i dramy*, 5. Moscow: Gosudarstvennoe izdatel'stvo khudozhestvennoi literatury, 1947.
---. "Strashnyi sud." *Guliston* 3 (1960): 5-7.
---. "Strashnyi sud." In *O vremeni, o sud'bakh, o sebe*, 135-138. Moscow: Sovetskii pisatel', 1962.
---. "Strashnyi sud." In *Izbrannye proizvedeniia*, edited by I. L. Mikhailov and N. G. Zakharenko, 310-313. Leningrad: Sovetskii pisatel' [Biblioteka poeta], 1972.
---. "Sud v Krasnodare." *Znamia* 11 (1945): 25-28.
---. "Sud v Krasnodare." *Krym Kavkaz Kuban'. Stikhi*, 147-155. Moscow: Sovetskii pisatel', 1947.
---. "Tol'ko ognem…" *Syn otechestva* 7 April 1944 [excerpt from "Ia eto videl!"].
---. *Tushinskii lager'*. Introduction by Aleksandr Gol'dshtein. *Zerkalo* 15-16 (2000). http://magazines.russ.ru/zerkalo/2000/15/14selv.html. Last accessed 20 February 2012.

---. "Ubiitsy rasplatiatsia svoei chernoi krov'iu. Novyi dokument of chudovishchnykh zverstvakh gitlerovskikh palachei." *Boevoi natisk* 30 March 1942, 2.
---. "Za rodinu, za Stalina." In *Ballady, plakaty i pesni*, 8-9. Krasnodar: Kraevoe izdatel'stvo, 1942.
---. *Rannii Sel'vinskii*. Moscow-Leningrad: Gosudarstvennoe izdatel'tvo, 1929.
---. *Pushtorg. Roman*. Moscow-Leningrad: Gosudarstvennoe izdatel'tvo, 1929.
---. *Ulialaevshchina. Epopeia*, 2nd ed. Moscow-Leningrad: Gosudarstvennoe izdatel'stvo, 1930.
---. *Ballady, plakaty i pesni*. Krasnodar: Kraevoe izdatel'stvo, 1942.
---. *Voennaia lirika*. Tashkent: Gosudarstvennoe izdatel'stvo UzSSR, 1943.
---. *Ballady i pesni*. Moscow: Goslitizdat, 1943.
---. *General Brusilov*. Moscow: Iskusstvo, 1943.
---. *Babek. Tragediia*. Moscow: Sovetskii pisatel', 1946.
---. *Livonskaia voina. Tragediia*. Moscow: Iskusstvo, 1946.
---. *Krym Kavkaz Kuban'. stikhi*. Moscow: Sovetskii pisatel', 1947.
---. *Lirika i dramy*. Moscow: Gosudarstvennoe izdatel'stvo khudozhestvennoi literatury, 1947.
---. *Izbrannoe*. Moscow: Pravda, 1948.
---. *Izbrannoe*. Moscow: Sovetskii pisatel', 1950.
---. *Tragedii*. Moscow: Sovetskii pisatel', 1952.
---. *Izbrannye proizvedeniia*. Mocow: Goslitizdat, 1953.
---. *Izbrannye proizvedeniia*. 2 vols. Moscow: Gosudarstvennoe izdatel'stvo khudozhestvennoi literatury, 1956.
---. *Arktika. Roman*. Moscow: Sovetskii pisatel', 1957.
---. *O vremeni, o sud'bakh, o liubvi. Stikhi*. Moscow: Sovetskii pisatel', 1962
---. *Lirika*. Introduction by Lev Ozerov. Moscow: Khudozhestvennaia literatura, 1964.
---. *O, iunost' moia! Roman*. Moscow: Sovetskii pisatel', 1967.
---. *Sobranie sochinenii v shesti tomakh*, vol. 1: *Stikhotvoreniia*. Moscow: Khudozhestvennaia literatura, 1971.
---. *Izbrannye proizvedeniia*, edited by I. L. Mikhailov and N. G. Zakharenko. Leningrad: Sovetskii pisatel' [Biblioteka poeta], 1972.
---. *Ia eto videl! Stikhotvoreniia i poemy*, edited by Vladimir Ognev. Moscow: Sovetskaia Rossiia, 1985.

---. *Stikhotvoreniia. Tsarevna-lebed': tragediia*, edited by Ts. Voskresenskaia. Moscow: Khudozhestvennaia literatura, 1984.

---. *Izbrannye proizvedeniia v dvukh tomakh*, 2 vols., edited by Ts. Voskresenskaia and I. Mikhailov. Moscow: Khudozhestvennia literatura, 1989.

---. *Iz pepla, iz poem, iz snovidenii*, edited by A. M. Revich. Moscow: Vremia, 2004.

"Sel'vinskii, Il'ia L'vovich." In *Kratkaia evreiskaia entsiklopediia*, vol. 7, 742-743. Jerusalem: Obshchestvo po issledovaniiu evreiskikh obshchin; Evreiskii universitet v Ierusalime, 1994. [Unsigned entry by Mark Kipnis.]

"I. L. Sel'vinskii." *Literaturnaia gazeta* 27 March 1968, 2 [obituary].

"Sel'vinskii, Il'ia L'vovich." In *Russkie sovetskie pisateli. Poety (Sovetskii period). Bibliograficheskii ukazatel'*, vol. 23, 4-61. St. Petersburg: Rossiiskaia natsional'naia biblioteka, 2000.

"Shcherbakov, Aleksandr Sergeevich." http://ru.wikipedia.org/wiki/Щербаков,_Александр_Сергеевич. Last accessed 30 January 2011.

Shcherbina, V[ladimir]. "Lozhnoe napravlenie." *Kul'tura i zhizn'* 31 December 1947, 3.

Sheremet, Oksana. "Za den' do svobody." *Bospor* 1 December 2011. http://www.bospor.com.ua/articles/4300.shtml. Accessed 27 January 2011.

Shevchuk, V[asilii] M. *Komandir atakuet pervym*. Moscow: Voenizdat, 1980. http://militera.lib.ru/memo/russian/shevchuk_vm/index.html. Last accessed 22 February 2012.

Shitova, Margarita. "Neiasnaia bol' nadezhdy." *Krymskie izvestiia* 4 November 2006. http://www-ki.rada.crimea.ua/nomera/2006/205/bol.html. Last accessed 7 April 2010.

Shirokorad, Irina. "Tsentral'naia periodicheskaia pechat' SSSR v gody Velikoi Otechestvennoi voiny, 1941-1945 gg." Avtoreferat. Moscow, 2002. http://www.dissercat.com/content/tsentralnaya-periodicheskaya-pechat-sssr-v-gody-velikoi-otechestvennoi-voiny-1941-1945-gg. Last accessed 27 October 2011.

Shmidt, O. Iu. "Pisateli na 'Cheliuskine'." *Literaturnaia gazeta* 28 June 1934.

Shneer, David. "Soviet Jewish War Photojournalists Confront the Holocaust." In *The Holocaust in the Soviet Union. Symposium Presentations*, 21-32. Washington, DC: Center for Advanced

Holocaust Studies, United States Holocaust Museum, 2005.
---. *Through Soviet Jewish Eyes: Photography, War, and the Holocaust*. New Brunswick, NJ: Rutgers University Press, 2010.
---. "Picturing Grief: Soviet Holocaust Photography at the Intersection of History and Memory." *The American Historical Review* 115.1 (February 2010): 28-52.
Shrayer, Maxim D. "The Shoah in Soviet Popular Imagination: Rereading Anatoly Rybakov's *Heavy Sand*." In *Jews and Slavs*, vol. 17: *The Russian Word in the Land of Israel, the Jewish Word in Russia*, edited by Vladimir Khazan and Wolf Moskovich, 338-347. Jerusalem: The Hebrew University Center for Slavic Languages and Literatures, 2006.
---. "Jewish-Russian Holocaust Poetry in Official Soviet Venues: 1944-1946 (Antokolsky, Ehrenburg, Ozerov)." Paper delivered at the Annual Conference of the Association for Jewish Studies (AJS). Washington, D.C., 21 December 2008.
---. "Selvinskii, Ilia Lvovich." In *The YIVO Encyclopedia of Jews in Eastern Europe*, 2 vols., edited by Gershon David Hundert, 2: 1684-1685. New Haven: Yale University Press, 2008.
---. "Pavel Antokolsky." In *An Anthology of Jewish-Russian Literature: Two Centuries of Dual Identity in Prose and Poetry, 1801-2001*, 2 vols., edited by Maxim D. Shrayer, 1: 580-581. Armonk, NY: M. E. Sharpe, 2007.
---. "Ilya Ehrenburg." In *An Anthology of Jewish-Russian Literature: Two Centuries of Dual Identity in Prose and Poetry, 1801-2001*, 2 vols., edited by Maxim D. Shrayer, 2 vols., 1: 180-182; 277; 529. Armonk, NY: M. E. Sharpe, 2007.
---. "Vassily Grossman." In *An Anthology of Jewish-Russian Literature: Two Centuries of Dual Identity in Prose and Poetry, 1801-2001*, 2 vols., edited by Maxim D. Shrayer, 1: 539-541. Armonk, NY: M. E. Sharpe, 2007.
---. "Lev Ozerov." In *An Anthology of Jewish-Russian Literature: Two Centuries of Dual Identity in Prose and Poetry, 1801-2001*, 2 vols., edited by Maxim D. Shrayer, 1: 573-575. Armonk, NY: M. E. Sharpe, 2007.
---. "Boris Pasternak." In *An Anthology of Jewish-Russian Literature: Two Centuries of Dual Identity in Prose and Poetry, 1801-2001*, 2 vols., edited by Maxim D. Shrayer, 1: 591-594; 597-598. Armonk, NY: M. E. Sharpe, 2007.
---. "Ilya Selvinsky." In *An Anthology of Jewish-Russian Literature: Two*

Centuries of Dual Identity in Prose and Poetry, 1801-2001, 2 vols., edited by Maxim D. Shrayer, 1: 226-227. Armonk, NY: M. E. Sharpe, 2007.

---. "Boris Slutsky." In *An Anthology of Jewish-Russian Literature: Two Centuries of Dual Identity in Prose and Poetry, 1801-2001*, 2 vols., edited by Maxim D. Shrayer, 2: 639-642; 794. Armonk, NY: M. E. Sharpe, 2007.

---. "Iosif Utkin." In *An Anthology of Jewish-Russian Literature: Two Centuries of Dual Identity in Prose and Poetry, 1801-2001*, 2 vols., edited by Maxim D. Shrayer, 1: 319-320. Armonk, NY: M. E. Sharpe, 2007.

---. "War and Terror" [Editor's Introduction]. In *An Anthology of Jewish-Russian Literature: Two Centuries of Dual Identity in Prose and Poetry, 1801-2001*, 2 vols., edited by Maxim D. Shrayer, 1: 509-512. Armonk, NY: M. E. Sharpe, 2007.

---. "In Search of Jewish-Russian Literature: A Historical Overview." *Wiener Slawistischer Almanach* 61 (2008): 5-30.

---. "Bearing Witness: The War, the Shoah and the Legacy of Vasily Grossman." *The Jewish Quarterly* 217 (Spring 2011): 14-19.

---. "Jewish-Russian Poets Bearing Witness to the Shoah, 1941-1946: Textual Evidence and Preliminary Conclusions." *Studies in Slavic Languages and Literatures*. ICCEES [*International Council for Central and East European Studies*] *Congress Stockholm 2010 Papers and Contributions*, edited by Stefano Garzonio, 59-119. Bologna: Portal on Central Eastern and Balkan Europe, 2011. http://www.iecob.net/main/pecobs-volumes/344-studies-in-slavic-languages-and-litera-tures-iccees-congress-stockholm-2010-papers-and-contributions-edited-by-stefano-garzonio

---. *The World of Nabokov's Stories*. Austin and London: University of Texas Press, 1998.

---. *Russian Poet/Soviet Jew: The Legacy of Eduard Bagritskii*. Lanham, MD: Rowman & Littlefield, 2000.

---, ed. *An Anthology of Jewish-Russian Literature: Two Centuries of Dual Identity in Prose and Poetry, 1801-2001*, 2 vols., Armonk, NY: M. E. Sharpe, 2007.

Shraer-Petrov, David [David Shrayer-Petrov]. "Karaimskie pirozhki. Il'ia Sel'vinskii." In *Vodka s pirozhnymi: Roman s pisateliami*, 272-282. St. Petersburg: Akademicheskii proekt, 2007.

---. "Tezka. David Samoilov." In *Vodka s pirozhnymi: Roman s pisateliami*,

282-297. St. Petersburg: Akademicheskii proekt, 2007.

---. *Vodka s pirozhnymi: Roman s pisateliami*. St. Petersburg: Akademicheskii proekt, 2007.

--- [as Petrov, David]. *Poeziia i nauka*. Moscow: Znanie, 1974.

Simonov, Konstantin. "Pis'mo iz Kryma. Posledniaia noch'." *Krasnaia zvezda* 9 January 1942, 3.

---. "Pis'mo iz Kryma. Predatel'." *Krasnaia zvezda* 10 January 1942: 3.

---. "V kontse voiny." In *Den' poezii 1971*, 169-174. Moscow: Sovetskii pisatel', 1971.

---. *Raznye dni voiny. Dnevnik pisatelia*, 2 vols. Moscow: Khudozhestvennaia literatura, 1982. http://militera.lib.ru/db/simonov_km/index.html. Last accessed 22 February 2012.

Sirota, N. A. "Otomstim za krovavye zlodeianiia." In *Zverstva nemetskikh fashistov v Kerchi. Sbornik rasskazov postradavshikh i ochevidtsev*, 23-31. Sukhumi: Krasnyi Krym, 1943.

---. "Kogda front priblizilsia vplotnuiu...." In *Kerch' geroicheskaia. Vospominaniia. Ocherki. Dokumenty*, 14-36. Simferopol': Tavriia, 1974.

Slesarev, P[avel]. "Bor'ba za Kerch'." *Krasnaia zvezda* 3 January 1942.

---. "Pokhorony zhertv nemetskoi okkupatsii v Kerchi." *Krasnaia zvezda* 11 January 1942, 3.

Slutskii, Boris. "Maiakovskii na tribune." *Oktiabr'* 3 (1941): 114.

---. "Seminar Sel'vinskogo." In *O drugikh i o sebe*, edited by Petr Gorelik, 232-235. Moscow: Vagrius, 2005.

---. "Sel'vinskii—broshennaia zona...." In his *Sobranie sochinenii*, 3 vols., edited by Iu. Boldyrev, 2: 207-208. Moscow: Khudozhestvennaia literatura, 1991.

---. "Tvardovskii." In *O drugikh i o sebe*, edited by Petr Gorelik, 215-221. Moscow: Vagrius, 2005.

---. "Zauchennyi, zachitannyi...." In *Sobranie sochinenii*, 3 vols., edited by Iu. Boldyrev, 2: 371. Moscow: Khudozhestvennaia literatura, 1991.

---. *Sovremennye istorii. Novaia kniga stikhov*. Moscow: Molodaia gvardiia, 1969.

---. *Neokonchennye spory*. Moscow: Sovetskii pisatel', 1978.

---. *Sobranie sochinenii*, 3 vols, edited by Iu. Boldyrev. Moscow: Khudozhestvennaia literatura, 1991.

---. *O drugikh i o sebe*, edited by Petr Gorelik. Moscow: Vagrius, 2005.

---. *Bez popravok...* Moscow: Vremia, 2006.

"Boris Abramovich Slutskii." In *Russkie pisateli. Poety (Sovetskii pe-*

riod). *Bibliograficheskii ukazatel'*, vol. 23, 267-397. St. Petersburg: Rossiiskaia natsional'naia biblioteka, 2000.

Snyder, Timothy. "Stalinist Anti-Semitism." In *Bloodlands: Europe between Hitler and Stalin*, 339-377. New York: Basic Books, 2010.

Solomatin, Mikhail. "My eto videli." *Zhurnal Mikhaila Solomatina* 21 October 2009. http://mike67.livejournal.com/261554.html. Last accessed 29 June 2010.

Solov'ev, Boris. "O novatorstve i traditsiiakh." *Znamia* 3 (1950): 141-167.

Sorokina, Marina. "People and Procedures: Toward a History of the Investigation of Nazi Crimes in the USSR." *Kritika: Explorations in Russian and Eurasian History* 6.4 (Fall 2005): 797-831.

"Spravka o mestakh massovykh ubiistv sovetskikh grazhdan nemetsko-fashistskimi okkupantami na territorii Kryma za 1941-19444 gody." In *Gor'kaia pamiat' viony. Krym v Velikoi otechestvennoi*, edited by V. K. Garagulia et al., 83-89. Simferopol: Krymskaia akademiia gumanitarnykh nauk, 1995.

Stepanov, A, Galyshev, S. "Operatsii Krasnoi Armii i Flota v Krymu." *Izvestiia* 1 January 1942, 2.

"Statistika o evreiiakh v sovetskoi armii vo 2MV." http://www.jewniverse.ru/biher/AShulman/30.htm. Last accessed 16 July 2010.

Sutzkever, Abraham. *Selected Poetry and Prose*, translated and edited by Barbara and Benjamin Harshav. Berkeley: University of California Press, 1991.

Svetlov, Mikhail. *Stikhotvoreniia i poemy*, edited by E. P. Liubareva. Leningrad: Sovetskii pisatel', 1966.

Sviridenko, P. P. "Stroka poeta v boevom stroiu (Iz frontovykh vospominanii)." In *O Sel'vinskom: vospominaniia*, edited by Ts. A. Voskresenskaia and I. P. Sirotinskaia, 115-121. Moscow: Sovetskii pisatel', 1982.

"Svora ubiits i grabitelei." *Krasnaia zvezda* 8 January 1942, 1.

Tanakh: A New Translation of the Holy Scriptures According to the Traditional Hebrew Text. Philadelphia: The Jewish Publication Society, 1985.

Taradankin, K[onstantin]. "Chto proiskhodit v Khar'kove." *Izvestiia* 11 January 1942, 2.

Tarasenkov, An[atolii]. "O natsional'nykh traditsiiakh i burzhuaznom kosmopolitizme. Stat'ia pervaia." *Znamia* 1 (1950): 152-164.

Tiaglyi, Mikhail. *Mesta massovogo unichtozheniia evreev Kryma v period natsistskoi okkupatsii poluostrova (1941-1944). Spravochnik.* Simferopol': BETs "Khesed Shimon", 2005.
---. "Kholokost evreiskikh obshchin Kryma v dokumentakh GAARK," Part 1. http://www.holocaust.kiev.ua/bulletin/vip1/vip1_2.htm. Last accessed 7 April 2010.
---. "Kholokost evreiskikh obshchin Kryma v dokumentakh GAARK," Part 2. http://www.holocaust.kiev.ua/bulletin/vip2/vip2_2.htm. Last accessed 7 April 2010.
---. "Kerch." In *Kholokost na territorii SSSR. Entsiklopediia*, 2nd ed., edited by I. A. Al'tman, 402-403. Moscow: Rosspen, 2011.
Turovskii, M[ark] and Antselovich, I[zrail']. "Zverstva nemtsev v Kerchi." *Krasnyi Krym* 24 January 1942, 2.
"Turovskii Mark Il'ich." In "Крымовед: Personalia." http://www.krimoved-library.ru/books/evrei-kryma14.html. Last accessed 27 January 2012.
"Tvorcheskii vecher Il'i Sel'vinskogo." *Suvorovets* 23 May 1945, 3.
Tynianov, Ui. N. "Promezhutok." In *Poetika, Istoriia literatury. Kino.* Ed. V. A. Kaverin, A. S. Miasnikov. 168-195. Moscow: Nauka, 1977.

Utkin, Iosif. "Ia videl sam!" *Literatura i iskusstvo* 18 April 1942.
---. *Stikhotvoreniia i poemy*, edited by A. A. Saakiants. Leningrad: Sovetskii pisatel', 1966.

Vaiskopf, Mikhail. "Liubov' k dal'nemu: literaturnoe tvorchestvo Vladimira Zhabotinskogo." *Vestnik evreiskogo universiteta* 29 [11] (2006). http://gazeta.rjews.net/Lib/Jab/vaisk.shtml. Last accessed 22 June 2010.
"V Krymu." *Izvestiia* 7 January 1942, 3.
Vishnevskii, V[sevolod]. *Sobranie sochinenii v piati tomakh*, edited by P. P. Vershigora et al., 6 vol. Moscow: Gosudarstvennoe izadatel'tvo khudozhestvennoi literatury, 1954-1961 [actually 6 vols].
---. "Dnevniki voennykh let (1943, 1945 gg.)." http://militera.lib.ru/db/vishnevsky_vv/07.html. Last accessed 8 July 2010.
Vol'fson, B.[entsion M.] "Krovavye prestupleniia nemtsev v Kerchi." *Istoricheskii zhurnal* 8 (1942): 33-36.

Voskresenskaia, Ts. A. and Sirotinskaia I. P., eds. *O Sel'vinskom: vospominaniia*. Moscow: Sovetskii pisatel', 1982.
Voskresenkaia, Tsetsiliia. "Oproverzhenie." *Canadian Slavonic Papers* 27.1-2 (1995): 281-282.
---. *Moi vospominaniia. Dokumental'yi roman*. Moscow: Vremia, 2006.
"V osvobozhdennoi Kerchi." *Pravda* 20 January 1942, 3.
Voznesenskii, Andrei. "Rov." *Iunost'* 7 (1986), 6-15.
--. "Rov. Dukhovnyi protsess." In *Rov. Stikhi. Proza*, 80-138. Moscow: Sovetskii pisatel', 1987.
---. *Rov. Stikhi. Proza*. Moscow: Sovetskii pisatel', 1987.
"Vtoroi Pribaltiiskii front." http://ru.wikipedia.org/wiki/2-й_Прибалтийский_фронт. Last accessed 8 March 2011.

"What the Advancing Russians Found." *Picture Post* 15.12 (20 June 1942): 7-9.
Wiesel, Elie. "Preface to the New Translation." In his *Night*, vii-xv. New York: Hill and Wang, 2006.

Zand, Michael. "Krymchaks." In *The YIVO Encyclopedia of Jews in Eastern Europe*, 2 vols., edited by Gershon David Hundert, 1: 948-951. New Haven: Yale University Press, 2008.
Zozulia, Efim and Aleksandr Chachikov, eds. *Stikhi i pesni o Staline*. Moscow: Zhurnal'nogazetnoe ob"edinenie, 1937.
Zverstva nemetskikh fashistov v Kerchi. Sbornik rasskazov postradavshikh i ochevidtsev. Sukhumi: Krasnyi Krym, 1943.

ACKNOWLEDGMENTS

The span of over fifteen years separating this book from *Russian Poet/ Soviet Jew* also marks the years I have been teaching at Boston College. I would like to thank Boston College for its support of my research over the years, and specifically for granting me a Faculty Fellowship for the spring of 2010. I thank the office of Larry McLaughlin, Vice-Provost for Research, for a subvention grant to defray some of the production costs of this book, and the office of David Quigley, Dean of the College and Graduate School of Arts and Sciences, for awarding me a research and travel grant. I also thank M. J. Connolly, chair of the Department of Slavic and Eastern Languages and Literatures at Boston College, for his support and encouragement. The completion of this project was made possible by the support of the John Simon Guggenheim Memorial Foundation.

I gratefully acknowledge the contribution of my former research assistant Leon Kogan, whose investigative skills are superb. Elizabeth Baker, a gifted Boston College undergraduate, assisted me in preparing sections of this manuscript. I am deeply indebted to Anne H. Kenny and Nina Bogdanovsky of the Boston College Libraries, and to Michael Swanson, Kerry Burke, and the staff of the Boston College Graphics and Photography Services. Kerry Burke helped design the map of Kerch and its environs, with reference to the Nazi occupation, that appears on pages 32-33.

My Boston College colleagues Dwayne E. Carpenter, M. J. Connolly, and Andrew Sofer have generously commented on drafts of my English translations of Ilya Selvinsky's poems. I alone am responsible for all of the translations' infelicities.

Lazar Fleishman, editor of the series in which the book appears and a scholar whom I admire, closely read a draft of this book and offered constructive criticism. I only regret not having been able to address all of his suggestions.

Joshua Rubenstein and Leona Toker generously commented on the entire manuscript. Igor Nemirovsky, Kira Nemirovsky, Sharona Vedol and all of their colleagues at Academic Studies Press have given this book a loving home; Sharona Vedol copyedited the manuscript with patience and verbal acumen. I am very grateful to them.

Early versions of sections of this book were presented at the 2008 Conference of the Association of Jewish Studies (AJS) in Washington, DC (December 2008); the 30th Conference on the Holocaust and Genocide, Millersville University (April 2010); VIII World Congress of the International Council for Central and East European Studies in Stockholm, Sweden (July 2010); the UCLA Conference "In the Memory's Reflection: The Encounters between Jewish and Slavic Cultures in Modernity" (May 2011); the International Conference "Tragicheskii opyt Velikoi Otechestvennoi voiny v istoriko-kul'turnom osmyslenii" at the Ilya Selvinsky Memorial Museum in Simferopol,' Crimea, Ukraine (December 2011); the University of Toronto International Conference "Jewish Life and Death in the Soviet Union" (March 2012); Institut für Slawistik—Humboldt-Universität zu Berlin (April 2012); the Tagung am Alfried Krupp Wissenschaftskolleg Greifswald Conference "Osteuropäisch-jüdische Literaturen im 20. und 21. Jahrhundert: Identität und Poetik" (April 2012), and Association Franco-Britannique pour l'etude de la culture russe: XXIIe colloque at Université de Caen Basse Normandie (May 2012). I thank the organizers of these conferences for giving me a chance to participate and present my findings.

Early versions of several sections of the book have been published as "Jewish-Russian Poets Bearing Witness to the Shoah, 1941-1946: Textual Evidence and Preliminary Conclusions," in *Studies in Slavic Languages and Literatures. ICCEES Congress Stockholm 2010 Papers and Contributions*, edited by Stefano Garzonio (Bologna: Portal on Central Eastern and Balkan Europe, 2011). I am grateful to the editor and the publisher.

* * *

Over the years, I have had the pleasure of discussing the development of this project with and learning from Antony Polonsky and Boris Czerny. I would like to express my gratitude to Zvi Gitelman, who kindly let me read his unpublished manuscript "What Soviet People Saw of the Shoah and How It Was Reported"; David Shneer, who generously shared with me his book *Through Soviet Jewish Eyes* in page proofs and responded to my queries about Jewish-Soviet photographers documenting the Nazi atrocities in and around Kerch in 1942; Joshua Rubenstein, who has given me many insights into the history of the Shoah in the USSR and the postwar onslaught on Jewish Soviet culture; Vadim Altskan, who has been very helpful in checking the files of the Jewish Anti-Fascist Committee (JAC) at the United States Holocaust Memorial Museum; Jonathan Dekel-Chen, who kindly answered my queries about the Jewish agricultural settlements in Crimea; Victoria Khiterer, who shared her unpublished work on post-occupation Kiev; Gennady Estraikh, who generously helped with a Yiddish source and with checking the digital database of *Eynikayt*; Christoph Eykman, who made working with several German-language sources less difficult; and Marat Grinberg, whose own work on Boris Slutsky has stimulated research for this book.

Over the past several years, I have had the honor of sharing the podium with Carol and John Garrard and of discussing with them what they call "art from agony." The Garrards' book *The Bones of Berdichev: The Life and Fate of Vasily Grossman* has been an inspiration, as has been their pioneering research on the Shoah in the Soviet Union.

Ludmila I. Daineko, director of the Ilya Selvinsky Memorial Museum (branch of the Central Museum of Taurida, Crimean Autonomous Republic, Ukraine) in Simferopol and her museum colleagues have been incredibly helpful and generous in furnishing me with rare archival materials and facilitating my on-site research during a visit to Crimea in December 2011, seventy years after the massacres at the Bagerovo anti-tank ditch. At the Selvinsky Museum, I thank: Irina Dobrovolskaya, Violetta Salamatina, Marina Dovzhenko, and Gennady Filippenko. I am tremendously grateful for everything my Crimean colleagues have done on behalf of this book. Specifically, Vladimir Gurkovich, Arkady Achkinazi, and Vladimir Sanzharovets were my guides during a field trip from Simferopol to Kerch and back. Vladimir Sanzharovets, a researcher at the Kerch State Historical and Cultural Reserve, subsequently shared valuable materials pertaining to World War II and the Shoah on the Kerch peninsula and answered my queries. I owe a particular debt of gratitude to Boris Berlin. A historian of the Shoah in his native Crimea who lost the majority of his relatives in the late autumn of 1941 outside Simferopol, an activist of the Crimean Jewish community and a person of unparalleled generosity, Boris Berlin was instrumental in facilitating my research with Crimean newspaper sources.

Tatiana Selvinskaya has enthusiastically responded to my queries

―――――― Acknowledgments ――――――

about her father. I am most grateful to her for her assistance, and for granting me permission to reprint her father's works in the original and to translate them into English, and also to reprint photographs, illustrations and archival materials.

Once again, I would like to thank all the individuals and institutions that assisted me in the process of the research, writing, and publishing of this book.

* * *

Without the love and dedication of my wife, Karen E. Lasser, and our daughters, Mira Isabella and Tatiana Rebecca, the pages of this book—of my life—would have remained blank.

My father, David Shrayer-Petrov, who as a young poet knew Ilya Selvinsky personally, was the source of my earliest knowledge of Selvinsky's poetry and personality, as well as of the life and verse of Lev Ozerov, David Samoilov, and Boris Slutsky. I thank my father and my mother, Emilia Shrayer, for their love and support.

This book is dedicated to the loving memory of my paternal grandfather Pyotr (Peysakh) Shrayer, who volunteered and spent 1941-1945 at the war fronts, finishing the war at Königsberg—like the hero of this book.

M. D. S.

Index

About Selvinsky, memorial collected volume 136, 240
Abramov, Vsevolod 21n45
Achkinazi, Arkady 48n87
Act of the Extraordinary State Commission 38, 79
Aduev, Nikolay 2
Adzhibegishvili, Aleksandr 55n99
Afanasyeva, S. 70
Agamben, Giorgio 103; *Remnants of Auschwitz: The Witness and the Archive* 103
Agapov, Boris 2
Akhmatova, Anna 216, 252
Aleksandrov, Georgy 156, 159
Aliger, Margarita 144, 173, 240n28; *Zoya* 144
Alov, Aleksandr 223
Altman, Ilya 38, 159n45
Altshuler, Mordechai 16, 73, 75n153, 232, 232n11
Altskan, Vadim 154n37
Amundsen, Roald 10
Andreev, Andrey A. 156, 185
Androsov, Sergey 75
Anfimova, Viktoria 257n65
Angrick, Andrej 43
An-sky, S. 5; *Dibbuk, The* 5
Anstey, Olga 116
Antokolsky, Pavel 116, 149, 171, 173, 189, 194, 195, 212, 219, 223, 236, 240n28, 256; "Death Camp" 189; *Son* 171
Antselovich, Izrail 58–61, 66, 70, 72, 78, 97, 98
Arad, Yizhak 38, 43, 73, 133
Arkharova, Maria 83
Arzumanov, Leon 55, 55n99
Aseev, Nikolay 7, 138, 139, 143, 163, 171, 216

Asmus, Vladimir 2
Atrocities of the German Fascists in Kerch: A Collection of Accounts by Victims and Eyewitnesses, collected volume 75–78, 79n163, 90, 97, 112, 172

Babel, Isaac 28, 250
Babenko, Vera xviii, 165
Babichenko, D. L. 155n42
Bach, I. S. 199
Bachinskaia, A. A. 193n14
Bagritsky, Eduard xv, xvi, 2, 7, 102n205, 179, 191, 216, 221, 222, 250, "Conversation with Komsomol Member N. Dementiev" xv *February* 191n12 *Lay of Opanas, The* 102n205
Balmont, Konstantin 192
Baltermants, Dmitri 53, 56–58, 70, 77
Bazhan, Mykola 216
Beethoven, L. van 199
Belikova, A. D. 38n78
Belotserkovskaya, Raisa 55–57, 68, 77, 88
Belugin, Dmitry 75
Berezin, Dmitri 21, 85, 86n178, 92n191, 95, 131, 152
Beria, Lavrenty 74
Berkhoff, Karel C. 166
Berlin, Boris 44n84, 44n84, 52, 73, 232n10
Berman, Grigory 54, 55, 55n99, 68, 71n143, 72
Bernshtein, Mikhail 167
Bialik, Hayim Nahman 100, 101, 101n204n205, 102, 112, 130; *Tale of a Pogrom* (Be Ir HaHarigah) 100
Black Book, The (Ehrenburg-Grossman,

eds.) 79n163, 172, 173, 189, 238, 238n22
Blanter, Matvey 261
Blium, Arlen 5, 159n45, 166
"Bloody Atrocities of Germans in Kerch" 37
Bloom, Harold 253
Boevoi natisk (Fighting Thrust) 21, 83n169n, 94n196, 95, 114n226
Bolshevik, Krasnodar Regional Party Committee newspaper 86, 87n180, 93n192, 115, 173, 175n87
Borodulin, Lev 53
Boryan, Gurgen 146
Brik, Lilia 173n80
Bronshtein, Mikhail 167
Bryusov, Valery 192
Bukharin, Nikolai 3, 7, 7n14, 8, 10, 15n34, 157
Byron, George Gordon 258; "Hebrew Melodies" 258

Central Committee of the Communist Party 6, 11, 13, 153n33, 154–156, 159, 161–163, 167, 174n84, 175, 184, 195, 212, 215, 217
Central Committee orgburo 13, 155, 156, 158, 215
Central Committee secretariat "About Errors in the Literary Works of I. Selvinsky" 159; "About I. Selvinsky's Poem 'To whom Russia sang a lullaby'" 162; "On Raising the Responsibility of [Executive] Secretaries of Literary-Artistic Magazines" 161; "On the Control over Literary-Artistic Magazines" 161
Chagall, Mark 178, 179
Chukovsky, Kornei 163
Conrad, Joseph 203; *Heart of Darkness* 203
Coster, Charles de 223; *Legend of Thyl Ulenspiegel and Lamme Goedzak, The* 223

Crimean Regional Committee of the Communist Party 76

Daineko, Liudmila xviii, 30n63
Dante Alighieri 102, 125
Dekel-Chen, Jonathan 224, 225
Derman, Abram 172
Directorate of Propoganda and Agitation (UPA) 6, 156, 161, 171, 174n84, 215, 220
Documents Accuse, collected volume 78
Dostoevsky, F. M. 142 "Pushkin Speech," 142
Dovzhenko, Aleksandr 160n49, 163, 171
Dzhafarov, D. 21

Egolin, A. M. 196n20
Ehrenburg, Ilya 8n18, 15, 15n34, 25, 26, 26n54n55, 28, 61, 61n108, 73, 79n163, 82, 88n184, 92, 130, 144, 153, 164, 168, 172, 173, 173n80, 179, 185n108, 187, 188, 188n2, 189, 190, 194, 212, 238, 246, 247, 250, 257
Fall of Paris, The 144; "On the Poems of Boris Slutsky" 8n18; *People, Years, Life* 130, 164, 187; "Signs of Distinction" 92; "To Remember!" 188; "To the Jewish Nation" 26; "To the Jews" 25
Einsatzgruppe D 34, 34n65, 43, 133
Einstein, Albert 242
Elling (Ofshteyn), Vladimir 154, 154n37
Engels, F. 246
Ermolaev, Herman 160n47
Estraikh, Gennady 154n37
Evtushenko, Yevgeny 254, 257; "Babi Yar" 254

Fadeev, Aleksandr 156, 157, 216, 216n64n65, 217, 221 "Goals of

Literary Theory and Criticism" 216
Falk, Robert 174
False Dmitri II 4
Fascist Atrocities in Kerch, propaganda booklet 78
Fedin, Konstantin 138, 164
Fedoseev, Pyotr 171
Fefer, Yitsik 70n140, 153
Fichte, I. H. 199
Filatiev, Eduard xviii, 147n21, 148, 150, 160, 165, 168, 181; "Secret of Lieutenant Colonel Selvinsky, The" 165
Fleishman, Lazar 3, 3n5, 8, 10
Forpost Baltiki (Forepost of the Baltic) 175
Frank, Susanne 10
Frezinsky, Boris 173n80
Friedberg, Maurice xix

Gabrilovich, Evgeny 2, 236
Gauzner, Grigory 2
Gavrilyuk, Vladislav 135
German, Aleksey 63n114 *Twenty Days without War* 63n114
German Barbarians in the Crimea, wartime collection 78
Gitelman, Zvi 166; "What Soviet People Saw of the Shoah and How It Was Reported" 166
Goebbels, J. 92, 92n191, 93
Goethe, J. W. von 29, 199
Goffenshefer, Veniamin 35, 67, 83, 83n171, 126, 127, 128, 133n246, 175n86, 276; "Bagerovo" 127; *Mikhail Sholokhov* 126
Gofman, Izya 56, 68, 81n165
Gold, Z. 48, 68
Goldfaden, Abraham 4; *Bar Kokhba* 4
Goldshtein, Aleksandr 5
Goldshtein, Mosya 53n95, 68
Goldshtein, R. 68, 77
Gorelik, Pyotr 248
Goriunova, Raisa 153n35, 180n99
Gorky, Maxim 25, 30, 155; "Song about a Falcon" 25
Great Patriotic War, The (USSR) xv, 24, 75, 92, 113, 138, 147, 215, 222, 229, 248
Griboedov, Aleksandr 211; *Woe of Wit* 211
Grin, Aleksandr 221, 222
Grinberg, Marat 233, 233n12, 235, 250, 250n49, 250n51
Grossman, Vasily 79n163, 82, 125, 144, 149, 151, 168, 179, 187–190, 203, 238, 257; "Hell of Treblinka, The" 125, 188, 203; "Old Teacher, The" 149; *People are Immortal, The* 144
Gruzinov, Vasily 62
Gubenko, Gitel 38, 38n79
Gudzenko, Semyon 234
Guliston 230
Gurkovich, Vladimir 48n87
Gutman, Il'ia 55n99, 81n165

Hegel, G. W. F. 199
Heine, H. 15, 88, 88n183, 164, 164n60, 261n69, 266; "Silesian Weavers, The" 88, 88n183, 266
Hicks, Jeremy 55n99

Inber, Vera 2, 138, 147, 173; *Pulkovo Meridian, The* 147
Isakovsky, Mikhail 138, 144, 203, 245; "The enemies burned the native hut…" 245
Ish, Lev 59, 61, 167; "Blood Atrocities of Fascists in Kerch" 61
Istoricheskii zhurnal (Historical Journal) 75
Iunost' (Youth) 254
Izvestia 7, 11, 25, 58, 59, 59n104, 63, 71, 140n8, 145–148, 160

Jabotinsky, Vladimir (Ze'ev) 4, 100, 101, 101n205, 202n205, 192, 258;

"In Memory of Herzl" 4; *Tale of a Pogrom* (tr., Bialik) 100
Jewish Anti-Fascist Community (JAC) 143

Kachalov, Vasily 91
Kaganovich, Lazar 11, 13
Kalinin, Anatoly 59
Kandyba, Fyodor 239
Kant, Immanuel 199, 200
Kataev, Valentin 160n49
Katina, Vera 1n2
Kedrina, Zoya 146
Kerch Worker, The (Kerchenskii rabochii) 65, 66, 127
Kerch-Eltigen Landing Operation 31, 152, 154
Kerchenskii rabochii (Kerch Worker) 65, 66, 127
Kerch-Feodosia Landing Operation 20, 52, 59, 62, 63n114
Kerler, Dov-Ber 166n66
Kerzhentsev, Platon 6
Khaldey, Evgeny 51, 53–56, 58, 72, 77, 129
Khatsrevin, Zakhar 167
Khelemsky, Yakov 117n235n236, 198, 199, 202n40, 208, 210, 210n51, 236; *Gulf of Riga* 202n40; *Kurland Spring* 208; "On the outskirts of Riga a ghetto died out..." 202n40; *On the Road* 202n40
Khodakovsky, Konstantin 51, 54, 58
Khrushchev, Nikita 235, 246, 254
Kirov, Sergey 11
Kirsanov, Semyon 3, 106n213, 256, 257n64
Klier, John D. 220
Kniga, Vasily 23, 24, 24n49
Kogan, Pavel 70, 234
Kolchak, Aleksandr 19
Kolganova, Ada xix
Kolosov, Mark 153
Komsomol'skaia Pravda (Komsomolskaya Pravda) 6, 59, 69, 71, 137, 140n8, 145, 148
Kornilov, Boris 13n31, 26
Korotkova, G.V. 43b83, 45n86, 53n93
Korzhavin, Naum 175n85, 196n22, 227n2
Kostyrchenko, Gennadii 152n29
Kotel'nikov, Petr 37n75
Kozlov, Dmitri 22, 23, 45n86
Krasnaia nov' (Red Virgin Soil) 3
Krasnaia zvezda (Red Star) 17, 59, 61, 61n108, 63, 64, 68, 86–88, 92, 107, 109, 112, 114, 137, 140, 146, 164, 167
Krasnyi chernomorets (Red Black Sea Navyman) 44, 126
Krasnyi Krym (Red Crimea) 59, 60, 76
Krenkel, Ernst 10
Krongauz, Anisim 234
Kucheryavenko, Mikhail 205
Kul'tura i zhizn' (Culture and Life) 220
Kulchitsky, Mikhail 234
Kursk, Battle of 135, 164
Kutuzov, M. I. 183
Kvitko, Leib 172, 172n79; "Story of Iosif Vaingertner, a Fisherman from Kerch, The" (ed.) 172
Kvyatkovsky, Aleksandr 2

Laar, Iosif 175–177
Lapin, Aleksandr 167
Lavrov Petr 88n183, 263n1 "Silesian Weavers, The" (tr., Heine) 88n183, 263n1
Leningrad, journal 191, 215, 216
Leonov, Leonid 138
Lermontov, Mikhail 19, 258
Levin, Abram 175
Lidin, Vladimir 71n144
Lifshits (Livshits), Sofiya 48, 68, 77
Likharev, Boris 215
Literary Center of Constructivists (LTsK) xv, 2, 144, 229
Literary Institute, Moscow 13, 17, 174, 174n84, 175n85, 196, 234, 238, 248, 261

Literatura i iskusstvo (*Literature and Art*) 55, 91, 238
Literaturnaia gazeta (*Literary Gazette, The*) 29
Literaturnaia Rossiia (*Literary Russia*) 241
Losev, V. 21
Lugovskoy, Vladimir 2

Machavariani, V. 21, 84, 84n174, 85, 92
Main Political Directorate of army (PUR) 11, 19, 154
Malenkov, Georgy 155n42, 156–158, 160, 167n68, 171, 171n75, 195, 196n20, 215
Markish, Shimon 187
Marshak, Samuil 216
Marx, Karl 9, 242, 243, 246; *Das Kapital* 8
Matrosov, Aleksandr 175, 250
Mayakovsky, Vladimir 3, 4, 216, 221, 230n5; "Anniversary Poem" 242
Medvedeva, Galina 236n20, 251, 252
Mekhlis, Lev 11, 11n25, 13, 17, 20, 22, 23, 137n1, 154
Melkov, Leonid 81n166
Merkulov, Vsevolod 162, 168; "On Writers' Political Moods and Comments" 162–163
Mikhalkov, Sergei 181
Mikhoels, Solomon (Shloyme) 143, 153
Military Commission of the Union of Soviet Writers 83n171, 116n232, 138, 145
Milton, John 261, 262, *Samson Agonistes* 261
Mishchenko, Vladimir 55n99
Mitrofanov, Vladimir 55, 55n100
Molotov, Vyasheslav 11, 13, 37, 63–65, 73, 112, 112n222, 196, 196n22
Moscow Art Theater 142–143
Moskovskii Bol'shevik (*Moscow Bolshevik*) 91

Mozart, W. T. A. 199
Murav, Harriet xix

Na razgrom vraga (*For the Defeat of the Enemy*) 197
Nabokov, Vladimir 219, 253n58
Narovchatov, Sergey 234, 236
Naumov, Vladimir 223
Nikulin, Yuri 63n114
Novalis 199
Novikova, Marina 1n2
Novy mir (*New World*) 189, 190, 236, 244
Nuremberg Military Tribunal 38, 55n99, 79, 232

Ogonek (*Little Flame*) 59, 259
Oktiabr' (*October*) 13, 93n194
Olonova, Elvira 240n28
Olshanskaya, Evdokia 116
Order of the Great Patriotic War 24
Order of the Red Star 24
Ortenberg, David (D. Vadimov) 17, 61, 62, 87, 88, 167; *Year 1942, The* 61
Oshurkov, Mikhail 55, 55n99
Ospovat, Kirill 113n225
Ovid 102, 125
Ozerov, Lev (Lev Goldberg) 14, 91, 92n189, 113n237, 149, 173, 189, 190, 194, 208, 212, 219, 220, 221n75, 223, 226, 229, 237, 237n21, 238, 238n22, 239–244, 256; *Babi Yar* 189, 219, 238, 240; "Glass of Ocean, A" 240, 243; *Downpour* 219; *Lyric: Selected Poems* (*Lyric: Selected Poems*) 238; *Portraits without Frames* 243; "Selvinsky's Wartime Lyrical Poetry" 91; "Should One Dream of Immortality?" 241 "Strength of the Word, The" 91
Ozersky, Izrail 58, 70

Panfyorov, Fyodor 29
Pasternak, Boris xv, 3, 7, 10, 11, 11n24, 25, 138, 139, 141, 142, 174, 175n85, 216, 221, 226, 227, 227n2, 228, 241, 252; "Artist, The" 11
Pavlenko, Petr 92, 92n189, 114, 115
Petrov, Ivan E. 154, 154n38
Fotogazeta Glavnogo politicheskogo upravleniia Krasnoi Armii (Photonewspaper of the Main Political Directorate of the Red Army) 71, 72
Picture Post 70
Pikach, Anatoly 256
Pinkus, Benjamin xix, 233n12
Platonov, Andrei 160n49
Pobeda za nami (Victory Shall Be Ours) 238
Poe, E. A. 192
Poliak, Lidia 171, 172; "On 'Lyrical Epic' of the Great Patriotic War" 171
Polikarpov, Dmitry 171, 196
Polonsky, Vyacheslav 3
Potyomkin, Vladimir 156
Poulsen, Niels Bo 79n164
Pravda 9, 11, 12, 37, 58, 63, 71, 92, 164, 188n3
Prokofiev, Aleksandr 11n24
Pupyshev, Nikolai 154, 195
Pushkin, Aleksandr 10, 19, 29, 99, 100, 141, 142

Rechkalov, Ivan 133
Redkin, Mark 58, 69, 70n140, 72
Reshetnikov, Fyodor (Fedka) 19, 44, 67, 68, 129
Revich, Aleksandr 3
Reznik, Osip 84n174, 85, 170n73
Rodin, V. 137
Rokhlin, Mosia 69
Romm, Aleksandr 126, 126n141, 127, 276
Romm, Mikhail 126

Rozenfeld, Mikhail 167
Rubtsov, Iurii 11n25
Rustemova, Ludmila 123
Rybakov, Anatoly 257
Rylsky, Maksym 144
Rza, Rasul 257n64

Samoilov, David (David Kaufman) 226, 234, 236, 236n20, 238, 243, 244, 248–250, 250n49n51, 251–253, 256; "In the Master Workshop of Poetry" 236n20, 251; *Memorial Notes* 251; *Nearby Countries* 249; "Our Teacher" 236n20, 251; *Solomonchik the Tailor. A Brief Life Story* 250, 250n49, 251
Sanzharovets, Vladimir 46, 48n87, 50n91n92, 51, 54, 55n98, 57, 58, 72, 78, 78n159, 112n222
Schiller, Friedrich 199
Seifullina, Lidia 172, 255; "One Survived" ("Utselel odin") 255
Selvinskaya, Berta 14, 16, 24n50, 100n202, 115n230n231, 153n34n35, 208n48, 236, 260
Selvinskaya, Tatyana 1n1, 5, 9, 14, 14n33, 17, 17n37, 20, 22, 132, 139, 160n50, 169, 169n72, 174, 174n83, 180n99, 198, 200, 200n37, 213, 213n56, 214, 218, 220, 226, 227, 228, 230, 233, 243, 244, 257, 258, 260n69
Selvinsky, Ilya
 "A Cossack Joke Song" ("Kazach'ia shutochnaia") 261; "A Soldier's Song" ("Soldatskaia pesnia") 200; "Anecdotes about the Karaite Philosopher Babakai Sudduk" 4; "Antisemites" ("Antisemity") 15; *Arctic: A Novel (Arktika: Roman)* 13; "Ballad of Laar, The" ("Ballada o Laare") 175, 176; *Ballads and Songs (Ballady i pesni)* 90, 140, 223; *Ballads, Posters, and Songs (Ballady, plakaty i pesni)* 29, 113; *Bar Kokhba*

4; *Chelyuskiniana* 10–12, 156, 201; *Crimea, Caucasus, Kuban* (*Krym Kavkaz Kuban'*) 107, 133, 153n35, 181, 190, 217, 218, 221; "Crimea" ("Krym") 152n32, 190 ; "Crimean Battle Song, The" ("Boevaia Krymskaia") 137; "Episode" 159, 159n46, 160n49, 162, 163, 223; "For Motherland, for Stalin" ("Za rodinu, za Stalina") 28; "From Palestine to Birobidzhan" ("Ot Palestiny do Birobidzhana") 4; *General Brusilov* 137, 174; *Fur Trade* (*Pushtorg*) 2–4, 6, 123, 163, 193, 196; "God of Poetry" ("Bog poezii") 223; "Great [or Pacific] Ocean" ("Velikii okean") 240; 230; "I Saw It!" ("Ia eto videl!") 30n63, 36, 53n93, 77, 81–84, 84n173, 86, 86n178, 87, 88, 90–93, 93n195, 96, 97, 99–101, 101n205, 103, 104, 105n212, 111, 111n221, 112, 112n223, 113, 113n223, 114, 116, 117, 117n235, 118, 125, 129–131, 134, 137, 140, 143, 154, 154n37, 164, 167, 171, 172, 175n86, 180, 190, 198, 199, 201, 202, 204, 209–211, 218, 220, 222, 222n78, 223, 239, 240, 240n28, 242, 243, 248, 256, 257, 266; "Jewish Melody" ("Evreiskaia melodiia") 258; "Jewish Question, The" ("Evreiskii vopros") 15, 15n34; *Kandava* 189, 191, 195, 202, 203, 205, 206, 207n46, 208, 210, 210n51, 211, 218, 229, 235, 248; "Kerch" 30, 30n63, 116, 117, 117n235, 118, 128, 145, 189–191, 204, 209, 210, 210n51, 239; "Königsberg Today (Travel Notes)" ("Kenigsberg segodnia [Putevye zametki]") 200; *Lay of Ulyalaev, The* (*Ulialaevshchina*) 2–4, 30, 102n205, 217; "Let Us Dream about Immortality" ("Davaite pomechtaem o bessmert'e", 1964–1966) 241; *Livonian War, The* (*Livonskaia voina*) 181, 195, 196; *Lyric and Drama* (*Lirika i dramy*) 165, 181, 218, 220; "Motke the Angel of Death" ("Mot'ka Malkhamoves") 4; *Notes of a Poet* (*Zapiski poeta*) 2; "Once Again on the Hitlerite Atrocities" 95, 114; "Portrait of My Mother" ("Portret moei materi") 4; "Reading Stalin" ("Chitaia Stalina") 181, 183–185, 192, 201; *Records* (*Rekordy*); 2; "Reply to Goebbels, A" ("Otvet Gebbel'su") 93, 129, 145, 223; "Russian Infantry" ("Russkaia pekhota") 158; *Sebastopol* (*Sevastopol'*); 191, 191n12, 192, 215, 218; "Stalin at the Microphone" ("Stalin u mikrofona") 28, 165; "Terrible Judgment" ("Strashnyi sud") 229, 230n4 ; "The Trial in Krasnodar" ("Sud v Krasnodare") 133; "There are regions which centuries cannot stir..." ("Byvaiut kraia, chto nedvizhny vekami...") 193 ; *Three Bogatyrs* (*Tri bogatyria*); 152; "To Russia" ("Rossii") 140, 142, 143, 145, 146, 151, 159, 162, 223; "To the Fighters of the Crimean Front" ("K boitsam Krymskogo fronta") 23n47, 145; "To the Jewish Nation" ("K evreiskomu narodu") 25; "To the Southern Slavs" ("Iuzhnym slavianam") 145; "To whom Russia sang a lullaby..." ("Kogo baiukala Rossiia...") 149, 165; *Tushino Camp, The* (*Tyshinskii lager'*) 4, 5; *Umka the Polar Bear* (*Umka — belyi medved'*) 13, 30; "Voice of Stalin, The" ("Golos Stalina") 29; *War Lyrics* (*Voennaia lirika*) 140, 173n80

Serman, Boris 77

Shakespeare, W. 4, 29 *Merchant of Venice, The* 4

Shcherbakov, Aleksandr 5n8, 153–157, 160, 160n50, 161, 164, 167, 171, 182, 185, 195
Shcherbina, Vladimir 220; "False Direction" 220
Sheldon, Richad 219
Sheremet, Oksana 53n93
Shevchuk, Vasily 44, 45, 85
Shirokorad, Irina 18n39
Shklovsky, Viktor 149, 227n2, 251
Shmidt, Otto Iulievich 10
Shneer, David 35, 36, 36n71, 56, 58, 69, 70, 70n140
Sholokhov, Mikhail 3
Shrayer, Maxim D. xv; *Russian Poet/Soviet Jew: The Legacy of Eduard Bagritsky* xv
Shrayer-Petrov, David 185n108, 191n12, 237, 250
Shuer, Aleksandr 167
Simonov, Konstantin 13n31, 62, 62n110, 63, 63n114, 85, 86, 133n248, 149, 174, 175n85, 181, 240n28, 250 "Letter from the Crimea" (2 parts) 62 62n111-112; screenplay for German's *Twenty Days without War* 63n114
Sirota, Naum 77, 77n157
Slesarev, Pavel 61, 62; "Funeral of the Victims of the German Occupation of Kerch, The" 62
Slutsky, Abram 167
Slutsky, Boris 14, 15, 173n80, 226, 229, 233, 233n12, 234, 235, 235n19, 238, 240, 243–248, 250n51, 253, 257 "The Pit of Cologne" 240; "Selvinsky's Seminar" 238n20; "Tvardovsky" 244-45
Smeliakov, Iaroslav 133n248
Smirnov, Lev 38, 79, 80, 80n165
Sobol', Mark 133n248
Sokol Rodiny (Falcon of the Motherland) 175
Solomatin, Mikhail 155, 163, 165, 215, 229
Sonderkommando 10A 133

Sonderkommando 10B 43, 48
Sorokin, Sergey 120
SS Chelyuskin Arctic Expedition 9, 19, 83, 129
Stalin, Joseph 5n10, 7, 8, 10, 11, 11n24, 12–15, 20, 22, 28–30, 59n103, 62, 73n146, 83, 92, 94, 95, 104, 111, 113–115, 142–144, 144n13, 148, 156–158, 160, 162, 165, 166, 167n68, 168, 169, 174n84, 177, 183–186, 196, 197, 200, 201, 213–215, 216n65, 219, 220, 223, 226, 229, 238, 243, 246, 247
Stalin Prizes, Committee 142
Stalingrad, Battle of 164, 184
Surkov, Aleksey 7, 8n15, 174, 240n28
Sutzkever, Avrom 105n212
Suvorov, Aleksandr 164, 183
Suvorovets (Suvorovite) 197
Svetlov, Mihail 178n95, 250
Sviridenko, P. P. 84n173
Syn otechestva (Son of Fatherland), newspaper of the 51st Separate Army 17, 18, 20, 58

Tanakh 107, 190, 261n72
Tarasenkov, Anatoly 221, 222; "On National Traditions and Bourgeois Cosmopolitanism" 221
TASS (Telegraph Agency of the Soviet Union) 37, 37n76, 58, 59, 128, 129
Terlovsky, Aleksandr 20
Tiaglyi, Mikhail 43, 79n164
Tikhonov, Nikolai xv, 7, 147, 216
Titova, Lyudmila 116
Tkachenko, Ivan 66
Trotsky, Lev 3, 157
Trud (Labor) 238
Tsiolkovsky, Konstantin 242
Turovsky, Mark 58–61, 72, 77, 78, 128
Tvardovsky, Aleksandr 174, 175n85, 185, 185n108, 216, 240, 244, 245, 247; "I Was Killed near Rzhev" 240

Tychyna, Pavlo 26, 216, 248n44
Tynyanov, Yuri 2n3, 149

"Undiscriminating Editors", by anonymous 145
Union of Soviet Writers 6, 155, 215, 257n64
Ushakov, Nikolay 236
Utkin, Iosif 177, 178, 178n95, 179, 180, 239, 240, 250; "I Saw a Murdered Girl" 180; "I Saw It Myself!" 180, 187, 240; "Listen to Me" 180; "Oath" 180; "On the Dnieper" 180; "Poplars of Kiev" 178; *Tale of a Red-Headed Motele* 177, 178

Vadimov D. — see Ortenberg, David.
Vaingardten (Vaingartner), Iosif 68, 77, 79n163, 172n79
Vaiskopf, Mikhail 102n205
Vakulin, Boris 59
Vasiliev, Ivan 205
Vilkomir, Leonid 167
Vishnevsky, Vsevolod 146, 147, 147n21, 189
Volfson, Bentsion M. 38n79, 44n84, 75, 75n153, 76, 77; "Bloody Crimes of the Germans in Kerch" 76

Voronsky, Aleksandr 3
Voskresenskaya, Tsetsilia 236
Voznesensky, Andrey 254–257; *Ditch* 254–256
Vpered k pobede! (*Forward to Victory!*) 23n48, 84n174
Vpered za rodinu! (*Forward for the Motherland!*) 23
Vurgun, Samed 216

Wiener, Norbert 242
Wiesel, Elie 103 *Night* 103

Yablonsky, Leonid 66, 77, 128
Yakovlev, Vladimir 81; *Crime. Struggle. Retribution* 81
Yashin, Aleksandr 115, 116n232, 146
Young Communist League (Komsomol) 59

Zarian, Nairi 28n59
Zelinsky, Kornely 2, 144, 236, 257n64
Zhdanov, Andrey 11, 13, 162, 168, 185, 186, 189, 215, 221
Znamia (*Banner*) 117
Zoshchenko, Mikhail 160n49, 161, 163, 216; *Before the Sunrise* 161

Praise for

I SAW IT: ILYA SELVINSKY AND THE LEGACY OF BEARING
WITNESS TO THE SHOAH

by Maxim D. Shrayer

"This beautifully close reading of a major Soviet poet restores for us an important vision of the Holocaust."

—Timothy Snyder, Yale University

"Comprehensive, meticulously researched, erudite, and up-to-date, with sober assessments and insightful interpretive comments, Maxim D. Shrayer's study of Ilya Selvinsky closes gaps both in the history of Soviet Russian literature and in the history of the literature of the Holocaust."

—Leona Toker, The Hebrew University of Jerusalem

"Ilya Selvinsky was a Soviet Jewish poet writer who wrote explicitly about the Holocaust at a time when most Soviet writers avoided the subject. Though Selvinsky was in and out of political trouble, his undeniable talent and Stalin's grudging admiration allowed him to survive. Maxim D. Shrayer tells his story vividly, comprehensively and convincingly. Unlike many literary studies, this deeply researched book is accessible, gripping and free of jargon. We learn not only about Selvinsky and other wartime writers, but also about Soviet policy toward the Holocaust and how it changed; the tense relations between the Party-State and writers; and the complexities of Jewish identities in the USSR."

—Zvi Gitelman, University of Michigan

"*I Saw It* is a major contribution to our knowledge and understanding of how Soviet Jewish writers and the regime in general responded to the Nazi massacres of Jews in German-occupied Soviet territory. As a soldier, poet, and journalist, Ilya Selvinsky was often on the front line, struggling to comprehend the enormity of the destruction and suffering around him. Based on painstaking and comprehensive research, Maxim D. Shrayer does a superb job of conveying the challenges of being a Soviet patriot and a Jew in the face of Hitler's onslaught."

—Joshua Rubenstein, author of *Tangled Loyalties:The Life and Times of Ilya Ehrenburg*

"Soviet Jews, serving on the Eastern front, were the first to document the German war against the Jews. The most memorable response was, indeed, the first: a Russian-language poem so immediate, so personal and so graphic, that even Stalin and his henchmen could not suppress the poem, nor, try as they did, the courageous poet who authored it. This is the remarkable story, never before told, of the Jewish-Russian poet Ilya Selvinsky, who despite all odds first taught his fellow Jews and Russians how to mourn their incalculable losses."

—David G. Roskies, Jewish Theological Seminary, The Hebrew University of Jerusalem

"Maxim D. Shrayer's searing account of the struggles of a famous Soviet-Jewish poet and military officer, Ilya Selvinsky, is among the most original and illuminating studies of the Holocaust as experienced by a generation of Soviet intellectuals who witnessed the atrocities and were at the forefront of Stalin's propaganda war against Nazism. Shrayer's research on Selvinsky is impressive and stunning. Scholars and students alike will appreciate Shrayer's presentation of Selvinsky's moving poetry, revealing diary entries, and rare family photographs—all of this rich material Shrayer contextualizes in a deep historical and literary analysis of this era's fanatical idealism and genocide. Standing at the edge of a mass grave of Jewish victims in his native region of Crimea at Kerch, Selvinsky followed his conscience by writing the poem, "I Saw It," to testify, and express his outrage and grief. In this penetrating book of Selvinsky's struggles, Shrayer pays a double tribute—to a shattered idealist and patriot who captured the soul of his people in his poetry, and to the victims of the Shoah whose voices like those of a generation of Soviet Jewish intellectual-witnesses were muted by postwar Soviet censors who suppressed the Holocaust."

—Wendy Lower, Claremont McKenna College

"In *I Saw It*, Maxim D. Shrayer meticulously and unflinchingly chronicles the Nazi massacre of Jews in Kerch, Crimea, and its reflection in Ilya Selvinsky's extraordinarily powerful poems. Selvinsky, a convinced communist generally willing to compromise, suffered considerably for his stubborn attempts to bring the Shoah to the attention of the Soviet reading public. Shrayer brings together social, political, historical, and poetic questions, producing a memorable book that will fascinate a broad range of readers."

—Michael Wachtel, Princeton University

"A sophisticated literary analysis of Ilya Selvinsky's texts, Maxim D. Shrayer's book demonstrates a deep knowledge of the history of the Holocaust in the USSR. It is the first study of poet's career in the context of Shoah memorization. Shrayer's book must be published in Russian translation."

—Ilya Altman, Russian Holocaust Center, Russian State University for the Humanities

ABOUT THE AUTHOR

Maxim D. Shrayer (PhD Yale University) is Professor of Russian, English, and Jewish studies at Boston College. A bilingual writer and translator, Shrayer has authored and edited a number of books, among them the critical studies *The World of Nabokov's Stories* and *Russian Poet/ Soviet Jew*, the literary memoir *Waiting for America: A Story of Emigration*, and the collection *Yom Kippur in Amsterdam*. He also edited and cotranslated three books of fiction by his father, the writer David Shrayer-Petrov. Shrayer's two-volume *Anthology of Jewish-Russian Literature* won a 2007 National Jewish Book Award, and in 2012 he received a Guggenheim Fellowship. He lives in Brookline, Mass. with his wife and two daughters. For more information, visit www.shrayer.com.

www.ingramcontent.com/pod-product-compliance
Lightning Source LLC
Chambersburg PA
CBHW071811230426
43670CB00013B/2429